伊利诺伊斯丁心社元

图书馆

厦门大厦学院 赠
2008·11·11·

Executive Editor: Shi Gaoxiang   施高翔

Cover & Illustrations: Dr. William N. Brown   Wen Xin   潘维廉 文心

魅力厦门
Amoy Magic
Dr. William N. Brown

Xiamen University Press

Xiamen Bay

Xiamen International Exhibition and Conference Center

Island in the Sun (Gulangyu Islet in Foreground)

Photos by Zhu Qingfu

Home Sweet Home!

Xiamen University

Zhongshan Park

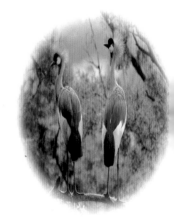

Fowl Play

Xiamen Botanical Garden

Photos by Zhu Qingfu

Zhongshan Rd.

Swords Into Plows...

Island Ring Road

Photos by Zhu Qingfu

Jimei Dragonboat Race

Xiamen Philharmonic Orchestra

Seaside Sculpture

Photos by Zhu Qingfu

Xiamen's 1st International Marathon (March 31, 2003)

Amoy Architecture

Amoymagic.com

Xiamen Museum (Gulangyu)

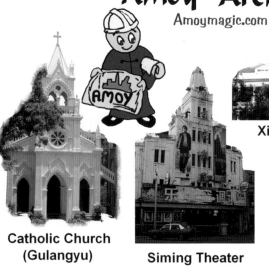

Catholic Church
(Gulangyu)

Siming Theater

Former U.S. Consulate (Gulangyu)

Gulangyu Guesthouse

Former British
Consulate

Former Dutch
Consulate

Former Ruifeng
Ginseng Store (1912)

Xinjie--China's First
Protestant Church

Amoy's Mascot
(Haihai 海海)

Enjoy Amoy!
The Garden Island

Go Fly A Kite!

Putt Around...

Read Amoy Magic On the Beach

Play Exciting Sports!

Dance With Dragons!
(Xiamen International School)

Cycle the Islang Ring Rd.

Nanputuo Temple Vegetarian Cuisine

Fun in Fujian

Amoymagic.com

China's Longest Reclining Buddha
God of Xiuxi? (Sanming, Shaxian)

China's Best Maritime Museum
(Quanzhou)

White Water Rafting!
(Changtai)

Rubies 'n
Sapphires
(Mingxi)

Floating Assets
Floating Villages of Sandu'ao
(Ningde)

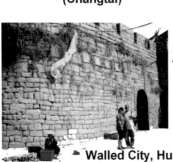
Walled City, Huian Maidens
(Chongwu)

Hakka Earthen Roundhouses
(Nanjing and Yongding)

Bamboo Rafting
(Mystic Wuyi Mtn.)

S. Shaolin Kungfu
(Zhouning, Ningde)

Tang Dynasty Mountain City
(Changting--"Li'l Red Shanghai")

Amoy Magic ©2003

魅力厦门

--The Compleat[1] Guide to Xiamen!

厦门指南

Many thanks to my intrepid wife, Susan Marie
Brown, who waded through Amoy Magic even in the
tub, though she dozed off several times; hence this
warning:

> **Warning**: Avoid Amoy Magic while bathing,
> driving, or operating heavy machinery.

And thanks to Sue for her new website, **http://www.Amoymagic.com!**

Special thanks for the many letters from Laowai and Laonei all over
the planet. But we're reprinting Amoy Magic in spite of their comments.

Muchas[2] Xie Xie! thanks to my hosts—the Chinese friends who put
the magic in Amoy.

Comments, suggestions, questions, corrections, or requests for additional
copies of Amoy Magic? **E-mail**: **bbrown@public.xm.fj.cn**
Snail Mail: Dr. Bill Brown, Box 1288, Xiamen University
Xiamen Fujian, PRC 361005
Complaints? Write my wife.

Enjoy Amoy!
Dr. Bill 潘维廉
MBA Center, Xiamen University

Table of Contents

Part One	**Enjoy Amoy**	**Page**
Chapter 1	Welcome Laowai—Intro	1
Chapter 2	Getting Down to Business	40
Chapter 3	Fun On-Island	60
Chapter 4	Gulangyu Islet	104
Chapter 5	Amoy Bushwalks	118
Chapter 6	Fowl Pursuits	128
Chapter 7	Museums	138
Chapter 8	Near Amoy Island	145
Chapter 9	Getting About (Transportation)	155

Part Two	**The Rest of Fujian**	
Chapter 10	Mythical Zaytun (Quanzhou)	171
Chapter 11	Zhangzhou	199
Chapter 12	Hakka Roundhouses	209
Chapter 13	Longyan (Dragon Crag)	213
Chapter 14	Fuzhou	225
Chapter 15	Putian and Xianyou	239
Chapter 16	Ningde	245
Chapter 17	Wuyi Mountain	257
Chapter 18	Scenic Sanming	267

Part Three	**Life in Amoy**	
Chapter 19	Chinese Foodfest	275
Chapter 20	Our Favorite Eateries	289
Chapter 21	Laowai Lexicon of Chinese Cuisine	309
Chapter 22	Home Cooking—Chinese & Western	316
Chapter 23	Laowai Life (Shopping)	330
Chapter 24	Chinese Festivals and Culture	367
Chapter 25	Mad About Mandarin (The language)	384
Chapter 26	Lords of Opium	397
Epilogue	Look Up	412
Supplement	Fujian Handicrafts & Shopping	414

New for this issue!

Amoymagic.com!

Get the latest updates on Amoy at Susan Marie's new website—and help Sue keep the magic in Amoy by e-mailing your own discoveries to **AmoySue@yahoo.com**.

Laonei (老内) Notes

at the end of each chapter help explain unusual or difficult words or sentences for Chinese, as well as for Brits like Scott Ballantyne (who have a tough time grappling standard American English).

Common Talk—

Xiamen Daily's Saturday English section, is the first of its kind in China! Submit contributions to the editor, Ms. Yayu Wu, at yy5188@vip.sina.com

Ms. Yayu, Editor of "Common Talk"
(Xiamen Daily, Saturday Edition)

Wasa Queen!

Try the beautiful new Star Cruises' cruise ferry between Hong Kong and Xiamen! The international crew is courteous, professional, and the trip is a great 20 hour respite from everything that ails you. The 440 foot long ship is only ten feet shorter than Noah's ark—big enough for hundreds of passengers, or two of every species of animal if we can't stop global warming.

Lifeline Medical System
来　福　诊　所

Lifeline Medical Clinic—

founded *by* Laowai, *for* Laowai! Also check out the Xiamen Tokushinkai Dental Clinic.

i

AXE! The **Association for Xiamen Expatriates** offers a welcome packet for newly arrived Laowai members, and hosts monthly coffee meetings (1ˢᵗ Tuesday of each month), sports activities, a book club, monthly shopping and cultural trips, and a monthly coffee to raise funds for UNICEF. For more information, phone: 139-060-28020, or write Eunice Chau at qp21@public.xm.fj.cn

And check out the monthly activities at Best Western Hotel's **International Children's Club.** http://bwxm.com/eg_main.html

Xiamen Shopping! Gone are the days (in Xiamen at least) when we must buy grain in the countryside and grind our own wheat on heavy stone mills. Nowadays we can buy bread, cheese, pepperoni—virtually anything a Laowai needs to keep body and soul together[3]. In addition to excellent Chinese supermarkets like Minkelong （闽客隆） we have two Trust-Marts (an Asian version of Wal-Mart), a new German-run Metro (near the airport), and the massive Philippine-based SM Mall (which has one of Xiamen's two Wal-Mart Supercenters). You want it, Xiamen has it somewhere!

Book City （厦门图书文化城）. We used to crave English reading material, but Xiamen now boasts Fujian's largest bookstore (SM Mall, 3/F). Book City even has foreign novels—everything from thrillers and chillers to "Chicken Soup for the Soul."

Gulangyu Islet, long a favorite shopping haven for both Laowai and Laonei, now has a delightful new mall, with traditional entertainers performing in the central square.

Xiamen Cuisine! In addition to local favorites like seaworms 'n jellyfish (which our oldest son Shannon actually likes; he's been here far too long), we now have cuisines from all over China, and the rest of the world as well. For example:

Xiamen's 1st American restaurant—The White Rose Café. Yiyuan Hotel (excellent Western cuisine), Little Saigon (Vietnamese), Sam's Barbeque (Singaporean-Filipino), Tutto Bene (Italian), Sarah's (French), Havana (behind the Philippine Consulate, it offers awesome Spanish cuisine), Burmese, Mongolian, deng deng!

More? Then follow the advice of Xiamen University's Bonnie Koenig:

> "We have found "Western foods" (baked beans, Campbell's soups, flour, etc...) in some of the "funniest" places - small shops that seem to buy an "odd lot" of something and then sell it until its gone. The prices are usually less than at the Restaurant Supply Store or hotels. You might want to suggest in the book (or on website) that people can keep their eyes open for these 'treasures'."

Explore magical Amoy—and then share your findings with the rest of the Laowai community by writing **bbrown@public.xm.fj.cn**

Last, but hopefully not least... Fujian Adventure!

After 3 years of preparation, the 440 page full color *Fujian Adventure* (Lujiang Publishers) is now available at less discerning bookstores everywhere. *Over 900 color photos*, drawings and maps help show what fun the rest of Fujian province has to offer—from Zhouning Highlanders' carp worshippers, China's largest waterfalls complex, and Baishuiyang (where even mortals like me walk on water), to the mystic heights of Wuyi Mountains, the birthplace of Southern Shaolin Kungfu, the Hakka haven "Lil Red Shanghai," Marco Polo's Silk Road of the Sea, and the well-rounded folks in the earthen round castles of Yongding.

Enjoy Amoy...and the rest of Fujian!

Dr. Bill

iii

Acknowledgements

Zhu Qingfu （朱庆福） The award winning photographer Zhuqing (his pen name) provided **all** of the fine color photos for the first 2 issues of Amoy Magic. For better or worse, this issue also includes my own photos, but to avoid damaging Zhuqing's reputation the fine photos are marked ZQF and the not-so-fine snapshots are marked BB.

Zhuqing was born in 1963 in Nankang City, Jiangxi Province, and joined the army in 1980. His first published work was *A Violinist*, in '81, and in '84 his *Heart-to-Heart Talk* received the Excellence Award at the Joint Youth Arts Exhibition of Eight Cities in East China. In '87, his *Grand Expectation* won the Excellence Award at the 1st Photographic Exhibit of East China's Army, Navy & Air Force.

In '94, he left military service to become a news photographer at Xiamen Business News. In '97, his masterpiece, *Chinese Man*, won the Gold Prize at the 18th National Photographic Arts Exhibition—the first prize Fujian has ever won in such a national exhibition.

In '97, the Fujian Literature & Art Association and Xiamen Literature & Art Association held a commendatory meeting in Zhuqing's honor, and in '98, the Ministry of Culture awarded him the Qunxing Award for outstanding achievement.

In 2000, Zhuqing received First Prize in the Fujian Province Baihua Literature & Art Awards, and his *Sweating for the Rainbow over Haicang* won the Silver Prize in the Photographic Works of China News Photo Awards. Also in 2,000 he published a beautiful pictorial, *Xiamen Charm*.

In 2001, the Fujian Provincial Government awarded Zhuqing the title of "Outstanding Youth Photographer in Fujian Province." And truly, he is more youthful at 38 years old than most people at 18!

Thank you, Zhuqing, for helping put the Magic in Amoy—and in *Amoy Magic*!

Dr. Jan Engsberg, a Xiamen University inmate since 1988, helped edit earlier versions of Amoy Magic, but not this one—so don't blame her for the current crop of mistakes. Jan's love for

Dr. Jan Engsberg

iv

Xiamen continues to be one of the many factors that prevent me from taking for granted the fact that we live in one of the most beautiful places on the planet. Thanks, Jan! Thanks too for being the U.S. Consulate's "warden" for Americans here (it just proves we are indeed inmates, Warden Jan!).

Veteran Bushwalker, Ms. **Trish Boman,** a lovely lady from the Land Down Under[4]wrote a fascinating section on Xiamen Bushwalks, including Foxtail Mountain (behind the Municipal Government offices). She's planning a Bushwalking book, and I look forward to reading it (if not walking it; I feel bushed just thinking about all that walking).   Thanks, Trish.

Amoy Magic.com My better 2/3,[5] Susan Marie, has burned the midnight oil[6] creating Amoymagic.com. It was a long row to hoe[7] because she knew nothing about website design (She thought HTML was an American health care plan[8]. But Sue persevered, and now we have **www.amoymagic.com** for the latest on Amoy dining, recreation, tourism, special performances, cultural events, sports activities, American warnings against Iraq, deng deng (Chinese for "etcetera"). Many thanks to those who abetted[9] Susan—especially Xiamen's *Wizard of the Web,* Mr. Frank Wei!

Frank Wei should spell his name **Frank Way,** because he is the kind of guy that finds a way to get anything done. Founder and Chairman of MTS, Frank graduated from Xiamen University in 1991 with an M.A. in English. He engaged in trade for Xindeco from '91 to '95, and was a trade rep in Boston and New York for two years. In '96, Frank became the Editor-in-Chief for the biweekly *Straits Info* (now *"Business Watch"*) and General Manager of Xindeco Business Information Co., Ltd. Also in '96, he conceived and directed construction of the highly popular and award-winning Chinavista.com (the 2nd English language website in China). Today, Frank is CEO of Master Translation Services Co., Ltd.. Check out their broad staff of translation and internet experts (also tested and certified in accordance with ISO 9000 compliance). Visit **www.xmmaster.com,** or write **frank@xmmaster.com**

Supplement
Amoy Gets the Gold!

Nations in Bloom, "The International Awards for Livable Communities."

"Recognizing environmental excellence in international communities"

In 2002, I was honored to take part in Xiamen's team that competed in Nations in Stuttgart, Germany. Over 40 cities from around the world made it to the finals, and Xiamen had some stiff competition—Chicago, Phoenix Arizona (which came in second in 2001 and was ready to win in 2002), and Hangzhou. Our competitors, especially Hangzhou, had many strong points, but in the final polishing of our presentation I focused on the one aspect that no city could possibly best Xiamen at—the speed and comprehensiveness of Xiamen's transformation. Over the past 20 years, Xiamen was China's #1 city in economic growth, and #2 in environmental sustainability—an incredible combination. And we basically started from scratch!

Over 1,000 years ago, Xiamen was part of Quanzhou, the start of the Silk Road of the Sea, and prospered. But the Japanese razed us in World War II, and the government put no money into Fujian Province, or Xiamen, until the early 80s because this coastal area was a buffer zone against the former military threat of Taiwan. When we moved to Xiamen in 1988, electricity was off

several days a week, water was off for days at a time, roads were potholed, or dirt, the city itself was dirty and grimy with soot. And within 15 years, Xiamen became China's cleanest city! Xiamen was first to give air quality reports via the media, one of the first to adopt international standards in quality and pollution control—Xiamen, in short, pioneered many areas in China.

I've loved Xiamen since we arrived in 1988, but only after helping put together the NIB presentation did I understand the full magnitude of Xiamen's accomplishments. And when I gave the presentation in Stuttgart, I was both honored and proud to be a "Xiamenese." And when Xiamen beat everyone to get the gold medal in this "Oscar of Environmental Communities," I was in 7th heaven[10]!

Dr. Bill and Alan Smith, Founder of NIB
(Stuttgart, Germany, Oct. 2002)

Many thanks to Xiamen and her people for allowing me to participate in this (and I am presently helping Quanzhou, my second favorite city in China, enter the 2003 NIB competition). And a special thanks to the founder of NIB, Mr. Alan Smith, who has since become a dear friend. Mr. Smith wrote the introduction to NIB that I enclose below especially for this issue of Amoy Magic!

Nations in Bloom

By Mr. Alan Smith, Founder and Director

Despite the possible interpretations of the name Nations in Bloom, it is NOT a flower show, but a unique international initiative concerned with all aspects of the local environment.

The objective of Nations in Bloom is the improvement in the quality of life through the creation of livable, viable communities, encouraged through international exchange of best practice. The international media has named Nations in Bloom as the International Benchmark for management of the local environment.

vii

Reasons for Creating NIB:

There is a long history of international meetings attended by world leaders and experts that have sought to reach agreement on environmental issues. But despite these meetings good intentions, too often the outcomes have been diluted to enable acceptance in many different political cultures. In the end, they often have little real impact on real communities.

There is no way of imposing penalties when countries break from previously made agreements, and there is no lasting ongoing commitment. The USA walked away from the Kyote Agreement because the previously agreed terms of this agreement did not suit the current Administration's political and financial aspirations.

Increasingly, local communities have sought to improve their environment, but have not had the essential network through which they could seek and exchange the best international practice.

Nations in Bloom was created to involve the main partners in the management of the local environment, including local politicians, local experts and the community.

Management:

Nations in Bloom is managed by a non profit-distributing Company that is a UK Registered Charity. Nations in Bloom is endorsed by the United Nations Environment Program.

Participation:

Nations in Bloom was piloted in 1996 and launched internationally in 1997. Each year new countries are represented in the Competition. Over 50 countries are now in the Nations in Bloom family.

Structure:

Participants compete in five Population Categories.

Communities are required to submit a 4,000 word report, which an international Panel of Judges assess against five criteria: Enhancement of the Landscape, Heritage Management, Use of environmentally Sensitive Practices, Community Involvement, and Planning for the Future.

The Judges invite a number of communities from each Population Category to compete in the Final, where they are required to make a verbal Presentation supported by slides and a video. Following the Presentation, communities face a series of questions from the Judges. The Judges then assess each community against the above criteria.

Benefits:
The writing of the Initial Report is a self-audit process, and highlights to municipal authorities both what the community is doing and is not doing. This initial Report has often been used as the basis for a community's long-term plan.

Management of the environment has more international implications than possibly any other community responsibility. No community faces unique challenges, and no community has all the answers. It is essential that anyone responsible for environmental management maintain an awareness of how communities in other parts of the world respond to similar challenges.

Environmental challenges have no national or cultural borders. Nations in Bloom is non political and therefore offers the only opportunity for communities to meet other communities from all parts of the world that are seeking an improved local environment.

There are many examples of communities meeting through Nations in Bloom that have formed agreements to exchange best practice, to exchange technical visits, or work together to address a common challenge. These partnerships have produced accelerated technical advances and significant financial savings.

The community has never before been better informed, had a greater desire to become involved, or had greater expectations regarding the improvement of their local environment. This increases the pressure on those responsible for the local environment to seek out international best practices.

Nations in Bloom is the only initiative through which communities can become aware of international best practices.

For full details, see www.nationsinbloom.com. For Registration Forms and general enquiries, please contact **nationsinbloom@aol.com**, or phone +44 118 946 1680. Closing date for annual competitions is May 31st.

Nations in Bloom, Globe House, Crispin Close, Caversham
Reading, Berkshire, RG4 7JS, England
Tel/Fax: +44 (0)1189461680   Email: nationsinbloom@aol.com
Web: www.nationsinbloom.com

Laonei (老内) Notes

[1] Compleat: variation of "complete," a highly developed or wide-ranging treatise on a subject.

[2] Muchas: Spanish for "much"

[3] Keep body and soul together: stay alive; survive

[4] Land down under: Australia

[5] Better 2/3: Americans often call their wives their "better half," but Susan Marie pulls much more than ½ the weight in our marriage—hence, "better 2/3"

[6] Burned the midnight oil: worked around the clock; similar to the phrase "burned the candle at both ends."

[7] Long row to hoe: seemingly endless amount of work ahead

[8] American Health Care Plan: HMO (Health Maintenance Organization) sounds similar to HTML.

[9] Abet: encourage, approve, support (often referring to an illegal activity, such as "abetted robbing a bank").

[10] 7th heaven: highest heaven (very happy!)

NOTE: For up-to-date English maps of Xiamen, Gulangyu, and Fujian, check local bookstores, or download from Amoymagic.com

Dr. Bill

X

Chapter 1
欢迎老外!

Welcome Laowai!—Intro

Get used to hearing, "Laowai (老外)!" This is Chinese for "venerable outsider," ("foreigner", 4/5 of our planet's population). I often respond with my own term, LaoNei! ©®™· (老内), which is "venerable insider." Some Chinese protest, "No such word!"

I answer, "Now there is!" ☺

Besides Laowai, you'll also hear folks calling out "Waiguo Pengyou!" (外国朋友). This means "Foreign Friend."

Maybe they think everyone since Nixon is a Quaker.[1]

But jesting aside, Chinese do welcome us Laowai as Pengyou (朋友, friend), and sometimes even as family. Perhaps this Chinese hospitality is

A Foreign Devil

why China gets in your blood for life (rather like malaria).

Our family has fallen in love with China, and especially with Xiamen (old Amoy). You will too, once you appreciate all that our adopted home has to offer. Hence this book.

In the early '90s, we doled out a hastily improvised "Xiamen Survival Guide" to newly arrived Laowai souls who staggered about intoning the **Laowai Litany**:

"Where can I buy cheese?" (there wasn't any), or,

"Where are the Western sit-down toilets?" (no squatter's rights then), or,

"What brand of toilet paper (TP) doesn't burn ones buns?" (China may well have invented TP 1,000 years ago, but Xiamen's recycled sandpaper-cum-TP used to make me wax nostalgic for a used Sears catalog[2]). [See "**Dethroned**" at the end of this chapter]

Xiamen Laowai no longer need a "Survival Guide" because life on the Garden Island is no longer 'survival' but fun and rewarding. (Just ask most of the 3,000+ Laowai community). Yet newly arrived Waiguo Pengyou still have lots of questions, like where to shop, or travel, or what to do on weekends.

Caviar Empty![3] It's getting harder to answer such questions because Xiamen changes almost daily. New restaurants, shops and tourist sites spring up like mushrooms (and like mushrooms, some wither overnight). So Caviar Empty! The best approach is to explore yourself on foot, or by bus or cab, because everything is subject to change—especially if you're depending on it.

With in mind, we still hope that Amoy Magic will answer all you ever wanted to know about Xiamen but didn't want to know bad enough to ask. For example, "Where'd the word "Amoy" come from?"

The world "Amoy" came from the Fuzhou dialect. After the Opium War of 1843, when Xiamen was opened as one of five treaty ports, a Fuzhou customs officer told Laowai that our island was called "Ah Moh," which sounds a bit like "Amen" spoken through the nose. Hence "Amoy."

End of Lesson One. ☺

Pop Quiz   What Chinese city won the gold medal in Stuttgart, Germany, at the 2002 "Nations in Bloom" (the "Oscar of Environmentalism")? And over the past two decades, what Chinese city was **#1** in economic growth *and* **#2** in environmental protection? What Chinese city has the best weather, the cleanest air, beautiful beaches and gardens, the planet's best seafood, a unique marriage of traditional Chinese, European colonial and modern architecture, the third fastest growing economy (thanks to one of the world's best natural deep-water harbors—which is also home to rare white dolphins), one of the nation's most advanced international airports, the only key university in a special economic zone—and unlimited business opportunities so you can afford to enjoy all of the above?   Nowhere but Xiamen, the "Garden Island"—our family's home since 1988.

Whether you're passing through or staying awhile, we hope you enjoy our enchanting island, which for centuries has woven her spell over Laowai and Laonei alike with her balmy climate, her rolling green hills dotted with gardens and pagodas and temples, and the infamous Anxi tea that played such a pivotal role in American Independence; we tossed it overboard during the Boston Tea Party.)

Seeing Red   It's hard to believe that until my 20s, I knew nothing about China except that most Chinese were either cooks named Hop Sing, or laundry men chanting "No tickee no laundry," or

Kung Fu adepts (I really thought David Carradine[4] was Chinese).

I heard that ¼ of the world's population was Chinese but I didn't believe it, because my family had four people and not one of us looked Asian.

It took the U.S. Air Force to *orient*[5] me.

In 1976, I was a 20 year old U.S.A.F. airman seeking solitude. I volunteered for two years on the world's largest island, icy Greenland, population a trifling 58,000.   And naturally, Uncle Sam packed me off to Taiwan, a small island teeming with twenty million people (20 million and one, after my arrival).

I had no idea which part of the planet Taiwan was in, so I thumbed through the "F" volume of Britannica to find Formosa (the old Dutch name for Taiwan, meaning "Beautiful Island").   When I learned that Taiwan was but 100 miles away from the Apocalyptic Yellow Peril, I wrote my will....

Words, not Weapons

Fortunately, by 1976 both sides of the Dire Taiwan Straits [6] were launching not weapons but words. And one bright Spring morning, a batch of colorful leaflets from a mainland propaganda balloon landed dead center on USAF headquarters. Frantic Taiwanese soldiers stuffed the leaflets in sacks and warned that anyone caught with the contraband would be jailed. So like any 20 year old American, I stuffed my pockets and hurried back to my room, where I huddled for hours, curtains drawn, poring over photos of happy Chinese farmers, and acrobats performing improbable feats. Of course, I knew the Communists viewed the world through Red-tinted spectacles, and I didn't believe a word—but a seed was planted (and I still have that leaflet in my MBA office!).

Island Fever

In just two years, I fell in love with Taiwan and her people. I hiked and biked the length and breadth of Taiwan, but like all gems, the Jade Island is small. Inevitably, a combination of contraband leaflets and Island Fever piqued my curiosity about the enemy island of Amoy, directly across the straits.

I sat on the beach for hours, studying the horizon, wondering what the "enemy" was really like. Who would have dreamed that a decade later, I'd not only visit Amoy, but also take up permanent residence with a wife and two infant sons. It was just like coming home—and no wonder.

I was surprised to learn that most Taiwanese' ancestors (over 70%) originated from Southern Fujian. So it is not hard to love Xiamen as much as Taiwan because they're basically the same people, with the same cultures, customs,

Taiwan, 1977

arts and crafts, deng deng (which means "etc." in Chinese; get used to it.). And the Taiwan Straits are getting narrower by the day.

A few years back, a mainland film company shot part of a TV series on a Taiwan occupied island 3 miles offshore. Imagine the director's dismay when he returned to Xiamen and found they'd left some things back in "Taiwan."

"We'll lose days," he moaned, as he envisioned a crew member returning to the island via Hong Kong, Taipei, Taichung, and Jinmen, and then retracing his steps to Xiamen.

A local fisherman said, "Bu Yao Jin. (Don't worry). I've got relatives over there." And under cover of darkness he put out in his little sampan, and returned with the missing items the next morning.

Angling, not Wranging.

Taiwan—so far at times, but getting closer. In September '98, we held our 1st annual Taiwan-Xiamen fishing contest. And afterwards, like fishermen the world over, both sides headed home to exaggerate the size of their catches and bemoan the big ones that got away.

It was nice to see both sides angling instead of wrangling. They're family, after all [and I'm told that by mid 2003 there will be direct tourism between Xiamen and Jinmen!]. But we Laowai are another kettle of fish[7]...especially here in the Kingdom of Snakes.

Fujian—the Serpent Kingdom

Xiamen is planted smack in the mouth of the Jiulong (Nine Dragon) River, so in ancient times she was called Xia Men (下门), or "lower gate to the sea." Inevitably, Xiamen became a haven for pirates and merchants (roughly the same occupation). Eventually the name was amended to Xia Men (厦门), or "Mansion Gate," which also means "Gate to China"—a title Xiamen well deserved for hundreds of years because Fujian Province, and especially Quanzhou, was the **Melting Pot of Asia**.

Let's set the record straight. Western history books go on about Shanghai, Canton and Peking, but for most of China's history, the heart of Chinese trade was Fujian Province, the ancient "Min Kingdom"—the Kingdom of Snakes.

The character Min (闽) means **"Snake in the door"**—and Fujian sure has its share of snakes. Ancient Fujianese kept snakes around the house to eat the rats that fed on their grains, but the province also has plenty of bamboo vipers, cobras, and pythons (which get up to 33 feet long!). So it's no wonder that Fujianese still have a high respect for snakes, even if they don't worship them much anymore—except in a wok, with a bit of soy sauce and ginger.

Chinese, by the way, eat anything edible. What isn't edible they boil and process until it is. What is truly indigestible is called medicine and ingested anyway. Which all goes to prove that Adam and Eve were most definitely not Chinese. Had Eve been Chinese, she'd have tossed the apple and eaten the snake, and Fujian would have never become known as the Serpent Kingdom.

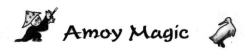
Fujianese—China's Adventurers   Over 2,000 years ago, the intrepid Fujianese founded China's maritime industry up near Fuzhou. Since then, the Kingdom of Snakes has given birth to, or at least been port for, many of China's greatest sailors and adventurers. They sailed virtually the entire world, and recently scholars have begun to accept the evidence that America was discovered not by Columbus but by one of Admiral Zhenghe's fleets.

Imagine how Columbus would have felt if his 85 foot long Santa Maria had come across Zhenghe's 440 foot long flagship (about the size of Noah's ark!). On Zhenghe's 7th and final voyage, he returned to the emperor with gifts of exotic animals like zebra and giraffes, but the emperor was unimpressed and closed the doors on Chinese trade and exploration, and literally sank the largest and most powerful navy that the world had ever seen.

Merchants and Militants   It's a good thing for us barbarians that the Chinese were more concerned with commerce than conquering, because we'd have not stood a chance against their fleets. The giant ships were accompanied by 100s of smaller supply ships (some carrying nothing but water for these 'cities upon the sea') and battle ships armed with the latest weaponry—like cannon and crossbows.

In addition, the Chinese used magnets to gain their bearings. When Europeans finally began using magnets, many captains forbade sailors to eat garlic, which they feared might interfere with the magnets' magical properties.

Chinese ships were also nearly unsinkable, with their many waterproof segmented compartments. The West did not adopt these until the 19th century, and even then the unsinkable Titanic went under.

Fortunately for China, her admirals used both magnets *and* common sense to avoid running full speed into icebergs.

Oh, Jack!

Columbus meets Zhenghe

B.B.

Vertical Fujian   Tens of thousands of ancient Fujianese sought their fortune abroad—and with good reason. Maybe they were trying to escape the 33 foot pythons, 350 pound Amoy Tigers, or legendarily strict wives (ancient tales of henpecked Han Chinese are legion). But the most likely explanation lies in our province's tortuous topography.

Fujian would be China's largest province if someone flattened it with a good heavy iron because the place is almost entirely vertical. As an old saying goes, Fujian is "8 parts mountain, 1 part water and 1 part field."

Fujian is a geological and botanical wonderland, with an abundance of critters and creepy crawlies that rivals the Garden of Eden (and bigger snakes than Eden had). But the one thing Fujian lacks is vertical land.

Farmers survived only by terracing, top to bottom, mountains that are so steep that some farmers probably have to tie themselves into their fields. Some fields are so steep that I suspect the only way they can be harvested is with help from the extra-terrace-strials that once frequented the province for Chinese take out.

Flat land is so scarce that, about 1000 years ago, the Fujianese engaged in a massive land reclamation project along the coast, but even that didn't solve the problem, so hundreds of thousands they went abroad to seek their fortunes. Their diligence and perseverance explains why, today, most of the wealth of Asia is in the hands not of the Japanese but of Overseas Chinese—most of whom trace their roots right here to the vertical province of Fujian.

Fujian—Babel[8] of China (普通话 或不懂话?) Fujian's vertical topography separated villages so well that the province has developed more idioms than any other place in China. The missionary J.E. Walker wrote, in 1878,

> "A native can hardly pass the limits of his own village but his speech will betray him... The tones seem utterly lawless."

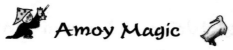
Over a century later, in 1993, Qiu Huang Xing[9] wrote,
"The dialects in Fujian count as the most complicated in China.
The twenty-six million people in Fujian speak the Minnan dialect
and the Puxian, Mindong, Minbei, and Hakka dialects, among over
thirty minor ones. As for the different dialects within each county,
they are simply too many to count. A friend from Fujian told me
that once when somebody in his village got married, he was asked to
go and borrow some dishes from a neighbor living in a village 1.5
kilometers away separated only by a hill and could neither
understand nor make himself understood."

Fujian has endless dialects and unique local customs, and is home to many
minorities like the She, Amei, Bunun, Paiwan, Miao, Hui, Manchu, and the
Hakka (who take great pains to prove they are Han, not a minority). And from
early times, Fujian has also had endless visitors from the four corners of the earth.

Silk Road of the Sea

B.B. Gobi Desert (enroute to Tibet, 1994)

"Silk Road" conjures up images
of the desert, but most trade with
ancient China was by sea because
the Silk Road of the desert was not
really all that silky. We navigated
part of that Not-so-Silky Road
in '94. Toy Ota is still in shock and
I'm still dumping sand out of my trouser cuffs. Sea trade had another
advantage. One ship could carry as much cargo as 700 camels (and ships didn't
spit in your eye). So while Fujianese sailed the seven seas, the rest of the
world sailed to China—via Fujian's Quanzhou.

A mere 70 miles north of Xiamen, Quanzhou was the starting point of the
Silk Road of the Sea. Called Zaytun (a homonym for peace), Quanzhou rivaled
Alexandria Egypt as the greatest port in the world. And UNESCO has called
Quanzhou a "World Museum of Religion" because it had representatives of
every major world religion (and a few that were not of this world). They
included Hinduism, Islam (7 mosques), Judaism, Franciscan Catholicism (at
least two cathedrals and monasteries), Nestorian Christianity, Jainism, Buddhism,
Taoism, Confucianism, and today the city has the last remaining temple to the
Manichaen religion, which was founded over 1700 years ago by a Persian
prophet who didn't make much profit before fellow Persians did him in.

[For more about this "Jerusalem of Asia," please turn to chapter 10]

Xiamen was part of Quanzhou back during Marco Polo's day, and given that
our city has one of the deepest natural harbors in the world, it is likely that many
of the great treasure ships anchored right off our shore.

For over a millennium, Xiamen and Quanzhou hosted foreign traders from all over the known world, as well as missionaries of every conceivable religion. Mohammed himself sent a quartet of Muslim missionaries to China; two set up shop right here in Minnan (Southern Fujian), because they saw that China's future was in Fujian. And so was her past. Fujian's history extends well back before the dawn of Chinese civilization 5,015 years ago (more or less; I was told that China is 5,000 years old, and that was 15 years ago).

China—Ancient and Ageless The weight of China's past is mind boggling. For Americans, an antique is a Barbie doll from 1959; for Chinese, it's a 2,015 year old brass horse—or even the woks and pans they cook with!

Sichuan sauces get tastier over time because the saucepots are never washed. Xiamen University's famed artist Tang Shao Yun told me that his family's sauce is 14 years old, and that a Chengdu family's sauce has been seasoning for over 200 years. The saucy rascal grinned slyly and said, "Their sauce is older than your country!"

An ancient nation sees age differently. On August 11, 1990, *China Daily* announced "China's Ten Outstanding Young People." One outstanding youth, Nie Weiping, world champion of go chess, was 39 years old.

Ponce de Leon, eat your heart out.

Little is known of ancient Fujian inhabitants like the Min because they left no written records, other than some Shang Dynasty (16th — 11th century B.C.) pictographs carved into a rock in the village of Hua'an. They also left some strange relics, like 4,015 year old boat-shaped tombs perched hundreds of feet high on the side of Wu Yi Mountain's vertical cliffs. I've been dying to know why they made tombs like that. Better yet, how'd they do it? It's a real cliffhanger of a puzzle. Had Eric von Danaken (author of *Chariots of the Gods,*) seen them, he'd have easily concluded that ancient extraterrestrials made frequent stopovers in Fujian, probably for Chinese take-out. Maybe NASA thinks so too.

"Sweet 'n Sour Pork -- To Go!"

NASA, having failed to find intelligent life on earth, is seeking it in outer space by sending interstellar greetings in many earth languages. Their message in the ancient Amoy dialect goes, "Friends of space, how are you all? Have you eaten yet? Come visit if you have time."

Maybe ET will come pay his respects to Wuyi's cliff tombs.

5,015 Years of Writing   Eventually, some ancient Chinese wit discovered how to write (or at least how to draw better; modern Chinese characters are still pictographs), and began recording Fujian's history back around the Warring States Period (475—221 BC). The Warring States Period was when the State of Yue (present-day Jiangsu and Zhejiang Provinces) was going at it with the State of Chu (Hubei and Hunan Provinces). After Chu

chewed up Yue, Yue hightailed it off to Guangdong, Guangxi, Vietnam, and Fujian, where they were called the Min Yue.

The Min were fair Fujian's first folk, but nowadays they share our province with nationalities like the She, which are a clan of the Miao tribe. Originally from the Yangtze River Valley, the She claim descent from a legendary emperor—hence their unique "phoenix clothing" and "phoenix hairstyles" (Chinese mythology associates phoenixes with royalty).

Fujian is also home to the Dan tribe, whose Mongol ancestors made the long trek to Fujian about 700 years ago. The Dan are no relation to the Israelite tribe of Dan, though China does have enough Chinese Jews scattered about that some experts claim they are remnants of the Lost Tribes of Israel. And given the state of our local maps, I can see how they got lost.

There was at least a small community of Chinese Jews in Quanzhou at one time, but whether the Lost Tribes are still wandering about China or not, the Lost Arabs certainly are.

Quanzhou, as you'll learn in Chapter 4, has at least 40,000 Muslim Hui, as well as communities of Ding and Guo, descended from Arab and Persian traders in ancient Zaitan (what Marco Polo called Quanzhou). With their curly hair and hooked noses, the Ding and Guo look more Laowai than Laonei. And it appears that Chinese Arabs are just as zealous as their Middle Eastern cousins.

Back when Iran was after Salman Rushdie's hide for writing the heretical "Satanic Verses," Chinese Moslems in N.W. China were after a Chinese writer's neck for the same crime—heresy. With so much running after folks, I guess that is why back in 1935 some wit changed Persia's name to "**Iran**."

Whether lost Jews or running Arabs, Abraham's descendants add a lot of color to Fujian, but just as fascinating are the Chinese Hakka ("guest families"). Over 1,000 years ago, entire villages of Hakka emigrated en masse from the Central Plains to remote areas of Fujian, where for hundreds of years they have faithfully preserved their unique language, costumes, customs, and cuisine. The Hakka now number about 60 million, and include among their luminaries such famous folk as Sun Yat-sen and his wife Soong Ching Ling.

The Legendary Chinese Jews

Jews probably first made their way towards China during the Babylonian exile 2500 years ago, when trade with China was already well established, but a 718 A.D. business letter, written on paper in the trade language of Judeo-Persian, is the first proof on paper (because paper was produced only in China).

In the late 9th century, ibn Khurdadbih, the "Postmaster of Baghdad," spoke of Jewish traders (Radanites) who traveled from Spain and France to China and back via land and sea. Marco Polo met Chinese Jews in Beijing around 1286, and in 1346, the Muslim traveler ibn Battuta entered Hangzhou through the "Jew's Gate. " He wrote of "Jews, Christians and sun-worshiping Turks, a large number in all."

During the mid 16th century, a Portuguese traveler wrote of China's "Moores, Gentiles, and Jewes, have all theyr sundry oathes," and that China's judges had them swear in courts "by the thynges they do worshyppe."

Matteo Ricci, the famed Catholic missionary, is credited with discovering the Kaifeng community of Jews, but they found him—and thought he was a Jew!

A Jewish Chinese mandarin, Ai Tian, left Kaifeng in June, 1605, seeking a better post in Beijing and a meeting with Ricci. Ai had read about Ricci's monotheism, and since Ricci stubbornly denied being a Moslem, the Chinese Jews had concluded he must be a Jew.

Ricci was thrilled to meet Ai, and since Ai was a monotheist but stubbornly denied being a Moslem, Ricci concluded he was a Catholic. Ricci led him into the church (which Ai thought was a synagogue), and knelt before paintings of Mary and the baby Jesus, and a young St. John. Ai decided they must be Rebecca, Jacob and Esau, and the ever courteous Chinese politely knelt. He remarked that his people did not genuflect, but he had no objections to Ricci's peculiar method of honoring ancestors.

Ai saw a painting of Matthew, Mark, Luke and John and asked why the painter didn't include Jacob's other sons. In the end they resolved the misunderstanding—to both party's delight. Though the Jews apparently still considered the Catholics a mere variation of Judaism.

In a 1608 letter to Ricci, the elderly rabbi of Kaifeng's synagogue (built back in 1163) objected to Ricci's insistence that the Messiah had already come. But he said their other differences were minimal, and he suggested that Ricci succeed him as chief rabbi of Kaifeng—provided that Ricci first quit pigging out on pork.

Kaifeng's Jews are thought to have originated from either the area of Persia or else India, Bukhara, or Yemen. The fact that Quanzhou and other coastal cities had Jewish communities suggests they arrived by sea, as traders, rather than overland. But the Ming shut down the silk road and the silk sea, and the Jews succumbed to isolation (though they were never persecuted by the Chinese, as they were in almost all other nations).

Today, the Kaifeng street on which hundreds of Chinese Jews still live is named, "The Lane of the Sect that Teaches the Scriptures."

But no lox and bagels.

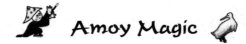
Xiamen on the Rise　　While
Jews and Arabs and Mongols and Han
Chinese were wheeling and dealing and
double dealing, Xiamen Island was in the
throes of a deadly battle for supremacy
between egrets and poisonous snakes. Or
so the legend goes.   The Egrets won,
earning Xiamen one of its many
nicknames, "Egret Island." Xiamen also

had tigers right up until the 30s, but today only 80 Amoy tigers remain in the
wild, and none on Amoy Island. (But we do have
rare white dolphins frolicking in our bay.)

Neither slithery snakes nor imperious egrets kept
away Song Dynasty farmers who were so pleased
with their rice crops that they nicknamed Xiamen
"Jiahe Island," meaning "Isle of Abundant Crops."
At that time, our verdant island was under the
jurisdiction of Tong'an County, Quanzhou Prefecture.
Nowadays the tables have turned, and Tong'an is part
of Xiamen County (and glad of it, given Xiamen's
deep pockets[10]).

Have you brushed lately?

The Citadel of Amoy

"Amoy is situated on an island of the same name. The city proper or
citadel is about one mile in circumference. Its form is nearly that of a
rhomboid or diamond. It is surrounded by a wall about twenty feet in
height, and eight or ten feet in thickness, built of large blocks of coarse
granite. It has four gates. The outer city, or city outside of the walls, is
much more extensive. Its circumference, I suppose, is about six miles. "

Rev. Talmadge, Amoy, 1847

Imperial troops were stationed on
Xiamen back in 1058 (Song Dynasty),
and in 1282, 1,000 soldiers oversaw
political and military affairs in the
"Thousand Households District."

As a defense against Japanese
invasion, Prince Zhou Dexing
enclosed "Xiamen Town" with 110

km of heavily fortified walls, and divided the 4,000 households into 22 wards governed by a city council. Sadly, that ancient wall was razed in 1928, but a few remnants remain here and there (Xiamen University has one).

City Wall at Zhongshan Rd.

China managed to fend off the Japanese fairly well, but Europe's Laowai were another matter. Portuguese began trading with Xiamen in 1516, and Zhangzhou and Quanzhou merchants, eager to resume the trade halted by the emperor a century earlier, began smuggling with the foreign devils on the island of Wuyu, at the entrance to Xiamen harbor.

The Spanish followed the Portuguese in 1575 with a mission from Manila to Fuzhou. When Fuzhou showed them the door, they turned their wills and wallets to Xiamen, where locals would do anything for a peso. And the rush was on.

The Dutch followed the Spaniards in 1604, and after seizing control of Taiwan in 1624, they began smuggling silk and sugar between Taiwan and Jinmen Island (an island now controlled by Taiwan and only a few miles off shore). But the silk and sugar trade proved neither smooth nor sweet once Koxinga came aboard.

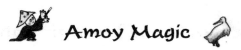

Koxinga, Pirate-Cum-Patriot

Every ship entering Xiamen Harbor is greeted by a massive statue that locals swear protects our port from rough seas and weather. The statue is of Zheng Chenggong (1624—1662), or Koxinga, as the Dutch called him—the pirate-cum-patriot who became one of China's most revered heroes.

Koxinga learned his trade from dad, Zheng Zhilong, who in his youth studied foreign trade in Macao, then sailed to Japan to apply Portuguese trade principles to piracy. Somewhere in Zhilong's busy pirating schedule he found time to marry a Japanese maid, Miss Tagawa, who bore a son: Fu Song, aka Zheng Chenggong, aka Koxinga.

After a stint of piracy in Taiwan, Zhilong returned seven year old Koxinga to Nan An, his hometown, for schooling. Like fathers before and since, he wanted his son to have what he did not have as a youth—namely, lots of homework.

Koxinga was indeed quite the scholar. He survived school and homework, and at age 21 headed off to Nanjing State College, never dreaming that his future lay not in scholastics but in piracy and politics—thanks to the militant Manchus.

After a peasant army overthrew the Ming dynasty, the Manchus waltzed into the power vacuum and created the Qing Dynasty. Their arrogance angered the Hans, who like most homo sapiens resented any arrogance but their own. They rebelled—futilely. After a fight in Fuzhou in 1646, Tagawa (Koxinga's mother) committed suicide, and Koxinga's father surrendered. Filial piety dictated that Koxinga also throw in the towel, but for unclear reasons he parted ways with his father and remained loyal to the Ming. And what better place to base his anti-Ming army than the very Gateway to China— Xiamen?

Koxinga changed Xiamen's name (yet again?) to Siming (思明, "Remember the Ming"), and even today one of Xiamen's main streets is called Siming Rd.

Gulangyu Islet's Sunlight Rock became Koxinga's command center, as well as training grounds for his legendary fighters. I once courted a hernia by hefting an ordinary soldier's 80 pound iron lance. But Koxinga's personal troops made ordinary soldiers look like Cub Scouts. He chose as his body guards ("Tiger Guards") only those who could pick up a 600 pound iron lion and walk off with it.

Koxinga's legendary fighters wore iron masks and iron aprons, wielded bows and arrows painted green, and used long handled swords for killing horses—a brilliant strategy he learned in school days while studying about the Great Wall. (The Great Wall was built to keep out not the barbarians but their horses, for while the Tartars were well nigh invincible on horseback, on foot the Chinese easily made Tartar[11] sauce out of them).

I said "IRON" Apron!

For years, Koxinga raised the battle cry "Remember the Ming," but on April 21, 1661, he set sail with 25,000 men and hundreds of war junks to drive the Dutch from Taiwan and return the island to the motherland. This mission cost him his life, but forever endeared him to Chinese on both sides of the straits.

On January 27, 1662, the Dutch surrendered their prize of 38 years. Chinese on both sides of the straits rejoiced, and Koxinga's men kicked back and played the "Mooncake Gambling Game" (you will too if you're in Xiamen or Taiwan during Mid-Autumn Festival). But patriotism had taken a greater toll on Koxinga's health than piracy had. He died five months later, on June 23.

One Chinese historian noted somberly that Koxinga "died of overwork."

May it be a lesson to us all.

Crashing the Gate—Both Directions

Taiwan's return to the motherland was a windfall for traders in neighboring Xiamen, which was soon the choice port of call for hundreds of Chinese and Portuguese merchant ships. In 1684, the Qing government finally legitimized Xiamen's title of "Gateway to China" by establishing a customs house. The British and then the Spanish flooded into Xiamen, and by the early 1700s, even the once reviled Dutch won a warm reception, coming this time as merchants, not conquerors (there's a lesson in there somewhere).

Slow boat to China

B.B.

While foreign devils flooded in, the Sons of the Dragon flooded out, much to the Emperor's dismay.

As early as 1728, the Emperor tried to halt mass emigration of Fujianese with a proclamation warning that Chinese who did not immediately return to China

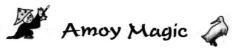
would be banished or, if caught, executed.   But naught stemmed the tide—in either direction.

By the mid 19th century, there were 2½ times more overseas Chinese of Xiamen origin than there were actual Xiamen inhabitants. Today, Xiamen is an ancestral Mecca for 350,000 overseas Chinese, and over 70% of Taiwan residents trace their origins to Southern Fujian — which helps explain why Xiamen and Taiwan people are so alike in dialect, dress, customs and cuisine. But the real problem was not Laonei flooding out but Laowai flooding in...

> "...About 60,000 people go out through Amoy each year on their way abroad, mainly to the Straits Settlements, Java, Borneo and the South Sea Islands... Amoy was the center for foreign trade almost earlier than any other city in the whole of China. The Dutch and the Portuguese traders came here as early as 1300. There are some graves of foreign men that date back to 1698, 1702 and 1710."   Paul Hutchinson, 1920.

Putting the Dragon to Sleep   By the 1750s, Xiamen was booming, and the once placid harbor was wharf-to-wharf foreign ships, but the Emperor placed a higher priority on stability and cultural integrity than mammon.   China unceremoniously ousted the entire rascally bunch of Laowai, and ancient Amoy was once again the sole province of farmers, fishermen, and gardeners – but even so exerted an influence that helped pave the way for American independence.

At midnight, December 16, 1773, irate colonists decked out as Indians boarded a British ship and tossed 342 chests of Anxi tea from Xiamen into Boston Harbor. Thus Xiamen catered the Boston Tea Party, but Britain made up for losing America by seizing Xiamen and the rest of China—not as a colony but as a market for her booming opium trade. (Lithograph by Sarony & Major, 1846).

Boston Tea Party (catered by Xiamen!)

Pigs 'n Poison   The Emperor pulled out all stops to halt the West's opium traffic. He appealed in vain to morality, and to the "Way of Heaven." As a last resort, Commissioner Lin Zexu burned Britain's opium on the docks. And Britain declared war.

During the early 1840s, British warships plied the coasts of China, razing cities and villages to the ground, plundering peasants of chickens and cows and ducks and daughters.   On their way out of smoldering villages, they posted placards that read, "Opium on Sale! An opportunity not to be missed!"   They even loaned peasants the money to buy it.

But the seemingly invincible British met their match in Xiamen! Soldiers and peasants, under the leadership of General Deng Ting-zhen, successfully repelled them.   Victory for Amoy!   Alas, it was a hollow victory. The corrupt Qing, which had failed virtually everywhere else in China, surrendered.

Under the Nanjing Treaty of 1843, Amoy was reopened as one of five treaty ports (the others were Guangzhou, Fuzhou, Ningbo, and Shanghai). The floodgates were opened, the Dragon sank into an opium-induced slumber…and Xiamen was transformed forever as she became a key player in the "Pigs 'n Poison" trade (coolies and opium).

The missionary, Talmadge, wrote that in the 1850s, "More than one-half of the men at Amoy are more or less addicted to the habit."   By 1900, ¼ of Chinese adults were opium addicts, and as late as 1925, half of European profits in Asia came from opium.   Britain abandoned her Hong Kong opium monopoly only in 1945, when the embarrassment began to outweigh the profits.

For well over a century, the West's major profit in Asia came from the opium trade—yet the average Westerner knows little or nothing about the two Opium Wars or the trade that started them. For a sobering but enlightening tale, read the "Lords of Opium" at the end of this book.

"Piggy (Coolie) House" Syme, Muir Co.
(Where "piggies" were "stored" during the "Pigs 'n Poison Trade").

HBR

Xiamen City Gate in 1840

Fashionable Amoy! Thomson took this photo of an Amoy couple back in 1873—4. He wrote,

"The costume and general appearance of the men and women of Amoy…the turbaned figure is an ordinary coolie, the type of the industrious laborer whose services are so highly rated in America and the other countries to which he emigrates. His habits of perseverance and economy gradually secure for him the reward of a modest competency, and if he resists the temptations of the opium pipe, and keeps aloof from the gaming tables, he will in a few years have amassed two or three hundred dollars, and with this he will embark as a farmer or a fishermen in his native land…"

The "Pig" Trade

"Most coolies came from the southern, coastal provinces of China, especially Fukien...large numbers of men where shipped out through Hong Kong, Macau and other ports such as Amoy. They were, from the very start, exploited by Chinese coolie shipping agents and ships' captains—over a third of whom were Americans—then abused and treated atrociously by their employers. The trade in these unfortunate souls was known colloquially as the " Pig Trade " : the 'Poison Trade' was slang for the opium business. Crowded into corrals like slaves they were, as the British Consul in Canton observed in 1852, frequently painted with letters such as P, C or S meaning Peru, California or the Sandwich Islands.

"Whilst some were convicts on release or kidnap victims (we still use the contemporary expression, 'shanghaied'), over 95 per cent were indentured workers who, having had $50 paid for their sea passage on their behalf by would-be employers who regarded it as a loan against future income, were offered a wage they never saw for their loan and deductions for living expenses exceeded their earnings. Their traveling conditions were grim but because money had changed hands they were not legally slaves so no action could be taken against their shippers. Many died en route: one British-owned vessel, the John Calvin, lost 50 per cent of its passengers whilst American ships were often known to have 40 per cent mortality rates.

"Women were sometimes part of 'Pig Trade' cargoes. Under Chinese law females could not emigrate but coolie employers overseas wanted women: the aim was to make their indentured coolies settle in their new countries, thus alleviating the need to import more. The women were mostly either kidnapped or purchases under a Chinese system, known as mui tsai, which allowed for the sale of young girls as servants or concubines-in-training. This aspect of the trade was invidious: in 1855, the British vessel, Inglewood, hove to off Amoy with a cargo of female children all under the age of eight. The crew, disgusted at what comprised their cargo, reported it to the British consul who arranged for the children to be returned home."

Martin Booth, *Opium—A History*, St. Martin's Griffin, New York, NY: 1996).

Note: the pig trade continues today, but instead of $40, Chinese pay "snake heads" as much as $40,000 USD to be smuggled abroad.

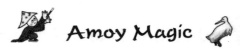

Gulangyu International Settlement, 1913

Gulangyu International Settlement Great Britain established her concession on Gulangyu Island in 1851, the Japanese established theirs in 1900, and the U.S. considered a naval base on the island but gave that idea up after taking over the Philippines in 1899.

One foreign country after another set up consulates and businesses in Xiamen, and in 1902, a Gulangyu municipal council of six foreigners and one token Chinese was "elected," and Gulangyu became an International Settlement with consulates for fourteen nations, including the U.S., Britain, France, Japan, Germany, Spain, Denmark, Portugal, Holland, Austria, Norway, Sweden, and the Philippines, and Belgium. Today, Gulangyu is a showcase of colonial architecture, attracting droves of Laowai and Laonei alike, including the "Father of Tropical Medicine," Dr. Patrick Manson. (Note: the photo on next page is from Xiamen, but is *not* Manson).

Dr. Manson, "Father of Tropical Medicine,"

made his monumental discoveries right here in Xiamen!

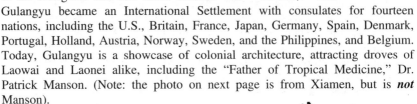

The intrepid Scotsman had a tough time gaining the locals' trust at first. For centuries, Chinese had told tales of how foreigners ate Chinese babies and used their eyeballs to line mirrors, so when Dr. Manson insisted he'd come to "serve" them, they may have thought he meant to serve them up on a platter. He gained their trust by operating a clinic that was open to the street so everyone could see that his surgeon's scalpel didn't come in a set, with knife and fork.

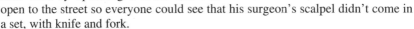

Over the years, the good doctor sought to solve the problems that plagued his beloved Amoy folk by dissecting everything from mosquitoes to corpses (in the dead of night, in graveyards, because Chinese frowned on cutting up corpses).

Manson was the first to link mosquitoes with malaria, and was very skilled at surgery for those suffering from elephantiasis. By the time he left Xiamen, he was loved by Laowai and Laonei alike. And in Hong Kong, he set up a school of medicine. One of his pupils was none other than Sun Yat-sen!

Another Illustrious Laowai   A Laowai from Gulangy International Settlement was destined to help shape the course of the 20th Century.   Dr. Walter H. Brattain, son of Ross R. Brattain and Ottilie Houser, was born in Amoy on February 10, 1902. After he obtained his Ph.D. from the University of Minnesota in 1929, he spent the rest of his life with Bell Laboratories, and with Dr. John Bardeen invented the point-contact transistor—the cornerstone of modern electronics!

The International Settlement became a shambles when the Japanese ravaged China before and during World War II.   American and British soldiers quelled a Japanese takeover in 1939, but in December 1941 Japan seized control of the island and established a puppet Chinese National Government.

After the War, Xiamen became yet again a typical Western settlement – a lawless enclave of bars, dance halls, trading companies, banks and brothels.   But the writing was on the wall.[12]

Britain had already surrendered its concession back in 1930 (while retaining rights in the International Settlement).   Japan surrendered her concession in 1945, and the last foreign rights were relinquished by 1946.   And then came Chairman Mao.

The Great Helmsman gained

HBR

Taking sick sons to Amoy Hospital

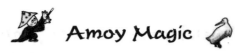

fame after leading thousands along the Long March (which was followed by a Short April). And then in 1949, Chairman Mao ousted us Laowai forever.

Well, not quite forever. We're back. But happily, this time we're not crashing the Gateway to China. The Chinese warmly welcome us Laowai—as Waiguo Pengyou!

Chiang Chin Bridge-God Temple, Amoy 1913

Post Liberation Xiamen — an Economic Power House

One of Beijing's top post-Liberation priorities was transforming Xiamen Island into an economic powerhouse. They began by ending the island's age-old isolation. Without even consulting the Chiang Chin Bridge-God, by the mid-50s, Beijing had connected Amoy to the mainland with a causeway (called a "causeway" 'cause it was the only way across). They followed up with a railway in 1958, and the establishment of Xinglin Industrial District.

Before 1949, Xiamen had produced products like cigarettes, wine, and matches, for its primary role was to serve Western merchants, bankers, and brothels. But by the late 1950s, several Xiamen firms were already engaged in producing advanced electrolytic capacitors, carbon resistors, fish detectors, deng deng. (Chinese for "etcetera," last reminder!) Xiamen's chemical industry set off in high gear in 1958, and now produces everything from rubber tires and synthetic ammonia to Chinese and Western medicines.

The textile industry was another resounding success, with production of various synthetic and natural fibers. The Municipal Grain Bureau was eventually created to oversee factories that today produce and export every conceivable foodstuff to dozens of countries.

Banks also flourished because Xiamenese have banking in their blood. Around the turn of the century, swarms of Chinese bankers trotted about Xiamen with baskets of money slung over their shoulders. By the 1920s, her "basket bankers" had expanded operations and opened over 100 "Money Shops." So the Central Government had no problem finding talented folk to staff Xiamen banks in the 1950s — but Xiamen's economic field-day ended all too quickly.

While Beijing was determined to build New China, Chiang Kai Shek was equally determined to recapture the Old China that his family had virtually owned for decades. Sin he didn't have a snowball's chance in Haiti[13], he vented his frustration by trying to bomb Xiamen back into the Stone Age.

Beijing eventually read the writing on the wall, put further construction on hold (why build up what the Generalissimo would just raze?), and beat its plowshares back into swords. While the rest of China continued to grow, Fujian Province, and particularly Xiamen, became a frontline defense against Taiwan. By the late 1970s, once glorious Fujian had become one of China's poorest provinces, and Xiamen was not the Gateway to China but one giant bomb shelter. Of course, by the mid-60s Taiwan was all but forgotten anyway, as the "Cultural Revolution" (1966—1976) raged for an entire decade, wreaking havoc throughout China, from Canton to Lhasa. Xiamen did not escape either.

Xiamen's Yundang Lake was once a small haven for ships and one of Xiamen's major aquatic production centers, but in 1971, during the throes of the Cultural Revolution, all development stopped and the port choked with silt. Some so-called experts actually argued that the lake was better off used as fields than as a harbor. It wasn't until the 1980s that China had come to grips with the forces that had almost torn it apart. Then national, provincial and municipal governments set out once again to achieve their long delayed dream of making Xiamen an economic and trade center.

Yundang Lake, by then a squalid, noxious mess, was cleaned up, and today is a recreational area that has hosted international sporting events. Every weekend, crowds throng the lakeside parks, listening to the music and watching the colorful Dancing Fountains.

A century ago, Sun Yat-sen dreamed of transforming Xiamen and Haicang into an "Oriental Mega-Port." It seems now that his dream will be fulfilled.

Geography Xiamen (aka "Egret Island," "Pearl on the Sea," "Isle of Prosperity," deng deng) is an island of about 130 sq. km floating a mile or so off Fujian's serpentine coastline, directly across from Taiwan Province. More precisely, we are at: 118°04' 04" East, 24°26' 46" North.

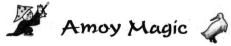 Amoy Magic

We are 695 nautical miles south of Shanghai, 287 nautical miles north of Hong Kong, 816 miles from Nagasaki, and a few thousand nautical miles from Tom's No. 5 Chili Burgers in L.A.

Locals claim Xiamen is shaped like an egret in flight, but I don't see the resemblance. Xiamen is almost round (13.7 km north to south and 12.5 km east to west). It looks to me more like an egret after a crash landing. *Splat!*

The northern reaches of this *Splat!* are mounds of volcanic rock reaching 150 meters above sea level, and the south is hilly, with Yunding Hill towering all of 339.6 meters above sea level.

Amoy's gardens bloom year round, thanks to an atmospheric alchemy that keeps the mercury at about 20.8℃—except from July to September, when it soars to 28℃ or more, and the humidity is so high you can suck the air with a soda straw.

Three or four typhoons per year, usually during July to October, add some excitement to an otherwise boringly nice climate, and help blow away some of the hot air that accumulates here.

But Typhoon Dan, in October '99, blew away more than hot air.

Typhoon Dan, and Disaster Preparedness   As Typhoon Dan headed for Xiamen, newly arrived Kodak engineer Rick Huntington asked, "Are typhoons bad here? We've never seen one."

"Nah," I said. "They always fizzle out over Taiwan, which acts like a buffer. Besides, Koxinga's statue guards the harbor."

Koxinga must have been out to lunch, because the next day I was huddling at home and eating crow[14].

Typhoon Dan was Xiamen's worst in 40 years; 250 mph winds atomized rain and whipped it about until it resembled a white laser light show. Giant banyans toppled, power poles and lines went down, window frames were ripped right out of the walls.

Amazingly, in spite of the devastation, utilities were quickly restored even at Xiamen University, which was worst hit.   But after going without power for four days, we'll no longer take warnings so lightly (neither will local fishermen; over 100 died).

Adopt the Boy Scout's motto, "Be Prepared."

Typhoon/Earthquake Preparedness Kit:

> Drinking water (3 days supply), a few dozen candles (and perhaps locally sold emergency lights), fresh batteries for the radio, canned fruits and vegetables, bread (bakeries may close); first aid kit (including a ten day course of oral penicillin, available without prescription in Xiamen pharmacies).

Even Typhoon Dan didn't affect our phone service, so you can probably call your work unit for updates and advice, or log on to the Internet at http://www.weather.com.

Dr Jan Engsberg, a Xiamen resident since 1988, suggests you also do a little earthquake preparedness (though after 7 years in Southern California, earthquakes don't shake me up that much).

Fortunately, though we average about 1.2 meters of rain annually, really bad weather is rare in Xiamen. But you'll need an umbrella during the rainy season (February through July)—unless you're like the two dapper fellows I encountered in Xiamen's airport.

When in Rome... wear Sandwich Bags!

I love Chinese' informality. Where but China would a university president pedal a 25 year old bicycle to work wearing cotton shorts, black socks and leather sandals, and a white straw hat with pink satin chin ribbon? Even Premiers hold press conferences without a tie, suggesting that the "Dress for Success" cult is all wet—or can be...

One morning it began raining cats and canaries (no dogs; they hit the wok before they hit the ground) just as Xiamen International airport disgorged a mass of passengers. They raced for buses and taxis, clad in complimentary, disposable plastic raincoats that looked like giant sandwich bags, but at least they were dry.

Then out marched two *Laowai*, shoulders back and heads high, clutching their expensive briefcases and Gucci bags. They surveyed the scurrying crowd of plastic wrapped locals, exchanged bemused grins, and stepped out boldly where no man with sense enough to get out of the rain had gone before. Within seconds their $400 pinstriped suits were soaked and their smartly padded shoulders had slumped, but they maintained their dignified march all the way to the taxi stand.

The quiet snickers suggested that no one was impressed.

So when in Rome, wear a sandwich bag. But I'll still pass on the cotton hats and pink chin ribbons.

B.B.

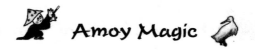

Amoy's Average Monthly Temperatures

Month	Avg.	Hi	Low
January	12	17	9.2
February	12.6	16.9	10.1
March	16	20.3	13.6
April	19.9	24.2	17.2
May	21.4	25.1	18.9
June	24.7	28.3	22.2
July	27.4	31.7	24.6
August	28.3	32.8	25.5
September	25.8	29.9	23.2
October	22.6	27.3	19.5
November	11.2	19	12.5
December	13.3	17.9	10.4

Temperature Conversion Chart

Fahrenheit to Celsius: subtract 32° and divide by 1.8.
Celsius to Fahrenheit: multiply by 1.8 and add 32°.
Or just cheat and use this handy-dandy conversion chart:

Centigrade		Fahrenheit	Centigrade		Fahrenheit
0.0	Freezing	32.0	37.5		99.5
10.0		50	38.0		100.4
12.7		55	38.5		101.3
15.5		60	39.0		102.2
18.3		65	39.5		103.1
20		68	40.0		104.0
21.1		70	40.5		104.9
23.8		75	41.0		105.8
26.6		80	100.0	Boiling Point	212.0
28.3		85			
32.2		90			
35		95			
36.0		96.8			
36.5		97.7			
37.0	Body Temp	98.6			

Historical Supplement!

Xiamen's Walking History Book

Hong Bu Ren, has compiled an amazing bilingual photo album entitled, *Old Photos of Xiamen*. (《厦门旧影》). It really brings to life Ole Amoy's rich heritage of Western and Chinese exchange (not all so pleasant, but all enlightening).

Hong Bu Ren...

...Xiamen's Walking History Book

B.B.

As one of China's first treaty ports, Xiamen was also one of the first places in Asia to have photos taken after the invention of the camera. And since his youth, Hong Bu Ren has devoted his life to collecting and preserving photos and written works about Xiamen's history. Professor Hong's two adjoining apartments are packed wall to wall with literature and books. Fortunately, his wife is a lot more patient than mine!

Hong Bu Ren is supposedly retired, but I feel pretired just watching him as he runs about advising governments, universities, and foreign researchers who are beginning to show a keen interest in Xiamen's rich past. He is an amazing man, with tireless energy and enthusiasm, and a sense of humor that reminds me much of my prankster grandfather (except for the eyes, he even looks like him!).

Professor Hong has very graciously allowed me to include photos from his book in *Amoy Magic*—but I hope they serve only to whet your appetite to buy his book (I've bought 25 copies!).

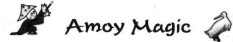

Colonial Amoy

From, *Old Photos of Xiamen* (《厦门旧影》)

Japanese Consulate

British Consulate
(built in 1844; photo
from turn-of-the-century)

HBR

Thirteen countries had consulates in

the bustling port of Amoy, which was said to have more wealthy people than any city on earth except Pasadena, California (thank, in large part, to the infamous "Piggy 'n Poison" trades).[15]

HBR

U.S. Consulate (originally built in 1844; this bldg. burned down in 1904)

Dutch Consulate
(Originally est. 1857)

HBR

German Consulate (1870)

From, *Old Photos of Xiamen* (《厦门旧影》)

Amoy (1905)

HBR

Amoy was wealthy in part because, for almost 1,000 years, she had been part of the Silk Road of the Sea, with one of the planet's deepest natural harbors. But as the rest of the world modernized, so did Xiamen. She even hosted the first round-the-world flight team—3 years before Lindbergh sailed the Atlantic!

New Amoy Dock Company, Ltd.
(British, begun 1858)

HBR

Osaka Steamship Company

HBR

Bustling Zeng Cuo'an Airport

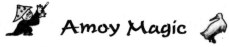

Amoy Magic

From, *Old Photos of Xiamen* (《厦门旧影》)

HBR — Gulangyu Municipal Council Police

British Police   HBR

Well-armed foreign police forces insured the stability that kept Amoy wealthy. They also enforced the now infamous "No Dogs or Chinese Allowed" signs that adorned some Xiamen clubs and parks. (We Laowai today are fortunate the Chinese are such a forgiving race!)

Chinese refugees hid in churches, schools and hospitals

HBR

Japanese soldiers search passengers on Gulangyu Ferry

From, *Old Photos of Xiamen* (《厦门旧影》)

Gulangyu's International Settlement wasn't the easiest place to get to before regular ferry service was established, but Longtou St. was as busy even back in the '30s as it is today.

Amoy-Gulangyu sampan (1921)

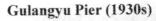

Gulangyu Pier (1930s)

Foreign Tombstones on Gulangyu

Longtou St., Gulangyu, 1930s

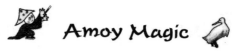

Amoy Magic

From, *Old Photos of Xiamen* (《厦门旧影》)

Zhongshan Rd. 1928   HBR

Amoy's Ancient Walls, which helped Xiamen repel centuries of pirates (and the British, for a while at least) were destroyed during the 1920s and 1930s to make way for urban renewal and expansion.

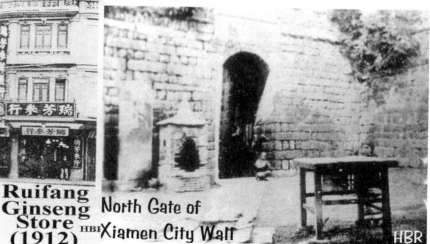

Ruifang Ginseng Store (1912)   North Gate of Xiamen City Wall   HBR

From, *Old Photos of Xiamen* (《厦门旧影》)

"New Street Chapel"--the 1st Church in China! (1948)

Gulangyu "Trinity Church" (begun in 1934)

Hope Hospital, Gulangyu
(Founded 1898 by American Missionaries)

"Bamboo Chapel" (1859)

Xiamen Mission School Pupils

While their countrymen traded in "piggies 'n poison," Amoy's missionaries built China's first churches and helped pioneer China's education of women, and introduced modern medicine (you read about Dr. Manson on p.20. Review, if necessary; you'll be tested later).

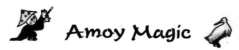

Amoy Magic

From, *Old Photos of Xiamen* (《厦门旧影》)

Bustling Laowai may have thought the local Laonei lazy, and going about life as usual, but not so. Amoy people were learning, and over the decades proved to be remarkably adaptable, and competitive, and excelled in not only commerce (like the Chinese-run Dutch Milk Cow enterprise below) but also athletics. And Xiamen is known even today for her world-class athletes. (I used to run[16] a lot myself—until I started boiling the water longer).

Street Scene

Dutch Milk Cow Enterprise

Rural Amoy kids eagerly await snack sellers

Yang Xiuqiong Swim Champion '35

Hysterical Supplement

Ming Dynasty Tales of Henpecked[17] Hans

We Laowai and Laonei are more alike than we realize, and nothing brings it home better than these ancient Ming Dynasty tales of henpecked Hans.   I hope Susan Marie doesn't read them...

Till Death Do We Part

A number of henpecked men were holding an emergency meeting to discuss ways to regain their dignity.   A bachelor prankster walked into their midst and said, "Your wives heard of this gathering and are all on their way here to deal with you." All but one panicked and dashed out the door.

"He's the only one with courage to stand up to his wife!"   the   bachelor exclaimed.   But   closer examination   revealed   he'd died of fright.

When I'm Ready.

After his wife had beaten him badly, a man crawled under his family bed. "Come out this instant!" his wife screamed.

"I'm not ready yet!"

"I am man enough to do as I please!" he said. "And I'll come out when I'm good and ready."

Grapes of Wrath

A magistrate asked his court clerk how he got the scratches on his face.   The embarrassed clerk said, "Last night, I was walking in the yard, taking in the cool night air, when a grape trellis fell on me and scratched my face."

The magistrate declared, "Only a wife could do this. Have her brought here this instant."

But the magistrate's own wife had been hiding in the next room, and hearing this she stormed into the court. The terrified magistrate shouted, "Court's in recess! Clear the court! My own trellis is coming down!"

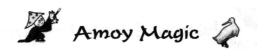

Nighty Nightsoil [18]   Two men terrified of their wives were moaning to one another. One said, "My wife has become so strict that now I even have to empty the night soil."

"What!" said his friend. "Why, if I were you –"

"—If it were you what would you do?" came his wife's voice from behind him.

"If it were I, I'd go empty it."

More ancient tales at the end of the next chapter!

**Warning: Amoy is Addictive—
but good for one's health!**

Supplement

Dethroned[19]
(written with hindsight)

B.B.

Squatter's Rights?

I love China, but I'm sometimes thrown for a loop by the most mundane things—like Chinese toilets. I was shocked when I learned they are little more than a white ceramic hole in the ground. "Where on earth do I sit?" I demanded.

"You don't sit," Susan Marie explained carefully, as if I were one of her sons, and not her husband. "You plant your feet on the raised rectangular or shoe-shaped platforms and squat."

"You're kidding!" I valiantly gave it a go—and lost face when I fell on my face.

When Sue learned that I could not squat flat footed without holding on for dear life to a wall or pipe, she demanded, "What do you mean you can't squat? I can do it. Your sons can do it. You're the only one in the world, Bill Brown, who can't squat!"

"Easy for you to claim squatter's rights![20]" I retorted. "You were born and raised in Taiwan, and Shannon and Matthew grew up in Xiamen. But I'm American, and I can't squat!"

Alas, years of comfortably ensconcing[21] myself upon the great ceramic, and sometimes cushioned, thrones of America have rendered my body too inflexible for flat-footed squatting, no matter how desperate the situation. While Barbie, Ken, and G.I. Joe[22] may be fully bendable, I am not.

Ironically, Chinese are the ones who invented the sit-down flush toilet that I so long for, though I must confess that the squat versions are indeed more practical and durable. Not much can go wrong with a ceramic hole, and there are no lids or seat rings to clean or fix (because seat rings often break when unenlightened souls squat atop the Western sit-down toilets in China's western restaurants). But practicality notwithstanding, I still miss the days of sitting pretty[23] upon the throne while browsing the newspaper or Reader's Digest (or, nowadays, Common Talk!).

Fortunately, while Chinese ceramic holes are still the norm, toilet paper has improved immensely. Not surprisingly, Chinese invented toilet paper as well as toilets. Almost 1,000 years ago, imperial households employed small squares of perfumed paper upon their royal rears. Even commoners used recycled paper—though one scholar firmly opposed using paper with poetry upon it. But when I came to Xiamen in 1988, I was hard pressed to believe that TP was a Chinese invention. Xiamen TP felt like recycled sandpaper, and it was months before our tender bourgeois bottoms could cope.

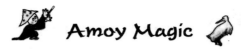

Fortunately, Xiamen firms now put out quality TP, and it turns out that foreign bourgeois buttocks weren't the only ones ready for pampering. Chinese also prize the new TPs, many of which have fragrances, and delicate prints.   An American lady in Quanzhou told me her favorite brand is "Mind Act Upon Mind," which boasts, "For soft and comfortable life you can really feel good."

But for life to be soft and comfortable for me, I need an American sit-down toilet, because Susan Marie's disdain notwithstanding, I still can't squat.

Laonei （老内） Notes

[1] Quaker: Nixon was a Quaker; also called "Friends," ("Society of Friends").

[2] Sears catalog: a century ago, poor rural Americans used the pages as toilet paper

[3] Caviar Empty: a play on "Caveat Emptor" (Latin for "Buyer beware")

[4] David Carradine: Caucasian who played a Chinese martial arts master in the TV series, "Kung Fu."

[5] Orient: a pun. Orient means both "Asia" and "to give direction to"

[6] Dire Taiwan Straits: a play on "dire straits" (tough situation)

[7] Kettle of Fish: troublesome, awkward or embarrassing situation

[8] Babel: ancient biblical city (probably Babylon) where God interrupted construction of a tower to heaven by confusing languages so builders could not understand one another; a confusion of sounds or voices

[9] Excerpt from, "A Cultural Tour Across China."

[10] Deep pockets: lots of money

[11] Tartar sauce: mayonnaise-based sauce for fish (Tartars were the ferocious Turkish or Mongolians during the Middle Ages).

[12] Writing on the wall: easy to see trouble was ahead. From a Biblical story in which God warned the King of Babylon by using his finger to write a warning on a wall. 圣经，但以理书 5:5-30

[13] Snowball's chance in Haiti: we usually say "hell" instead of "Haiti" (it's too hot for snowballs to survive in either hell or Haiti without melting).

[14] Eat crow: retract something one has said; be defeated.

[15] Piggy 'n Poison (coolie and opium trafficking)

[16] Run: also means "suffer from dysentery"

[17] Henpecked: strict control by wife; often expressed by the Chinese pun Qi guan yan (妻管严)

[18] night soil: human excrement collected as fertilizer
[19] Dethroned: we often call the toilet the "throne. "
[20] Squatter's rights: the right to squat (though here, "squat" is means to occupy a piece of land).
[21] Ensconce: settle securely or comfortably
[22] Children's dolls, with jointed limbs, that are advertised as "fully bendable!"
[23] Sitting pretty: successful

Chapter 2
Getting Down
to Business

"Everyone lives by selling something."
Robert Louis Stevenson

Time Magazine(May 11, 1998, p.16):
"To understand where China is heading, check out Peking University. Long a hotbed[1] of political activism, the school these days is buzzing. But what's got students hopped up[2] isn't politics but getting ahead....Like the rest of China, Peking University is remaking itself for a modern, market-driven age.

"...Biology major Lei Ping sums up the new spirit. 'We are not as preoccupied with politics as our predecessors, but at heart we are just as patriotic, ' she says. 'We are more pragmatic. After all, we're in a new era now. '"

Actually, Chinese pragmatism is nothing new, for over the past 5,015 years the Sons of the Dragon (driven perhaps by their wives) have invented everything from Pi to Ice Cream[3].

π &

Pi and Ice Cream "Necessity is the mother of invention" explains why Chinese have come up with everything from exact pi to ice cream. The age-old struggle for survival on limited arable[4] land has forced China's teeming millions to be both pragmatic and innovative. And they're still innovating today.

In a remote Shandong Province town, we came across a poor mayor's version of a modern street sweeper. A handmade tractor lugged an iron and wood contraption from which whirled a dozen handmade straw brooms. And it worked. That poor hamlet's main street (it's only street) was spotless.

Peasant or urbanite, Chinese are resourceful, resilient, and persistent, and if Cathay's future even remotely mirrors her past, we can expect some marvels in the coming century — particularly in commerce.

Commerce, not Conquer We Laowai are fortunate that Chinese have always emphasized commerce over conquering. For centuries, Chinese merchants sailed the seven seas in the world's most advanced ships. They were virtually unsinkable, thanks to innovative watertight compartments, but China could have easily sunk the barbarians' boats with such Chinese inventions as gunpowder, rockets, and cannon, and finished off survivors with innovative crossbows.

The 1,000 mile Grand Canal, earth's longest manmade waterway, led Chinese to invent suspension bridges, canal locks, and the segmental arch. And China's canals and rivers, not Twain's Mississippi, hosted the first paddlewheel ships, so Chinese merchants never had to worry about being up a creek without a paddle.[5]

Venetian blinds came from China, not Venice. Pasta originated in China, not Italy, as did the use of coal for cooking it. Speaking of fuel, Chinese invented deep drilling for natural gas and salt. They invented the rotary crank, the waterwheel-driven bellows in steel smelting, and the seismograph.

Given their penchant[6] for paperwork, it is no surprise that Chinese invented paper, as well as paper money. (The note below was printed in Amoy). And our planet's first newspaper, the *Peking News*, ran from A.D. 363 to 1935. (Chinese reporters may well have been the first to fight deadlines, thanks to mechanical clocks which originated not in Europe but in Tang Dynasty China).

While we're on a roll[7] on paper, over 1,000 years ago, Imperial behinds luxuriated in 4″ squares of perfumed paper—the world's first TP! (toilet paper)—though a famous poet warned against using paper which had writing on it. And they probably did their business[8] while court musicians serenaded them on a two-stringed Erhu—the world's first violin.

Chinese, not Gutenberg[9], first printed with movable type. And contrary to Britannica CD, the first greeting cards were not European Valentine cards but Chinese New Year cards, invented centuries earlier by noblemen tired of too many New Year visits.

Another lesson for Britannica: it wasn't the French in 1783 who first used parachutes, but Chinese acrobats way back in 1306.

And if you think Laowai Life is sometimes a zoo[10], there's good reason. China invented zoos way back in 1150 B.C.

While my Nordic ancestors huddled in bark shelters and caves and cowered at moon-devouring eclipses, Chinese plotted the courses of sun, moon and stars. Records of solar and lunar eclipses are found on bones and tortoise shells dating from the Shang Dynasty, over 3,015 years ago, and Chinese astronomers recorded every one of Halley's Comet's 27 appearances over the past 2,100 years.

Chinese came up with both the decimal system and binomial mathematics, and about 1500 years ago, the mathemagician[11] Zu Chongzhi calculated the ratio of a circle's circumference to its diameter to be 3.1415926.

Last but by all means least, Chinese invented "zero," which is really handy in Xiamen, now that her GDP has so many zeroes behind it.

Overlooking Xiamen Harbor just after Liberation

Xiamen—China's Mother Lode   Chinese pragmatism is still alive and well, making the Middle Kingdom a gold mine for entrepreneurial Laowai. And Xiamen Special Economic Zone (SEZ), the Gateway to China, is becoming the mother lode—for many reasons:

1. **Natural and Situational Assets** The best overall weather in China, combined with one of the world's best natural deep-water harbors, has helped rank Xiamen's 81 berth port in China's top ten (#7 in China, #40 worldwide). We handled over 27 million tons of cargo in 2,002 (half of which my wife bought in Xiamen's new shopping centers). Xiamen is a natural port of call for ships linking over 60 ports in 40 countries—315 voyages each month!

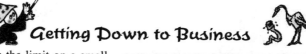

But land's the limit on a small gem like Xiamen, so we've invested almost 3 billion Yuan on the Haicang Suspension Bridge to connect Xiamen Island and the new 100 sq. km. Haicang Investment Zone (which a century ago, Dr. Sun Yat-sen envisioned as an **"Oriental Mega-Port"**).

Stretching 1,108 meters across Xiamen Harbor, Haicang is the second longest suspension bridge of its type in the world.

Haicang's natural port extends along 26 km. of coastline, and for 5.5 kilometers the average depth is over 10 meters.   A bay extending 3 nautical miles, and a string of offshore islands that act as a natural breakwater, create an ideal haven for ships.   Back in Dr. Sun's day, America's "Mobil" consortium and Britain's "Asia" had invested in Haicang and were using it as a petroleum transfer station and marine refueling base, but only now are Haicang, and Xiamen, becoming the super-port that Dr. Sun dreamed of—attracting even ships from Taiwan, now that direct shipping has resumed.   (I'm still hoping for the day that passengers can just hop a boat back to Taiwan).

Xiamen's extensive natural harbor, combined with her strategic proximity to Kong Kong and Taiwan province (a mere 100 miles as the fly flies[12]) makes Xiamen the natural gateway for overseas Chinese and others seeking to stake a claim in China.   But just in case the slow boat to China isn't fast enough, Xiamen also has one of China's top airports, Xiamen Gaoqi International Airport. Over 22 airlines handle 400 flights a week to 89 domestic and international destinations, including Singapore, Penang, Kuala Lumpur, Manila and Jakarta. We also have direct cargo flights to cities in China, Hong Kong, Taiwan, Singapore, Nagoya of Japan, and Chicago. And planes

landing at Xiamen's new airport are a far cry from the four that landed in Xiamen Bay way back in 1924—on the **first round the world flight.**

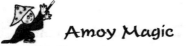 **Amoy Magic**

Round the World—and China Too! On April 6th, 1924, 3 years before Lindbergh crossed the Atlantic, four specially built Douglas World Cruisers took off for an around the world flight. They must have had more layovers than a cheap Korean Air flight at Christmas because it took two full months to reach Amoy.

Zeng Cuo'an Airport

On June 7th, they flew from Shanghai and landed in Amoy Harbor, refueled at the Standard Oil depot, dined with the American consul, and flew out the next day. Fortunately, modern planes no longer land in Xiamen bay.

At least, not intentionally.

2. Social and Cultural Assets Gumption, more than geography, explains why over 350,000 overseas Chinese (and 70% of Taiwanese) now trace their ancestry back to coastal South Fujian. It took unusual gumption for tradition-bound Xiamen peasants to cut their ancestral apron strings[13] and sail to every corner of the globe in search of work. Most of them toiled at menial labor, but many of them saved every penny, peso, and peseta to build industrial empires that even today exert great global influence. (I was not surprised when *Time Magazine* reported that overseas Chinese, not Tokyo, wield the greatest economic power in Asia today).

Most Chinese, of course, stayed behind in Xiamen. Maybe the prospect of capital punishment dampened their pioneering spirit. But they did not lack drive and initiative. They simply redirected it, and having proved themselves adept in the rice fields, they're now going to town in the fields of industry, making Xiamen uniquely blessed by an abundance of highly motivated and qualified laborers, both skilled and unskilled.

3. Education in Xiamen At least 10% of Xiamen's urban residents have higher education, thanks to 120 scientific research institutes, 8 universities and colleges, 12 poly-technics—and Xiamen University's excellent **MBA** program! (Phone: 218-6441).

For those with Little Laowai running about, Xiamen International School offers comprehensive education from grades 1 ~ 12 (a trump card that has helped win

firms like Dell, General Electric, Linde, deng deng).   And when you're little ones start spouting unintelligibly in Mandarin, don't panic.   You can always sign up for full and part-time language courses in Xiamen University's Overseas Correspondence college, which offers study in everything from anthropology to acupuncture (for more details on OCC, turn to page 67).

4. Economic and political   Xiamen, as an SEZ, has been granted Provincial level authority and autonomy in economic administration and local legislative power. This gives Xiamen's leadership unprecedented flexibility in guiding the development of this 1,516 sq. km. district, and insuring the best business environment for both domestic and foreign enterprises in Xiamen.

When we stepped off the slow boat to China in '88, Xiamen was a dirty backwater town with inadequate and unreliable water, frequent power outages, heavy pollution, and abysmal infrastructure. The only tall building in town was the harbor's Seaview Building, and foreign enterprises were not coming but going. But Xiamen did an about face after the arrival of Mayor Hong Yong Shi, who like Teddy Roosevelt "speaks softly but carries a big stick."

After a close encounter of the worst kind with a Xiamen traffic jam, Mayor Hong moved infrastructure to the top of his to-do list.   The pitiful path that was once Xiahe road is now six lanes wide (bike lanes alone are as wide as the original road). The beautifully landscaped island beltway relieves congestion while providing mile after mile of beaches and manicured parks.

Our mushrooming skyline has prompted son Shannon to say, "Xiamen is now like a little Hong Kong."   Fortunately, Xiamen has also retained its distinctive colonial architecture, which draws droves of Laowai and Laonei alike. But look closely because some of the beautiful "colonial architecture" was built not in the 1840s but the 1990s. The original structures were in such bad shape that the government razed them and built duplicates. (The best examples are the buildings on the corner of ZhongShan and Siming Roads.).

By 1996, Xiamen had approved 71 foreign invested projects with a total investment volume of USD 1.36 billion, and 94 domestic projects with a total investment volume of RMB 2.343 billion, and by 1996 the industrial output value of Haicang Investment Zone had reached RMB 3.2 billion. Mega-Port, and mega-bucks.

Current Events In the early '90s, electrical blackouts were almost routine. When we had power, it could drop to 160 volts when a neighbor half a block away fired up an electric teakettle, and surge up to 280 volts when they unplugged it. We used to fry[14] more computers and printers than fish and vegetables. But power is no longer a *current* problem, thanks to Songyu Power Plant's two 300,000 KW generators, which supplement our Fujian Electric reserves (Xiamen also has three reserve power plants).

Giving Us a Line[15] Phone service has improved too. In 1989, I made only two phone calls, across campus. Neither got through. But now we have direct dial service to 1800 Chinese cities and over 210 countries or regions. And no more $500 U.S. deposit and 3 year wait for a phone. Now its about $100, and installation is often same-day. In less than a decade, we've gone from tin-can phones to having two phones at home, plus cell phones, fax, internet, e-mail... We're so well connected that I sometimes long for the peace of yesteryear.

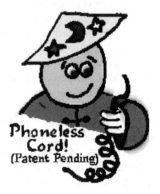

Phoneless Cord!
(Patent Pending)

Maybe I can buy a phoneless cord?

It's nice to have dependable water too—no more catching water from mountain runoffs behind Xiamen University. Xiamen's daily water capacity is 915,000 tons, which according to official sources is adequate to the year 2,005.

So in 2,006, it's back to the mountain runoffs?

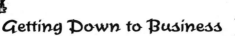

And Xiamen's really cooking nowadays, thanks to dependable sources of natural gas and propane—and every other kind of gas, from oxygen to nitrogen, argon, carbon dioxide, hydrogen, coal gas and flatulence. Pass the beans?[16]

Growing, but Green.

Basic utilities no longer worry Laowai, and health and health are looking up too. Xiamen has almost 1300 medical establishments, including an advanced eye care facility utilizing the latest laser surgery. Zhongshan Hospital is so advanced that on Nov. 7, 2002, they performed an artificial heart implant on three year old Zhou Boling (the implant for the poor son of migrants was funded by donations from local citizens).

Zhongshan Hospital also has a "Laowai Clinic," and the Lifeline Clinic has foreign doctors and English-speaking staff. But our 1300 medical facilities may have less business now that Xiamen has cleaned up her act.

Back in 1990, Xiamen was less than pristine. Her streets and sidewalks were covered with litter, and a film of black coal soot coated much of our town, and our lungs as well. Mary Poppins[17] might see romance in coal-black, but it's a different kettle of soot in real life. But someone must have heard that "Cleanliness is next to Godliness," because by the mid '90s, Beijing had recognized Xiamen as the cleanest city in China, with the purest air. Xiamen has received awards like "National Sanitary City," "National Garden City" and "Model City for Environmental Protection." Over the past 20 years, Xiamen ranked #1 in economic growth—and also #2 in environmental sustainability!

To avoid what it calls the West's 'pollution before solution' model of development, Xiamen's core guideline has been:

"No projects that create severe pollution are admitted into Xiamen. The municipality's unremitting policy has been that Xiamen should not sacrifice its environment for economic prosperity."

Talk is cheap, but Xiamen puts her money where her mouth is. Since 1997, investment in environmental protection has equaled 3% of Xiamen's GNP. The biggest payoff is seen at Yundang Lagoon.

Yundang Lagoon   Yundang Lagoon was once so smelly that we, literally, held our nose whenever we got near. But thanks to a 400 million Yuan face-lift, Yundang Lagoon is now the cultural center of Xiamen, attracting tourists, real estate developers, and the wildlife that had fled over the past few decades. Xiamen is once again an Egret Island.

The Yundang clean-up received not only praise from the Central Government, but was also chosen by the Development Program of the United Nations as a demonstration site of the "Regional Program for the Prevention & Management of Marine Pollution in the East Asian Sea."

Xiamen's environmental policy allows only low emission, low energy consumption, technology-intensive high-tech industries on the island.   Labor-intensive industries are relegated to the less populated and more spacious off-island Xinglin and Jimei Districts, and raw material and energy industries are restricted to the Haicang Investment Zone.

Xiamen was 1st **in China** to offer daily air quality reports through the media and the internet!   We also, early on, banned the use of phosphorus detergents, nonbiodegradable Styrofoam fast food containers, and persistent pesticides.

Xiamen had the cleanest air of any major Chinese city for a while.   The record slipped a bit, but in the Spring of 2003, Mr. Pan, our vice-mayor (responsible for vice?) announced that Xiamen would again have pristine air—and he gave a deadline of ten days to do it. It must have worked because I can breathe easier already.

You can keep up-to-date on our environment with real-time internet updates, or the monthly, quarterly, semi-annual and annual reports and bulletins.   And…if you have little ones, send them to one of our summer ecology camps.   This Xiamen 4th grader actually received a patent for his used battery disposal system!

"And Silence, like a poultice, comes To heal the blows of sound."
Oliver Wendell Holmes, Sr.

The Sounds of Silence. Xiamen has attacked not just air and water pollution but also noise pollution. For years I envied the quietude of Gulangyu Islet, which forbids motor vehicles and bicycles. Many a Chinese city has tried to ban auto horns, but unsuccessfully, for every driver in China has a motive a minute for joining the raucous ranks of honkies. But Mayor Hong decreed, "No horns." and it was Silent Night overnight. (Neighboring cities still seek the sounds of silence!)

Clean air, clean water, quietude. Xiamen is finally living up to her "Garden City" reputation, and attracting not just tourists but businessmen seeking a city that's as nice to live in as to invest in. It's even nicer if we all obey Xiamen Government's Ten Commandments.

Xiamen Municipal Government's Ten Commandments

1. Don't litter.
2. Don't spit.
3. Don't abuse the greenery.
4. Don't damage public property.
5. Don't run red lights.
6. Don't be unruly on buses.
7. Don't use coarse or inappropriate language.
8. Don't smoke in public buildings.
9. Don't honk automobile horns on the island.
10. Don't affix unauthorized posters in public places.

The Ten Bu's

The list of foreign firms now in Xiamen reads like a "Who's Who" of industry. I typed this book on a Dell assembled in Xiamen; We take photos with film produced by the most advanced Kodak plant in the world—here in Xiamen. When my wife shops, we unload our van, **Toy Ota**, with a Linde forklift from Xiamen. (Just joking!)

While retaining a small town flavor, Xiamen has become a mini metropolis that is host to Hyundai, Ikea, Marubeni, Matsushita, ABB, Swire, and deng deng. By the end of 2002, Xiamen had 5,714 enterprises from 50 countries and regions, with a total investment of US $ 20.11 billion. They account for 84% of the city's total industrial output, 60% of the export value, and 40% of tax revenue.

Canton and Shanghai, eat your heart out. In early 1998, following an inspection tour of Xiamen, the Energy Research Corporation (ERC) picked Xiamen as its premier location for investment in China. ERC will form a joint venture with Nan Ya Plastics Co., Ltd. and Xiamen Battery Factory to manufacture the cutting edge (and green) Nickel-Zinc batteries. They will also license their Nickel-Zinc technology for use in pollution-free electrical vehicles (a priority for Xiamen municipal planners; Xiamen has already started converting many buses to 'green' LP fuel).

Xiamen's track record and future prospects landed her the opportunity to be China's first pilot city to introduce ISO14000. To date, ABB Switchgear (Xiamen) Co., Ltd., Matsushita Audio (Xiamen) Co., Ltd. and Xianglu Fibers (Xiamen) Co., Ltd. have already been granted the ISO14000 license.

Since the central government approved Xiamen Special Economic Zone in 1980, Xiamen has had one of China's highest economic growth rates, with a **20%** annual growth in GNP and a per capita GDP that is now $3,800—the third highest in China. And Laowai and Laonei alike have plenty of places to store all that cash they're raking in.

Xiamen's turn-of-the-century Basket Bankers would rest happier in their urns if they knew how much Xiamen was urning with the help of over 600 financial institutions from around the globe. In addition to domestic varieties like Bank of China, Industrial and Commercial Bank of China, Bank of Communications, and the Agricultural Bank, we also boast Singapore's United Bank, America's Citibank,

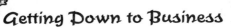

Holland's ING Bank, the Philippines' Allied Bank, the U.K.'s Standard Chartered Bank, France's Credit Lyonnais Bank, Thailand's Bangkok Bank, and Japan's Dai-ichi Kangyo Bank Ltd.

But if you prefer "basket banking," we have a nice basket in our Xiamen University apartment.*

(*Heavy penalties for early withdrawal; offer
void where prohibited by common sense.)

Investment Opportunities in Xiamen are almost endless, but not without rhyme or reason. Xiamen government has carefully selected 4 pillar industries: chemical, electronics, power and machinery. The sprawling 100 square kilometer Haicang Investment Zone has been carefully subdivided into four districts with the following emphases:

New Urban District (development of commerce and trade, finance, real estate, tourism, recreation and leisure).

Harbor District (port facilities, energy industry, bonded facilities and warehousing & storage).

South Industrial District (petrochemicals).

Xinyang Industrial District (machinery, electronics, chemicals and building materials).

According to the 1998 *Investment Guide to Xiamen SEZ*, Xiamen's Ninth Five-year Plan is focusing on 7 key industries: advanced-technology industry, transport, commerce and trade, banking and insurance, tourism, real estate, and information and communications. Priority areas for foreign investors include:

1. Infrastructure facilities
Construction and management of port facilities (with Chinese party holding controlling stock);
Urban light rail (with Chinese party holding controlling stock);
Highways, tunnels; LNG receiving station;

2. Mechanical manufacturing, electrical equipment, and metallurgy
Manufacture of components for passenger vehicles and motorcycles;
Ship repair and building, as well as manufacture and repair of port handling equipment;
Manufacture of machinery for environmental protection and engineering transport equipment, machinery for road construction and spare parts;
Aircraft maintenance and repair;
Manufacture and repair of airborne equipment and manufacture of aeronautical materials;

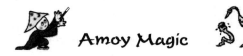

Tooling R & D;
Basic mechanical equipment;
Photo-electromechanical products;
Hard alloy cutters;
Electrical engineering equipment;

3. Electronic information industry

Manufacture of computers and peripheral equipment (including high-density hard disk drives, soft disk drives, CD drives, mainframe boards, top-end monitors, laser and ink-jet printers and components, UPS, etc.);
Computer application systems;
Network equipment and products;
Terminal multimedia products;
Specialized business computers, patent smart cards, etc.;
Software development and production;
Digital and fiber-optic communication equipment and systems;
Digital mobile communication products;
Micro-electronics and components;
Automobile electronic components;
Green lighting products.

4. Chemicals and petrochemicals

Basic organic chemical raw materials and midbody;
New synthetic materials, products and auxiliary materials;
Functional plastic products;
Synthetic rubber, synthetic resin;
Radial tire and processing of other automotive rubber products;
Fine chemicals such as sensitized goods, auxiliary chemicals, and electronic chemicals, deng deng;
Film separation technology products.

5. Pharmaceutical and manufacture of medical equipment

Drugs sourced from chemical raw materials and specialized pharmaceutical midbody;
Highly effective Western medicine and patent medicine;
Biochemical pharmaceuticals;
Advanced and top-end medical apparatus and instruments;

6. Light industry and textile industry

New and high quality light industrial products for daily use;
Production of synthetic perfumes and mono-isolate;
Specialty foods;
New specialized chemical fibers and products;
Fine spun combed knitting yarns;
Knitted apparel of superior quality;
Post finishing of printing and dyeing of woven and knitted goods;
New shell fabric and premium quality apparel;
Specialized industrial textile products;
High power and high capacity battery and automobile fuel cells.

7. Building materials

Deep-processing products of glass;
Fiberglass and fiberglass reinforced plastic products;
High-grade ceramics and ceramic raw materials;
New and light building materials, wall materials;
Advanced chemical building materials and decorative and finishing materials of high quality.

8. Pioneering industries

Microelectric technology;
New materials and bio-engineering technologies;
New sources of energy and energy efficient technologies;
Isotopic element radiation and laser technology;
Oceanography, technologies for comprehensive treatment and utilization of ocean resources; comprehensive utilization and renewal of resources;
Advanced environmental protection technology:
Technologies for the development and utilization of resources and 'green' energy.

9. Tourism

Construction of such tourist facilities as theme parks and amusement parks;
Development of tourist resources.

10. Service Industries

Economic and scientific and technological information consulting services (joint venture or cooperation only);
Institutions of financial consulting service;
Development of new and high technologies, technical service;
Maintenance of precise instruments and equipment;
Warehousing and storage service;
Education (joint-venture or cooperation only) and facilities for physical education;
Special hospitals of higher level and distinguishing features.

11. Agriculture
Irrigation works;

Introduction, breeding and population of new varieties of high-yield crops;

Large livestock & poultry production and processing bases;

High-quality feed and additive agent;

Cultivation of rare aquatic products and ocean fishery

New technologies for preservation, refrigeration and processing of farm products, animal by-products and aquatic products;

Flower planting bases;

Production and processing of advanced agricultural chemicals and chemical fertilizer.

Alas, no cheese yet! ☹

12. Real Estate
Urban renewal projects; Residential housing projects.

China Trade Fair (CIFIT)
— The Window on Chinese Investment Opportunities! Did

you know that you can prospect for gold in every province in China in just one day?!

At our Annual China Fair for International Investment and Trade (every September 8th), pavilions for every province in China give the lay on investment opportunities from coastal Fujian to the Himalayan heights of Tibet-- and everything in between.

Over recent decades, CIFIT has been responsible for *over half* of the foreign investment to small and medium enterprises, and quite a chunk for large businesses as well. The past five CIFITs have brought in over 50 billion USD in investment (that's more than I make in ten years!). In 2,002, the 6th CIFIT had over 50,000 participants and 10,107 business guests from almost 100 countries and regions. The 663 contracts signed were worth almost 7.3 billion USD! Speakers at the CIFIT International Forum have included top Chinese leaders, Nobel Prize winners, U.N. officials and vice premiers of various countries.

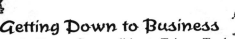

You should also try the Export Commodities to Taiwan Trade Fair (held April 8-12).

Municipal government officers are glad to provide information and materials on investment opportunities, and other Laowai and Laonei businessmen should also have a good handle on how to go about setting up shop, and home, in Xiamen.

Or contact with **China (Xiamen) International Investment Promotion Center.**

Address: 2/F, Foreign Trade Bldg. Hubin Road N., Xiamen, China 361012.

Phone: 0086-592-5079898-631, or 5068459

Fax: 0086-592-5129898, or 5146205

Website: http://www.chinafair.org.cn

E-mail: ciipc@public.xm.fj.cn

Ancient Tales of Business Conquest   For those who
think Chinese are new at the business game, think again, because these ancient tales prove otherwise.

Limited Partnership   (Ming Dynasty Tale)
Two brothers planted wheat together and at harvest time discussed how to share the yield. The older brother said, "I'll take the top half and you take the lower."

"But all the wheat's on the top!" said the younger brother.

"Ok, if you don't feel its fair, next year I take the bottom half and you take the top!"

The younger brother agreed, and the next year they planted potatoes.

If the Shoe Fits Share It   (Ming Dynasty Tale)
Two brothers saved up enough to buy one pair of shoes, which they shared. The older wore them from morning till night. The younger, to get his share of the benefit, waited till his elder brother went to bed then put the shoes on and walked all over the countryside until dawn.

When the shoes were worn out, the elder brother asked, "Want to buy another pair of shoes?"

"No, thanks. I need to get some sleep."

Moral to the above two stories: if someone says, "We're like brothers," hide your wallet!

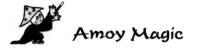

Don't Wine[18] About it   (Ming Dynasty Tale)

Two men decided to make wine together. One said, "You supply the rice and I'll supply the water." The second said, "If I provide all the rice, how do we divide the results?"

"I will be absolutely fair. When the wine is ready, we get back what we put in. I'll take the liquid and you keep the rest."

On "Caveat Emptor" ...

Mosquito Amulet   (Ming Dynasty Tale) A man bought an amulet to ward off mosquitoes but when it didn't work he returned to the vendor. The vendor said, "You have to use it in the proper place for it to work!"

"And where is that?"

"Under a mosquito net!"

On reading the fine print...

Peace and Quiet (Song Dynasty Tale)

A man who loved peace and quiet lived between a blacksmith and a coppersmith and the noise was driving him nuts. Many times he offered to throw them a fine banquet if they'd move. Finally they took him up on his offer. After a lavish banquet, the man asked his unruly neighbors where they were moving to. The smiths answered in unison, "I'll move to his shop and he'll move to mine."

On Labor Relations...

Asking Only Workman's Wages   (Qing Dynasty Tale)

A rich old miser refused to hire a servant because he did not want to have to pay and feed him. A friend finally offered, "I have a diligent servant who needs neither pay nor food. I'll lend him to you for free. Will you take him?"

The man thought about it. "If he doesn't eat won't he starve?"

"An immortal taught my servant the secret of inhaling wind and passing smoke as excrement. He is never hungry."

The man pondered this, then said, "No, thanks. I don't want him."

"Why not?"

The miser complained, "I would like to use the servant's nightsoil for my fields, but he only passes smoke."

On Discount Promotions...
Half Price! (Qing Dynasty Tale)
When the goldsmith's assistant delivered two gold ingots to a government official, the official asked, "How much?"

"Normally, such and such, but we are giving them to you for half price!"

The official smiled, then handed one ingot back to the assistant. The assistant just stood there and the official exclaimed, "What are you waiting for? I've paid you already!"

"What?"

"You said you would take only half the normal price. Fine. I returned one of the gold ingots to you. I've kept my part of the bargain. Now get out."

On "One Wife, Two Systems"...
Eat in East, Sleep in West (Ming Dynasty Tale)
A young girl was torn between two suitors, the rich but ugly young man who lived East of their farm, and the poor but handsome neighbor who lived to the West. She moaned to her mother, "If only I could marry both, and eat in the East and sleep in the West."

Man of the People (ancient Chinese tale) A newly appointed official decided to impress folks with his moral virtues by writing three phrases on the walls of his office:

1. Don't covet money.
2. Don't desire promotions.
3. Don't fear death.

A few days later some wit added two characters to the bottom of each:

1. in small quantities.
2. unless it's much higher than this one.
3. But I want to live as long as I can.

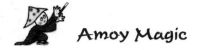

Amoy Magic

Getting a Bead on Business[19]

Chinese have been boning up[20] on business for thousands of years, and they have that beaded wonder, the beaded abacus, to prove it.

While Xiamen folk wholeheartedly embrace the future, they still cling to their cheap, energy-saving, immensely practical and highly accurate abacuses (or abacusi), which in skilled hands are faster, and deadlier, than an electronic calculator.

Special for you!

I marvel every time a businessman or clerk flicks the black wooden beads up and down the brass rods faster than a Buddhist monk fingering his rosary. And when they present it to me for my verification, I never let on that it's Greek to me.[21]

I bought my first of many abacuses in Los Angeles' China town, and set about relearning the skills my first grade teacher, Ms. Magruder, had allegedly imparted to me years earlier. And after reading the foolproof instruction booklet 3 times, I shelved the beaded bane[22]. Years later, in Xiamen, I bought a miniature abacus in the hope that smaller ones were easier, but it was still worse than Rubik's cube. No wonder they were invented by ancient Babylonians. Who but Saddam Hussein's ancestors would have dared?

The abacus began as a sand-covered board for scratching merchants' ciphers. Eventually someone scratched out some lines and added counters for tens, hundreds, and *deng deng*. Then the Romans added grooves to make it easier to slide the counters. Modern Chinese merchants now use wires to string up the counters and to string along their customers. And the beads are still pushed by Middle Eastern, Chinese and Japanese businessmen, and schoolchildren, and desperate economists.

I still can't figure out the abacus, but I have a nice collection of them. In fact, I have a whole case of the miniature brass and jade versions, packaged in Chinese silk boxes. I present them to friends, along with the idiot-proof instruction booklet so they will have no excuse for failure.

Misery loves company.

Laonei (老内) Notes

[1] Hotbed: environment that encourages fast growth or development

[2] Hopped up: excited

[3] Pi & ice cream: we often eat pie (as in apple pie) with ice cream.

[4] Arable: able to grow food on it; 适于耕种的, 可耕的

[5] Up a creek without a paddle: lacking the means to solve a problem

[6] Penchant: strong liking, inclination; 倾向; 嗜好; 爱好

[7] On a roll: already started, or already experiencing sustained success or luck (and toilet paper comes in rolls)

[8] Do one's business: euphemism for going to the toilet

[9] Gutenberg: German printer considered by Westerners to be the inventor of movable type because he printed the Bible in 1455.

[10] Life is a zoo: very hectic, 乱

[11] Mathemagician: no such word. I coined it by combining mathematician and magician.

[12] As the fly flies: a play on the common phrase "as the crow flies" (meaning the most direct route)

[13] Cut ancestral apron strings: to cut off all ties with home (we usually say, "Cut mother's apron strings").

[14] fry computers: power surges burned them out

[15] Give someone a line: insincere talk, usually to deceive or impress (here used as a pun while discussing a *phone* line)

[16] Pass the beans: eating beans causes flatulence (gas)

[17] Mary Poppins: a Walt Disney movie character who befriended chimney sweepers.

[18] Wine about it: a play on 'whine' about it (whine = complain).

[19] Get a bead on: take careful aim at

[20] Bone up: improve

[21] Greek to me: unintelligible

[22] Bane: cause of injury, worry; a poison

Chapter 3
Fun On-Island

"Boredom is always counter-revolutionary.
Always."   Guy Debord, French philosopher

Once upon a time
(the early '90s or so), the
most exciting pastime in
Xiamen was swatting
mosquitoes in the dark, or
amateur wrestling matches
in crowded post offices and
banks [1]. But there's no
longer any excuse for
counter-revolutionary
boredom in Xiamen.
Xiamen boasts hundreds of hotels and guesthouses, thousands of restaurants,
dozens of theaters featuring the latest Western films, scores of bowling alleys
and billiard halls, and several PGA class golf courses and resorts.

Good Sports   Our city has just completed a new sports stadium—not
surprising, given the locals' athletic prowess. Xiamenese have been getting a
kick out of soccer since the British introduced it here in 1898, and local big
shots[2] are happy now that Xiamen has set world records in shooting.

Another Xiamen athlete set a world record in track and field. All told,
three athletes won a total of 19 world championships. And during the Fall of
1999, a guy from Xiamen TV returned from an endeavor that is poles apart
from track and field. He made a cool trek to the North Pole! Or the South Pole,
or East Pole, or May Pole—I know it was a pole somewhere. Maybe Poland?

On Gulangyu Island, you can try your hand at windsurfing or parasailing,
and not a week goes by that art lovers can't enjoy a performance by a Chinese
or foreign orchestra, or an opera, or a ballet performance—or the London
Circus. Lil' Laowai love our 30 nice parks and zoo, amusement centers, one of
China's best marine aquarium, a Go-Kart racetrack that has held international
competitions, a water park with slides 'n pools 'n such, deng deng.

Much to see... but I suggest your tour begin with Xiamen University...

Xiamen University

Xiamen University (1930s) B.B.

"This school [Xiamen University] is entirely a Chinese institution, with no foreign teachers and no foreign connections, and right out in a small Chinese village. The course of study is being made very practical… When we think of the future days, it is one of the most encouraging things to be seen in the whole of China."
Paul Hutchinson, 1920s[3]

Xiamen University (厦门大学, or Xiada) gets top billing in *Amoy Magic* for three reasons:
1) Its China's most beautiful campus;
2) Its China's most strategic university (the only key university in a Special Economic Zone);
3) Its my home.

I rest my case!

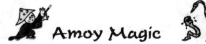

Xiada's 400 acres, nestled snugly between the Five-Old-Men Mountains and the sea, are as tranquil as the sprawling Nanputuo Buddhist monastery right next door—except on April 6. Then the campus springs to life to celebrate its founding in 1921 by Mr. Tan Kah Kee, a patriotic overseas Chinese with a big heart and an even bigger wallet.

To add to the festivities, Xiada's birthday follows on the heels of the **April 5th Tripleheader**: 1) Grave Sweeping Day; 2) the anniversary of Chiang Kai Shek's death; and 3) my birthday, the latter being the most important.

Mr. Tan Kah Kee acquired his fortune not from Tan Kah Kee Fried Chicken but from rice and rubber. At age 17, he and his father opened a rice shop in Singapore. From this humble beginning he saved enough capital to diversify into shipping and canning, but it was rubber that really stretched his fortune.

Band of Rubber Barons   Mr. Tan was one of the four members of the rubber band that founded Malaysia's rubber industry, and one of Southeast Asia's few millionaires, with business dealings in 48 countries.   But this rubber magnate rubbed Westerners the wrong way[4] by donating most of his fortune to China (money was supposed to come out of China, not go back in).

Mr. Tan held his own against attempts to shut him down, but rubber prices plummeted during the Depression. Mr. Tan's rubber interests never bounced back, so before his checks bounced[5] instead, he closed up shop, sold some large buildings, and put the money into a trust fund for Xiamen University. After Japan's invasion of China in 1937, he founded the Southeast Asian Overseas Chinese Relief Association, and spent the rest of his life raising money for China. At one point he almost single-handedly financed Chiang Kai Shek's Nationalist army—a feat he probably regretted later when Generalissimo Chiang and the Madame fled to Taiwan with his money and everyone else's.

Mr. Tan's contributions to China were many, but Xiada was the apple of his eye (or as Chinese say, "bright pearl in ones palm", 掌上明珠, "Zhangshang Mingzhu"), even when Xiamen University was no longer in Xiamen!

In 1937, during the war against Japan, Xiamen University relocated to Fujians's Changting County, out in the Western boondocks bordering Jiangxi Province (a beautiful little riverside town today — give it a visit!). After 1945, Xiada returned to Xiamen, and the new president and eminent biologist, Dr.

Wang Deyao, immediately set out rebuilding and expanding the campus. Tan's money and Wang's vision paid off.   In 1963, Xiada was designated a key national university and has been mushrooming ever since.

Xiada now boasts nearly 20,000 full-time students and a few thousand part-time students, who pursue 61 majors in 34 departments, with master's degrees in 108 majors, and doctoral degrees in 59.

One student earned so many degrees I call him Dr. Fahrenheit.

A university brochure rightly boasts, "Xiada's tens of thousands of graduates and postgraduates have been highly recognized both at home and abroad as outstanding in their fields."

Of course, local farmers are out standing in their fields too.

To appreciate Xiada's impact on Chinese science, arrange a tour of the Laboratory for Physical Chemistry of Solid Surfaces, one of China's key strategic laboratories, where renowned scientists (7 of whom are in the Chinese Academy of Sciences) wield such hi-tech devices as scanning tunneling microscopes to perform research in bioelectrochemistry, spectro-electrochemistry, and other esoteric stuff I can't even spell correctly.

The laboratory is located in the five-story concrete and bathroom tile covered edifice across the street from our Economics College (and not far from our MBA Center). Website: **http://pcoss.org/english/about/e_intro.htm**

A tour of beautiful Xiada should include the anthropology museum, which is holding its own even though budget cuts forced the anthropology department to be shut down a few years back.

Standing beside the anthropology museum is the statue of the patriotic poet, writer and all around good guy Lu Xun. Behind Mr. Lu Xun is our campus' best photo spot—the majestic granite structures of the original campus, which curve around the soccer field and face the sea.

By now you're hungry or thirsty or both, so take a break for lunch or dinner in the International Academic Exchange's (Yifu Bldg) dining room. They have great hot pot, and the best spicy fried shrimp in town (coated in spices and deep-fried, you can eat the shells and all—though Sue balks at eating the tail, but that's another tale). Phone ahead for large groups, or to reserve a private dining room: 208 7988.

Wind down your whirlwind tour with a stroll around our serene mid-campus lake, which mirrors the Five-Old-Men Mountains and the Oriental architecture of the student dorms (and walls of weeping willows until Typhoon Dan flattened them). On a small island are statues of Tan Kah Kee surrounded by students— and the occasional Laowai listening in.

By day, the lakeside is host to dozens of students standing alone, textbook in hand, memorizing English dialogues. By night, the lakeside is still host to dozens of students, this time in pairs. And they aren't studying English. In the

Xiamen University

B.B.

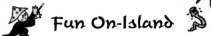
early 90s, university regulations forbade
males and females (my wife and I included!)
holding hands. But men held hands...

I Wanna Hold Your Hand? [6]

I nearly fell off my trusty rusty Forever Brand
bike when I saw a gate guard sitting in another's lap,
arms about him, eyes locked intimately.

Chinese men are very intimate — unlike us Westerners who
religiously defend our inviolable body space (about 30 inches, according to space cases
who study such stuff).

Chinese view privacy and body space differently because with 1.3 billion people
there isn't a lot of room for either one. Men have no qualms holding hands, arms, or
bodies, which is all well and good for Chinese who know the ropes, but not for
foreigners.

Consider the simple handshake. Americans grab, squeeze, pump for oil 3 times,
and escape, but Chinese may grab your hand and hold it intimately in theirs, even
stroking it throughout the entire conversation. It still unnerves me, even after 12 years.

I eventually gave a lecture on how not to shake hands or other body parts with
unsuspecting Laowai. And the very next day, I ran into Foreign Affair's Lao Huang,
(Lao means "old" or "venerable"), one of my sons' favorite Chinese grandfathers, and
handholder par excellence.

Lao Huang grasped my hand and caressed it for a good 15 minutes while he chatted
away. He eventually asked, "Xiao Pan" (which means "Little Pan," not "Unvenerable
Pan"), "Do you feel awkward holding my hand?"

"A tad," I confessed.

He roared with laughter, threw his arms about me (that I could handle), and
confessed, "I heard about your hand-holding lecture yesterday!"

And ever since then, the old rascal has greeted me with an American pumping-for-
oil handshake—and a sly chuckle.

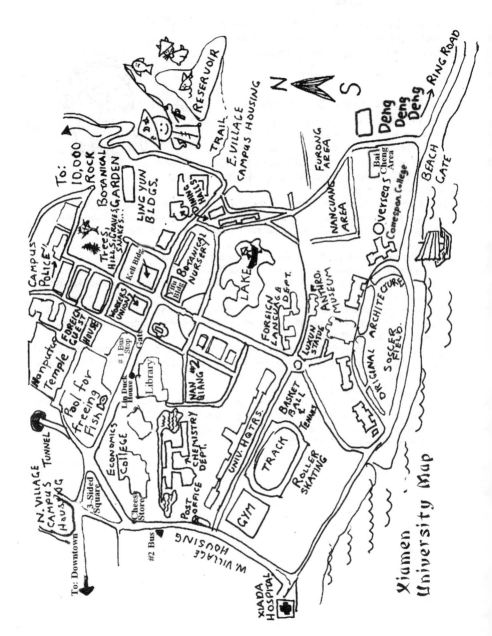

Xiamen
University Map

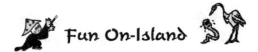

Xiada's Overseas Education College

To make the most of magical Amoy, bone up[7] a bit on the language. A few choice phrases like "Ni Hao!" (你好!) will have your beaming hosts exclaiming, "Your Chinese is wonderful!"—even if you've massacred both tones and pronunciation (see Chapter 10, "Mad About Mandarin").

You can pick up Mandarin from friends or a tutor, but it's hard to keep at it on your own, so check out Xiada's Overseas Education College (OEC), where I spent my first 5 months in Xiamen.

Since its establishment in 1956, the OEC has taught over 20,000 students, both face-to-face and by correspondence. Subjects include not just Mandarin but also Xiamen dialect, Chinese language and literature (2~6 years by correspondence), and Traditional Chinese medicine (1~5 years, both correspondence and face-to-face).

So doctors graduate quicker than literature students? Comforting.

The OEC also has some sharp professors of acupuncture and moxibustion (1~3 years, correspondence and face-to-face), as well as history, archaeology, anthropology, tourist management, law, higher education, economics, sciences, engineering, deng deng.

The OEC has mushroomed right along with Xiamen's expat population. In 1999, the center had 400 Laowai, many of them businessmen, as well as their wives and dependents.

In 1988, when our family arrived here, the OEC was on a drive to lure foreign students. They were so successful that they ran out of housing and we were forced to live off campus. But thanks to the new ten-story Overseas Students' Dormitory Building (replete with A/C, in-room phones, and dining hall), and other facilities both on and off campus, there is now plenty of room in the inn. OEC also has modern new classroom facilities, thanks to contributions from alumni like Indonesian correspondence student, Lin Lianxing.

Sixty of the OEC's eighty staff are full-time teachers with at least 10 years teaching experience; 36% are professors and associate professors; and every one of them is dedicated to helping you master everything from Mandarin to moxibustion. So do yourself and your hosts a favor by giving the OEC a ring at (592) 218-6211, 208-6139   E-mail: **xmuoec@jingxian.xmu.edu.cn**

Xiada Alumni Association of North America: http://www.xmuaaa.org

Xiamen Univ. MBA Center... For a classless society, the MBA Center sure gives me a lot of classes (especially considering that Susan Marie says I have no class at

all). Whereas in the early 90s we had to literally drag students in, now we have them coming out our ears. How times have changed since Xiada MBA awarded **China's 1st MBA** degrees! (We beat Nankai Univ. by one week).

Our MBA program began in 1987 as a joint project with Dalhousie, Saint Mary's, and other Canadian universities with the support of the Canadian International Development Agency. The first 30 MBAs graduated in July, 1990—and some

MBA Center

still write me. I've received their Chinese New Year and Christmas cards from such diverse places as Beijing, New York, and Helsinki Finland!

Xiamen University's School of Management has 7 undergraduate programs in accounting, business administration, corporate finance, human resource management, e-commerce, management science, and tourism management, as well as 5 postgraduate MBA programs, and 3 doctor-degree programs in accounting, business administration and tech-economics & management. The school has over 1600 undergraduates and 1200 graduates. Exciting times—unless you're trying to remember their names!

Our students have included the CEO of Xiamen Electronics, the Director of Fuyao Glass Industry, and graduates are working in such firms as Kodak, Dell, Nokia (China), GE China, Credit Lyonnais Bank. Some are pretty big potatoes now. (Don't forget your teacher!).

Give our ultramodern facilities a visit while you're touring the campus—and hire some of our students!

Phone: (0592)218-6441 218-2873 218-7182

E-mail: **xdmba@jingxian.xmu.edu.cn**

Website: **http://sm.xmu.edu.cn**

Chinese European Art Center (厦门大学艺术学院，中国欧洲艺术中心)

Seeing as how it was the Dutch who opened up Xiamen back about 1300 A.D., its appropriate that they are in the forefront of opening Xiamen yet again as they help Chinese Laonei and European Laowai better understand one another's culture and arts.

Ms. Ineke Gudmundsson iniated the Art Center in 1999 as a joint venture with Xiamen University Art College.   Works by well respected European artists have included Teun Hock's painted photographs ("stills of the theater of life"), JCJ

Vanderheyden's "fragments of reality," Pieter Holstein's drawings, Marcel Kalksma's handmade prints, Arni Gudmundsson's sculptures, as well as the works of Chinese artists like Xie Lai, Wu Yiming and Wen Bin.

When I visited the art center this morning, Jean Bernard Koeman was busy, drill in hand, setting up his exhibit entitled, "Mental Architecture (a travel survival kit), which included photos, Chinese characters, and oddly designed cubicles (designed, he said, to fit well in planes, and to form a sphere when stacked).   It was a bit too much architecture for my mental capacities (or lack of them), but I enjoyed the photos, and his infectious enthusiasm. I did ask one person why

Jean Bernard Koeman

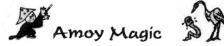
Xiamen Univ. doesn't have an American-Chinese Center and they said it was because we Americans don't have any culture. That isn't true. I've had cultures[8] many times; I've used them to make yogurt.

Exhibits change frequently, so check out the latest offerings at their website, or phone. Tel: 218-0850, 218-5860

    website: **http://www.ceac99.com**   E-mail: **ceac99@public.xm.fj.cn**

    Center Hours: Wed. thru Sunday, 10 AM – 12 Noon, 3 – 5 PM

Lu Xun—"Father of Modern Chinese Literature"

Beside Xiamen University's Anthropology Museum is a statue of Lu Xun (1881—1936), author of *True Story of Ah Q* and other modern classics.   Lu Xun (a pen name for Zhou Shuren, 周树人) broke 5,015 years of literary tradition with his first story, *Madman's Diary*, because he wrote in the language of the people—which is worlds apart from the hallowed written language that scholars had perfected over the centuries.

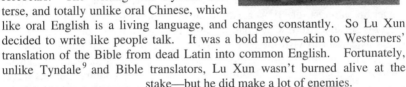

For over 2,000 years, any scholar worth his salt mastered the classics of Confucius and Laozi, and then wrote brilliant essays about the brilliant essays written by his forebears.   The writing was stylistic and terse, and totally unlike oral Chinese, which like oral English is a living language, and changes constantly.   So Lu Xun decided to write like people talk.   It was a bold move—akin to Westerners' translation of the Bible from dead Latin into common English.   Fortunately, unlike Tyndale[9] and Bible translators, Lu Xun wasn't burned alive at the stake—but he did make a lot of enemies.

Lu Xun taught in Xiamen University the last few months of 1926, but he disliked the professors' constant bickering and politicking (common on any campus, in China or elsewhere!). He wrote curt essays like *How to Write?* (怎么写?). And having said his piece, and having disturbed what little peace the place had, he packed his bags and moved to Guangzhou in January, '27.

In *Old Tales Retold*, Lu Xun wrote, "In some places the narrative is based on passages in old books, elsewhere I gave free reign to my imagination.   And having less respect for the ancients than for my contemporaries, I have not always been able to avoid facetiousness."

You can pick up Lu Xun's works in SM Mall's Book City (3/F), or even download some from the internet!

Zhongshan Park (Sun Yat-sen Park) is on Zhongshan Road (where else?), just over the hill and past the new Cultural Palace (while it was being rebuilt we were temporarily without culture; in fact, Sue says I still don't have any).

Zhongshan Park visitors (free admission!) are greeted by Dr. Sun Yat-sen's statue, which bears his granddaughter's inscription, "The Great Democratic Revolutionary Pioneer Dr. Sun Yat-sen." I suspect she was biased, but so are 1.3 billion other Chinese. Every two-ox town [10] in China has a ZhongShan Road — and obligatory Liberation Street, Si Ming ("Remember the Ming") Street, People's Street, deng deng.

Dr. Sun Yat-sen

Bonnie Koenig said her kids especially enjoy Zhongshan Park's bumper cars, but I get enough bumper car thrills just driving Toy Ota around Xiamen. Zhongshan also has nice rental rowboats. If you're afraid of being up a creek without a paddle[11], try the swan shaped fiberglass pedal boats (but avoid the hottest days lest your pedaling be to the tune of your swan song[12]). Enjoy numerous gardens, the flower exhibition hall, the bridges and pavilions, and drop by the small zoo, which has small hippos, lions, tigers, deng deng. You might also want to visit the park on holidays - especially on Lantern Festival (the 15th day of the first lunar month), when the park is thronged with special performers, displays, and exhibitions from all over the country. Folks travel from all over Fujian to see Zhongshan Park's Egret Island Lantern Show, the parades, the Dragon Lantern Dance, Lion Dance, deng deng.

In the wee hours of the morning, every park in China is full of folks "shadow boxing." They are exercising their Qi (life force) with TaiQi—one of the many styles of Kung Fu. I did Kung Fu in Taiwan—or it did me...

Feel the Force, Grasshopper!

My intro to Chinese philosophy was the '60s TV serial "Kung Fu," starring David Carradine. I was 22 before I discovered that he wasn't Chinese. I've still not quite forgiven Carradine for being Caucasian, but at least he helped pique my interest in China—and martial arts.

While I was a young airman in Taiwan I studied Kung Fu for 2 hours each evening with a bunch of bald Buddhist monks. I coveted a black belt, but advance came only by defeating students of higher levels, and the only belts I ever landed were to my poor bruised body.

There are over 100 different styles of martial arts, using knives and spears, swords and clubs, deng deng. In addition, there are external styles, emphasizing strength, and internal kung fu, which stresses one's mind and one's life energy, or Qi.

In theory, as one ages one progresses from movement to stillness, from firmness to softness, and Qi becomes both more powerful and more focused than brute force. Or so I was told, but I was skeptical of the soft soap about soft force—until Master Lin put my doubts on ice with a 200 pound block of ice.

I often chuckled at Master Lin's roly-poly physique, which betrayed the fact that he moonlighted as a candy maker, but he could stand back to the wall and touch the wall above his head with his feet. And after he demonstrated the power of Qi, I quit chuckling altogether.

While his students watched silently, Master Lin poised his hand, palm downward, about one inch above the giant block of ice, and concentrated. Then without warning, he slapped the ice and it shattered.

I could not have duplicated the feat with a sledge hammer.

Pass the candy, Master Lin!

I no longer laughed about Qi. But I still don't think much of it as a self-defense technique. After all, what self-respecting enemy is going to lay on his back and wait half a minute while you lay your hand above his chest and charge up your Qi?

Note: Want to build up your own Qi? Read on...!

Kungfu Kicks in Xiamen? If you've ever wanted to master martial arts, Xiamen is the place to start! (Southern Shaolin Kungfu originated in Fujian; the jury is still out[13] on whether in Fuqing, Putian, or Quanzhou).

Styles and weapons vary enormously, and it seems that each village boasts its own particular style, which is taught only to members of that village, with a certain clan's surname. For example, the unique Kungfu style of Zhouning (the carp village) is taught only to those surnamed Zheng.

What Style? With so many unique styles and variations, its tough to continue training if you move elsewhere in China, or return home. So one option is to study an internationally standardized style, like Korean Tae Kwondo. And fortunately, Xiamen has Karate masters as well.

Master Que Jiangsheng

Master Que Jiansheng （阙建生教练）, a 7th degree black belt, teaches Shannon and friends. Born in poverty in Zhangzhou in 1963, his father died at age 5 and his mother moved to Taiwan. He studied Chinese martial arts, but fell in love with Karate, and is now zealously promoting the art in China.

He has several locations in Xiamen, and very reasonable rates. Give him a call! Phone: 891-6169 Mobile: 13666080730

Master Que (flying!)

Shannon meets his match!

B.B.

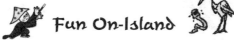
The 10,000 Rock Botanical

Garden, perched behind the Monument to Revolutionary Martyrs, has more rocks than you can find in our university cafeteria rice.

Below ground are dozens of caves, and strewn across picturesque hills are giant boulders with names like "Laughing Rock." When you've seen enough rock stars, stop and smell the roses, because there are even more flowers than rocks. You can spend days exploring beautifully landscaped trails, visiting the 20+ nurseries, and marveling over 4,000 kinds of tropical and subtropical plants, many found nowhere else on earth (or China either).

B.B.

Down the garden path...

The gardens are reached most easily by taxi, but more adventurous souls hike over the mountain behind Xiada. Ascend the serpentine trail, a relic of Japanese occupation days, up the mountain past the "Heavenly Bestow Mineral Water Co.

'Laughing Rock
Xiamen Botanical Garden
B.B.

Cross the bridge and continue past the sign that says "No foreigners beyond this sign." The trail eventually crosses the forested crest, where tigers roamed 60 years ago, and where not long ago they found a 30 foot reticulated python.

But fear not! Reticulated pythons are rarer than Monty Pythons[14], and fear us more than we fear them. Or so I'm told. But has anyone told them? Two hours north, in Koxinga's hometown of Nan An, a python ate a farmer and two kids (in separate sittings). I suspect the locals now find the 'snake fears man' story a bit hard to swallow.[15]

Military Museum Trek up the Five Old Man Mountains behind Xiada, and just over the crest you'll come to the military camp. You'll hear it before you see it; budding buglers blow their brass day and night. While there, visit the **Military Museum**. Sons Shannon and Matthew give it rave reviews, but every time I've visited it has been closed for one reason or another. It's worth a try, though. At the least, you can enjoy the tank, fighter and large guns out on the lawn.

After the military museum, take the right fork, descend the hill, and take a pit stop[16] in the ancient tea garden, then saunter down the beautifully laid out trails through the gardens and past the Buddhist nunnery (strategically separated by an entire mountain from Nan PuTuo monastery, lest wifeless monks have nun). Splash in the streams a bit, take turns treading the footmill, enjoy the wide lawns and rose beds and orchids, then head out the main gate. The Martyrs Memorial will be on your right, but go straight and you'll come to Zhong Shan Park, and eventually to the harbor and Gulangyu Island. (Take the ferry, otherwise it's a long swim)

Martin Thorman inspects Military Museum

Tea time!

Back to the Garden
A True Tale of "the Cultural Revolution"

Zhang Li set his clay teacup on the brown plastic tray and said, "I was a Red Guard, you know. As insolent as they came. But I was given a new heart in the 10,000 Rock Garden.

"During 'the Cultural Revolution', public property was up for grabs by any Red Guard who wanted it. We used to seize whatever we wanted and no one dared stop us.

Zhangli

And one day, my friend and I decided we wanted rare and beautiful flowers for our room, so we each grabbed a sack and headed for the Botanical Garden.

"In the green house we were overwhelmed by the variety and beauty of the tropical flowers. I was about to put a beautiful plant in my sack when I heard a noise and turned to see an old lady bent over some plants, weeding them.

"We didn't fear her, because no one dared question or hinder a Red Guard. But when she looked up at us she didn't seem fearful either, or surprised that we had barged into her greenhouse, or that we obviously planned to steal some flowers. In fact, she smiled!

"Before I could move she walked over and picked up the plant I had been eyeing and held it before my eyes. 'Isn't it beautiful?' she exclaimed. 'These are very rare and come from South America. They are difficult to raise, but well worth the effort. Do you like it?'

"I was speechless! I glared at her and headed for another exotic plant, but before I could even reach for it she had set the other plant down and rushed up to my side, and asked, 'Do you know what this plant is called?'

"'No,' I snarled. She was getting on my nerves.

"She smiled, and patiently explained the plant's name, origin, and how to keep it alive. She concluded, 'It is very beautiful, isn't it?'

"I stomped away, frustrated, but every time we reached for a plant she was beside us, smiling, patiently explaining the plant's origins, habitats, and needs. She never raised her voice, and when I picked up a plant anyway and started to put it in my bag, she just looked at me silently, with a little smile, but sad eyes.

"I melted. I had been so angry and bitter, and determined to take it out on society, but her gentleness and patience defused my anger, and my friend's too, and we walked out, leaving our sacks behind us, defeated, and renewed.

"We were so glad when the Cultural Revolution ended soon afterwards. It has been two decades now, and I've returned to the garden many times hoping to see the lady, to tell her how much she changed my life, but I've never seen her again. Maybe she's dead now. But I'll never forget her…"

 **Amoy Magic**

Nanputuo Temple (686 A.D.)

B.B.

NanPutuo Temple, right outside the #1 Bus terminus and Xiada's old gate, sprawls across the Five-Old-Men Mountains like a Chinese miniature landscape on steroids. The complex's original structures were built over 1,000 years ago, during the Tang Dynasty, and now include the Heavenly Emperor Palace, the Grand Majestic Treasure Palace, the Buddhist Scripture Pavilion, and the Great Benevolence Palace – all of which you can tour once you've made it past the Benevolent Ticket Seller.

NanPutuo ("Nan" means "South", and "Putuo" is one of China's four sacred mountains, up in Zhejiang) is home to a few hundred monks — and a few hundred statues as well, like the Reverend Three-Life-Cycle Budda, the Four Heavenly Kings, the Eighteen Arhats, and Bodhisattva, aka the Thousand Handed Guanyin (patron saint of glovemakers, perhaps).

Merry Maitreya [17]

Upon entering Nanputuo you are first greeted by the pot-bellied Maitreya (Mi-le-Fo in China). He's the "god of wealth (but looks to me more like the god of maternity). The Buddhist Sutras say Sakyamuni, the first Buddha, will rule for 10,000 years. When international morality reaches a high level (like the Spice Girls entering a nunnery), Buddhism will

"Well, Milo, that explains the pickles and ice cream!"

die out. Eight million years later, Maitreya will come to preach.

Let's hope his sermons are shorter than his grand entrance.

Maitreya last incarnated 1,000 years ago as the Linen-Bag Monk of Zhejiang Province. He traveled nonstop, preaching to all and sundry, free from cares and smiling in all circumstances. He believed that he was Maitreya incarnate, and so did everyone else—at least after he died.

Behind Nan Putuo's Maitreya statue stands Wei Tuo (Boddhisatva Skanda), the deity responsible for safeguarding those two pillars of most religions: doctrine and finance. And Wei Tuo's staff is the reason Nanputuo has attracted millions of pilgrims over the past 1,000 years.

Tradition has it that when Wei Tuo holds his staff horizontally in his arms, he's suggesting, "Try elsewhere." But at Nanputuo, Wei Tuo's staff is aimed at the ground, indicating the temple is wealthy and offers both room and board. So pilgrims pack in by the hundreds of thousands. And happily for Wei Tuo, they leave their millions behind. Maybe this fellow is playing a lute to encourage more loot? And why not—because it appears they all have money to burn…

Money to Burn[18] Nanputuo has more pilgrims than Wei Tuo can shake a staff at[19], busily sacrificing paper houses, paper furniture, paper cars, even paper microwaves, all to be used by ancestors in the afterlife. They also burn stacks of "hell money." With each banknote worth a 100 Million Dollars or so, one stack could easily top Bill Gate's fortune, yet they are printed on the cheapest paper and sold for a pittance by hawkers outside the temple. They figure that demons and deities down under can't tell real money from fake—but it must make for some hellish inflation down there!

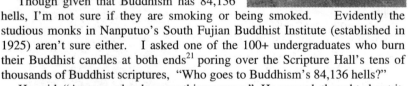

"Hell to pay..."

Demons, deities and dead ancestors get the short end of Wei Tuo's stick[20] not just with money but with edibles as well. Peasants offer rice or choice fruits in a 15″ basket with a 12″ false bottom, because folks down below don't know the difference.

Smoke clouds rise day and night from Nan Putuo's eternal offerings. But maybe the smoke is more symbolic than the offerings, given that China has 300 million smokers. If they use paper houses and microwaves in the next life, why not tobacco too?

Though given that Buddhism has 84,136 hells, I'm not sure if they are smoking or being smoked. Evidently the studious monks in Nanputuo's South Fujian Buddhist Institute (established in 1925) aren't sure either. I asked one of the 100+ undergraduates who burn their Buddhist candles at both ends[21] poring over the Scripture Hall's tens of thousands of Buddhist scriptures, "Who goes to Buddhism's 84,136 hells?"

He said, "Anyone who does anything wrong." He paused, thought about it, and added with a wry smile, "Everyone, I guess."

"Is there a Buddhist heaven?" I asked. He said "Of course," so I asked, "Who goes to heaven?"

He pondered this, and said, "Just a minute." He pushed his Gandhi spectacles back up on his nose, and flipped through pages of a massive, musty volume for a good ten minutes, then said, "No one has ever asked me that. I'll have to get back to you."

Monkish Munchies[22] These monks may not be much on heaven, but they certainly offer some heavenly cuisine! A set fee in their famous vegetarian restaurant will land you tasty dishes of vegetarian "meats," fungi, and vegetables—culinary creations with names like "Half Moon Sinking Down the River," "Treasure Hidden in Scented Clay," "Golden Lotus in the South Sea," or "Two Mushrooms Competing for Beauty."

Deng Xiao Ping's Favorite

If you decipher their menu, let me in on it.

One of their best dishes is taro, the tuber from which Hawaiians make their staple food, poi (which looks like library paste but doesn't taste as good). Deng Xiao Ping liked Nanputuo's taro so much that he had his personal chef take 200 pounds back to Beijing. And in truth, taro is tasty. But never eat it with beef—because that's taro-bull[23].

For restaurant info, phone: 208-6587.

Devilish Deductions The gift shops offer Nanputuo knickknacks like chant cassettes, glow-in-the-dark plastic Buddhas, and wood or stone rosaries. Unlike American religious merchandising, there isn't any "Suggested love offering," or tax deductible receipt. But given the state of economic affairs down below, you can just add a few zeros to your receipt and make an outlandish deduction after you die. The Infernal Revenue Service[24] will probably never know the difference.

But don't try to pay with Hell Money, or there'll really be hell to pay.[25]

B.B.

Nanputuo Knicknacks
(Hell money not accepted)

NanPutuo's real excitement is not inside the temple grounds but outside the massive gates, where street vendors cry, "Candied crab apples on a stick!" and "Fresh sliced pineapple!" and "Tea eggs 3 mao (cents) each or 2.50 Yuan a jin" (a jin is about 1.1 pounds). Shoe repairpersons from far off Sichuan resurrect weary pilgrims' weary soles with glue and thread, and TongAn peasants puff rice with a coal-fired cast iron contraption that goes off like a cannon every few minutes. The liveliest trade, of course, is in the Buddhist paraphernalia - incense sticks, candles, and "Hell Bank Notes." There's also another trade that strikes me as a bit fishy…

Freed Fish & Fireworks

In front of Nanputuo lies the shimmering mirror of the Buddhist pool for freeing captive fish. At least in theory, Buddhists are vegetarians, and opposed to taking any kind of life (though enterprising peasants may allow calves to strangle themselves on a short leash, then enjoy guilt-free beef 'n green peppers).

If there is merit in not taking life, there is even greater merit in saving it, so many pious pilgrims buy live fish from fishermen and release them into Nanputuo's murky pond, thus freeing the finned folk from a dire

Pool for freeing captive fish

fate. But given that this goes on day in and day out, one wonders just how many fish can one pond hold? I suspect the monks afford their new Noki cell phones by recycling the fish to the waves of pious pilgrims that flock in each day.

A Bang and a Whimper[26]   The unending emancipation of captive carp goes on largely in silence, but not so the monastery's other activities. Monks drive off devils, both domestic and foreign, by banging drums and cymbals day and night. And before fireworks were banned in Xiamen, the temple grounds emanated an eternal cacophony of firecrackers that reverberated off the adjoining Xiada Foreign Expert's Guesthouse walls, and the denizen's pounding craniums.

Chinese have been enamored of fireworks since before the dawn of recorded time 5,015 years ago, when ancestors shooed demons by burning bamboo stems, which explode when air heats up in the hollows between the joints. Somewhere down the line, an enterprising soul stuffed bamboo with gunpowder, and eventually someone else replaced the bamboo with rolls of heavy paper, giving us the modern fireworks we hear today—or

used to hear. During the mid 1990s, a stroke of the pen banned this perennial pastime in many major cities. Now Chinese must either shoot off their fireworks in the countryside and small towns, or pop strings of balloons, or play tape recordings of firecrackers over massive sound systems.

The ambiance just ain't the same.

Buddha's Bugs   (A Qing Dynasty Tale) A Buddhist monk vowed to offer his blood to feed other living things, but after mosquitoes had bitten him for hours the itching got to him and he began swatting them with abandon.

"What happened to your vow?" asked a bystander.

The monk sighed. "Some of them have started coming back for seconds."

B.B.

World's Largest Cannon!
(Huli Hill Fort)

B.B.

Huli Hill Fort — China's Doorstep Huli Hill Fort, located strategically on the beach behind XiaDa, has always been considered the door to Xiamen. And given that Xiamen is "China's Gateway," that makes Huli Hill Fort China's doorstep.

Huli Fortress was started in 1891 and took five years to build. It's virtually impregnable, thanks to its construction of sand, clay, camphor tree juice, lime and glutinous rice (during a prolonged siege defenders could eat their fort).

Huli Fort boasts The World of Exotic Stones (3,850 exotic stones with 'natural pictures on them, including the Emperor Qianlong's Pet Rock), and an exhibition of ancient armaments. The 455 weapons include guns, swords, and cannons, including a 12th century cannon reputed to be the world's oldest. But its real claim to fame is the world's largest cannon. (Guinness lists a cannon in Moscow, but we're working on changing that!). The German-made Krupp coastal defense gun, installed by some big shot[27] back in 1896, weighs 60 tons, is 13.96 meters long, and cost 60,000 taels of silver. And in taels lies another tale...

A Tale of Taels and Mus

It annoys me no end to read in the guidebook that the Huli Fort cannon cost 60,000 taels of silver. What on earth does that mean? Even if you do know that a tael was about one ounce, what was the exchange rate for silver in 1896? The endless references to taels is about as bad as using mu in English translations. Assuming they

didn't mean a Xiamen park was the sound of 1,400 cows (moo!), I checked the dictionary. The only entry for Mu was, "The 12th letter of the Greek Alphabet." You'd think that whoever puts stuff in English could also condescend to delineate mu and tael, but I won't hold my breath. Just last week I saw that the Xiamen #1 Department Store spent a pretty penny on a beautiful new English sign that boasts, "Xiamen First Yibai Store." Do they think Yibai is English, or do Laonei deliberately use Yibai, Mu and Tael to befuddle barbarian Laowai? Well... back to my *gushi*.

During the Opium Wars, China had over 100 cannons, but Huli Hill's behemoth is the only well preserved coastal cannon left. With a range of 16,640 meters, it could easily lay into Taiwan-occupied Jinmen island, a mere two miles offshore. Though since we've lived here, it has been Xiamen, not Taiwan, taking the shelling.

When Chiang Kai Shek fled to Taiwan in 1949, he left a sizeable force behind on Jinmen Island. Jinmen is so close that with binoculars we can read Taiwan's propaganda billboards, and watch patrolling KMT soldiers.

During the 1950s, Taiwan loosed hundreds of thousands of shells on Xiamen Island and her neighbors—especially Da

Compliments of Taiwan!

Deng Island, which now has a marvelous museum. (This Xiamen house is still lived in by the family of one of my students).

Little 8th Army! (小八路!) Sometime back during the hostilities, a Taiwan attack upon the village of Hecuo (site of the bombed out house above) destroyed the communications lines. Inway, my MBA student, said the young students of Hecuo Primary School rushed out and, with their bare hands, joined the wirses together and held them until they could be repaired! (I thought Inway was just giving me a line, but the story was true; maybe this was the current thing to do back then?). Since the elementary heroic exploits of these elementary students, this elementary school has become a museum for the

Little Heroes. It is the only primary school in China that boasts heavy artillery and machine guns on the sports grounds, and a military museum. My student asked me if any American primary schools had weapons like this on display. I said, "Of course not. If American kids had them, they'd use them!"

B.B.

Hecuo Elementary School Sportfield Artillery!

After the PLA in Fujian announced a ceasefire and cessation of all hostilities, Taiwan's bombing gradually decreased. But the calm was deceptive.

Xiamen folk were still rebuilding homes and lives when, on January 24, 1984, Jinmen pounded Jiaoyu Island with 120 shells. "A soft answer turneth away wrath." In spite of civilian casualties, the PLA refused to retaliate, and Taiwan abandoned its bombing — until 1994.

Kaboom! Our family was in our hillside XiaDa apartment on November 14, 1994 when we heard the explosion reverberate across campus. "Dynamiting or war games?" we wondered. But no games this time.

Two bombs from Jinmen pounded Xiamen's Huangcuo village, wounding 4 workers. Western media shrugged it off as an accident, but when the

Nov. 14, 1994

PLA fired missiles into the open sea near Taiwan, what an uproar that created! It seemed like the entire world bemoaned China's militancy, and politicians seeking re-election votes demanded U.S. Naval intervention.

Ironic, to say the least. Taiwan bombs our home and the world shrugs. China bombs open ocean—and hawks[28] don war paint. But times are changing....

When we arrived in 1988, Amoy's perimeter was studded with granite tank traps and concrete bunkers, but over the past decade Xiamen has turned her swords into plows[29] – and roads.

Our shoreline facing Jinmen is now garlanded with a beautifully landscaped ring road. The tank traps have been replaced by lawns and gardens, and paths for hikers, bicyclists and roller bladers.

Take a bus or taxi to one of the picnic areas, and have lunch on the broad grassy lawns that front the miles of beaches. Enjoy the sand and surf, and the backdrop of islands and freighters, and majestic two-masted mahogany Chinese junks gliding gracefully through the channel, or fishermen's sampans bobbing like corks in a giant basin. And if you're lucky, you might even catch a glimpse of the **rare white dolphins** that frequently frolic in our bay.

A Tidy Suggestion: hit the beach two hours before high tide, when the water is clearest. To calculate high tide, multiple the lunar date (find it on a Chinese calendar, or in the *Xiamen Daily*) times 0.8. After the 15th of the month, subtract

Roughing it on the Island Ring Road!

15 from the date, and multiply it by 0.8. Example: 1st = 1 × 0.8, or 0.8 (about 00:50 a.m. 12:50 p.m.). The 15th = 15 × 0.8, or 12 (12:00 midnight and 12:00 noon). The 18th = （18 − 15） × 0.8, or 2.40 (roughly 2:25 a.m/p.m.).
Deng deng.
If the Luny Calendar befuddles you, ask any Chinese 7-year-old to calculate it for you.
(**Note**: for even more great Fujian beaches, try Chongwu and Yakou to the north, or Dongshan Island to the south).

Or skip the picnic and have tea or a meal by the beach, where you can rent beach umbrellas, floats, mats, rubber boats, deng deng. After your swim, rinse off in one of the many modern public facilities, and then get high—on a rental hot air balloon or motorized glider.
Or go fly a kite![30]...

Go Fly a Kite?

If someone has told you to do just that, head for the beach, because offshore breezes make Xiamen's Ring Road the perfect place to take part in this ancient Chinese sport—or art, or science, it's all of the above. I marvel at the kite adepts who with a flick of the wrist send silk dragons skywards,

Family Outing

B.B.

and then by subtly tugging on one of the control strings, cause it to perform dizzying acrobatics, diving so close to the ground that the ants and spiders duck, then soaring back into the skies. Personally, I'm happy just to get a kite up and keep it up; when my kite descends it's not with a kiss but a crash.

Kites, like just about everything else on this planet, were invited by the Chinese some few thousand and fifteen years ago. (Dr. Needham even lists kites as one of China's greatest scientific inventions). In 478 B.C. the Chinese philosopher Mo Zi spent 3 years making a wooden hawk that actually flew. Poor fellow. Were he around today he could just log on to **www.pincle.kite.com** and buy one of the delightful hi-tech fiber-glass spar and silk kites produced right here in Xiamen! (E-mail: pincle-kite@pincle-kite.com).

In 200 B.C., General Han Xin flew a kite over a city he was besieging, and then measured the string to see how far he had to tunnel under the city to take them by surprise. Yet another general tied harps to kites, flew them over a city, and had his spies in the city spread the rumor that the waling from the heavens was from the gods, who were angry and would visit a bitter defeat upon them the next day. They of course fled in terror, totally unaware the enemy was just stringing them along (or feeding them a line, etc). This may have helped lead to the Chinese name of kites: fengzheng (wind musical instrument).

Kites were used to send signals, and very large kites allowed archers to rain arrows into fortified cities. Marco Polo wrote that Chinese sea captains tied folks to a kite and sent them aloft. If they stayed up, smooth sailing was ahead. If they wobbled or crashed, it was a bad omen and

the ship delayed setting out. I'm not sure what they did for the poor fellow who came down with the kite; if it were me I'd be pretty up in the air about it.

Chinese also believe that kite-flying can bring good luck—and the higher the kite, the better the luck. Personally, I'd have to be higher than a kite to believe that. But lucky or not, kite flying is fun. For me, it's like fishing with a sail instead of a hook, surfing invisible currents seeking to catch evasive updrafts.

Kite flying was banned during the "Cultural Revolution," but in cities like Xiamen the beautiful sport is again catching on. I like watching the kite masters just outside the Mandarin Seaview (beside the Exhibition Center). Some of the kites soar so high they look as if they could land in Jinmen. Now there's a thought! If Taiwan and the mainland don't get the Three Links worked out soon, maybe I'll just take a kite back to Taiwan…

A kite's view of Jinmen

B.B.

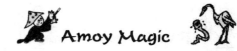

Chinese Opera. Just past Huli Hill Fort, on the right, is an open-air stage where you can catch one of the locals favorite pastimes: a unique version of Chinese Opera that has resulted from centuries of collaboration between artists in Taiwan and Southern Fujian. [The photo below is of retirees who give open-air performances each week by the Gulangy ferry].

After Koxinga's unpeaceful liberation of Taiwan from the Dutch in 1662, Fujian folk migrated to Taiwan and introduced their folk music, which eventually developed into Gezi Opera (which was influenced by Liyuan Opera, Gaojia Opera, Peking Opera, and Opera Winfrey). Eventually, Gezi Opera recrossed the Taiwan Straits to Xiamen and Southern Fujian, and after some innovation it was renamed "Xiang Opera."

In town and country alike, audiences are enthralled by the lively, melodic stories told in simple language. Favorites include *"Liang Shanbo and Zhu Yingtai,"* which is China's version of *"Romeo and Juliet."* Others include *"Dumb Girl Sues," "A Tale of the White Snake," "True and False Princes,"* and *"Five Daughters Offer Birthday Felicitations."*

Xiamen folk also enjoy Gaojia Opera. This lively combination of singing and acrobatics originated over 200 years ago in Quanzhou, and used to be called Songjiang Opera because it is about Songjiang, chief hero of the classic *"Outlaws of the Marsh."* Clowns are the heart and soul of this cynical yet comical opera.

South Fujian has many forms of indigenous music, played on such instruments as the pipa, erhu (two-stringed violin) and sanxian, but the most popular music is "Nanyin," which dates back over 1,000 years to the Sui Dynasty. In 1713, Fujian performers played "Nanyin" for Emperor Kangxi's 60th birthday, and the delighted emperor awarded them a silk banner embroidered with, "Delightful Melody Before the Throne." (I've made delightful melodies *on* the throne—especially after eating beans).

Want to sample Nanyin's delightful melodies while on your throne[31]? A 1989 Xiamen guidebook assured us that Nanyin gramophone recordings are available at home and abroad.

But where on earth (or China!) does one get a gramophone?

B.B.

While we're on the subject, Xiamen also excels in modern music. The **Xiamen Philharmonic Orchestra**, established only in 1998, has already made a name for itself, thanks to the able direction of internationally renowned conductor Professor Zheng Xiaoying. In spite of their motto, "Highbrow art will be increasing popular," lowbrows like meself enjoy the over 100 works performed by the 60+ musicians.

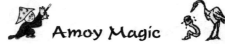
The Chinese Theater

Rev. John Mcgowan (In and About Amoy, 1889[32])

"A theatre has been planted in this, one of the busiest streets of the town. For forty or fifty yards on each side of it the people are packed like herrings, gazing with rapturous, upturned faces at the actors. They are just concluding a farce, and ever and anon bursts of laughter show how keenly the fun is appreciated by the crowd....

"The acting before us is first-rate, for the Chinese are natural, born actors... What specially strikes one about these actors is the coolness and ease with which they perform their parts, and the natural life-like way in which they act the characters they have taken. Two women for example are quarrelling and scolding each other. As women are not allowed to be actors, two men have assumed their dress. The looks, the gestures, the feminine toss of the head, the rising tones that grow shriller and shriller as their passions become excited, are exactly such as may be witnessed in the quarrels of women almost any day in the streets of Amoy. We forget, in the reality of the scene before us, that these persons are actors. They have impersonated an actual event in human life so realistically, that the stage seems to have vanished, and we are standing in one of the narrow streets of the city, with the crowd around us, watching two women so completely absorbed by their passions as to have become oblivious of the many eyes that are fastened upon them."

Beggars
—Some of Amoy's Best Actors

"Xiamen is as bad as Calcutta!" an American tourist complained to me. "Beggars everywhere!"

Many of Amoy's beggars have genuine needs, but some are simply actors, employing ingenious incapacitations as props, with more skill than you'll find in any theater in town! Consider this fellow I met in Zhongshan Park...

Prodigal Daughter, Lost Son

A nicely dressed man in Xiamen's Zhongshan Park clutched his bag and groaned softly. "Is anything wrong?" I asked.

"No, nothing," he said, and he looked at me dolefully, like a beagle puppy. But as Susan and I turned away he said, "I arrived yesterday from Nanjing to visit my daughter. All I had was this address," and he flashed a crumpled, grimy envelope. "I can't find her, and I've spent my life savings to get here."

"That's terrible," Susan exclaimed, and I reached for my wallet.

"Don't help him!" a man said, and he turned on the distraught father. "Have you no face? How can you take advantage of foreign guests?"

"But he needs help!" I protested.

"He's a con man!" the man said. "Don't give him a penny."

As a crowd gathered, the unfortunate fellow clutched his black bag and shuffled off, glancing at me reproachfully over his shoulder. For weeks afterwards, Susan and I questioned whether we were right in heeding the callous advice of others. In fact, I never quite got him off my mind—until I met him again two years later.

He was clutching the same black bag as he spoke to a cornered foreign businessman at the harbor. "I just got here yesterday from Shanghai," he said. "I came to visit my son but I can't find him, and I spent all my money—"

The foreigner was reaching for his wallet as I rushed up, clasped the con man around the shoulder, and said, "Hi, remember me? We met two years ago in a Xiamen park after you'd spent your life savings to find your daughter. Your children really give you a hard time!"

The crowd roared with laughter as he stalked off. I didn't see him for over a year, but last week he zeroed in on me outside Xiamen University's gate (you'd think he'd know better—but maybe we foreigners do all look alike!).

"I need your help," he said. "I just—"

"—You just got here looking for your son?" I asked. "Did you ever find the daughter you lost a few years ago?" He glared at me, and stormed off.

Amoy Beggars Guild, 1847

Back home in Los Angeles, beggars and con men are a dime a dozen. Every country has them, and China is no exception. In fact, way back in 1847, the missionary John Talmage wrote about Amoy's notoriously efficient beggars' guild. The 18 "Beggars Chiefs" were actually appointed by the magistrate, and held their office for life (unless removed for bad conduct. Businesses that paid their monthly "beggars tax" were entitled to display a placard that exempted them from harassment by the city's 2,000 "official" beggars, who lived in the "Beggar's Camp" and operated throughout the 18 beggar districts.

So begging is nothing new in Xiamen! But when tourists tell me that China is as poor as India's Calcutta because it has so many beggars, I feel obliged to note that not all of those with their hands out really need a hand out. But the question is—how do we tell professionals from the cons?

Some American businessmen in Xiamen actually flew to Anhui Province to verify one beggar's woeful tale—and ended up becoming a great help to his family. But I, personally, am torn between giving to all or giving to none— especially when I've seen the same beggars working the same beat on Zhongshan Road for over a decade!

I hope that Xiamen's government can one day find a way to help those with true needs—and to send the rest packing! While it is one thing for China's visitors to run the gauntlet of the truly needy, it is quite another to contend with those who have made a profession out of being needy.

Who's Begging Who?

Like their American counterparts, teachers in China are underpaid—and even the beggars know it! A nicely dressed lady on Zhongshan Rd., smoking an imported cigarette, approached me and said, "Help me out with a little money."

"Sorry, but I don't have much money on me," I said.

She smirked and said, "Come on. Foreigners are all rich. Just a few Yuan."

"I'm not a rich foreigner," I said. "I'm just a teacher at Xiamen University."

She laughed. "I'm so sorry. If I'd known you were a teacher, I'd have given you money instead." And she set off after another more promising victim.

Hongshan (Swan Mountain) Park (鸿山公园) Take any

bus from Xiada and get off just past the train tracks.[33] After you've seen how people on the other side of the tracks[34] live, visit Hong Shan Park, which has everything from a small Buddhist temple (for small Buddhists) to beautiful gardens, an old fashioned Carousel, and a Ferris Wheel, where for once you'll go in circles and not mind it (though I've been told the Ferris Wheel has been down for awhile).

On a clear day, Hong Shan Park's Ferris Wheel, on the 125m peak, offers the best panoramic view of Xiamen.   And on a rainy day, the peak's unique wind currents blow rain both vertically and horizontally, simultaneously, creating a unique phenomenon that locals have dubbed 'knitted rain.'

1st Church of China

(新街礼拜堂) Every two-horse-town in America has a First Baptist or a First Methodist, but there is only one First Church of China — right in Xiamen!   China's oldest Protestant church, XinJie Church was built in 1848 at # 29 Tai Guang Street (台光街 29 号), which is now a narrow, winding alley behind the Chinese Drug Store at the corner of Zhongshan Rd. and Siming Rd.   Phone: (0592) 207-2383.   The same year, 1848, saw the first two Chinese to be baptized—a maker of silk flowers, in his sixties, and his son.

Just off the harbor, near XiaHe Rd., is the Bamboo Church (1848), and Gulangyu Island has a large Catholic church (with English services) and the popular Sanlitang Protestant Church.

Xiamen has several of China's oldest churches, but also boasts one of China's largest, the New Territories Good News Church.   Out in Jiangtou District, past LianBan, this 10 million Yuan edifice looks like Frank Lloyd Wright's version of Noah's Ark.   But the architect should

The Ark   B.B.

have taken some advice from Noah, because this ark is sinking! It once stood proud and tall in an empty field, but now is slowly submerging in a rising sea of skyscrapers. Taller cross, perhaps?

Pastor Iap
(1st Chinese pastor in Amoy)

With 3,000 in attendance on Sundays, it's almost standing room only, so get there early (take the #7 bus from the train station).

Pew Perils　　Xiamen church pews are packed on Easter and Christmas, when even the Buddhists enjoy the choirs' special music.　Get there half an hour early for a good seat.　At Christmas especially, the time will pass quickly as you listen to recordings of such classic holiday hymns as Silent Night, The First Noel, Frosty the Snowman and Jingle Bells. (They fit right in with the "Santa Bless You" Christmas cards sold in book stores.).

Do get there early!　Otherwise, Laowai-loving ushers will oust some 90 year old granny from her front row pew so the foreign friend can see the service better, and so everyone else can see the foreign friend better.　Of course, you can always gallantly refuse the granny's seat and perch on a red plastic stool on the front porch.　But then you're a sitting duck[35] for that sect which believes "speaking in tongues" means mastering English.

They'll grab a stool and pull it up beside you and spend the entire hour, nonstop, practicing English. I've actually had prayers go like this:

"Our Father who art in —"
    "—What country are you from?"
"Thy kingdom come, thy will be —"
    "—Where do you work?"
"Give us this day our —"
    "—How much money do you make?"
"And lead us not into temptation."
Like murder!

Chinese Communion... For 2000 years, Christians have " broken bread [36] " together during Communion. Well, some have. B.B But what about those who don't have bread to break?

"Instant Noodles?"

When we first came to Xiamen Christians celebrated communion with little squares of noodles. I liked the chewy texture, and the Chinese wine did more for you than the grape juice we sip back home (though I learned why communion cups are so tiny; enough of that wine and you're in the spirits, not in the Spirit).

Alas, Xiamen has modernized, and that includes churches. Now they use the round, flat imported bona fide communion wafers that look and taste like Styrofoam. Granted, they look nice, with the little cross stamped on them. It would be tough stamping crosses on wet noodles. Still, I kind of miss the noodles.

Laowai 3rd Degree [37] In 1990, an American complained, "I'm tired of nosy Chinese! They ask me almost non-stop, 'Going to work?', 'Coming home?', 'Going shopping?', 'Eaten yet?'"

I looked about furtively, then whispered, "Do you know why they ask Laowai so many questions?"

He looked surprised, and whispered back, "No. Why?"

"Because they're Communists, and they have to report on us."

"Really?" His eyes widened as paranoia took a toehold.

"Not really!" I said, laughing. "That's just how Chinese greet one another!"

Westerners usually greet one another with a simple and non-invasive

"Hello" or "Good Morning" or "Nice weather today!" But not the Chinese. They are seldom content with "Ni Hao" (How are you?) or "Zao Shang Hao" (Good morning). Rather, they ask what you are **doing**. And unlike Americans, who don't want an honest answer to "How are you?" Chinese *do* expect an answer.

I've never asked anyone how much money they make. I don't even know my own sister's salary. But Chinese have no qualms homing in on a strange Laowai and firing off in rapid order the **Laowai 3rd Degree**:

1) "Hello, what is your name?"   2) "Where are you from?"
3) "Is it cold in America?"   4) "Where do you work?"
5) "How much do you earn?"   6) "Will you teach me English?"

It's culture, not nosiness. But with 1.3 billion Laonei pitted against a handful of Laowai, it gets to you sometimes.

Laowai Radar   I was standing armpit to sweaty armpit on a hot bus when it screeched to a halt to let on a youth. He still had one foot in the door when his Laowai Radar picked me out of the crowd. With an ear to ear grin and eyes nailed to me as if I were the Holy Grail[38] (or the Worshipful Wok), he wormed his way towards me, the Laowai 3rd Degree on the tip of his tongue. As he sidled up under my arm and opened his mouth I preempted him with, "I'm Pan Wei Lian from America, which is like China. Hot in the south, cold in the north. I work in Xiamen University, and earn enough to pay taxes but not enough to avoid them. Have I missed anything?"

So much for Sino-American friendship. His jaw dropped, he slunk away, I felt like a cad, and I have regretted it ever since.

The Solution! Nowadays I just answer the questions, with a smile. But I have a **solution**! Make life easier for Laowai and Laonei alike by just printing the answers to the Laowai 3rd Degree on the back of your business cards, and keep a stack at all times. But even though Chinese have no qualms in asking "personal" questions, they also have no aversion to answering them. In a way, their candor is refreshing, and we Laowai could learn from it. But not in Church, please!

 Fun On-Island

The Amoy People In August 1889, the missionary John Macgowan published his *The Story of the Amoy Mission* in London. I marvel at how he captured the heart and soul of the Amoy people, whom he so clearly admired. He wrote frankly of the poverty and problems, and of the problems between Laowai and Laonei, but he also brought to life the Amoy people's passion and drive and, above all, their "English sense of fair play." So rather than subject you to my own impoverished prose, here is a selection from his marvellous memoir!

Chinese stare at the foreigner, sometimes with skepticism or even thinly veiled contempt, but once they know you, "The crowd becomes sympathetic. The sneer dies out of their faces. There is nothing that touches the Chinese heart so mightily as practical benevolence. It is a virtue they highly appreciate. Their stolid, emotionless features begin to light up with genuine feeling, and the eyes of some are twinkling and flashing as their hearts are moved...[what] has just happened has been a mighty revelation. It has brought you closer to the Chinese heart than you were before, and it has revealed to you the wondrous possibilities of the future..."

"The Amoy people... are sturdy representatives of their race....They are very fiery and passionate when any injustice or wrong is attempted, but generally they are fair-minded and amenable to reason. They have an Englishman's sense of fair play, and they have an intense respect for virtue and goodness of every kind, and they will pay devout homage to any one in whose lives these are conspicuous."

William Burns (Scottish missionary who greatly influenced Western attitudes toward the Chinese)

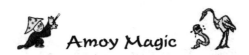
Recreation on Island

Bowling

Big Egg Bowling Alley, above the department store at 358 Xiahe Road, has the cheapest games in town (ranging from Y5 to Y20, depending upon the time of day).   Big Egg supplies shoes but bring your own socks.

After a few games of bowling, you can get your mind out of the gutter by playing billiards in an adjacent room. Better yet, see how many laps you can manage on the indoor gasoline go-carts before you succumb to the carbon monoxide (piece of cake for L.A. natives). (More go-karting below!).

Hua Yi Bowling Center, on N. Hubin Rd., has at least 40 alleys, with much nicer equipment than Big Egg's. But it's also much more expensive. (Unlike Big Egg, it must cater to Big Potatoes).

Phone: 512-3777

Golf

Southern Wood Golf & Country Club, 50 kilometers out of Xiamen towards Zhangzhou, gives you sand traps and salt air in one package. Call (596) 688-1555 to arrange a day, or stay for a weekend in a bungalow.

The Kai Kou Golf Club, between Jimei and Tongan, was supposedly designed by that man of many hats, Greg Norman.

Phone: 701-1679

Go-Karting
The Big Egg Bowling Alley has a nice little in-door go-kart track, but for a real Indianapolis 500 feeling, try the Indy Go-Karting Center—a large outdoor track in the Bailu Zhou  recreation area (on Yundang Lake).   Those little cars are **fast**—but safe. Rates are cheaper before 6:00 p.m. Phone: 508-1333 or 508-2333.

Xiamen Water Park （厦门快乐谷水上乐园）

Xiamen Water Park has enough water slides and pools to keep you busy for hours on a hot summer afternoon. It's located in Huli, just down the road from the big double tunnel.

Address: Xiamen, Huli District, Huarong Rd. Huli Park East Entrance. 厦门湖里区华荣路湖里公园东大门　Phone: 565-6967

Swimming Pools （游泳池, Youyong Chi）

— Holiday Inn and Marco Polo have nice pools but a less expensive route is to buy a 30 visit pass, for only 300 RMB, at the Huli Sports Center (湖里体育馆). It's near the corner of HaiTian Rd. and Huli Park, behind the theater. Phone: 602-5886.

Xiamen World Gardens （厦门景州乐园, Xiamen Jingzhou Leyuan）

, or "Taiwan Folk Village," as I think it's now called, is out on the beach road, in Huangcuo Village (黄厝村). The boys like the wood and rope obstacle courses (a maze of swinging bridges, nets, balancing bars, deng deng). We also enjoyed the wild animal shows, and Taiwan folk dance performances.

Phone: 256-0115 or 256-0112

Laonei (老内) Notes

[1] Wrestling matches: pushing and shoving because no one likes to wait in line

[2] Big shots: important people

[3] Hutchinson, Paul, Ed., "A Guide to Important Mission Stations in Eastern China," The Mission Book Company, Shanghai, 1920

[4] Rub wrong way: annoy, anger

[5] Check bounce: not enough money in the bank to cover a check (支票)

[6] I wanna hold your hand: name of popular Beatles song

[7] Bone up: practice, improve upon

[8] Culture: colony of bacteria, such as the lactobacillus used to make yogurt)

[9] Tyndale: William Tyndale (1494-1536) burned at the stake for translating the Bible (New Testament) from Latin into English. Keeping the Bible from the masses gave priests the same power as Confucian scholars enjoyed by keeping the language, and literature, out of the hands of common Chinese (hence the importance of New China's 'simplification' of Chinese, in spite of its drawbacks).

[10] Two-ox town: small town (variation of American phrase "one horse town")

[11] Up creek without a paddle: in difficult situation with no solution

[12] Swan song: legendary, beautiful song sung only once by a swan, at its death.

[13] Jury is still out: undecided

[14] Monty Python: British comedy program

[15] Hard to swallow: difficult to believe

[16] Pit stop: rest (racing cars make 'pit stops' for repairs)

[17] Pickles & Ice cream (in cartoon): pregnant women crave strange foods, like pickles and ice cream together.

[18] Money to Burn: so much money one can afford to burn it

[19] Shake a staff at: from the phrase "shake a stick at" (slang for "point out, designate, or name").

[20] Short end of the stick: worst side of an unfair deal

[21] Burn candle at both ends: work around the clock

[22] Munchies: snacks (小吃)

[23] Taro-bull (sounds like "terrible"

[24] Infernal Revenue Service (America's Internal Revenue Service collects income tax). Infernal (rather than internal) refers to hell.

[25] Hell to pay: big trouble

[26] A bang and a whimper: in the poem "The Hollow Men," (1925) T.S. Eliot wrote, "This is the way that the world ends, not with a bang but a whimper; but with Chinese fireworks we have both the bang *and* the whimper (aching ears).

[27] Big shot: slang for "important person"

[28] Hawks: politicians who favor military force for foreign policy

[29] Swords into plows: Biblical phrase [Isaiah 2:4] referring to future peace [圣经, 以赛亚书 2：4,他必在列国中施行审判,为许多国民断定是非. 他们要将刀打成犁头,把枪打成镰刀。这国不举刀攻击那国，他们也不再学习战事。]

[30] Go fly a kite: sometimes a euphemism for "get lost" ("get out of here!")

[31] On the throne: "throne" is another word for "toilet"

[32] Mcgowan, Rev. John, "The Story of the Amoy Mission," Butler & Tanner, The Selwood Printing Works, Frome, and London, August, 1889.

[33] Other side of the tracks: euphemism for people of a different social class (usually lower)

[34] From the other side of the tracks: euphemism for low class people

[35] Sitting duck: easy target (a duck is easy to shoot when it is not flying)

[36] 圣经,路加福音 22：19：[耶稣] 又拿起饼来祝谢了,就劈开递给他们,说,这是我的身体,为你们舍得。你们也应当如此行,为的是纪念我。

[37] 3rd Degree: mental or physical torture used to interrogate a prisoner

[38] Holy Grail: legendary cup from which Christ drank during his last meal; it was sought by Medieval knights because of its supposedly miraculous powers

Chapter 4
Gulangyu Islet

A mere 500 meters as the fly flies from downtown Xiamen's harbor lies the
famous 1.77 square kilometer island of
Gulangyu (or "Drum Waves," because the
breakers pound the rocks like drums).

The 10 minute ferry ride to Gulangyu
costs nothing unless you sit upstairs, where a
ticket lady will collect about twice nothing.
But unless you can swim, you have to pay
the piper[1] for the return trip-which at is still a
better deal than Hong Kong's Star Ferry,
New York State's Island Ferry, or Disney
Land's "Pirates of the Caribbean."

It won't take you long to understand why
Laowai chose this tiny island for their
International Settlement. And even today
Gulangyu possesses one asset almost unheard of elsewhere in China: **quiet!**
Vehicles and bicycles are forbidden on the tiny island, so people walk, and
commerce is done with pull carts. But on this silent isle, the one sound you *will*
hear is pianos!

Pianos & Preachers   In the 1840s, Christian
missionaries came with Bibles in one hand and pianos
in the other (very big hands!). Today, this tiny
community of 20,000 has more pianos per capita than
anywhere else on the planet — hence Gulangyu's
nickname "Piano Isle."

Early on, Protestants started several churches on Amoy
and Gulangyu Islands. Catholics were busy too. The
Vicariate Apostolic of Amoy (created in 1883 under the
Dominicans) oversaw 11 European and 8 Chinese priests,
32 churches or chapels, 3 orphanages, and 13 schools (and
included Taiwan in its domain). The piano played an
integral part in all religious services, and Gulangyu folk

have been hooked on them ever since.

It is no surprise that Gulangyu has produced an inordinate number of famous pianists. The tiny islet has more pianos per capita than any other city in China (perhaps even in the world)—over 350 pianos, or one *in every five homes!* Famous pianists have included Zhou Shu in the '20s, Lin Junqing in the '30s, Wu Tianqiu in the '50s, Xu Feixing in the '60s, Xu Feiping in the '80s, and Chen Zuohuang and Xu Xing in the '90s. And we're still putting them out today, because not an evening passes that some family's budding pianist is not holding a recital. And many go on to study in the Amoy Music Academy, and from there to play in London, New York, Paris—or the local churches from whence the pianos came in the first place. It's no wonder that Gulangyu has *Asia's largest piano museum.*

Xiamen Piano Museum
-- Largest in Asia!

Descend Sunlight in the harbor, or taking a bumpy speedboat tour around the island. Then visit Dragon Hill, Hoisting Flag Hill, or the many parks and gardens where Chinese colleagues eagerly point out the ancient engraved inscriptions that immortalize every rock and boulder (for after 5,015 years, Chinese have analyzed and written poems about every mountain, rock, river and lake in China).

Savor Gulangyu's silence (punctuated by a few hundred preschoolers practicing scales or "Chopsticks" [2]), then steal a glimpse of the magnificent harbor and skyline by climbing Gulangyu's Sunlight Rock. (You'll really wish you had "stolen" that glimpse when you fork out 40 Yuan for the entrance ticket).

Rock's sweaty heights and cool off by windsurfing

Sunlight Rock
Gulangyu Islet

Underwater World Xiamen （厦门海底世界）, just to the right as you get off the ferry on Gulangyu Islet, has more fish than you'll find in Hubin North Road's Cantonese restaurants. The greatest variety of fish in any aquarium in China, over 10,000 finned folk of 350 fresh and salt water species swim about in 17 large and small tanks, a rock pool, a cylindrical tank, and two immense shark and reef tanks. And you don't have to be able to walk on water to get in on the action. Two 80-meter tunnels allow you to walk under the tanks

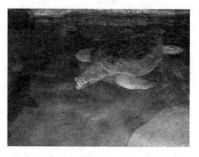

(and sharks!) without getting soaked by one million liters of water.   Visit the Penquin and Freshwater Fish Hall, Ocean Fish Hall, Sperm Whale Hall, and Dolphin and Sea-Lion Performance Hall.

    A joint-venture with Singapore Xingwang Holding Limited Company and Gulangyu Beauty Spot Construction Company, the facility is open daily, 8:30 AM to 8:00 PM. Present a valid student card for a discount. Address: Gulangyu Island, #2 Dragon Head Road（鼓浪屿龙头路 2 号）. Phone: 206-7668

Gulangyu Mall, straight ahead of the Ferry, may look Colonial but the beautiful building was finished in 2001! Enjoy the top floor buffet and a great view of the harbor, visit the shops, sample some of the popcorn and

At Gulangyu Mall B.B.

cotton candy in the square below, and enjoy live traditional music performances.

B.B.
Longtou St. (Gulangyu's 'main street')

Longtou （龙头, Dragon Head) **St.,** which winds past the Mall, has been Gulangyu's 'main street' for at least a century. Longtou is lined both sides with shops selling tea and teapots, Chinese art and handicrafts—even a bookstore. At the intersection by the bookstore, hang a left. Pearl World, a favorite with Laowai, will be on the left at the T intersection.

Gulangyu Architecture Take a leisurely couple hour stroll along Gulangyu's paved, 4 kilometer ring road. Enjoy the beach on one side and the eclectic architecture on the other— bungalows built in English, French, German, Japanese, Spanish and Chinese styles. I like the Gulangyu Guesthouse, where Nixon stayed during his historic 1972 trip. I've been in three TV mini-

series filmed in this wonderful estate. (I asked a Shanghai director why I always played the bad guy and she said, "Because foreign devils did not have any good guys!).

Xiamen spent 76 million Yuan on our Gulangyu Islet Architectural Protection Plan to preserve sites like the French style Lin House, the neo-Gothic Catholic church, the geometric Art-Deco court building, the Filipino Huang Yongyuan Mansion, and Gulangyu Shifan University (which was designed by the American architect Henry Murphy, who was famous for his marriage of Chinese and Western architecture). While on Gulangyu you can even walk on water at Shuzhuang Gardens…

Renovating Gulangyu Bldg.

Shuzhuang Garden's "9 Bend 44 Bridge" snakes across the water at Garden like a befuddled bamboo viper. Shuzhuang (bean plantation) Garden was built by a Taiwanese businessman who moved here with his family during the Sino-Japanese War of 1894—1895. With all of the stone bridges and walkways zigzagging over the sea, Chinese say it is "a garden in the sea and a sea in the garden." After enjoying the delightful diversity of flowers and shrubs, sip tea in the tea house and enjoy the sea view, or enjoy the golden beach. Open daily, 7am-8pm (except when it isn't).

Address: No. 45 Huangyan Rd., Gulangyu 鼓浪屿晃岩路 45 号   Phone: 206-3744

Website: **http://www.shuzhuang.com.cn**

Gulangyu Catholic Church is as beautiful inside as out, with intricately interwoven wood domed ceilings. I had never seen the inside of the church until Susan and I played a Mother Superior and a Catholic Priest in a TV series that was filmed partly on Gulangyu Island. It was quite an experience, and Sue still think she's a Mother Superior or Superior Mother or something.

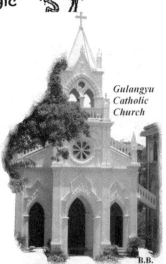

Gulangyu Catholic Church

Holy Father, maybe.
But Mother Superior?!

If two-hour hikes aren't your cup of coffee, you do have alternatives. You can be hauled around on a bamboo litter by bearers wearing unique numbered uniforms, just like the Good Ole Days when their ancestors hauled our forebears to public parks and private clubs that even in Xiamen bore signs, "No Chinese or Dogs Allowed."

At least nowadays the litter bearers are well paid for their services. And they give camera-- loving Laowai some good photo opportunities.

Gulangyu Islet electric tour buses

If bamboo litters aren't your style either, take one of the electric carts—or a boat. The 8 kilometer cruise around Gulangyu offers tantalizing glimpses of Monkey Isle, Baozhuyu (Pearl) Isle, and Huoshaoyu Isle (or " Burning Isle," because it is an extinct volcano).

Gulangyu Shopping   Laowai and Laonei alike pick up great buys on Gulangyu handicrafts.   Pearl World offers rock bottom prices (if you know what you're looking for).   Former U.S. President Jimmy Carter was amazed by the Chinese bottles and globes (and delicate Christmas balls) hand painted on the inside. "Miraculous!" Jimmy said.   (Get your name hand painted on the inside if you wish).

Just across from the Music Hall, around the corner from Pearl World, is a small shop where a lady sells shells, coral, knickknacks, and exquisite paper parasols from Fuzhou, which is where they originated centuries ago (the Japanese borrowed and refined the idea, and are so taken with them that they make even paper beach umbrellas).

Also check out the artists who will transform your name into a Chinese painting!

But the greatest attraction is not the shops but the traditional entertainers in the new Gulangyu Mall, and jovial shopkeepers like Mr. Fu Zhongjun (傅重军, photo to the right), who invariably invite foreign friends with, "He cha!" "Have some tea!" (Or, "m 'dei" in the local dialect—hence the English word "tea").   Give Mr. Fu a visit at #25 Huangyan Rd. (晃岩路 25 号), for ships in bottles, leather items, and a nice chat over some local Oolong tea.

"Have some tea!"
(Gulangyu shopkeeper)

"Chinese Inside-Painting is Miraculous!"
--Jimmy Carter

B.B.

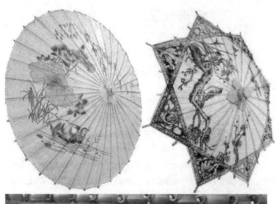

B.B.

Business gone to *pot...* B.B.

The Former U.S. Consulate is on northeastern Gulangyu

near the Sanqiutian tourist landing pier. Built in the 1930s with bricks imported from the U.S., it was taken over after '49 by an oceanography institute, and by the Chinese Ministry of Foreign Affairs in 1992.

Today, you can spent the night there because it is now the Jinquan Villa, run by the Xiamen Yongshun Company, which offers aquatic activities (parasailing and skiing) and electric cars for touring the island. Address: No. 26 San Ming Lu. Phone: (0592) 206-5621/2/3/4

Book electric cars: 2069886 (day); 2060833 (night).

Book aquatic activities: 2066833, 2066896

Sleight of Hand[3]- Puppets!

Marco Polo's fabled port of Zaytun, just 70 miles north of Xiamen, has long been the marionette capital of China, and ancient Zhangzhou, just to our west, is famous for its hand puppets. But Zhangzhou puppets are also now made right on Gulangyu Islet by a company that arranges private performances!

B.B.

Blowing Smoke B.B.

These aren't the run of the mill[4] hand puppets we toyed with as children. Nor are they like the 'rock 'em sock 'em' boxing George Bush and Saddam Hussein puppets that our friend Dave Hollinger bought in a Gulangyu shop, and has been playing with ever since. Zhangzhou puppets, in the hands of a master, are the closest thing you'll find in this life to real life little people!

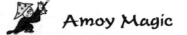

One puppet puffs a long pipe, and then blows smoke out his mouth. Another pours him a cup of tea with a steadier hand than I'll ever have—and the liquid goes right into the pinky sized cup. Puppets did the dragon dance almost as well as the Xiamen International School students' legendary performance. And they performance astonishing comic routines and acrobats—throwing spinning plates into the air and catching them on two poles, or juggling a barrel on their heads, tossing and flipping it—or tossing each other!

No Puppets, No Fireworks Chinese were amused at the childlike delight I took in the puppets' antics. One told a friend, "It's because America doesn't have puppets like this."

He reminded me of the Longyan farmers who saw us happily firing off half a ton of fireworks. One sagely told another, "Look how excited they are! They don't have fireworks outside of China, you know."

For the record[5], Americans *can* buy fireworks, but in China they don't cost an arm and a leg[6]. And we do have hand puppets—though perhaps not the magic to bring them to life. I eventually snuck behind stage to reassure myself the critters[7] were not alive.

Be sure and take in a Zhangzhou puppet show—and take home a handcrafted puppet for only 100 Yuan or so. Or arrange a Zhangzhou puppet show in Xiamen! Contact the Natural Sciences Museum's （厦门自然科普博物馆） Mr. Hong Ming Zhu (麦明章) to arrange puppet performances, or to purchase a genuine made-in-Xiamen Zhangzhou hand puppet.

Backstage Magic B.B.

Phone: 206-9933, or 897-3331. Mobile: 13666008151

Address: 2 Zhong Hua Rd （中华路二号） Gulangyu Islet.

Gulangyu Islet Sites

Chinese cities' glossy tourist brochures usually make boasts like, "1,043 Scenic Sights famous at both home and abroad." Quanzhou boasts over 2,000!. But with Gulangyu, it's no brag, just fact. Gulangyu has dozens of great sites, like The Overseas Chinese Garden for the Introduction of Subtropical Plants, which has over 1,000 species of plants, one experimental horticulture nursery, and a refrigerated room (a really cool[8] site). Also visit the 1,000+ Western style buildings put up by Laowai during the heydey of the opium trade, and check out the Numismatic Museum around the corner from Pearl World (to the right).

Here are some of Gulangyu's main attractions. (According to Dr. Jan Engsberg, somewhere between sites # 26 and # 36 is a former underground Japanese jail; if you visit it, be sure and take your cell phone). Vendors near the ferry sell English maps, or check Amoymagic.com.

1. Ferry Quay
2. Former English Consulate (1844)
3. Underwater World
4. Book Store
5. Former Spanish Consulate (1850)
6. Xiamen # 2 Hospital
7. Catholic Church (1917)
8. Piano Island Hotel
9. Beautiful Island Hotel
10. Bank of China
11. Concert Hall
12. Xiamen Music School
13. Marine Environmental Forecasting Center
14. Library
15. Former Dutch Consulate
16. People's Stadium
17. Gulangyu Hotel
18. Dragon Head Hill
19. Sunlight Rock
20. Zhengchengong Museum
21. People's Primary School
22. Xiamen Trinity Christian Church
23. Qin Dynasty Statuary Exhibit
24. Gulangyu Local Government
25. Cavern of Horror
26. Bishan Park
27. Xiamen #2 Middle School
28. Stadium
29. Xiamen Museum
30. Longshan Cave
31. Former U.S. Consulate (1865)
32. Former Salvation Hospital (1898)
33. Yanwei Hill
34. Xiamen KLI Cactus Amusement Park
35. Post Office Training Center
36. Jide Palace
37. Fujian Arts & Crafts School
38. Gulangyu Experimental Ctr. of Fujian Provincial Agricultural Research Institute
39. Langdong Hill
40. Gulangyu Fishery Shipyard
41. Gulangyu Villa
42. Gulangyu Villa Ferry (C.T.S.)
43. Gulang Rock
44. MeiHua Beach
45. Xiamen Overseas Chinese Subtropical Garden
46. Bird Garden
47. Piano Garden
48. Cable Cars to Sunlight Rock
49. Gulangyu Naval Sanitorium
50. Gulangyu Army Sanitorium
51. Gusheng Tunnel
52. Gangzaihou Beach
53. Gospel Hall
54. Yanping Park
55. Shuzhuang Garden
56. Cadre's Sanitorium
57. Seaview Garden Holiday Resort
58. Former Denmark Telegraph Offic
59. Seaview Villa Ferry
60. Seaview Villa Beach
61. Yu Garden
62. Former Yude Girl's School (1880)
63. Dadeji Beach
64. Cadres' Economics & Trade School
65. Lodge Cabin
66. Zhengchenggong Stone Statue
67. Bright Moon Park
68. Fuding Beach
69. Flag Raising Hill
70...Finished!

Supplement
– Umbrella Streets

"The streets [of Amoy] are not so wide as the sidewalks in Brooklyn. Some of them are so narrow that, when two persons, walking in opposite directions, meet each other, it is necessary for the one to stop, in order that the other may pass on." Rev. Talmadge, Amoy, 1847

Umbrella St. B.B.

One of my favourite pastimes is strolling Xiamen's narrow, twisting lanes. Over 100 years, a missionary wrote that they were so narrow one could not even open an umbrella in them.

Xiamen has changed so much the past 15 years. Xiahe Road used to be so narrow, and congested with street stalls, I could barely navigate it by bicycle. Today it is a six lane highway. But there are still plenty of "umbrella streets" to explore. Just take your pick; most of them lead to treasures like China's oldest church, Xinjie, bustling night markets, quaint barbershops, tailors using 100-year-old Min River sewing machines—or folks like Mr. Huang Tianhua (黄天华), the Bamboo Master of Hengzhu (横竹 horizontal bamboo) Rd.

100 Years Ago

Today

Sheer heaven for basketcases

This business is for the birds... B.B.

Bamboo Master of Hengzhu Road

We were in our favourite night market, on Ding An Rd. (定安路 between Trust-Mart and the Zhongshan Rd./Siming Rd. intersection), when Sue saw a man selling exquisite wrought iron and rattan baskets and shelves for a pittance. Susan Marie is a basket case[9] for basket buys, and the next day we visited their Hengzhu Lane warehouse.

We had visited their main shop many times over the years, but had no idea this shop had been started by the

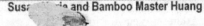
Sus... ...ie and Bamboo Master Huang

owner's father way back in 1953. They had even been written up in local newspapers several times. (*Xiamen Daily*, May 7th, 2001, for example). So Sue sifted through the piles of basketry, and I eventually wandered over to chat with Mr. Chen Yangsheng, who was playing Chinese chess with a young friend. I asked Mr. Cheng where he learned his excellent English and he said, "From the radio." Alas, Mr. Cheng was laid off from his store job, and had not found a new one yet. I'm happy to see China's emphasis on efficiency, but it's a shame to see such talented middle-aged folk put out to pasture, and I hope the government can find ways to recognize and use such talents.

Bamboo Shop address: #29 Hengzhu Lane (横竹路 29 号). Phone: 204-0144
Mobile Phone: 13906035727

B.B.

Yet Another Supplement!
(free of charge!)

B.B.

Rubbed the Right Way[10]

Umbrella road exploration can do a number[11] on your feet, but therapeutic foot massages are good for both sole and soul (especially when someone else foots[12] the bill). Or get a full body massage at one of Xiamen's blind body massage centers. They're inexpensive (about 30 Yuan an hour), and the masseurs don't stare at the folds of flesh they so expertly knead.

Chinese foot massages may not be as soothing as you'd expect, but long term they do wonders for both sole and soul! Skilled lasses plop your feet into a wooden barrel of steaming water spiked with herbs and medicines, and perhaps rose petals. They then scrape your feet with a wooden blade. I can't

Shannon likes foot massages-- *if Dad foots the bill!*

stand this, as I'm ticklish (which they think is funny; for Chinese, being ticklish signifies one is henpecked).

We often have dinner at the Shuyou (树友) Restaurant on Hubin N. Road (by Bank of China), then get a 70 minute foot massage next door at Tian Tian (天天).

Address: Wenwu Bldg, Hubin N. Road # 40 (湖滨北路 40 号, 文物大厦)

Phone: 507-9716

Blind Body Massage
(Address: 湘江花园 2 号楼明珠阁 6 层). Phone: 513-3477.

New massage shops seem to open almost daily. Across from the Overseas Chinese Museum is a delightful new place that offers a 90 minute foot/body massage for only 50 Yuan—and that includes tea, coffee, fruit and snacks (Chinese dumplings, soups, noodles).

Address: Siming S. Road # 384—390 (思明南路 384-390 号). Phone: 257-4818

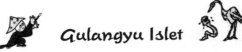

After a good massage, you'll be ready to take on another Amoy adventure—like tackling Amoy tigers on one of Trish Boman's Bushwalks (next chapter!).

Trish "Bushwalker" Boman

Laonei （老内） Notes

[1] Pay the piper: pay a debt (often long avoided; from the old European "Pied Piper" tale in which the villagers of Hamlin refused to pay the piper after he rid the town of rats, so he took their children in payment).

[2] Chopsticks: Waltz written in 1871 by English composer Arthur de Lulli

[3] Sleight of hand: fast or skilful tricks by a magician; legerdemain,

[4] Run of the mill: ordinary

[5] For the record: To embrace or support a position, officially, openly

[6] Cost an arm and a leg: very expensive

[7] Critter: creature (pronounced this way in rural mountain areas of the South Eastern U..S.,. and in fact close to the way it was spoken in Shakespeare's day).

[8] Cool: excellent (slang)

[9] Basket case: crazy (Sue's crazy about baskets)

[10] Rubbed the right way: variation of the phrase "rubbed the wrong way" (which means "to annoy, harass, or vex" someone).

[11] Do a number on: wreak havoc on; defeat; abuse; injure

[12] Foot the bill: pay the bill

Chapter 5
Amoy Bushwalks

Take a Hike!

Fujian has lured Western naturalists since the 18th century. Our province is home to rare creatures like the majestic Amoy Tiger, which reaches 8 ′ 7 ″ in length, almost **Amoy Tiger (Berlin Zoo, early 1900s)** 400 pounds in weight, and is considered the ancestor of all tigers (and if he isn't, I sure wouldn't tell him so).

Amoy tigers are nearly extinct now, though some can be seen in a West Fujian reserve (where two cubs were born in September, 2002!).

Fujian also has butterflies and insects seen no where else in the world. But if insects bug[2] you, then consider our snakes. We have king cobras, bamboo vipers, and reticulated pythons that reach 33 feet in length and have been known to eat farmers that didn't eat them first!

If you are like me, and think snakes are for the birds[3], then check out the birds. Marc Mueller, a teacher at Xiamen Education College and a veteran bird watcher, has delighted in the many species of birds to be bound on our island (at least 174 varieties of Amoy feathered friends were identified by Western naturalists over 150 years ago).

Allow me to introduce you to Amoy's delightful birds and animals. But first… you've got to hit the trail. And the perfect guide for Amoy's trails is veteran Aussie bushwalker, Trish Boman, who has kindly allowed me to print her delightful accounts of perambulations about Amoy. I haven't tried them all myself; I get bushed just thinking of all that walking—but they're on my "2 Do List."

But first, Bushwhacker Bushman's (Boman, I meant) Bio—so you'll know what you're getting into and who got you into it! And after her accounts, I'll introduce you to the fowl and fauna of Amoy that you just may meet on the way.

Bushwhacker Boman's Bio

"My hometown is Brisbane, Queensland, Australia, though I was born in a smaller city, Rockhampton, beside a mountain range which inspired my first day long walk when I was about 14 (not that our mountains are anything to skite[1] about on the world scale.)

"I am not a mountain-climber in the Everest sense, nor do I do any fancy rock-climbing, though I've abseiled[2] and hauled myself on ropes and chains up volcanic cones, and even Uluru (Ayers Rock, in the centre of Australia).

"Brisbane is surrounded by other mountain ranges (referred to as "hills" by visitors to our fair city) variously covered with dry eucalyptus forests, or temperate rainforest. I especially love rainforest bushwalking and can deal with ticks, leeches, mud, and wait-a-while vines. I also lived in Cairns, in Queensland's far north, which has dense tropical rainforest. This really sparked off my love of bushwalking, beginning with trekking to pristine waterfalls, and swimming in fresh water creeks among the boulders and fresh-water crocodiles.[3]

"In Xiamen, I found a like-minded person who began showing me around the Five Old Men Mountain behind Xiamen University, and from then on we would choose a different hill each week and go out and find a track to climb it. In Xiamen, many of the hills end in army bases, and have savage dogs and guards, so I've been turned away from several of them.   I began to fear I'd be considered a particularly persistent spy who kept turning up in the wrong places!!"

Trish Boman, the Bushman

Insights on "Strine" (Aussie Slang)

After am futile browsing of the dictionary to decipher Trish's Aussie English, I e-mailed her. Trish responded as follows:

"I LOVE explaining "Strine" (Australian), so:

"...a chook is a chicken/hen, also used to fondly or cruelly chide someone: 'Silly old chook!' Also a common nickname mostly among men.

"'Skite' is to boast and a skite is a boaster. (Both noun and verb)

---

[1] Skite: see Trish's explanation of Aussie slang on the next page, or go palaver with the Aussie native herself.

[2] Abseil: technical word for 'descend,' I think; again, not in dictionary!

[3] If Trish swims with crocs, I'd think twice about bushwhacking with bushwalker!

"'Wait-a-while vines' are rainforest vines with many barbs on long shoots that are sent out across the clearings. When you walk by, they catch on clothes, skin, hair and pull you up to 'wait a while'. The only way to escape is to back yourself out the way you got into it. It's pretty vicious stuff. Eventually they grow up to become lawyer cane, the kind teachers used to hit kids with.

"Congratulations for including some Australian slang in Amoy Magic. I feel our existence is acknowledged somehow."

Bye,
Trish

Well, folks, I was so intrigued by Boman's bushwacking of the English tongue that I surfed the internet to learn more about Strine, and found her down under euphemisms were just the tip of the Strine iceberg. Here are a few more Aussie expressions. Get these under your belt and you just might be able to make heads or tails of the Aussie song, "Waltzing Matilda!" (cartoon on right from an 'Aussie mousepad')

Amoy's Kiwi-Tony Hale
(He says the dangling wine corks ward off pesky NZ blowflies)

Dr. Bill's A—Z Aussie Slang

Airy-Fairy (hare-brained), Al Capone (telephone), Arvo (afternoon), barney (argument), battlers (honest, hard working people), beano (celebration), billy (container for boiling tea), bludger (lazy person), Bluey (nickname for redheads!), chinwag (conversation), chook (chicken), chuffed (delighted), corker (something very good), crook (sick, ill), digger (Australian soldier), dinkum (genuine), doona (quilt; 被子), dunny (outside toilet), furphy (rumor), good guts (accurate info), grog (alcohol), grouse (very good), hooroo (see you later), illywhacker (con man), Irish (wig), jumbuck (sheep), knackered (exhausted), loo (toilet), motza (large amount of money), mozzie (mosquito), mug, or nong (a fool), nick off (scram), onkus (bad), ol' cheese (Mother), open-slather (anything goes), Pom (Englishman), rubbity dub (pub or tub, depending on context), sanger (sandwich), seppo (American), Sheila (girl), snog (to kiss and cuddle), swagman (itinerant worker), thingy (thing), tucker (food), up the duff (pregnant), wog (derogatory for foreigner), wowser (killjoy, prude), yonks (long time ago).

Trish Boman's Bushwalk #1
Shangli (Half Day) Commencing from Shangli.

Take the number 20 bus to the end of the line at the Railway Workers' Sanitorium. Walk out of the compound back across the small bridge you came over and there's a major road under construction to the left. Follow this road along, noting the eucalypts and sally wattles that grow on the hillsides. In the early mornings there is a strong smell of the lemon-scented gum, giving a little Australian experience for those who know it. On the right, you may catch a glimpse of the long, snake-shaped reservoir whose administration buildings you pass on the right.[4] (At the end of this reservoir there is a fork on the right which is covered in the final paragraph below.)

After about a kilometer from the starting point, with the city buildings in view ahead, there is a fork on the right leading uphill. A few hundred metres along it, there is a rustic stone gate on the right, with the characters: (Ban Ling Gong) in reverse order. This is a Daoist-style temple name, characterized by the word "gong", so it gives the appearance of leading to a Daoist temple above. Stone steps leading up through the trees wind away invitingly into the greenness.

Follow the winding stepped path, which is accompanied by a set of Railway Department white posts equipped with red numbers, from about 41 up, until you reach a fair-sized Buddhist temple under construction. The only sign of the Daoist temple is a small shrine to the left, crowded with Daoist figurines whilst above it, a quite magnificent red brick Buddhist temple is being built. A magnificent view of the valley with the new road cutting through it can be enjoyed from the temple forecourt. The view extends as far as the city buildings and is filled with greenness. Military installations beam out from the opposite hill top.

Descending the steps from the temple, you can take another set of steps on the left which will lead back to the trench at a more southerly point.

---

[4] It leads eventually to downtown Xiamen, coming out at two places, either Wenzao (right fork) or Wenyuan Road (left fork) if you care to walk that far. No 83 bus will start before then and it will go to the Railway Station.

From here you can return to your original point and carry on to downtown Xiamen, or you can return to Shangli the way you came.

If you still feel energetic, return to the turn-off at the end of the reservoir, mentioned above. This fork is a connecting track to the main Xiamen Cross-Country Track (see Qianpu Walk). Along the way, you come to a rural dwelling, with chooks[5] and dogs, and the dirt track going by it on the left leads to Dong Ping Shan, a main village in the heights of Xiamen. At the T-junction, turn right to go to the back of the Taiwan Village Park. At the next fork, be sure to turn left in a downhill direction, or you'll find yourself in an overgrown and fairly impassable track further on up the hill.

When you reach the Taiwan Village, you will probably be stopped by the workers whose job seems to be to look out for people getting in the "back door" of the Village, though if no one is around, you could try going for a little look-around. The gate-keeper will require you to exit via the nearest track which will bring you out in Huang Cuo Village. There's a restaurant down the road to the right, (the restaurant is on your left) and it boasts some comfy upstairs rooms with air conditioning, lounges and TV which will restore lost energies.

Once restored, keep going down the lovely tree-lined road towards the Huan Dao Lu and there's a bus stop just a little way to the left that will return you to Xiamen University or Hulishan Cannon Fort termini for your connections.

CHIEF ATTRACTIONS:

1. It seems the builders are constructing an excellent walkway along the creek below the new road, complete with artistic touches and cross-bridges. When finished this will keep traffic and walkers well apart.
2. The stone stairway to the temple is green and leafy with bird song, fresh smells and rustic appearance.
3. The views from the Buddhist temple at the top of the stairs are especially spacious and green, facing down into the valley.
4. Because of links to the main Xiamen Cross-Country track, there are possibilities for full-day walks of varying lengths.

---

[5] Chooks: See Dr. Bill's A-Z Aussie Slang

Trish Boman's Bushwalk #2
Da Lun Shan, Tong An District.

This is an easy half day bus ride and stroll. Catch the Tong An number 18 bus at the railway station or any stop on the main road between Hulishan Paotai and Jimei. After about an hour's travel, get off in Tong An at the Fan Tian Temple stop. The entrance road to the temple is across the street a few yards on from the bus stop.

After reaching this township temple, which has no entrance fee, you can investigate the various worshiping activities in the different halls, gradually moving higher up the Da Lun Mountain. Finally there is a new, lavishly decorated temple building with a path leading up the hill on the right. You can also go the left, but the path is rougher. This path leads to the top of the mountain where there is a small resting pavilion with a view of the surrounding countryside. It's a peaceful little walk, leading past several typical graves in their horse-shoe shaped settings.

CHIEF ATTRACTIONS:

This is an insight into a non-touristy township temple. The locals are friendly and a little surprised to see visitors, but do not intrude. There are no beggars or fortune-tellers waiting to pounce on you.

1. The bus trip opens up the Xiamen experience by revealing an outlying district of the city.

Trish Boman's Bushwalk #3
Xianyue Mountain - Tianzhu Temple

Xianyue Mountain is one of Xiamen Island's larger range of hills, being a barrier between downtown and the Huli District. It offers a leisurely all-day, or a brisk half day outing. The use of a car to get to the temple can make the journey considerably shorter if time is limited. There are several ways to get to the temple, the easiest being up Qiaoyue Rd, which is an extension of the larger Lianyue Road which can be found at the farthest eastern point of YongDang Lake, crossing Hubin North Road. Buses 13, 31 and 33 also turn the corner of Lianyue and Xianyue Roads. The road can be climbed on foot, but there is an off-road shortcut where the road first turns to go up the mountain. There is a "no lighting fires in the forest" sign in Chinese by a lane which is the only indicator of the entrance to the road. Once you reach the top of this shortcut, you rejoin the vehicle road just below the temple. The temple area is a busy one, with an enormous construction site begun for a major new temple. The present ones are a mixture of makeshift and elderly buildings doing a brisk trade in ancestor worship with copious amounts of holy money going up in smoke. There's a map and plan of the new temple on display. Toilets are rudimentary, though there's a new one built but not open yet further up the hill.

If you want to continue on to the wonderfully constructed walk to the western end of the range, go on to the left (east) beyond the temple. There are several lookouts and trails leading off from the main track, including one which overlooks the city from an attractive pavilion. You'll also notice several "scientific experiments" among the trees, collecting insect samples and warning of poisonous contents. At the farthest point you'll come to an unsignposted[4] collection of paths. To get down the mountain at this point, take the path on the right (Huli side) and you'll eventually emerge at a staircase at the back of a residential unit. Follow the road ahead, turn left and then right at a jeep training ground, and you'll find yourself out on a bypass road that goes under the Haicang Bridge approaches. The number 15 bus calls in just to your right and will take you all the way back through Xiamen city to Xiamen University.

CHIEF ATTRACTIONS:

1. This is one of the largest downtown hills, offering excellent views of both the city and port sides of the hill. It can keep you occupied for a whole leisurely day if you take some food and drink and occupy one of the small pavilions either at the temple or along the path towards the Dongdu end of the range.

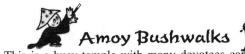
2. This is a busy temple with many devotees carrying out traditional worship activities.
3. There are several side paths that can be explored if you have time.

Trish Boman's Bushwalk #4
Foxtail Mountain (Huwei Shan)

Huwei Shan is a continuation of Xianyue Mountain on the western side of the Haicang Bridge approach. It is a relatively compact walk that could occupy a leisurely half-day and boasts a neatly developed lookout, toilets and picnic tables with a great view of the City Government buildings and beyond.

There are two main ways to this mountain: the walking path which begins from Feng Huang Villa (凤凰, Phoenix[5]) grounds in Hubin Beilu, and the vehicular

City Hall (Foxtail Mtn. in back)

road that starts in Haishan Road, (off Dongdu Road, a block past beyond Hubin Beilu T-intersection) and ends at the TV Station via the Meteorological Station on the western part of the hill. Despite being for cars, it's quite a nice walk, and a walker can link up with the forest track that links up with Feng Huang Villa. To do this walk, you can catch bus 87 and get out in Hubin Beilu at the Xiamen City Administration Building stop.

If you prefer to keep off the vehicular road, then just stick to the walking path beginning from Feng Huang Villa grounds. The gate is about half a block from the City Government office building towards Dongdu (west). Check with the security guard and say you want to climb the mountain and it will be okay. Go straight ahead until the road curves around a couple of times and keep an eye out for the forest sign that marks an upward-leading set of stone steps. These steps will lead the vehicular road, but if you continue on across the other side, you come to a half-finished pavilion, and beyond that the road peters out at a worker's hut at the mountain top. Retrace your steps and instead of crossing the road, turn left on to it and take the stone pathway just a little way back down the road on the left. This will lead to the lookout and picnic area. The meteorological station is upwards from the picnic area while the exit is downhill. But you can return the way you came and go back to Feng Huang Villa and avoid the traffic.

Trish Boman's Bushwalk #5
Nanputuo Temple and Five Old Men Mountain.

Besides being one of the major temples of Fujian, Nanputuo Temple also backs on to a very attractive and path-riddled mountain called Wulao Shan. Allow quite a lot of time for this walk, as it can also lead to a trek through to Xiamen University, Ten Thousand Stone Botanic Garden (Wanshi Zhiwuyuan, 万石植物园) and link up with a number of other very interesting walks, probably too many for just one day. If you want to spend a half day, then just stick to Nanputuo's Wulao Shan and go back down OR walk through to the Botanic Gardens and come out at its entrance. This walk will be described first.

Catch any bus that goes to Xiamen University, e.g., 1, 15, 71, 45, etc. Nanputuo Temple is very visible as you arrive. Pay 3 Yuan to enter the main gate, and you will pass a number of very fine Meditation and Worship Halls—usually a crowded area. Keep advancing towards the rear. Don't worry which route you take because there are many, and they all lead upwards. Signboards show where you are, but just keep taking any stairs that go UP and don't stray too far to the left or right edges, unless you want to explore the many fascinating pavilions, grottoes and lookouts that abound in this marvelous place. As you get higher, there are more lookouts, including one magnificent railed platform on top of a great boulder. Go on until after about half an hour of steady climbing on well-crafted stone steps, you reach the rest area at the top of Wulao Shan. There is a little refreshment stall there, as well as a gate for paying your entrance fee into the Botanic Gardens. It is possible to bypass this gate by heading off to the right of the summit but the track is not well developed and there are many forks to help you get lost. Unless you have local assistance, better to pay the money. This track goes down dale and up hill, crossing a concrete road that leads to an army base nestled among the many little peaks on this rugged and complex set of hills. Keep your eye open for the Cactus Garden, housed in a glass house. To the right of this, there is a back track that goes through another mountain, offering great views and joining up with another road that meets the Botanic Garden track in a different place. When you meet any track, keep taking left turns if you want to end up in the Gardens and not in the army base or eventually, Xiamen University, though these are well worth a visit, though perhaps on another day.

And now, a pastime that's definitely *for the birds*[6]...

Laonei （老内） Notes

<hr>

[1] Take a hike: can be a euphemism for
"Get lost!" ("Get out of here!") A similar
phrase is "Go fly a kite!"
[2] Bug you: annoy you
[3] For the birds: English slang for
"objectionable or worthless" (although
here, I emphasize that the study of birds is
definitely of great value).
[4] Unsignposted: lacking signs (I suspect this word to be Trish's creation, though it
might well be an example of Strine)
[5] Phoenix: mythical Egyptian bird that lived in the desert for 500 years, consumed
itself by fire, and then rose again from the ashes. In English, Phoenix also refers to
a person or thing of unsurpassed beauty or excellence.
[6] For the birds: objectionable or worthless (slang). Please note, however, that I do
love bird watching, and do not think bird watching is for the birds! (I just could not
pass up the chance to play with the words. Sorry!).

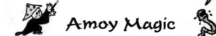

Chapter 6
Fowl Pursuits

"The Crane"
(Xiamen
City Bird)

For the Birds!

Bushwalkers should always carry a pair[1] of binoculars because Xiamen is heaven

for veteran birdwatchers like Mr. Marc Mueller (a teacher at Xiamen Education College). Xiamen bird watchers have formed the Observe Birds Association (OBA), and each March the OBA promotes "Care for Birds Week," and offers field trips for bird watchers of all ages. Back in 1860, Mr. Swinhoe, the British Consul in Amoy, reported 174 kinds of birds on Amoy! I'll let Mr. Swinhoe introduce his fowl and fauna, but first a brief intro to the great naturalist himself.

Bird Master Marc

Robert Swinhoe was born in Calcutta, India on 1 September 1836 to a family who had served British interests in India for many years.   His father was a lawyer and his brother was a colonel in India.

After university in England, Swinhoe went to Hong Kong at age 18, and studied Chinese, as well as Chinese natural history. He moved to Amoy in 1855, learned the local dialect, studied the local fowl and fauna, and kept as

Seeking the rare
Tweetum Birdiensus

pets a civet cat[2], pangolin[3], great owl, and a young falcon[4]. During a trip to Taiwan, he recorded, during only two weeks 93 new birds and 17 mammals.

Swinhoe returned to Amoy, where he helped found the short-lived Literary and Scientific Society of Amoy. At their first meeting, on 17 November 1856, Swinhoe

read his first published paper, *A Few Remarks on the Fauna of Amoy*. (I include an edited version of this at the end of this chapter).

Swinhoe was the first British consular official in Taiwan. He became ill and returned to England in 1862, where he set up an award-winning "Formosan Booth" at the London Exhibition, and gave lectures for many societies.   Charles Darwin, in one of his writings, noted the pigeon skin specimens sent to him by Swinhoe.

Swinhoe returned to Amoy in 1866, returned to England again in 1869 on sick leave, and in 1875 had a stroke in China. He decided China was for the birds and returned to England, but died anyway in 1877 at the tender[5] age of 41.

Robert Swinhoe
Amoy Consul

Birdie

Amoy's Feathered Friends

Eurasian Cuckoo

Dusky Warbler

Dalmatian Pelican

Eurasian Tree Sparrow

Eurasian Sparrow-Hawk

Brown Hawk Owl

Crested Myna

Common Hoopoe

Eurasian Marsh Harrier

Blue whistling thrush

Blue and white flycatcher

Collared Crow

Chestnut-eared Bunting

Buzzard

Blue-breasted Quail

Barn Swallow

Woodstockus
Peanutsiensis

Peregrine Falcon

Eureka!
I found
him!

Taiwan Blue Magpie
Susan Marie's Favorite!

Pintail Snipe

Little Egret

Mew Gull

Light
vented bulbil

White-throated
Kingfisher

Spot-billed
Duck

Osprey

Long-tailed Shrike

Japanese
White-eye

Masked Laughing
Thrush

Horned Grebe

Gray Heron

Amoy Tigers

"Tigers possess magical qualities; their claws are talismen[6] against devils, their bones and tendons potent medicine for healing and strength. They are sovereign because the Chinese discern the character for king on their foreheads...

"Two things in Fukien impressed Marco Polo: the beauty of the women and the size of its tigers...the Fukienese hunted tigers in the rock caves of the island's high spine. The conservative hunted in pairs; one took a flaring torch into the tiger's lair, walked on until the tiger's eyes reflected in its flame, then quickly stepped aside for his companion to spear or shoot. The modern-minded strapped electric lamps to their foreheads, and practised the hair-raising sport alone. There were still quite a lot of tigers on the island, the fishermen said, but their numbers were dwindling."

A Race of Green Ginger, p. 68, 69[1]

Little Nancy & the Tiger – a true tale of Gulangyu!

"...It appears that little Nancy Theobald had run in from the garden crying that there was a tiger in the bamboo patch. For this she had been severely reprimanded by her mother, who believed that 'let's pretend' was the thin end of lying and deceit. But Nancy, whose busy imaginative life had already

"Why, Dinah! How you've grown!"

caused her parents some anxiety, insisted that she spoke nothing but sober truth. Mr. Theobald entered upon a scene of exhortation, tears and temper, masterfully to declare that he would deal with his child once and for all. 'Come and show me this tiger,' he had said to Nancy, giving his wife to understand that it was as simple as that.

"Nancy, delighted with unexpected parental support, hoping that the beast had not gone, led her father in all hasten to the bamboo and to the tiger, who lay asleep there..."

A Race of Green Ginger, p.94

While I do pity their demise, I'm thankful that eight-foot Amoy Tigers no longer lurk to bushwhack bushwalkers. (One of my local friend's aunts was killed

---

[1] Race of Green Ginger, by Averil Mackenzie-Grieve, Putnam, 1959 (the author lived on Gulangyu in the 1920s).

by a tiger in the 1960s!). The most dangerous thing you'll encounter nowadays in Amoy's hills is snakes (cobras, bamboo vipers), and that rarely. For the most part all we see is birds, blue-tailed lizards, chameleons and geckos (which I catch and turn loose in the house so they can eat mosquitoes), chameleons, and francolins[7] (which I've seen in the woods with chicks, and which locals chase down for supper). But 150 years ago the hills were alive with exotic creatures like the ones recorded in the November 17, 1857 paper, A Few Remarks on the Fauna of Amoy. It was presented by H. Stevenson, Esquire, to the Literary and Scientific Society of Amoy. Here are the 'few remarks' (though edited to make them considerably fewer!).

A FEW REMARKS ON THE FAUNA OF AMOY
Robert Swinhoe (1857)

"…Who has not wondered at the bare hills of Amoy, at the first glimpse he obtains on entering the harbor, and, seeing the great boulders of rock rise one another in endless confusion, thought to himself with a shudder, Can animal life be there? But though animal life is there to a small extent, it is to the plains, which are inhabited and cultivated with such care by the natives, that we must look for most that will interest us in our science.

"The **wily fox** is the first animal which we have to consider, for, low as he stands in the natural series of Mammals, he is here prominent as the largest of the Carnivora we possess…

"The greatest devastator among the poultry of the poor is an animal belonging to the **weasel** [8] family (Mustelideae), and, though generally distributed, is very rarely seen. It measures about a foot and a half in length, has buff-coloured fur, with a black muzzle, and is the Hwang-shoo-lang of the Pun-ts'aou, and the Chiah-ch'oo (tawny rat) of Amoy men…

"Before leaving the Carnaria it would be as well to mention a curious animal that was brought alive to me by a native, and which I kept some months in confinement. It evidently belonged to the **civet** family (Viverridae), measured in length one foot and a half, having rather long fur of a dingy brown colour, and a black head with a white line down the snout; the tail was tipped with white. ..

"We have also heard certain stories about the **sea-otter** that is occasionally seen prowling about on Six Islands, seeking his finny prey at the dead hour of night, and avoiding the light of day...

"...The next quadraped... is the scaly ant-eater or **pangolin**...Ours is a small species (probably Manis brachyurus), measuring in toto only two feet and three inches, of the tail takes one foot. Its gait is most peculiar - with the body bent in a bow, and the head and tail downwards, as it runs along on the sides of its fore feet. ..Large prices are given by the native

doctors for this animal, for its flesh and bones are employed for various medicinal purposes; and one of its scales, fastened to the end of a stick, is sold as a safe instrument to be used in scratching without fear of producing ulcers on the skin. ... and also the Cetacea, the Phocaenae or porpises of which order are well known to us even in the harbour, where at times they may be seen showing their round white backs in a line, and then disappearing, to be seen again at a further distance.

"... the Aves. The **peregrine falcon** (Falco peregrinus) is a straggling visitor, but a pair built their eyrie last year on the high hill of Nan-tai-woo (on the summit of which stands the pagoda).... A species of **sparrowhawk** ... There is also a buzzard (Buteo), and the hen harrier (Circus cyaneus) of Britain is seen not unfrequently in the early winter...An **osprey** (Pandion) is sometimes seen even in the harbour, but little is known of him. I have seen him strike a fish

close under the bows of a vessel, and bear it away in triumph.

The **great owl** (Bubo maximus) ... A **sparrow owl** (Nyctipeles, Swain.), and a small tawny Scops owl (probably Scops rufiscens of Horsfield), are seen occasionally in winter. ...

"...the **blackbird** and **rock thrush** (Petrocincla violacea) are always with us, the former enlivening our gardens by his rich full notes, and the latter enchanting the lonely wanderer among the bleak hills with his wild minstrelsy, as he sings from the summit of a monstrous boulder, or springs lightly into the air, trolling forth his merry roundelay. It may be mentioned that the blackbird here, though very similar, is yet not the same as our black-bird at home; he differs not only in being of greater size, and in the colouring of the female, but also in his call-note.

"The rock thrush and blackbird are taken by the Chinese for one and the same, and called Ok`ee, though one is blue and red, and the other black. The most familiar and perhaps the best known is the magpie robin (Gryllivora), a small bird of the pied plumage of a magpie, with the habits and peculiarities of a robin. Its song, poured out at early morn or sunset from the roof-tops of our houses, is occasionally pretty, but abounding in harsh and jarring notes…

"…The most diminutive of all stands next, the little **tailor-bird** (Orthotomus), remarkable for its long pointed bill, which serves as a needle in sewing leaves together round its nest; the underside of a long leaf of the Alpinia nutans is often chosen, the edges of which are drawn together by thread made of spider's web and fibres. The prettiest construction of the kind I have seen was a nest flanked in by three orange leaves, and placed in the extremity of the boughs of an orange-tree.

"Flocks of the beautiful **white egret**, or paddy bird, as they are familiarly known to us (Herodias Garzetta), often attract our attention as they wing their way slowly through the obscure blue of a summer twilight, from the fields where they have been feeding, to their selected nest-trees, on which they settle

like masses of snow among the dark green leaves. The **yellow-headed egret**, while with us in summer, is commoner, and roams about in larger flocks than the latter. A third and solitary species, **Herodias flavirostris**, is also found, and may be distinguished by its yellow bill, and the tuft of snowy feathers which surmounts the occiput. We have, besides, five or six other species of **heron**, nearly all remarkable for their elegance and beauty.

"The egret is much admired by the sentimental Chinese, and is often alluded to in poetical compositions by the style Loo-sze; and the Island of Amoy is often poetically called Loo-mun, Loo-keang, and Loo-taon, from the number of these snow-like birds that annually frequent it. Of the ninety-two species of Insessores found here, nine are British birds. Seven species of the Grallatores, and nearly all the Natatores, with the exception of the **pelicans**, **albatrosses**, and a few **gulls** and **terns**, are identical with those found in Great Britain…

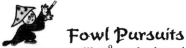

" ...It is unnecessary to dilate[9] on the beauties and delights of the study of Nature: the heart of every man naturally throbs in the contemplation of the Creator's handiwork, and thrills with joy at the discovery of some new manoeuvre in the wondrous economy which so beautifully modulates and arranges all animal and vegetable life upon the globe.

"Solomon said, "There is nothing new under the sun;[10]" so, probably, there is not; but a great deal of what passes around man is new to him, and astonishes him when brought to his notice, simply because he has not made use of those powers of observation that he has been endowed with. In conclusion, I cannot do better than quote the words that Milton[11] puts in the mouth of the Divine Author of Nature[12] in his address to our first parent:— "Is not the earth With various living creatures, and the air, Replenish'd; and all these at thy command, To come and play before thee?" Robert Swinhoe

A sampling of Swinhoe's 174 Amoy Birds

[I include some of his lengthy descriptions so you can appreciate just how serious were the birdwatchers of yesteryear!]

1. **Buzzard** (Buteo vulgaris) A regular winter visitant.

2. **Osprey** (Pandion haliaet) Lives on the rocks at the mouth of the harbor and comes occasionally to Amoy, but very shy and unapproachable. I have never been able to produce a specimen.

3. **Perefrine Falcon** (Falco peregrinus) Breeds in the neighbourhood and is not unfrequent.

10. **Brown Hawk Owl** (Ninox scutellatus) A straggling winter visitant, common in summer at Fouchow where it breeds. The immature plumage is brown, banded with ochraeous.

11. **Great Owl** (Bubo maximus) Occasionally seen of a winter's evening. Breeds somewhere in the neighbourhood, as every early spring the young are sold in the streets of the town.

17. **Swift** (Hirundapus nudipes) A straggler in spring during rain-storms.

18.**Barn Swallow** (Hirundo rusticas) This appears to be merely a degenerate variety of the European species. It is a summer resident here and pretty numerous, building mud-nests shaped like a half-dish, and lined with straw and a few feathers, over the doors of Chinese huts, where they are revered as the harbingers of good luck.

19. **Red-rumped Swallow** (Hirundo daurica, alpestris) A few passing flocks spend a day or two in Amoy during winter. In Formosa it takes the place of the common species, and builds domed nests of clay and mud under the roof-tops

21. **White-throated Kingfisher** (Halcyon smyrnensis) A common resident; called "Fey-tsuy" by the Chinese, who glue the feathers, chiefly

those of the wing, over ornaments worn by their women. Thus treated the lustrous blue feathers give the appearance of turquoise stone. The bird is shy and remarkable for its loud screeching cry.

24. **Pied Kinfisher** (Ceryle rudis) Very common on the river; where it rises on the wing at a height above the water, and drops suddenly on its scaly prey. I have also seen it strike obliquely when flying close to the surface of the water.

27. **Prinia** (Prinia sonitans) I have named this from the crackling noise it produces when hopping or flying from twig to twig...

34. **Dusky Warbler** (Phylloscopus fuscatus) Common during winter... its most frequent note is "chick chick."

56. **Blue Whistling Thrush** (Myiophonus caeruleus) Lives among rocky caverns; not common, and very shy; native name Aw-chuy.

64. **Masked Laughing Thrush** (Garrulax perspicillatuas) Length 12 inches. Wing 4 7/10. Tail 5 2/10. Bill 9/10, to gape 1 3/10...This large Butcher-thrush is common in some parts of the country, building a nest a good deal like that of the Blackbird. It is a shy bird, but may be known a long way off by its loud cry of Teo-teo, uttered from time to time, or followed by a liquid guzzling low chatter.

65. **Spectacled Thrush** (Garrulax sinensis) This is the Hwa-mei of the Chinese, by whom it is prized for its fine vocal powers, as well as for its pugnacious propensities. It is, strictly speaking, a hill-bird, and very abundant on the hills near Fuzhou, but as I have, on more than one occasion, met with it in the bushes here, I must include it in my list.

79. **Long-tailed Shrike** (Lanius schach) Very common; has a great habit of shrieking. This is a much larger race than that found in the Indian archipelago, and is no doubt worthy of specific distinction...

82. **Collared Crow)** Corvus torquatus) Amoy's only crow.

83. **Magpie** (Pica media) Very common.

84. **Crested Myna** (Acridotheres cristatellus) A very common species from Hongkong to Shanghai; builds in holes of trees or walls, or makes large oval nests in trees; learns to speak with facility and soon becomes docile.

94. **Finch** (Ligurinus sinicus) Half goldfinch, half greenfinch; not uncommon all the year, has a pretty tinkling note; and feeds on thistle-heads as well as grain, &c.

120. **Little Egret** (Herodias garzetta) The common resident species; building in company on large banyan trees.

147. **Goose** (Anser segetum) Frequents the mouth of the river in immense flocks during winter.

151. **Spot-billed Duck** (Anas poecilorhyncha)

162. **Albatross** (Diomedea brachyuran)

164. **Mew Gull** (Larus canus)

168. **Loon** (Gavia Kittlitzii)

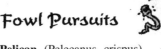
173. **Dalmatian Pelican** (Pelecanus crispus) Common in winter.

175. **Archaeopteryx** Extinct bird of the Jurassic period. If you see one of these flying about, you'd better lay off the rice wine.

Laonei （老内） Notes

[1] Pair of binoculars: an odd way of saying it! You just need one binocular, but a binocular has two eyepieces, so we say "pair" of binoculars.

[2] Civet cat: small wild cat; 麝猫；麝猫香

[3] Pangolin: a kind of scaly anteater; 穿山甲

[4] Falcon: bird of prey often trained to hunt small animals; 猎鹰

[5] Tender: young (implies "premature")

[6] Talisman: object that gives magical protection; 护身符, 辟邪物

[7] Francolins: related to quails; 鹧鸪之属

[8] Weasel: 鼬鼠

[9] Dilate: speak at length

[10] Nothing new under the sun: quoted from the Bible, Ecclesiastes 1:9（传道书 1: 9, 已有的事，后必再有。已行的事，后必再行。日光之下并无新事。）

[11] Milton: John Milton (1608-1674), blind English poet and scholar best known for the epic poem Paradise Lost, written in 1667, which describes humanity's fall from grace. The blind poet dictated the masterpiece to his daughter.

[12] Divine Author of Nature: Creator, God

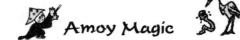
Chapter 7

Amoy Museums

Xiamen has 139 cultural and historical preservation sites. And having been up a tree[1] most of my life, I was pleased to learn that Xiamen has 533 protected ancient or famous trees. The city also has 18 historical temples and churches, as well as 17 museums—including Asia's largest Piano Museum, the Coin Museum, and the unique Bridge museum located, appropriately, beneath Haicang Suspension Bridge.

Overseas Chinese Museum, about 2 km south of Zhongshan Rd. on S. Siming Rd. (just over the hill from Xiamen University), was proposed by Tan Kah Kee, founder of Xiamen University, and built in 1956. It opened to the public in May of 1959. The 30,000 square feet area has over 7,000 items in displays documenting the lives of overseas Chinese through different historical periods.

The museum is divided into six sections, from relics of old China to photographic and pictorial evidence of *Huaqiao* (overseas Chinese) exploration. The ground floor's three halls contain paintings, photos and documentation of the Fujianese life abroad, an interesting way for us *laowai* (foreigners) to see the other side of the coin. Some of the pottery and bronzes date back to the Shang Dynasty (1600—1100BC— or, more accurately, 1615—1115BC).

Over 2.5 million overseas Chinese, in over 50 countries, claim to have their roots in Fujian Province! Open daily, 9 a.m. – 4:30 p.m.

The Xiamen Museum, on Gulangyu Islet, is Xiamen's largest, and housed within the circa 1907 "Eight Trigrams Tower" (named after its round red roof). The museum has over 10,000 artefacts, including jade and porcelain, and ancient weapons.

Xiamen is now building a 300 million Yuan Xiamen Museum in the Yuandang Lagoon area (which is fast becoming the city's cultural center).

Asia's Largest Piano Museum

Asia's Largest Piano Museum is on Gulangyu Islet (within Shuzhuang Garden). Thirty of the over 70 historic pianos were provided by Mr. Hu Youyi, a piano collector from Australia whose hometown is Gulangyu Islet.

I enjoy the old player pianos, and the barrel organs that organ grinders used to play as their monkeys scampered around the crowds collecting donations.

The pianos came from Britain, France, Germany, America, Austria and Australia. The museum also has over 100 piano lamps. The displays are in two separate buildings, so be sure to catch the exhibits in the rear building.

Address:
No. 45 Huangyan Rd., Gulangyu
鼓浪屿晃岩路 45 号
Phone: 257-0331
E-mail: glygqbwg@sina.com

B.B.

Pasquale Street Piano (London, 1899)
Also called "barrel piano," because it used a barrel filled with different lengthed nails, they were used downtown for monkey shows and street performances.

Xiamen Bridge Museum

Bridges are fascinating because they show us the routes people used for travel and trade. And Xiamen is a great place for a Bridge Museum because our province has some of the finest bridges on the planet—both old and new.

Quanzhou's Luoyang Bridge (see the Quanzhou section) was built 1,000 years ago of massive granite slabs—some of them ten meters long. This bridge is one of the first examples of biological engineering (they used the secretions of live oysters to cement the granite blocks together).

Anping Bridge, just south of Quanzhou, was the world's longest bridge during the middle ages.   But I most enjoy the delightful wooden covered bridges that are all over northern and Western Fujian—especially the 700-year-old structure northwest of Fuzhou (on the way to Zhouning).

The Xiamen Bridge Museum, located right beneath the Haicang Bridge, has attracted both tourists and experts with its introduction of famous Chinese and foreign bridges (including the iron arch bridge over the Thames River, the Normandy Suspension Bridge, deng deng).   About 1/3 of the indoor area is devoted to fascinating exhibits about the construction of Xiamen's beautiful Haicang Bridge. I'd tell you more about this suspension bridge but I want to keep you in suspense.

Fujian Bridges

B.B

"Launching 1,000 Ships!"

Jinquan Coin Museum

(金泉钱币博物馆)　　The former British Consulate is now a coin museum!

Fujian Coin (1912)

Xi'an's Jin Quan company has transformed the beautiful colonial building (built around 1870) into Fujian's largest coin museum, with over 5200 exhibits dating from the New Stone Age to New China (1949). It also includes a fine selection of Fujian coins.　　This fine museum, opened September 28, 1991, must be right on the money[2] because it has attracted coin experts, dignitaries and tourists from throughout Asia. Jin Quan Coin Museum (金泉钱币博物馆) is located at #5 Zhongshan Rd., Gulangyu Islet.

The Koxinga Museum has 23 national level historical relics, as well as one local historical relic who sells tickets.　(Read about Koxinga on pages 18,19).

Art in the Park

Museums are nice, but Xiamen has also worked to move art and culture out into the open, where the people are.　Our city has 119 traditional and modern sculptures scattered about downtown areas, open amphitheatres, along the beach, in picnic areas, and in parks. Favorites include "Egret Fairy," "Koxinga," and "3 Generations of Helping Hands."

15 Minute Walk—or Five?

In our presentation for the Nations in Bloom Competition in Stuttgart, Germany, in October 2002, we wrote, "Xiamen citizens are never more than a 15 minute walk from a park."　So imagine my surprise when, two days before our presentation, the mayor of Stuttgart boasted, "Stuttgart citizens are never more than a 5 minute walk from a park."

Talk about stealing one's thunder![3]　But I stole it back. During the presentation I said, "In Xiamen, citizens are never more than a 15 minute walk from a park." I paused, then added, "I know the Mayor of Stuttgart said that his people are only a 5 minute walk from a park—but fortunately for us, Xiamen people don't have to walk so fast!"

A Modest Proposal!

Amoy Maritime Museum? There isn't one—but there should be! Or at the very least, a life-size sculpture of Zhenghe's 440 foot treasure ships—especially since Gavin Menzies 2002 publication of "1421—The Year China Discovered America."

Chinese as well as foreigners know little about China's great seafarers like Zhenghe, thanks to the Emperor destroying most of the records. But China had the greatest navy, the largest ships, the most powerful weapons, and could have easily conquered the world had it so desired. Fortunately, the Chinese, then as now, were interested in cultural exchange and commerce, not conquering.

Columbus' Santa Maria beside Zhenghe's Flagship! B.B.

While in Germany for the Nations in Bloom presentation, I shocked people by comparing Zhenghe's 440 flagship with Columbus' 85 foot Santa Maria.

Most of China's foreign trade took place on the Maritime Silk Road, which began in Quanzhou, 70 miles north of us. And since Xiamen was part of Quanzhou back then, and had the best harbour even then, it is quite likely that the largest ships were anchored right here in Amoy! (even Zhenghe mentioned Xiamen's great port).

Only two years ago, most foreigners knew little about Zhenghe, or China's ancient ships, and the Silk Road of the Sea. But that has changed since the publiscation of "1421." Gavin Menzies book has turned Western academia on its head with his claims, based on years of painstaking research, that Chinese explored virtually the entire world—decades before Columbus discovered America. He writes about ancient Chinese treasure ships, scientifically dated back to 1410 A.D., discovered in South America, San Francisco, the Mississippi River, Australia, and about the Chinese settlers in these areas.

Most exciting to me was the drawing on the inside cover, in which, like me, he compared the Santa Maria to Zhenghe's flagship. It is an awesome comparison. And Xiamen could go one step further…with a **Treasure Ship Sculpture.**

A full-size but simple, relatively inexpensive steel outline of Zhenghe's ship, and the Santa Maria, anchored off the beautiful Ring Road, with sails and flags flying, would dramatically convey China's past maritime greatness—and highlight China's role in it.

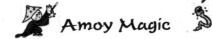
Foreign Precedents   Such an exhibit might pay for itself in the long run. For example, Columbus, Ohio has created an entire industry around its full-size Santa Maria in Battelle Riverfront Park.   **(http://www.santamaria.org**; photos at **http://www.santamaria.org/virtualship/photo.html**).

San Francisco has twelve historic ships, San Diego has five, Seattle has eight, London has a replica of the Golden Hinde (in which Sir Francis Drake circled the globe). **http://www.goldenhinde.co.uk/jubilee.html**

. Tampa Florida has drawn crowds for decades with its magnificent H.M.S. Bounty, a Hollywood replica built for the movie. They are now restoring the 1945 "American Victory" as a memorial and museum. Tampa Florida has drawn crowds for decades with its magnificent H.M.S. Bounty, a Hollywood replica built for the movie.

Cities around the world, from Australia to Turkey, have bolstered tourism and enhanced their image with historic ships, or replicas. But no one has done this with Chinese treasure ships. Xiamen should be the first.

The initial investment for a Zhenghe/Columbus sculpture, while costly, would be relatively small compared with the vast sums we have spent on our Island Ring Road—and it would be the crowning jewel of our Garden Island, capturing our great past while conveying our dreams for a greater future.

I hope to see it built—and just to drive the point home, I include the proposal in Chinese (thanks to Joe, an MBA student who translated it for me).

Laonei (老内) Notes

[1] Up a tree: helpless; in difficult situation
[2] Right on the money: precise; appropriate, correct (from betting)
[3] Steal one's thunder: outdo someone, steal attention from someone

Chapter 8
Near Amoy Island

Qingjiao Ciji Palace For a different perspective on religion in Xiamen, head across the Haicang Suspension bridge, hang a left, and visit Haicang Township's temple honoring Wu Tao, a Chinese medicine man back in the Song Dynasty. Wu spent his life treating people for free and gained, according to a local guidebook, "a world-wide reputation" (probably over the internet).

Hanging by a Thread

He even cured the mother of Emperor Rengzong, whose life was hanging by a thread[1]—literally!

Physicians were mere commoners, and not allowed to touch royalty. So in keeping with custom, Dr. Wu diagnosed her illness by holding one end of a silk thread tied to her wrist. I'm not sure if he really felt her pulses through the thread (Chinese doctors claim they feel 18 different pulses) or was just at the end of his rope and pretended. In any event, the patient lived, and Dr. Wu was a hero.

B.B.

After Dr. Wu died, villagers honored him with the title of "Medical Saint," and pooled their funds to build a hall and statue in his memory. In 1161, the emperor granted the hall the title of Ciji Temple, and in 1241 it was renamed Ciji Palace.

Qingjiao Ciji Palace

B.B.

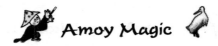
Today, thousands of pilgrims make the trek to pay homage to him, though given that he died at only 57, one wonders how good he really was. But maybe he was like the doctor in this ancient tale:

Heal Thyself (Qing Dynasty Tale)
A dying doctor cried out, "If any doctor can cure me, I will give him a dose of my secret elixir of immortality and he will live for centuries!"
Someone asked, "If you have such a miraculous drug, why not take it yourself?"
He looked surprised. "A good doctor doesn't write prescriptions for himself!"

Just for fun, here are a few more Classic Chinese Doctor Tales....

Classic Chinese Doctor Tales

First Things First — A Ming Dynasty Tale (1368—1644) A doctor was detained by the furious relatives of a patient he had killed with the wrong prescription, but he escaped by night and swam across a wide river to reach home. When he saw his son studying medical texts, he said, "Don't be in such a hurry to study medicine. First things first. And first, learn to swim."

First things first

Quack² Compensation — A Qing Dynasty Tale (1644 —1912) When a quack doctor's treatment killed a family's son, he was forced to give them his own son. He lost his daughter in the same way. One day a man knocked on his door and asked his help. "Who's the patient?" the doctor asked.
"My wife."
The tearful doctor told his wife, "Sweetheart, I fear someone has taken a fancy to you."

Getting the Boot³ — A Ming Dynasty Tale (1368—1644) A heavily laden woodcutter stumbled into the local doctor on a narrow path. When the doctor drew back his fist to hit him, the woodcutter dropped to his knees and begged, "Please kick me instead."
A bystander asked, "Why would you rather him kick you?"
The terrified woodcutter replied, "Treatment by his hands would be much deadlier than with his feet!"

"Anything but the hands!"

Nantai Wu Mountain and the Giant's Footprint!

Take the car ferry at the end of Hubin N. Road across to and you can visit the giant's footprint impressed in the granite peak, or enjoy the silky white sands by Longhai volcano (more on than in the section on Zhangzhou). The beauty of this area is brought home clearly by the elegant description given by Rev. John Macgowan in his *The Story of the Amoy Mission*.

"The island of Amoy is on the southern coast of China, and about three hundred miles to the north-east of Hong Kong. It is about thirty miles in circumference, and is beautifully situated in the midst of a very extensive bay. Seaward, it is protected by a chain of islands, the largest and most important of which is about the size of Amoy, and is called Quemoy, or "The Golden Gate." This acts as a natural breakwater, and prevents the heavy seas that are raised by storms and typhoons from rolling into the bay and injuring the shipping that lies anchored there.

"On the south the bay is bounded by a low range of mountains, from the midst of which rises abruptly Lam-tai-bu, the "Great Southern Warrior."

"This is the most beautiful sight in the whole of the landscape, for there is a never-ending charm in its varying moods, as seen in storm or sunshine. In fine weather its summit is bathed in great floods of light, and it stands out clearly against the sky as it looks down upon the blue waters of the bay, which dance and sparkle beneath the rays of the great eastern sun. When bad weather is coming on, dense masses of cloud, tumultuous and agitated, as if clinging to it for protection, gather round its head and far down its sides, and then the waters of the bay, dark with the shadows cast upon them, seem to be in sympathy with them, as though they feared the coming gale...

"The city of Amoy is a walled town of the third degree in rank."

Chapter 2, "Amoy and its People"

Jimei (集美) is just across the Xiamen Island Causeway. It is called the Causeway 'cause it was the only way across before we built the Haicang Suspension Bridge. They're planning a second suspension bridge to Longhai but they haven't said when it will be finished. I think they want to keep us in suspense.

Jimei University

Tan Kah Kee, Xiamen University's patriotic and deep-pocketed[4] benefactor, was born and buried in Jimei. Jimei is a college town if there ever was one. In this small hamlet, Mr. Tan built 12 schools, a science center, gymnasium, library, hospital, and a navigation club. While Mr. Tan was Chinese to the core and proud of it, he was also quick to appreciate the best of the West— particularly its architecture.

Tan Kah Kee's Home (Jimei)

Mr. Tan's buildings are all a marriage of Western and Chinese architecture, using red brick, white stone, and glazed tiles. But the new Jimei University makes a radical departure from the Tan tradition. This campus looks more like a posh Oriental Holiday Resort than mere hallowed halls of learning. And Jimei U. seems intent on giving Xiamen University a run for its money, what with its nine colleges covering everything from navigation, aquaculture, finance and economics to teacher training.

A Grave Undertaking "Turtle Garden" (Jimei)
I was surprised to learn Tan Kah Kee's "Turtle Garden" is a major tourist site. I'd have thought the idea of an island mausoleum to be dead in the water.[5] The island is shaped like a turtle, a common shape for graves, because the turtle suggest longevity. But I don't

understand the point since the deceased within the graves are dead already (eternally dead, maybe?).

Cool Friezes [6] Turtle Park has a delightful display of Hui'an style stone carvings lining both sides of the entrance hall. These friezes depict in stunning detail various historical scenes and personages from ancient and modern China. One carving of a political session around a round table (rather like a Socialist's Last Supper) looks so 3-

A Cool Frieze! (Turtle Garden, Jimei)

dimensional and lifelike you can almost hear them debating about how to run us foreign devils off.

While you're in the museum, take in one of the performances (every half hour) of ancient music played upon brass bells, chimes, and zither. The costumes are as intriguing as the music. Best of all, the performance hall is air conditioned, and the show is free.

The museum's gate attendants require you to exit from a gate clear on the opposite side from where you entered. This forces you to wander the narrow street lined both sides with shops that sell everything from fashionable clothes to VCDs, dried fruits and Chinese herbs, and sundry handicrafts.

Mini-buses make the 30 minute jaunt to Jimei almost around the clock from Xiamen University, the harbor, or the train station.

Dragon Boat (龙船) Races are Jimei's real drawing card. Held every fifth day of the fifth Luny month, these races have been held for at least a couple thousand years, and teams from all over the world compete in Jimei's exciting event. For more, turn to the section on "Chinese Festivals."

And after you've had your fill of Jimei, head north a few minutes to Tong'An, home of Su Song, and Film City!

Ancient Dragon Boat Race
(Quanzhou Maritime Museum)

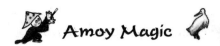
Tong 'An Town (同安, "Common Peace")

Around 1,000 years ago or so, Xiamen was part of the thriving town of Tong An, which today is home to over 3 million Overseas Chinese.   Tong'An was home to Su Song (1019-1101), who invented the world's first astronomical clock—a device I suspect my students still use because some are astronomically late to class.   This Renaissance man[7] was also

into herbal medicine, and in 1061 he compiled the *Illustrated Canon of Materia Medica* (bencao tujing)—the definitive guide for those who believe the grass is always greener on the other side.   He explained, for example, when and where to find "dragon's blood" (from a plant of the Dracaena family), a plant which Chinese today claim lives for 8,000 years:

Su Song's Astronomically Old Clock

"**Dragon's blood** is from plants. The fine looking trees are dozens of feet tall. The red resin (from which it derives the name 'Dragon's Blood') oozes from the trees like glue and congeals. Harvest time varies."

Dracaena

Visit Su Song's home, and then take in the ancient Confucian Temple, Fantian Temple, deng deng.   The Beichen Mountain Tourist District has a reservoir and the beautiful "12 Dragon Waterfalls."   For a special treat, enjoy Tong An's excellent local cuisine at the Tong 'An Guesthouse.   The rather plain décor is misleading, because they offer some of the finest dishes in Minnan.

And now, the hottest item for Sole and Soul, Tong 'An Firewallking....

B.B.
Confucian Temple (Tong 'An)

B.B.
Ancient "Garfield"
Confucian Temple, Tong 'An

Tong 'An Firewalkers—Soul 'n Sole   The firewalking that still occurs in Overseas Chinese communities, and which practitioners claim is as good for the soul as the sole, began right here in Tong'An. Firewalking is usually done on the 15th day of the 3rd Luny month—the birthday of Tong'An's "God who protects life" (Bao–sheng Dadi, 保生大帝).

Baoshen (or, Wu Ben) was born in 979 A.D. in Tong'An. As a youth, Ben read voraciously, and could recite long passages after reading them only once. After serving as an Imperial Censor, he became a hermit in the mountains.

During the great famine of 1032, he had rice sent to the starving peoples of Quanzhou and Zhangzhou, and miraculously cured a great epidemic the following year. Alas, Ben laden with cares, he died four years later at the ripe old age of 58.

His home village built the "Temple of Wu" honouring the "True Man" (Taoist term for "perfected person"). Almost 400 years later, gentle Ben showed up in disguise and cured Emperor Yong Le's mother of an incurable illness. The grateful Emperor had Ben's temple enlarged to palatial proportions, and gave him the humble title of, "Palace Censor who Ascended to Heaven, True Lord of the Miraculous Way of Compassionate Salvation, and Eternal and Unlimited Lord who Preserves Life." Today, Wu Ben has temples all over the mainland and Taiwan.

On Wu Ben's birthday, small idols of the god are placed in palanquins, with great care to insure the god is both physically and spiritually secure (because if the god were to get heated up over something, the firewalkers are likely to get the hot foot as well). Hundreds of pounds of charcoal are burned for an hour or so, and then levelled off to form a path about six feet wide and thirty feet long. A Taoist priest purifies himself, and the firewalking area, and then a procession of men in white, bearing the deity in his palanquin, parade around the fire's perimeter. The priest then kneels at the south end of the fire, wearing only black shorts, and wielding his divine sword. He performs esoteric gestures, and then rock salt his shovelled on to the hissing coals. After the priest runs across the coals, the procession kicks ash as well, while bearing the heavy palanquin and idol. And afterwards, onlookers scoop up the coals and take them home for good luck.

Firewalkers earn much merit, but not always without a few blisters and burns. Unlike other firewalkers, Tong 'An firewalkers are not in trances, and attribute their success to the Taoist priest's preparations, strict diet, and purity.

So they either toe the line[8] or toast their tootsies[9].

Nowadays, Westerners are also on fire[10] about firewalking's benefits for sole and soul. Websites and training schools are popping up everywhere. They say it does as much for the soul as for the sole; personally, I think it will all fizzle out.

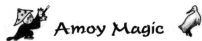
Tong 'An's
Film City! 影视城
By Trish Boman

I visited Film City on a Friday morning, along with about 3,000 primary school children and their teachers. This meant that along with the Forbidden City, Summer Palace, Nine Dragon Wall, Qing-Ming Street, and other old Beijing attractions, I became an extra object of fascination, with children rushing up to surround me and shout, "Hello, how are YOOUUU!"

Unwanted celebrity status aside, it was a pleasant outing. The recreation of the Forbidden City is quite spacious and impressive, giving plenty of room to roam around and take photos in famous settings. Many buildings seem to be almost full-size - at least I couldn't tell the difference, and it's a little far to run and check. The different Halls recreated there are now inhabited by photographers with their costumes and photos-for-a-fee stalls, including sedan chairs, and for an extra payment you can even sit on the Emperor's throne.

Qing-Ming Street is complete, right down to the advertisements on the walls for insect powders and beauty products, and there are a few amusements and souvenir stalls. Behind the street, if you can find the stairs at either end, is a mini-Great Wall from which to view the entire scene. I could just imagine myself as a movie director calling the shots for the

Film City, Tong 'An

street scene of a kung-fu film, with exotic beauties flirting with the local heroes in the bustling marketplace, while in the palace forecourt, mandarins bow and scrape before Dowager-Empress Cixi.

The extensive park is big enough for hours of leisurely strolls, but there is little else to do, and refreshments are minimal. Perhaps if a film was actually being shot, it could be really exciting. But otherwise it's still a fairly peaceful interlude that lets the mind wander back to the old days of Beijing.

Entrance fee: 25 Yuan.

Bus 618 from Zeng Cuo'An Village ends up right at Film City's Gate.

Jinmen Island （金门岛）

Jinmen Island, at its closest point, lies only 2310 meters from Xiamen. So close, and yet so far, because at present it lies under the control of Taiwan Province. With good binoculars, you can see the soldiers patrolling the coast of the 148 square kilometre island, and when I was in the U.S. Air Force in Taiwan, from 1976-1978, Jinmen was quite a hot spot because it lies right inside of Xiamen bay. Now that I've lived in Xiamen for over a decade, it amazes me that America can justify considering it part of Taiwan!

Happily, some tour groups have now visited Jinmen from Xiamen, and I'm looking forward to the day when we can travel freely back and forth, because from what I've read and heard it's a beautiful island.

Jinmen, population 50,000, has a fairly long history (at least by Western standards, though 1600 years is nothing for the Chinese). In 803, a Tang Dynasty official, Chen Yuan, led 12 families to settle the island. It became part of Fujian Province's Tong 'An county in 935 A.D.. Since the Ming Dynasty, the island has been called Jinmen, meaning "Strong gate of gold." In 1914, Jinmen came under Xiamen's jurisdiction, and today the people share pretty much the same customs and festivals as those of Minnan, particularly Zhangzhou and Quanzhou. This is not surprising since, by and large, they are relatives. One particularly unique element of Jinmen culture is their worship of lions, which are seen as the guardian angel of the island. Many village entrances have stone lions in armor, or gowns (depending, perhaps, on whether the lion's getting ready for battle or for bed?).

Centuries ago, Chinese gave Jinmen such names as "Fairyland in the Sea" and "Beautiful Haven of Peace." Favorite scenic spots include Taiwu Peak, Yanping Sword, Lying-on-Cloud Hall and Xianying Waterfall. Jinmen also has 18 ancient buildings with the beautiful ornamentation and upturned eaves typical of Minnan (Southern Fujian) architecture.

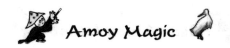
Laonei （老内） Notes

[1] Hanging by a thread: barely surviving (as if clinging to a cliff by a small thread)

[2] Quack: fraud (or poorly trained or skilled)

[3] Getting the boot: getting laid off, fired, kicked out

[4] Deep-pocketed: lots of money; rich

[5] Dead in the water: hopeless, futile (like a boat with a dead engine).

[6] Frieze: decorative band along the upper part of a room

[7] Renaissance man: a person with broad intellectual interests, accomplished in both arts and sciences.

[8] Toe the line: conscientiously obey guidelines or rules; conform

[9] Tootsies: feet (slang, a variant of footsies).

[10] On fire: excited

Chapter 9
Getting About (Transportation)[?]

On vehicle-less Gulangyu Islet, you either walk or lounge on a bamboo litter, but the best way to tour the rest of Xiamen is to hop on a new double decker bus and see where it takes you.

If you're less adventurous or pressed for time (like a mummy), take the 20 RMB scenic tour. (For details, call 2100070 or 5095442).

Of course, taxi drivers are also willing to take you for a ride[1]. And it could be a lot longer ride than you expect if you don't beware of **Odd & Even Days!**

Left turns are forbidden at most Xiamen intersections, which means the shortest distance between points A and B could very well take in point Z. And to reduce downtown traffic, ZhongShan Road and Siming Road are restricted to cars with even numbered license plates on even days, and odd numbered plates on odd days. Our van, for example, has an odd plate, so I can only drive downtown on odd days. Which is fine since I usually have odd passengers. And as son Shannon so sagely observed, odd plates get more days than even plates. (Think about it).

So if you feel a taxi driver is taking you for a ride, bear in mind the restrictions on them. And next time try the bus. If you learn the Chinese characters for the four primary bus terminals you can get almost anywhere in Xiamen:

Main Bus Terminals

			Pinyin
Train Station	=	火车站	(Huo Chezhan)
Harbor	=	轮渡	(Lun Du)
Xiamen Univ.	=	厦大	(Xia Da)
Jimei	=	集美	(Ji Mei)
Huli Bus Station	=	湖里车站	(Huli Chezhan)
Airport	=	飞机场	(Feijichang)
Exhibition Center	=	会展中心	(Huizhan Zhongxin)
Haicang	=	海沧	(Haicang)

? Why does Hawaii have interstate highway signs?

Main Bus Routes

When we arrived in 1988, there were only 3 or so bus routes. The old tandem buses belched smoke like an asthmatic dragon (and much of the smoke drifted up between the cracks in the warped wooden floors). But nowadays we have dozens of sparkling new buses, including some delightful doubledeckers. Few are smokers; indeed, buses on 20% of the routes use clean LPG! Modern indeed—though they still drive with their lights off at night.

Lights Out! Before we moved to China in '88, a Shanghai Chinese friend in Los Angeles told us that Chinese buses did not use their headlights at night. We didn't believe him, but he was right. And police ignore them even today—but they'll stop you in a heartbeat for driving *with* headlights on in the daytime! (Too dangerous, they say).

When I drove to Dongshan Island with my MBA students, I forgot to turn off my lights after exiting a tunnel. A policeman pulled me over and said, "It's against the law to have your lights on in the daytime."

"Really?" I said. "May I ask why you allow buses and trucks to run without lights at night?"

The policeman glared at me, then said, "Show me your license."

"Good answer!" I acknowledged. Will I ever learn?

Here, to my knowledge, are the main bus routes as of April 14, 2003, 5:03 p.m. (tomorrow may be an entirely different story):

#1 Bus Xiamen University (Xiada) → Overseas Chinese Museum → Zhenhai Rd. (Holiday Inn) →ZhongShan Rd.→ Siming N. Rd.→ Douxi Rd.→ Train Station (and back).

#2 Bus Xiamen University (Beach Gate)→Xiada Hospital→ O.C.Museum→ Zhenhai Rd.→Zhongshan Rd.→ Harbor (and back)

#3 Bus LianHua Village→#2 Lianhua Village→ Lianhhua Middle School→ Train Station→ Zhongshan Park→ Cultural Palace→ Zhongshan Rd.→ Harbor (and back).

#4 Bus Harbor→ Zhongshan Rd.→ Cultural Palace→ Zhongshan Park→ Train Station (and back).

#5 Bus Train Station → Hecuo Village （何厝） (and back)

#6 Bus Train Station → Wu Tong Village （五通村） (and back)

#7 Bus Train Station → Zhong Zhai (钟宅) (and back)

#8 Bus Huicheng（汇成）→ Xiahe Rd. → Harbor (and back)

#9 Bus Huli Bus Station→ Huli Boulevard→District Government→ "100 Amusement Park"→South Hill (Nanshan)→ Dongdu Harbor→Xiamen Municipal

Government→7-Star Rd. (Qixing)→Personnel Center→Postal Communications Tower→ Hudong→ Train Station (and back)

#10 Bus Jiangtou N. District→Harbor (and back)

#11 Bus Harbor→ Datong Shijia

#12 Bus Dongdu District-→Bank of China Building→Municipal Government→ Trade Center→ Bailu Zhou→ Central Hubin Road→ People's Insurance Company→ Zhongshan Park→ Cultural Palace→ Zhongshan Rd.→ Harbor (and back).

#13 Bus Train Station→ Central Hubin Road→ Taiwan Hotel→ Sports Center→ Sports Center East Village→Train Station

#14 Bus Shi quan Ganxiusuo (石泉干休所)→ Train Station (and back)

#15 Bus Xiamen University→ O.C. Museum→ Zhenhai Rd.→ Zhongshan Rd.→ N. Siming Rd.→ Construction Bank Building→ Long Distance Bus Station→ Electronics City→ Jiannan Tower→ People's Palace→ Jianxing Rd.→ Municipal Government→ Trade Center→ 7-Star Road→ Postal Communications Tower→ Sports Center... (and back)

#16 Bus Yueyang District (岳阳小区)→ Wanshou Rd.

#17 Bus Train Station→ 10,000 Rock Botanical Garden→ NanPuTuo Temple→ XiaDa Hospital→ Xiada BaiCheng→ Beach Road (and back)

#18 Bus Xiamen University→ O.C. Museum→ ZhenHai Rd.→ ZhongShan Rd.→ Cultural Palace→ ZhongShan Park→ #1 Middle School→ Train Station→ LianBan District→ LianHua Intersection→ Airport Intersection→ District Government →Jimei (and back)

#19 Bus Exhibition Center → Wenyuan Rd. → Harbor (and back)

#20 Bus Xiamen University→ West Village→ Xiada Hospital→ Xiada Beach Gate→ Huli Mountain Fortress→ Shangli (and back)

#21 Bus Xiamen University→ O.C. Museum→ Zhenhai Rd.→ Zhongshan Rd.→ Cultural Palace→ Zhongshan Rd.→ #1 Middle School→ Train Station (and back).

#22 Bus Huli Mtn.→ O.C. Museum→ Zhenhai Rd.→ Zhongshan Rd.→ N. Siming Rd.→ Dongdu District→ South Hill→ Haitian Intersection→ "100 Amusement Park"→ District Government→ Huamei→ Port Area (and back)

#23 Bus #5 Lianhua Village→ #3 Lianhua Village→ #2 Liangua Villa→ Lianhua Middle School→ Lianhua Intersection→ Lianban→ Hudong→ New Village (Xincun)→ Zhongshan Hospital→ Electronics City→ Long Distance Bus Station→ Construction Bank Building→ N. Siming Rd.→ Zhongshan Rd.→ Harbor (and back)

#24 Bus (If you see it, get your eyes checked, because there isn't one).

#25 Bus Jiangtou District→ #3 Lianhua Village→ #2 Lianhua Village→ LianHhua Middle School→ Lianhua Intersection→ Lianban→ Train Station→ Douxi Rd.→ N. Siming Rd.→ Zhongshan Rd.→ Harbor (and back)

#26 Bus Train Station→ Central Hubin Rd.→ New Village→ Bailu Zhou→ Trade Center→ Municipal Government→ Bank of China Tower→ Dongdu

District→ South Hill→ Huli Bus Station→ Huli Boulevard... (and back)

#27 Bus Harbor→ Zhongshan Rd.→ Cultural Palace→ Zhongshan Park→ #1 Middle School→ People's Insurance Bldg.→ Central Hubin Rd.→ New Village→ Hudong→ Train Station→ Lianban→ Lianhua Intersection→ Airport Intersection→ Airport Boulevard→ Airport (and back)

#28 Bus Train Station→ Douxi Rd.→ N. Siming Rd.→ Datong Elementary→ Lujiang Blvd.→ Harbor (and back)

#29 Bus Xiamen University→ West Village→ Xiada Hospital→ Xiada Beach Gate→ White Rock (Baishi)→ Coastal Highway to Huangcuo Village→Qianpu District (and back)

#30 Bus Harbor→ Lujiang Blvd.→ N. Siming Rd.→ Construction Bank Bldg.→ Long Distance Bus Station→ Electronics City→ New Village→ Hudong→ Lianban→ LianQian→ Dragon Hill Bridge→ Qianpu →Exhibition Centre (and back)

#31 Bus Harbor→ Lujiang Blvd.→ N. Siming Rd.→ Dongdu District→ Bank of China Tower→ Municipal Government→ Trade Center→ Personnel Center→ Postal Communications Tower→ Sports Center→ Sports Center East Village→ Sibei Bus Station→ ... (and back)

#32 Bus Harbor→Huicheng (and back)

#33 Bus Dianqian Village (殿前村)→ Train Station (and back)

#34 Bus Huli Bus Station→ Huli Blvd.→ District Government→ "100" Amusement Park→ Guili Flower Garden→ Huli Park→ Central Elementary→ Kangle Hualian→ Kang Le New Village→ #3 Lianhua Village→ #2 Lianhua Village →Jinshang District (and back)

#35 Bus Xidi Port (西堤码头) → Huli Mountain (湖里山)

#36 Bus Exhibition Center → E. Port (Dongdu, 东渡) (and back).

#37 Bus Train Station → Jinshang Rd. (金尚路) → Airport (and back)

#38 Bus Train Station → Dongpu (东浦)

#39 Bus Caitang → Yuan Mtn. (园山, Garden Mountain)

#40 Bus Baoshui District (保税区)→ Xianyue Rd. → #2 Lianhua Village (and back)

#41 Bus Airport → Baoshui District (and back)

#42 Bus Wenbing (文屏) → N. Jiangtou District (江头北区) (and back)

#43 Bus Baoshui District → S. Hubin Rd. → Train Station (and back)

#44 Bus Qianpu (前埔) → Xiahe Rd. → Harbor (and back)

#45 Bus Jinshang District → Xiamen University (and back)

#46 Bus Jinshang District(金尚小区) →Train Station

#47 Bus Xiamen University→Qianpu

#48 Bus Train station ←→ Baicheng (on the beast beside Xiada).

#49 Bus Yueyang District (岳阳小区) → Shitou Pishan (石头皮山)(and back)

#50 Bus Xinglin (杏林) → Harbor (and back)

#51 Bus (Ain't one!)

#52 Bus Sibei（思北）→ Xinglin（杏林）(and back)

#53 Bus Sibei → Jiaowei（角尾）(and back)

#54 Bus Sibei → Bantou（坂头）(and back)

#55 Bus Sibei → Tong An Yuanhua Film City（同安远华影视城）(and back)

#56 Bus Sibei → Dadeng（大嶝）(and back)

#57 Bus Xinglin → Haicang (and back)

#58 Bus Xinglin → Xin An（新安）(and back)

#59 Bus Xingmei（杏美）→ Huagong School（化工学校）(and back)

#60 Bus Xingnan（杏南）→ Xiting（西亭）

#61 Bus Jimei Gongshanju（集美工商局）→ Haicang Guanweihui（海沧管委会）（and back）

#62 Bus Haicang Guanweihui → Kodak（柯达）(and back)

#63 Bus Xingmei → Gaopu Village（高浦村）

#64 Bus Jimei Train Station → N. Jimei Industrial District（集美北部工业区）

#65 Bus Xingnan → Jinyuan Houpu

#66 Bus Xinglin → Huli → Harbor (and back)

#67 Bus Tong An Film City → Harbor (and back)

#68 Bus Tong An → Da Deng Island (and back)

#69 Bus Tong An Bus Station → Jimei → Xinglin (and back)

#70 Bus Xinglin → Tong An (and back)

#71 Bus Xiamen University → Haicang Guanweihui (and back)

#72 Bus Train Station → Haicang Guanweihui (and back)

#73 Bus Songyu→ Haicang Guanweihui (and back)

#74 Bus Jimei Dragonboat Pool（集美龙船池）→ Houxi（后溪）

#80 Bus Baoshui District → Xianyue Tunnel → Train Station

#81 Bus #2 Lianhua Village → Airport

#82 Bus To be continued… !

Tourist Bus Routes

To **Gulangyu and Harbor**:
   Numbers 2, 3, 4, 10, 11, 12, 23, 25, 27, 28, 30, 31, 32, 42, 47, B
To **Nan Pu Tuo Temple and Monastery**:
   Numbers 1, 2, 15, 17, 18, 20, 21, 22, 29, 35, 45, 48, 87, B
To **10,000 Rock Botanical Garden**:
   Numbers 3, 4, 12, 17, 18, 21, 27, 32, 35, 87, B
To **Jimei**: Numbers 18, 52, 54, 55, 61
To **Beach Road**: Numbers 17, 20, 29
To **Tong An Film City** Numbers 55, 67

Travel Services

Xiamen has plenty to keep you busy, but if you're raring to see the rest of our province, visit a local travel agency for advice, tickets, and itineraries. (And read chapters 4 and 5 of Amoy Magic for some great destinations in Fujian Province and the rest of China).

Dr. Jan recommends FASCO, in the United Bank Building (Dahua). They set up shop in Xiamen after ten years experience in Shanghai, and can do international ticketing over a month in advance!
   You might also try:

China Youth Travel Service
65 Bai Lu Road (白鹭路 65 号)
Phone: 205-3188   Fax: 202-0024   CABLE: 2274

Sino Pacific International Travel Co.
Bldg. D 4/F North Block,
Hongshan Building, N. 287 Siming S. Rd)
Phone: 205-5648

China International Travel Service
N. Hubin Road, Zhenxing Mansion, 15th Floor.
   (湖滨北路振兴大厦 15 层).   Phone: 505-1825 505-1822

Airlines In Xiamen

Feeling flighty? [2]   *Call ...*

Xiamen International Airport Information
602-0017 (automated) or   602-8357×6017

Amoy Airlines There isn't one—but there should be! (it's next on my to-do-list).

All Nippon Airways Phone: 573-2888 (9:00-5:00)

China Eastern Airlines Phone: 213-0375
  Fax: 202-8940

China Northern Airlines Phone: 509-6973 Fax: 509-6980

China Southern Airlines   Phone: 212-7815 or 212-7816
  Internet: http://www.xmcz.com

Fly Amoy Airlines!

Shandong Airlines Phone: 513-9777

Shanghai Airlines Phone: 221-0600 Fax: 221-1591

SilkAir (Regional Wing of Singapore Airlines) 205-3280
  205-3257 205-3275 Fax: 205-3273

South East China Airlines   Phone: 506-4941 Fax: 506-4944

Xiamen Airlines Phone: 573-9888 Fax: 573-9777
  Toll Free (From Mainland China only; will not work from HK)   (800) 858-2666
  Local Ticketing (11 Lines) 508-3666

Xiamen International Airlines
  Phone: 602-2936

Train Tickets 515-4386
  Information   505-4340

Plane Tickets   It used to be that we could buy roundtrip plane tickets only for domesticated[3] destinations, but that's changing, and local Chinese travel agents can now get you better international fares than you can from bargain basement ticket hackers in Hong Kong or Los Angeles.   Ask your Chinese colleagues or fellow Laowai for the best agents.   Dr. Jan recommends the outfit located in the Dahua Bank Building.

Xiamen to HK flights take only 50 minutes, but cost 4-5 times as much as bus tickets.   It's much cheaper to fly to Shenzhen or Guangzhou and take the train into Hong Kong.   Either train provides a relaxing, scenic South China excursion.   But go to the W.C. before reaching Shenzhen or you'll have to hold it until you disembark (or disembowel) in Kowloon; the bathroom is locked the last hour to keep you from soiling Hong Kong tracks.

Yet another alternative: Guangzhou has daily 3-hour jet foil boats to Hong Kong, as well as a romantic overnight cruise.

Exit Warning!   If you travel outside of China, make sure you have your reentry visas, otherwise your return can be more difficult than reentry for Russian cosmonauts on a post-USSR shoestring[4] space budget. (But don't knock cosmonauts! NASA spent $100,000 designing a zero gravity pen; Russia solved the problem by using a nickel pencil).

Slow boat to China

When leaving China, you must present your Baggage Declaration Form.   Beware that whatever you bring into China must be taken out when you leave.   If you have a cold when you enter, you'll have to catch another cold, or upgrade to the flu, before you may depart.

For at least the past seven years, airport officials have routinely confiscated Residence Books with the promise that you can pick them up when you return.   Don't believe it.   I learned the hard way.   After they'd promised us this, we returned only to be told the residence books are disposed of after they are confiscated.   We had to pay an arm and a leg for 3 new residence books, and new visas.   In 1993, an American businessman pressed the issue, and after a long wrangle, they admitted his Residence Book was still at the airport, and they returned it to him as they'd promised.

Avoid this hassle by just getting a re-entry visa before you leave Xiamen.

While immigration officials in China's most advanced airport offer less than advanced service, officials at Heping Port (和平码头) were always courtesy incarnate—so I much preferred the boat!   I navigated the harbor's customs and immigration dozens of times, and they bent over backwards to avoid causing themselves, or me, inconvenience.   Alas, as of Spring 2000 the boat is no more-- but for nostalgia's sake, here is what she was like...

A Flighty Travel Agent!

In this story, long term Amoy resident Scott Ballantyne, of ABB, reminds us of the old phrase Caviar Empty!⁶   Unfortunately, Scott is from England, and therefore, like bushwalker Trish Boman neither speaks nor writes standard American English, so you'll have to bear with him.   To make matters worse, he wears a skirt! Well, actually it's a kilt. He's Scottish. ☺

"Mary, an old friend who lived next door, used to visit my apartment each day after work. One day, she told me she was leaving Friday for a long weekend to Hainan Island in southernmost China, and would return on Wednesday afternoon. When she did not show up until Thursday afternoon, I asked her why she was so late.

"She looked flustered and angry, and she said, 'I got to Haikou airport in plenty of time for my flight back to Xiamen on Wednesday morning, but there was no plane. I don't mean the flight was delayed, or even cancelled. I mean there was no flight. In fact, they told me that there had **never** been Wednesday flights from Haikou to Xiamen, and probably never would be!

Scott Ballantyne

"I was livid. I changed my ticket for a flight the next day, but I had very little money left, so I ended up staying in a really cheap, dirty hotel, with just enough money for a bowl of noodles for dinner. So, I am going to the travel agent who sold me the ticket and I am going to demand that they pay me for the extra night I spent in Hainan and for one day's loss of pay - I was supposed to be teaching today, you know.!'"

"And off she stormed to the travel agent.

"Later that night she called in at my apartment. I asked her if she had got her money from the agent. She glared at me as though I had asked her a perverted question and replied, 'No I didn't. Apparently it was all my fault!'"

"'How come?' I naturally asked.

"'Well, I told them that they had given me a ticket for a flight that did not exist and they told me that this was correct. Then I told them that I wanted them to repay my hotel and loss of pay for one day. Then, they reminded me that when I went to book the tickets last week I told them that I wanted to leave on Friday and return on Wednesday, so they gave me exactly what I wanted. I should have known that there was no return flight on Wednesday, therefore, it was my fault. They only did what I asked them to do!"

"Of course, Mary did not get her money back.!"

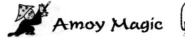
Slow Boat From China

The most convenient and leisurely means to Hong Kong used to be the "poor man's cruise," which I took at least 30 times. Buses were cheaper, but you were stuck in a seat all day watching videos of gory Hong Kong gangster movies or Karaoke tapes, and you got in at night just in time to fork out $100 U.S. on a Hong Kong hotel room. (If you go to Hong Kong, by the way—stay in the Kowloon YMCA! Great prices, great rooms, awesome view, and located next door to the Peninsula Hotel, of James Bond fame). With the boat, I was free to roam about, or relax in the cabin, and a morning arrival saved one day's accommodation.

First class, which ran about 500 RMB, gave us a cabin with a window and a private bath--and included, at no extra charge, a cabin mate who was inevitably a chain smoker.

Second class saved us 60 RMB, and was also two to a room, but there was no window or bath, though we had a sink to soak our head in when the tobacco smoke got to us. Bear in mind that our roommate, like us, was cost conscious (that's why he too was in 2nd class), so he smoked a cheaper, more noxious grade of Chinese tobacco—like Petunia Cigarettes, or Great Ceiling.

Third class saved yet another 60 RMB and landed us in a room with 18 to 20 people in bunkbeds. Smoking was not allowed while lying in bed, so everyone sat up in bed and smoked. The token foreigner was always assigned the upper berth in the corner where the smoke collected, but if you complained they just thought you were blowing smoke. Third class mattresses were a ¼" thick piece of foam laid on top of plywood; authentic "room and board."

Fourth class, the lowest you could go in our classless society, landed us an assigned chair on deck. I tried it, and then threw decorum out the port hole and slept on the floor like a bug in a rug (or at least with the bugs in the rug).

Dinner and breakfast were are available for a fee, and two shops sold snacks, alcohol, and cigarettes to resupply our chain smoking cabinmate.

Jesting aside, we loved the boat, if for no other reason than we could bring tons of luggage (like cheese!) and not pay a lot of overweight.

The 18 hour Slow Boat to China was a pleasant interlude in our all too busy life -- except during typhoons. Those prone to seasickness could get "seasick pills" at the front desk. Those who could not say Yun Chuan Yao (晕船药) got the message across by throwing up on the desk.

Alas, the MV Jimei is no more. But now we have the Star Cruise Lines ferry cruiser, Wasa Queen—and it beats the previous boats by miles (or knots, or leagues, or somesuch).

Wasa Queen, at 155.7m long, is just a tad longer than Noah's ark, and is big enough for either 1,100 passengers or two of every kind of animal if scientists don't stop global warming.

It's a delightful ship, with an international crew that speaks English and are easy to please.

As of this writing, the ship makes the trip to Hong Kong and back once a week, but they generally manage to change the schedule to conflict with whatever travel plans I've made in advance. For the latest information, contact"
Star Cruises: 9G, International Plaza, No. 8 Lujiang Rd., Xiamen
Phone: 592 226 1189 Ext. 3030 (Ms. Zhang Jie Ling, Serena)
www.cruise-ferries.com.cn

Hint: the best rooms and view are first class, 6th level, midship, but if I had more cents than sense I'd take the luxurious suites near the ship's bow (that's the pointy end).

Holiday Travel Warning!

In just 200 years, America has come up with a dozen holidays, so imagine how many the Chinese have thought up after 5,015 years! And those of us in Xiamen enjoy following a few traditions not found anywhere else in China - like the mid-autumn festival "Cake Gambling."

Bearing in mind that Koxinga is reputed to have died of overwork, foreigners' favorite antidotes to the rat race include the Dragon Boat Festival (watch the International Dragon Boat Races at Jimei!), National Day (October 1st), Spring Festival (the break during which China literally shuts down for a week--and school is out for a month), and mid-Autumn festival (cake gambling time).

Holiday travel is difficult, especially during the Spring Festival, because boat and plane tickets are booked up months in advance. During Spring Festival, Overseas Chinese flood into China to usher in the New Year in their ancestral home. While incoming boats are packed, outgoing boats are deserted, so this is a good time to visit Hong Kong. But beginning the day after Chinese New Year, it is the reverse.

This state of affairs suits foreigners quite well, since many prefer to spend Chinese New Year in Hong Kong. But take care, for even in Hong Kong, many markets shut down for 3 or 4 days during Chinese New Year. Stock up in advance with 4 or 5 days worth of meat and veggies, or you'll end up with the crowd of folks subsisting on burgers and fried chicken.

 Amoy Magic

Travel Supplement 1

The Arcane Art of Mini-Bussing

Our first long distance bus trip, to neighboring Zhangzhou and back, was supposed to take 1½ to 2 hours, but that obviously didn't include the hour they spent packing us on the mini-bus. If only we could have figured out which bus was leaving first.

One would think the fullest bus would pull out first, but not so. Sometimes a half empty bus will race off, the strategy being to pick up more victims down the highway, while a bus that is packed to the gills[7] like a sardine tin might wait another half hour to find some soul willing to fry their fanny on the blistering engine cover.   On a 30 seat bus, they can cram 50 victims, who sit on laps, or stand, or squat on tiny bamboo stools in the aisles.

The ticket hawkers all squawk in unison, "Hurry up! We're leaving right now!" And drivers inch forward a few feet to prove time is of the essence. "Aiyah!" they scream. "Kuai Lai!"

I asked one lady, "Do you have A/C?"

"Of course! See the sign? Get on quick! We're leaving!"

Sue and I scrambled aboard and squeezed into a tiny seat in the back, between two farmers and their baskets of carrots, cabbage and Chinese celery.   The ticket seller snatched my money and the driver switched off the engine.

"I thought you were leaving right now?"

"As soon as the bus is full," she said.

"It's packed now," I argued.   But she ignored me like yesterday's news, and stuck her head out the window like a turtle straining from its shell for a feeble-minded fly, and she screamed at all and sundry, "Hurry up! Get on board. We're leaving now!"

Several passengers snickered, and I knew I had been had.

A youth who was obviously wiser than I eyed the bus suspiciously and said, "You've not filled up the aisle yet."

The ticket lady rolled her eyes. "Of course we haven't. We'll pick

"Get aboard! Plenty of room!"

up more people down the road.   The driver started his engine and inched forward. The youth puffed his chest and led his girl onto the bus, sat on a bamboo stool in the aisle, forked over his 20 Yuan, and the driver switched the ignition off.

"Hey, you said we're leaving now!" But the agent was again deaf, dumb and blind. I could barely keep from joining the snickers.

Twain's Duke and Dauphin[8] would have been proud.

Fully 45 minutes after we had been told, "Hurry, we're leaving!" the van lurched off down the road. I asked the ticket lady, "Why haven't you turned on the air conditioning?"

"Open windows are cool enough when we're moving."

"But you said the bus has A/C!"

"It does!" she said, "But we don't use it when we're moving."

Snicker, snicker, all around me.

The bus slowed every few minutes as the ticket hawker poked her head from her yellow shell and screamed, "Get on board. Plenty of seats! Hurry!" One wily peasant dubiously eyed the collage of faces peering dolefully from the windows like nonAryans on the cattle car to Auschwitz. He timorously put one foot, clad in Playboy socks and plastic flip flops, onto the rusted bus step. The lady grabbed him by the collar, yanked him inside, slammed the door, and said, "Ten Yuan!"

"You said there was plenty of room!"

"There is room," she said, and pointed to the battery box, which was coated in greenish gray cottony corrosion and grease, and squeezed between the hot engine cover and the wheel well.

Those of us with enough room to expand our rib cages snickered softly.

There was no order to her people packing, so every time the bus stopped to disgorge a victim, we reshuffled the deck of dog-eared bodies; parents lost children, husbands lost wives; one lost a wallet. But we made it to Zhangzhou in one piece, more or less.

After a pleasant afternoon in Zhangzhou, we returned to the bus stop, where we saw a bus inching forward. The sweetest little granny shouted, "Hurry, we're leaving."

"Susan, this old granny can't be like the rogue on the last bus. They really are leaving." We boarded the bus, paid our pesos, and the driver cut the engine. We sweltered for 20 minutes until sweet old granny had packed her bus.

Susan snickered.

When we reached home that night we discovered that we had been gallivanting about the countryside on Friday the 13th[9].

Someday I'll write about Saturday the 14th.

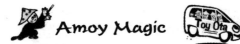
Travel Supplement 2

The Arcane Art & Science of Darwinian Driving

Darwinian Driving
"Survival of the fastest"

Americans, who are used to traffic cops writing tickets for something as small as causing another driver to hit his brakes[10] (for any reason), suspect driving in China to have neither rhyme nor reason[11]. But a decade of driving in Xiamen has taught me that this is not the case. It is simply a matter of, "Darwinian Driving—Survival of the Fastest[12]." This is immensely

"He who hesitates is lost."

logical and practical—especially in a nation of 1.3 billion people, where auto warfare does double duty as population control.

It is simply a matter of knowing the rules…

Rules of Darwinian Driving

1. First has right of way—whether driver or pedestrian. This explains why buses, cement trucks or 18-wheelers will career blindly out of side streets, neither looking nor slowing down, right into the path of oncoming traffic. If they are hit by another vehicle, they are innocent because they were there first (obviously—or they would not have been hit).

Of course, if they hesitate, the oncoming traffic with the so-called 'right of way' will speed up to cut them off. This is logical. Even as we must take every opportunity to cut in front of others, it is imperative we also prevent them from doing the same to us. It is a matter of the Golden Rule: do unto others, but do it first. For example, if your car breaks down, be sure

Diagonal Intersection Block Tactic

B.B.

to stop in an intersection—preferably diagonally to block as much traffic as possible. After all, you're not going anywhere, so neither should the competition. And when making left turns, do it from the far right lane—but do it fast, because of rule #2.

2. He who hesitates is lost. Physics plainly teaches that only two objects may occupy one space at a time. Of course, sorting out who is first can get sticky, especially when five cars abreast try to enter a two lane road. If none hesitate, all may usually merge nicely using the Zipper Tactic, though at times this formation does come unzipped. To insure the zipper moves

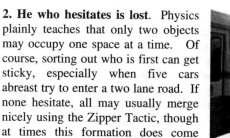

8.8 Darwinian Driving—"Zipper Tactic"

smoothly, it is crucial to avoid hesitation, as well as that peculiar Western weakness known as 'defensive driving.'

3. Offensive, not defensive driving. General Patton said, "A good offense is always the best defensive." It gives you a psychological edge. I learned this the hard way. When I edged to the right to let large trucks pass me on mountain

Unzipped

roads, they interpreted it as weakness and ran me off the road. Now I hog the middle till the bitter end. (Chinese call this 'hero car;' Americans call it 'playing chicken'—though here, no one is playing).

4. Don't pander[13] to pedestrians (lest you get them killed) Pedestrians have no qualms in stepping right in front of a car without looking. Indeed, they will deliberately not look, or even look the other way. This is because they know that 1) First has right of way, 2) Only one object can occupy a space at a time, and 2b) If they occupy that space first and you run them down, they will retire

So who needs sidewalks?

Street | Sidewalk

on the lawsuit. If they are killed, their entire extended family will retire on the lawsuit, and worship their ashes forever on the ancestral shelf. This explains why pedestrians ignore wide sidewalks and walk down the middle of busy streets. They seek retirement. Hence rule 5...

5. Avoid so-called Courtesy or Caution—especially with pedestrians, lest we get them killed. In my formative[14] years, I often stopped for old ladies and women with babies. They invariably hesitated, suspicious of my motives. The few who did get the nerve to cross were nearly run down by the vehicles that raced around me from behind. So give no quarter[15]. But in all you do, avoid looking the opponent in the eye.

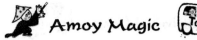
6. Face is foremost. It is hard for Americans to fathom[16] how Chinese drivers and pedestrians keep so calm while waging war on each other. In America, road rage is so endemic that people get shot simply for tapping their horn or looking the wrong way at an opponent. But Chinese avoid such extremities by avoiding direct eye contact. This keeps warfare impersonal, allowing both parties to save face during no holds barred[17] battle. It is a unique ability, honed over 5,015 years by hundreds of millions of people co-existing in cramped quarters.

Lesson? Relax, enjoy, and don't take it personally. Once the rules of the road are understood, driving in China is as easy as in America—and lots more fun. With cars, who needs Nintendo or Gameboy?

Laonei (老内) Notes

[1] Take you for a ride: a euphemism for 'cheating someone'
[2] Flighty: unstable, given to irresponsible behaviour, capricious
[3] Domesticated: tamed (as in "domesticated dog")—a play on "domestic" (国内)
[4] Shoestring budget: very tight financially (as if hanging from a cliff not with a rope but with a shoestring).
[5] Flighty: irresponsible, capricious, unstable
[6] Caviar Empty: a play on the Latin phrase "Caveat Emptor" (Buyer beware)-the basic principle that the buyer alone is responsible for the quality of a product or service
[7] Packed to the gills: common euphemism for "completely filled"
[8] Duke and Dauphin: Two swindlers in Twain's Huckleberry Finn (to regain some face, their victims helped trick their fellow towns people—but in the end they all ganged up to seek revenge against the alleged Duke and Dauphin).
[9] Friday the 13th: considered a very unlucky day (because Christ was crucified on Friday, and including his 12 disciples they numbered 13).
[10] In America, any driving that causes another driver to need to hit the brakes is considered potentially unsafe, and can get the driver a ticket
[11] Neither rhyme nor reason: absolutely no logic, sense
[12] Survival of the fastest: a variation of Darwin evolution's, "Survival of the fittest."
[13] Pander: cater to lower desires or tastes of others, or to exploit their weaknesses
[14] Formative years: young years, why ideas were easily shaped or formed.
[15] No quarter: pity, mercy (often used in the context of combat, like sword fighting)
[16] Fathom: understand
[17] No holds barred: no limits (in wrestling, some extreme or dangerous holds are illegal).

Chapter 10

Mythical Zaytun (quanzhou)

—Start of the "Silk Road of the Sea"

Magical Amoy has more than enough to keep boredom at bay, but if you do get island fever[1], explore the rest of fascinating Fujian Province—beginning with the Minnan Golden Triangle, which comprises the 28,700 sq. km. between Xiamen, Zhangzhou to the west, and mythical Zaitan (Quanzhou) and Putian to the north.

Minnan, population 12 million and a few thousand Laowai, was settled by the Min-Yue people over 5,015 years ago, and in some places little has changed. Minnan mountains and valleys are blanketed by primeval forests inhabited by 33-foot pythons, and rare species like ant-eating pangolin—seldom seen outside of zoos and Cantonese restaurants.

Every inch of verdant valley floor is planted in bananas and sugarcane and rice, and that most versatile of plants, bamboo. The mountains that cover most of Fujian have been carved into precipitous terraces so steep that farmers are in danger of falling out of their fields. On these vertical fields they plant rice, and longyan (Dragon Eye fruit), and tea bushes. Not a wasted inch in the province!

Marco Polo's mystical, magical port of Zaytun is our first stop in Minnan. To his dying day, Columbus thought he had reached Quanzhou. Alas, he never did.... but you can! It's but a 70 mile drive north of Amoy. Piece of cake (provided you are adept at Darwinian Driving).

---

[1] Island fever: boredom (from being in a small place)

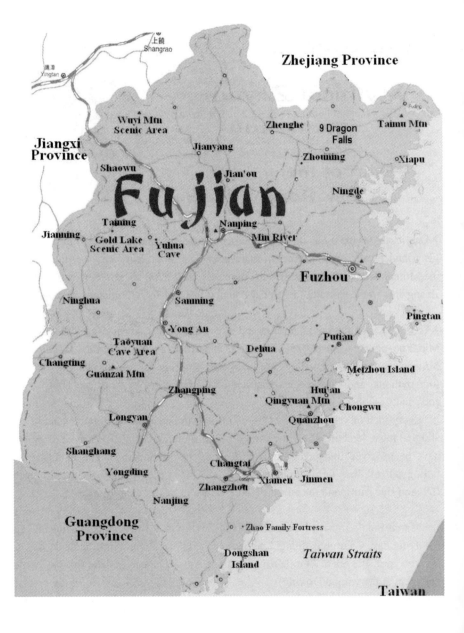

"East is East, and West is West,
    and never the twain shall meet."
                Rudyard Kipling

But they *did* meet once – in Quanzhou!

Quanzhou – Melting Pot of Asia!

Quanzhou, not New York City, was our planet's first great melting pot—and probably stirred by Tong 'An firewalkers. Quanzhou was open to foreigners as never before or since. Laowai became Chinese citizens, intermarried, and held leadership positions even at the provincial level. It was good for both Laowai and Laonei. The Arab with Chinese citizenship who managed China's trade had such good guanxi (relationships) back in camel country that at one point his operation accounted for ¼ of China's entire revenue!

Not surprisingly, the government appreciated its foreign experts, and conferred honors on them similar to those doled out today. Laowai and Laonei mixed freely, trading commodities, culture--even religions!

The Emperor actually financed foreign missionaries, helping them to build Muslim mosques and Franciscan Catholic cathedrals. Andrew of Perugia, the Franciscan Bishop of Quanzhou, wrote that the Emperor's budget for these 'cultural activities' exceeded the entire annual budget of some European countries. (Read more in my book, "Fujian Adventure", still available in less discerning bookstores everywhere!).

Quanzhou (泉州)

China's first major international port was Guangzhou, to the south of Amoy, but merchants soon had enough of the corruption and wars, and moved to the more stable Quanzhou (which Marco Polo called **Zaitan**, and from which we get our word "satin"). Zaitan boasted one of the world's best natural harbors. Better yet, it was closer to Hangzhou, the silk capital of China (though as you'll see in the supplement at the end of this chapter, Fujian's silk was as good or better!).

Over 1,000 years before Christ, the West valued Chinese silk more highly than gold. The poet Horace wrote of the silks from the legendary land of Seres (the

Marco Polo

Roman name for China), and the poet Lucan wrote of Cleopatra's "white breasts... revealed by the fabric ... close-woven by the shuttle of the Seres."

Once Romans and Greeks got a glimpse of Cleopatra's undies[1], the demand for silk mushroomed. So did the silk supply, thanks to mythical Quanzhou, the starting point of the Maritime Silk Road, since one ship could carry as much silk as 700 cantankerous[2] camels on the not-so-silky Silk Road of the Desert. (Fujian also produced excellent silk! See supplement at the end of this chapter).

"Forget silk roads! We want a Silk Highway!!!"

Made in China 　B.B.

By the mid 1300s, Quanzhou had 500,000 people of every race, creed and color imaginable. Historians wrote that "100 large ships and numerous small ones" anchored in the harbour. Marco Polo, who sailed for home from Quanzhou, claimed it rivalled Alexandria Egypt as the planet's largest and busiest port.

"A gift for European traders!"

Magnetic compasses, which helped Chinese sail the seven seas., eventually attracted the attention of Europeans, but sea captains often banned the eating of onions, which they feared could interfere with miraculous devices' properties. Their understanding of magnetism was poles apart from that of the Chinese.

Chinese merchants brought home ivory, pearls, hawksbill turtles and rhinoceros horns, and they sold satin, tea, iron wares, and the other Chinese treasures in great demand throughout the known world. Quanzhou's Dehua 'blanc de chine'[3] porcelain was prized highly, and the Mogadisu and Kilindini in East Africa almost worshipped blue and white porcelain. But the broadest demand was for Chinese silk (Quanzhou and Zhangzhou silk were legendary). Damask and red and green silk went to Vietnam; printed silks to Thailand; colored satin to Malaysia; floral designed silk to Indonesia; brocade to Burma; colored brocade and white silk to India; green brocade to Iran; colored thin silk to Kenya; and colored brocade to Iraq, Egypt, Morocco, and Saudi Arabia.

For a good feel of what it was like to sail the world in a Chinese junk, visit the recently excavated ancient Chinese vessel on display in a museum beside the famous 1,000 year-old Kaiyuan Buddhist temple. The ancient

Excavated Song Dynasty Ship (24m x 9m) Quanzhou

ship, which lay at the bottom of Quanzhou bay for 700 years, was 24 meters long and 9 meters wide, had 13 cabins, and boasted a 200 ton capacity.

Quanzhou Maritime Museum has a world-class display of exhibits on China's marine developments and explorations, as well as the astonishing history behind this ancient port.   The museum displays hundreds of religious artefacts, including Islamic, Catholic and Nestorian tombstones, Hindu statues, and Manichaean pieces.   After reading so much about the Bishop of Quanzhou, Andrew of Perugia, I was excited to see his headstone on display! Though I do wonder where the Bishop now rests his head.

Quanzhou Maritime Museum

"World Museum of Religion" is what UNESCO named Quanzhou in '91, and with good reason.   Over 1000 years ago, all world religions prized this "Jerusalem of Asia" for 3 reasons: she had the greatest market of souls; she was prosperous; she was easily accessible through unparalleled trade networks on land and sea.   Even Mohammed himself set his sites on China – particularly Quanzhou.

Mohammed's beliefs were outlawed in his own homeland, so he coped with poor domestic demand by exporting, and the biggest market was China. Between 618 and 626, the persecuted prophet sent one missionary to Guangzhou, one to Yangzhou, and two to Quanzhou.   You can pay them a visit in the Sacred Tombs of Islam (on Ling Mountain, just outside the city's East Gate).

Tombstone inscribed in both Chinese and Arabic

For 1300 years, the tombs have been well-kept by faithful members of Quanzhou's 40,000 strong Muslim community – many of whom frequent the oldest mosque in Southeast Asia.

Tomb of Muslim Saints   B.B.

Tushan Street's imposing mosque was constructed of blue and white granite in the year 1004 (400 by the Muslim calendar). It was an imitation of a mosque in Damascus, and included the Fengtian Altar, Mingshan Chamber, and Prayer Hall. The dome above the Fengtian Altar collapsed

during a 1607 earthquake, but the 20m. high vaulted entrance and four walls remain, and the faithful are working on restoring the place.

Nestorian Christians made their China debut about the same time as the Muslims, and they both had their work cut out for them competing with the missionaries of Taoism, Hinduism, Buddhism, and the proponents of esoteric Manichaeism—as well as representatives of Tibetan Lamaism, Jainism, Confucianism, deng deng!

Star of David?

This stone, with what resembles a Star of David, was unearthed in 2001, and may be the first archaeological proof of the ancient Jewish community. While Jews weren't the first to use the six-pointed star (Hindus also use it, with the Tamil "Om" in the center[4]), an excavated synagogue in Roman era Capernaum had a "Star of David" architectural motif, so its possible.

Ancient "Star of David?"

Workers have also found over 300 Hindu fragments. Many were found near the Tonghuai Gate, suggesting that the city had a Hindu temple. The elephant in the photo below is offering flowers to Shiva's lingam (stone phallus). Given the population problem, I'd think Indians would find another area of the anatomy to worship.

Nestorian Christian Angel

Hindu art in Kaiyuan
Buddhist Temple

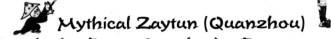

Break the Pots, Scuttle the Boats... is how Laonei say

"burn one's bridges." And that's exactly what happened to Quanzhou …

While strolling down Jubao (Treasure Trove) Street, it is hard to believe that at one time this was our planet's center of international trade in jewels, pearls and gold. But Quanzhou's fame and prosperity, and a little help from us Laowai, turned out to be her undoing.

For at least three centuries, a mix of merchants, emissaries, missionaries and sailors lived in the Fanfang (Foreigners Living Area), which was an eclectic hodgepodge of architecture - temples, mosques, churches, houses. A raucous community of Arabs, Persians, Indians and other Southeast Asian Laowai mixed freely with the Chinese. In fact, foreigners actually ruled!

The ruling Mongolians were too much in the minority to control Quanzhou's Han Chinese, so they passed the reins to Quanzhou's Chinese Arabs. That was eventually their downfall.

During the early Ming Dynasty, the Arab troops mutinied. When the Ming sent in troops to suppress them, disgruntled Han Chinese seized the opportunity for revenge. But the Ming made a fatal move – attacking the Arab's religion.

Quanzhou descended into chaos as inter-racial feuding escalated. The Ming Emperor responded by breaking the pots and scuttling the boats – literally. Like rulers before and since, he valued stability above all else. So he burned and sank the world's greatest fleet of merchant ships, forbade foreign trade, and Alexandria's glorious Asian rival began her long slide into anonymity.

Quanzhou never recovered. Neither did China. While the world moved on, China closed herself off from the barbarians outside. And from that time on, Chinese have feared (with reason, sadly to say) foreign influence in her affairs.

Fujian Province did not give Permanent Residence to another Laowai until 1992, when I got it. Now they might wish they'd have waited another 1,000 years or so. Fuzhou's Mrs. Elise Glickman also got PR! Only two, but it's a good start.

This time, I hope we Laowai and Laonei both make a better go of it.

Happily, Quanzhou's glorious past remains alive yet today – in her people. Many Quanzhou citizens are direct descendants of mixed marriages between Chinese and Arabs, who once lived together in peace. But faced with increasingly xenophobic Chinese neighbors, many Laowai adopted Laonei names to avoid trouble. Even their Arabic writing took on a Chinese slant. Islamic tombstones scattered about Quanzhou are engraved with fanke mu - 'foreign guest's tomb.' The words are written in an Arabic script that strangely resembles Chinese characters.

The Arabs are still here today, in a way. Quanzhou's Baiqi Island has over 10,000 descendants of Arabs, though you'd never know it from their surname of Guo. The Ding clan in Chendai village are also of Arab descent. Their ancestral hall is built in southern Fujian architectural style, but the decorations are Islamic.

Some Quanzhou residents had no idea they were of Arab descent until historians told them.   Only recently, the Bu and Huang people of Yunlu Village were informed that their common ancestor was none other than Pu Shougeng, an Arab in

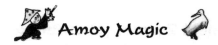
charge of foreign trade during the Song and Yuan Dynasty, and eventually the assistant to the Fujian governor.

Quanzhou Sites   Quanzhou's official tourist brochure spreads it a little thick with[5] its boast, "2,000 tourist sites famous at home and abroad." Still, there is definitely enough to keep you busy a few days!

Main attractions include:

Mulberry-Lotus Tree & Kaiyuan Temple

During the Cultural Revolution, Zhou Enlai issued orders to protect Kaiyuan Temple (and many other relics) from destruction by zealous Red Guards. They also spared the famed Mulberry-Lotus tree.

Legend has it that a monk asked the owner of a mulberry garden to

Kaiyuan Temple

donate his land for a temple. The rich man said, "I'll donate the land if this mulberry tree sprouts lotus flowers within 3 days." To his dismay, it did, so he coughed up the land for Kaiyuan Temple.

Multiculturalism inevitably bred syncretism, traces of which can still be found in Kaiyuan Temple's Mahavira Hall, where two carved stone poles bear carvings of Shiva the Destroyer, a member of the Hindu trinity (the other two are Brahma and Vishnu). The poles were transported to Quanzhou from a collapsed Indian temple.

Mahavira Hall has 24 bat-winged flying apsaras, arms outstretched and holding not harps but Nanyin musical instruments. These Oriental angels (from Batman heaven?) have bat wings because bats, according to legend, bring good fortune.

Buddhist Angels

The East and West Pagodas which flank KaiYuan Temple were originally built of wood and stone, then brick, and later stone. They have withstood 1,000 years of earthquakes and tourists, thanks to their Song Dynasty reconstruction, which took 22 years. Today, they are the best preserved stone pagodas in China.

The East pagoda is named Zhenguo ("nation-protecting") and the West is Renshou ("merit and longevity"). Both of the five story octagonal structures are carved top to bottom with vivid relief sculptures, and warriors are carved into the niches of each story.

The stone carvings are an unusual combination of Chinese and Indian styles-not only because China's contacts with India were frequent, but also because the Chinese monk supervising reconstruction died when only four stories had been completed, and a monk from India took charge.

I particularly like the Monkey King carvings. The novel "Journey to the West," which originated the Monkey King tale, was not written until the 16th century, so some argue that the legend of the Monkey King originated right here in Fujian. (More likely, he was borrowed from the monkey-god Hanuman in the Indian epic, Ramayana).

Weasel the attendants into unlocking the pagoda gates and enjoy a marvelous view of the city from the top – and a view of Spirit Mountain to the north.

Spirit Mountain, aka "Fujian's Fairy Land," is a great place to go when someone tells you to take a hike. It's an enchanting park of winding paths, pagodas, temples, and 36 caves perched precariously on precipitous hillsides. Before the Red Guards got to them, pilgrims used to worship the hundreds of statues in the 36 caves. Now they worship the empty caves. (Maybe because they're holey[6]?).

Old Stone Saint, near Spirit Mountain, is a granite statue of a Song Dynasty Taoist saint (some claim he is Lao Tzu, Taoism's founder). The fellow is 5.5 m. high and 7.3 m. wide. Legend has it that if you rub his nose you'll live 120 years; rub his eye and you'll reach 160. They also used to say you'd die early if you rubbed his mouth, but this didn't go over well with tourists so now they've changed

Ye Olde Stoned Saint

B.B.

it to "Rub mouth, get good luck." But 1,000 years of rubbing Lao Tzu the wrong way[7] was rubbing his nose away, so a few years back they fenced him off and hired a guard (though if you rub his palm with a few Yuan, you can still rub noses with the Old Stone Saint). Whether you succeed or not, I'm sure you'll never again take life for granite.

There's a lot of rubbing going on in China. In a narrow defile of Yunnan Province's Stone Forest, a guide told me, "Get through without touching either side and you'll live to be 100." After I brushed the left face, he said, "No problem. You'll reach 95."

Then I banged the right face. My imperturbable guide assured me, "You'll still live to 90."

I guess he didn't want to rub me the wrong way.

The Little People

Spirit mountain may well be "Fujian's Fairy land" because I've seen real fairies in Quanzhou. (No, not the San Francisco variety).

As a child, I firmly believed in "little people" (like leprechauns, fairies, brownies, elves, gnomes, civil service workers). I'm still not certain they don't exist, especially after visiting Quanzhou, where I've seen little folk less than two feet tall. Quanzhou has long been the marionette capital of China, with more puppets[8] than Parliament.

Be sure to take in a puppet show, where Chinese puppeteers perform miracles with hand-painted wooden puppets, which strut and fret and dance across the stage with more abandon than Macbeth. (They use from 16 to over 30 strings!).

And visit a puppet factory (around the corner from the Overseas Chinese Hotel, past KFC) and watch the uncannily lifelike woocden heads take shape, or girls embroidering the intricate costumes. Also visit the Chen family's Puppet Museum (behind Ashab Mosque).

Zaytun Night Life Early travellers claimed that Zaytun was virtually intoxicating, and no wonder, with travellers from all over the known world converging on this port city. You wanted it, Quanzhou had it. Marco Polo even noted that the city was the tattoo capital of China!

Quanzhou still comes to life at night, though I'm sure it's a lot tamer. Bright lights are strung through the trees, and across buildings and pagodas. And every night the city has traditional artists performing music or drama on stages at major intersections. We enjoy the streetside artists painting, or sketching caricatures in charcoal, or transforming names into beautiful works of calligraphy. Vendors offer snacks, both traditional and modern— everything from Xinjiang raisings and chestnuts to popcorn and cotton candy, and barbeque chicken. 0020

And Quanzhou night markets are a shopper's paradise (and perhaps her husband's nightmare!). The city is also a haven for fortune tellers—once the lowest rung of Chinese society, right next to barbers. Some of them look pretty down on their luck; maybe they're not allowed to tell their own fortunes?

Cotton Candy Man

Fortune Teller

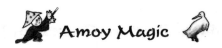
Water World (水
上乐园, Shuishang
Leyuan) in Quanzhou is
a real hit with our family.
You won't find Kevin
Costner here, but you will
find the wee folk—and
the big ones too. Our
family spent 11 hours one
summer day on water
slides, and paddling boats,
and playing in the tidal
pool (though I've had bigger waves in our bathtub). Water World's sole drawback
is that there is neither escape nor respite from the nonstop Chinese pop music
played at 200 decibels from speakers strung up every ten feet. When we begged
them to turn it down a tad, they turned it up. Maybe take some wax ear plugs?

After a nice wet day, try the local Pizza Hut (only a block from a puppet shop
and factory), then head home on the new Quanzhou-Xiamen Toll-way to recover
from your sunburn. Or else head north to Luoyang Bridge…

Luoyang Bridge, just north of
Quanzhou, was the first stone beam bridge in
China. This 1.2 kilometer bridge has stood
over 1,000 years, and may be one of the
oldest examples of biological engineering:
they wedged live oysters between the granite
blocks to cement them with their secretions. I
asked how they trained the oysters but they
clammed up on me.

Legend has it that Cai Xiang tried ten
times to lay the foundation, but each time it
was swept away by the powerful tides. In frustration,
he sent an officer to find the Sea God and ask advice.
The officer returned from who knows where with a one
word suggestion, "Venigar." Cai Xiang took it to mean,
"Lay the foundation on the 21st." He did, and was
successful, and ever since Chinese have said, "You may
not believe a gentleman but you may well have belief in
the Venigar."

Personally, I'd watch my purse with either one.

Not far way is the Five-Mile Bridge, a similar
structure but longer - the longest in the world, in fact,

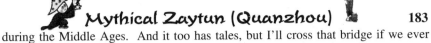
during the Middle Ages. And it too has tales, but I'll cross that bridge if we ever get to it.

Sisters-in-Law Tower South of Quanzhou is the city of Shishi 石狮 (Stone Lion City), which in the early '90s was a backwater haven for smugglers, pirates and counterfeiters but today, naturally enough, is a modern center of commerce and industry. Shishi is also the garment capital of Fujian. A few kilometers south of Shishi, in Yakou, is one of the finest stretches of sand in China. After a day of sun and surf, visit the Sisters-in-Law Tower.

Legend has it that way back in the Song Dynasty (when Dehua pottery went for a Song and a dance), a man sailed forth to Southeast Asia to seek his fortune and promised to return in 3 years. His wife and sister missed him so badly that they piled up stones by the river and watched for him, year after year, but he never returned. The two girls died of grief, and the sympathetic villagers called the rock pile "Sisters-in-Law Tower." And somewhere along the line, the rock pile metamorphosed into a 4-story pagoda that is a landmark even today.

Anhai Manichaean Temple Not far from the Sisters-in-Law Tower is one of the world's last bastions of the Persian religion Manichaeism, "The Religion of Light" (an esoteric combination of Gnosticism, Zoroastrianism and Christianity.

Long before George Lucas wrote, "Use the Force, Luke!"[9] the Persian founder Mani (216-276 A.D.) taught that existence is but the eternal battle between the two sides of good and evil, light and dark. He adopted elements of many religions, reasoning that each contained at least a grain of truth. Mani's malleable metaphysics appealed to St. Augustine, who followed the religion for a decade until his conversion to Christianity.

St. Augustine, as a youth, knew too well the eternal battle between good and evil. The intellectual genius partied by night and prayed by day, "God, grant me chastity—but not yet!" After his illegitimate teen-age son died, he entered the clergy, denounced Mani, and then became a bishop and a saint, though it is not clear whether he ever achieved chastity.

"Use the Force, Auggie!"

The "Religion of Light" found increasing acceptance around Quanzhou for 600 years – until an Emperor snuffed the light out. Emperor Taizu, who ruled from

St. Augustine

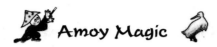
1368-1398, banned the Religion of Light because "ming" (明), the Chinese word for "light," also happened to be the name of the Ming Dynasty, and in one of the earliest arguments for intellectual property rights, the emperor decreed that only he could use the name. Thus was the world's very last stronghold of Mani's light extinquished, though locals continue even today to worship the Manichaeist deity in the Cao'an 'Thatched Nunnery' (which some take to be the popular Goddess of Mercy). This temple also boasts the last Manichaeist carving in China - of two angels holding lotus flowers and a cross (a combination of Greek, Persian and Chinese mythology).

It appears that the Persian's followers made their way into China in the late seventh century, at the same time as their arch rivals, the Moslems and the Nestorian Christians. The Manichaean Temple was built in 1339, after villagers had spent 26 years carving statues of Mani all over the cliffs of Huabiao Mountain. Evidently the artists didn't have a photo to go by, because Mani bears a striking resemblance to the standard issue Chinese deities found elsewhere - except that he sports four braided dreadlocks. Still, the statues are unlike any others in China.

But for something really unique, visit one of the temples to Mao or Deng…

God, not Man?

A few years back, one of Mao's ex-bodyguards wrote, "Mao Ze Dong—Man, not God," but it appears some folks are now having a change of heart. Throughout China, people are offering up sacrifices in temples to Mao, Deng Xiao Ping, and other extinguished revolutionary leaders. A Buddhist priest lamented, "Nowadays, temples to Mao bring in a lot more money than temples to Buddha."

An ancient Chinese proverb used to go, "The man who carves the Buddha does not worship him." But nowadays one might say, "Why not make a buck off the Buddha." Or Mao, or Deng. Deng deng.

If you don't think Chinese are more business-oriented than even us hard core capitalists, visit Shaoshan, Mao's hometown. Peasants perch on the very tombstones of Mao's parents and hawk cheap plastic souvenirs—a grave undertaking if I've ever seen one.

Yang Amiao's Former Home 杨阿苗古居—Steer clear!

Pascoe Trott, Chief Rep for Oxford Instruments up in Beijing, visited the place and received the rudest welcome imaginable from the man and woman out front playing mahjong. They said, "We did not invite you, and did not put the sign up. Get out!" When Pascoe tried photographing the house from the public highway, with a telephoto lens, the man ran after him, ready to "come to blows."

Quanzhou's city grandfathers should strike Mr. Yang's house from Quanzhou's "2,000 sites famous at home and abroad." But the indefatigable Mr. Trott said a sight not to be missed is the beautifully preserved Minnan Village just down the road.

Minnan Village Cultural Landmark (蔡资深建筑群)

is just before Guanqiao, and 2 km west of the 324 highway. Pascoe Trott writes,

"It consists of a small village of beautifully preserved 100 year old "Minnan" houses. They were all built at the same time with money from Mr Cai Zishen who had made it big in the Philippines. I heard about this place from an article in a Chinese travel magazine. I would say that it was well worth a visit. The curator / caretaker was very friendly and knowledgeable, and a 5th generation Cai himself. There are still about 200 people living in this tidily laid out settlement but of course many others have moved out to the city or newer homes. There are many beautifully preserved stone and wood carvings both inside and around the doorways..."

Just a few months back I visited the village with MBA Dean Wu Shi Nong (a Quanzhou native) and the Mayor of Nan "An. It was delightful! No wonder Minnan folk have the saying, "You can have lots of money but still not have a house like Mr. Cai." The sprawling complex is one vast museum of intricate carvings in stone, wood and tile. We toured the rooms, enjoyed Minnan tea, and then listened to some elderly musicians as they gave an impromptu performance.

Cai Mansion (Nan 'An)

Nan'An Mayor and MBA Dean Wu Shi Nong enjoy local music

Exquisite furniture! (Buy copies at the Xianyou Arts Crafts Town--later in this chapter)

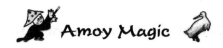
Ꭰaꜟeng Island (大嶝岛)　　In 1988, I was so entranced by my Chinese-English dictionary's 'model English sentences' that I read it cover to cover twice! (Read some of them on page 218). For example, how would you use the word "suppose?" The dictionary suggested, "I *suppose* she's gone to practice grenade throwing again."

What a hot date she'd make! But after visiting Dadeng Island's Cross-Straits Conflict Museum, I understood what got China's lassies hot under the collar.

Local lore has it that the mainland and Taiwan used to bomb each other on alternate days, with Sundays off for rest. Whether true or not, DaDeng certainly took its share of bombs during Taiwan's "bomb them into the stone age" period.

Tour guides will explain the museum's photos and displays, and guide you through the long underground reinforced tunnel. They pipe in, loudly, the sound of strafing bombers, and exploding missiles, and air-raid sirens.　　It was almost too realistic. If our vote-seeking politicians had to walk that tunnel (or had family trying to survive in the villages that are targeted each time), they'd think twice about waging wars.

Along the beach outside the museum, the government is

'turning swords into sandcastles' by creating a resort. A large concrete pad has been designed for setting off fireworks (every year, the Taiwanese and the mainlanders vie over who has the biggest display).

For information, contact **DaDeng Island Tourist Center** (大嶝旅游接待中心). Phone: 86 (592) 709-5125. Fax: 709-5125

If this museum leaves you feeling bombed ou[10]t, boost your spirits by visiting DaDeng's unique Cross-Straits market, which boasts products from all over China—including Taiwan Province's Jinmen Island. For $20 U.S. you can pick up a set of Jinmen's famous kitchen knife sets. They are beautiful, functional, and inexpensive, and purportedly made from one of Jinmen's most common resources: bomb casings.

After shopping, drop by one of China's most unique temples...

Taoist-Confucian Temple　Given that Taoism and Confucianism, two of China's main religions, are 180 degrees apart in philosophy, it's surprising that DaDeng Island has a temple where pilgrims manage to worship both! (Confusionism, perhaps?)

Unlike Confucianism, which emphasizes absolute obedience, conformity, standards, and education to preserve them, Taoism is the Montessori approach to enlightenment. Taoism means "The Way" (New Testament Christianity was also called "The Way"), and is based on the teachings of Lao Tzu in 6th Century B.C. China. But with Taoism the way is relative for there are no standards for proper behavior or right and wrong. All is relative. The emphasis is individual freedom, loose government, and mystical experience.

Not surprisingly, the powers that be preferred Confucius to Lao Tzu--though not in his own lifetime.

Confucius employed his youth mastering poetry and history classics, and the six arts (ritual, music, archery, charioteering, calligraphy and arithmetic). Then in his 30s, he became a teacher and devoted his life to insuring that Chinese for the next 3000 years followed suit.

Confucius humbly claimed that he was an ordinary man of ordinary intellect, so all people could follow his lead in seeking perfection through study and conformity to society. The problem was that no one wanted to follow his lead because he was usually jobless, homeless, and half-starved.

Confucius' failures often ate at him. He once said, "It is these things that cause me concern: failure to cultivate virtue, failure to explore in depth what I have learned, inability to do what I know is right, and inability to reform myself when I have defects."

I think what really ate at him was his wife, because she too was usually homeless and half-starved – not exactly choice ingredients in the immortal's elixir of marital bliss.

While claiming to be just one of the boys, the unemployed Confucius also said he was unstoppable and immortal until his heavenly mandate was completed. "If Heaven does not intend this culture to be destroyed, then what can the men of K'uang do to me?"

Not much, except to keep him unemployed. So at age 56 he left the inhospitable leaders of Lu, who still weren't hiring, and spent the next 12 years traveling about with a slowly growing following. He returned home at age 67 and died 6 years later, leaving behind 3,000 disciples who were usually jobless, homeless and half-starved. But they kept alive the teachings dear to 2400 years of imperial hearts.

Confucians taught that moral community begins by cleaning up one's own backyard (and ignoring the emperor's). The foundation of society is filial piety. Obedience to father and elders and magistrates and emperor guarantees social order, stability, and peace; deviations of any kind insure anarchy.

They learned that lesson only too well.

A few centuries back, a young man saw a girl drowning in a river. He debated whether or not to save her because society forbade young men, under penalty of death, from touching young women. In the end he leaped into the raging torrent, rescued her, and was promptly arrested. The magistrate said, "Saving life is good, but arbitrarily disobeying society's rules is not. You will not be killed, but for your dangerous precedent, you are banished for life."

Not much of a concession; for Chinese, banishment is worse than death.

Emperors have always loved Confucius's emphasis on obedience, but his warning that revolution would topple unjust governments never went over well. In 231 B.C., the emperor tried to eliminate Confucius' influence by destroying every book in China. But someone missed a few volumes. Confucians crawled back out of the woodwork, regained the upper hand, and have been stacking China's deck ever since (while being careful to remove all the wild cards).

B.B.

Jiuri Mountain (九日山) The official starting point of the Silk Road of the Sea was actually Jiuri (9th Day) Mtn in Nan 'An, just to the west of Quanzhou City. Yanfu Temple, at the base of the mountain, is Fujian's oldest Buddhist Temple, built during the 9th year of the Taikang of the Jin Dynasty (the barbarian-befuddling way of saying 288 A.D.).

My Chinese guide boasted, "Every meter of this cliff is covered in ancient calligraphy!"

"We have the same thing in New York City subways," I said. And to add to it, in 1991 a UNESCO Maritime Silk Road Expedition visited Jiuri Mtn. and left an English inscription, with signatures in many Western languages.

The Stone Buddha (石佛厅) is 300 years older than the Old Stone Saint in Quanzhou. His head was destroyed during the Great Proletariat Cultural Revolution, but Hui'an artists replaced it with a cement head. I'm not sure why they didn't use stone. Maybe they thought this material would help cement relationships. Or maybe they wanted the Stone Buddha to have more concrete ideas. Whatever the case, this is certainly one Buddha who won't take getting ahead for granite.

Stone Buddha (Cement head promotes a concrete philosophy)

Hui'an   "...an out-of-the-way village, in the county of Hui'an, or Gracious Peace. The situation of this village is a most picturesque and beautiful one. Just outside of it, Toa-bu, or the "Great Mother" rises abruptly from the plain, and towers up amidst the peaks and mountain-tops that range themselves around it... In front of it there flows a stream that comes out of the heart of the mountain, its waters pure and sparkling, and as yet undefiled by their touch with the outer world. It never dries up, for its fountains repose deep in the bosom of those everlasting hills; and no summer's drought, nor fiery-faced sun can penetrate to where they lie. Its music, too, never dies out, for jutting rocks, and stones worn smooth, and curves and winding passages, and miniature falls make it sing an endless song."

MacGowan, "The Story of the Amoy Mission, (1889, p.127)

Hui'An (惠安) **Beauties 'n Beaches**   Just up the coast from Quanzhou is quaint little Chongwu Town 崇武, one of only two ancient Chinese village walls still completely intact.

Ancient Chongwu is situated on the horn-shaped Chongwu Peninsula and was originally an easily defended sentry post prized by famous heroes like Koxinga. The first Ming emperor, Zhu Yuanzhang, changed the name from Dousai to Chongwu, which means "advocation of arms," (which suggests the Emperor was a Republican).

Standard issue concrete, glass and bathroom tile high rises are springing up like mushrooms in the surrounding fields outside of the 1,000 year old battlements, but within, the old town remains a maze of winding, narrow roads, less than 8 feet wide at points, apparently laid out to confuse enemy troops and foreign tourists (who love the long, white beaches).

Walled City of Chongwu

The 2.4 km. Chongwu wall has 1,300 battlements, averages 7 meters in height, and has a 3.5 meter deep granite foundation. It is easily the best preserved Ming Dynasty wall in existence, and constructed entirely of Hui'an's greatest natural resource: granite. By day and night all throughout Hui' An, young and old alike chip away with stone and chisel to create everything from intricate temple dogs and garden lanterns to Mickey Mouse statues.   They also build their homes of granite, and I know for a fact they're cold in the winter! (And the poor men have no one to snuggle up too—as you're about to learn).

Hui'an's greatest economic asset is a resource harder than granite - her hardworking women, who fascinate Chinese as much as they do foreigners.

Chongwu's isolated position meant that the ancient Baiyue inhabitants never quite assimilated into the Han culture, so much of their unique culture and dress still survives today.   Many a Chinese social scientist has camped out in Chongwu, studying the unique fashions and strange marriage customs.

The women's colorful jackets are tight and short, leaving bare bellies above skintight black hip huggers that flare out baggily on the legs. While bellies are bare, heads are almost completely covered by colorful kerchiefs and yellow bamboo hats that are often decorated with emblems resembling the butterflies that their ancestors once worshipped.

Chinese call this bare belly/covered head custom 'democratic bellies and feudalistic heads.'   I think it's just a tantalizing 'revenge.'

Legend has it that long ago, a young girl refused to marry a wealthy man so he bound her and married her anyway. (Now that's how to tie the knot!) [11].   Today, the designs around shirts' sleeves and waists remind girls of their tragic ancestor's bonds, and their wedding traditions (once common throughout China but disappearing elsewhere) are a form of eternal revenge upon all men.

Democratic Belly B.B.

B.B.

According to ancient custom, bride and groom may not stay together on their wedding night. The groom stays in a friend's house. On day two, the bride pays respects to the groom's family and gives gifts to the elders. On day three, the groom's sister leads the bride to the communal well to draw two buckets of water. After five days of obeying various customs, she returns to her parents' home. Bride and groom are not allowed to live together until she bears a child. But here I conceive a problem: when does she conceive?

Until she has a child, she is neither allowed to stay with her husband nor even to talk with him. If she meets him on the street she must treat him as if he were a stranger, and if her husband visits her home, she must avoid him, waiting in back until he leaves.

The newlyweds are allowed to stay together only 3 times a year: Spring Festival, Grave Sweeping Day, and Mid-Autumn Festival.

I bet they really make hay on the holidays.

"Not this year, dear. I have a headache."

While Hui'an lassies are bothersome brides, they are also indefatigable laborers. They clean house by night and spend all day lugging ponderous loads of rock or grain on baskets slung over their deceptively petite shoulders. Meanwhile, the men fish, or chisel stone in quarries, or hawk victims for their motorcycle taxis, or hang out in tea shops moaning because their bride just told them, "Not this year, dear. I have a headache."

There are other restrictions on marriage that apply not just to Chongwu folk but to everyone in China. Just inside one of the ancient city gates is a blue enamel sign with row upon row of tiny, white Chinese characters explaining in detail the rules governing marriage and child-bearing. Girls must be at least 20 years old to marry, and boys must be 22. To bear children, girls must be at least 20 years and 10 months, and boys must be at least 22 years and 10 months.

I'd have never imagined that boys bear babies at any age. This may explain China's burgeoning population, or how Chongwu couples have children when they don't sleep together. Men just grin and *bear* it.

Religion is a big part of Chongwu life, and with wives like theirs, I see why. On festivals, Chongwu people light candles and incense and offer sacrifices in the Temple of the 12th Lord, but nowadays, many also attend the newly renovated and expanded Protestant church, which was first built in the 1880s. As late as 1995, members sat on pews made of tree trunks split in half, but now the church has been rebuilt and expanded, and equipped with genuine pews, much to my derriere's delight.

Hui'an Art   Hui'an folk have been stone masons for at least 1700 years, and folks come from all over Asia to buy up their stone carvings, furniture, deng deng. Buy a nice stone statue to take home in your carry on (after you've courted a hernia lifting it, you won't take it for granite[12]!).

B.B.

B.B.

Shadow Carving is a recently developed Hui'an stone technique. They can reproduce virtually any painting or photograph on a smoothly polished marble slab by tapping out the design, dot by dot, and then coloring it in. The carvings of Michael Jordan look like they could pop right off the stone!

Give them a family photo and they'll copy it for you, and mail it to your home! Try the little green souvenir shop just to the right of the stone gate with the elephants in

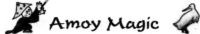
front. An 8 × 10 will run about 200 to 300, depending on the quality desired. But make sure the photo is top notch, or they can't reproduce it.

B.B.

Chongwu's "Earth Art"
(Seems fishy to me)

Walled City Most Chinese tourists come for the 'official' tourist stuff, like the forest of 500 new statues portraying events in Chinese history and literature. But I think the best part of the walled city is... the Walled City! Starting from the church (the original was built in the 1880s), walk up the narrow road, and enter the gate.

At the "T" intersection, hang a right and go all the way to the temple at the end. Note the tailor you pass on the left. He uses a 100 year old Min River sewing machine—much the same as those used a century ago. And, in fact, newly minted machines are made the same. But why reinvent the wheel? They work!

100 Years Ago **Today**

Ascend the wall, and head left to the lighthouse, from which you get a great view of the walled city, and of the large crescent of a beach, with its fine white sand (Hui'an has miles of beautiful beaches). Then either return the way you came, or walk along the top of the wall.

As you explore the city, you'll pass unique old architecture—homes that are hundreds of years old new. Though the people live much like their forebears, folks like Granny Chen also have the most up-to-date kitchens to engage in that most Chinese of all endeavours—cooking, and eating! And indeed, the Chens have long been making and selling Chongwu's famous fish rolls; buy a few jin, take them home, slice them thin, fry them, and enjoy.

Granny Chen's delightful new kitchen (Chongwu)

Dehua (德化) Porcelain

Paradise, in the mountains northwest of Quanzhou, has been one of China's key porcelain producers since ancient times. Since 1949, archeologists have over 180 ancient porcelain kilns, dating from the ancient Song Dynasty to the recent Qing. These ancient kilns have sure fired the imagination of

guidebook authors, who have written of the 17 chamber Qudougong Kiln, "Such a large-scale kiln of ancient times looks like a dragon crouching on a hill, magnificently."

The old dragon went to pot, but modern Dehua kilns still offer every porcelain product imaginable, provided you've a limited imagination: fine dishes, statues of deities and demons, and gigantic vases big enough to hide in.

If you arrange it in advance, factories are quite happy to give you a tour, and perhaps even a souvenir to remember them by.

The drive is as interesting as the destination. The nicely paved concrete road snakes through valleys and past unique villages. One village is dusted in crimson, as if the Red Tide had become a red snowfall. They make incense (I'd be incensed[13] if I had to live with that; at the very least I'd see red[14]).

I also enjoy watching the folks in the kilns making bricks— endless rows of them, formed by hand in wooden molds.

Robert H. Blumenfield, an American collector of Dehua's blanc de Chine, wrote the 240 page, "Blanc de Chine—the Great Porcelain of Dehua."   Amazon.com offers the book for $52.50 (compared with the $75 retail price).

Kilns near Dehua

BLANC de CHINE

THE GREAT PORCELAIN OF DEHUA

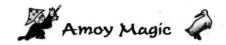
Supplement
Fujian's Famed Silk Industry!

"The people [of Jianning 建宁, Fujian] live by trade and manufacture and they have great store of silk which they weave into various stuffs." Marco Polo

"Zhangzhou in the Middle Ages was the seat of a great silk manufacture and the production of its looms, such as gauzes, satins, and velvets, were said to exceed in beauty those of Soochow and Hangchow."
George Philip, former British Consul at Amoy, 1889[15]

Quanzhou Silks

A century ago, villagers near Minhou (outside Fuzhou) were well known for raising silkworms, the foundation of Fujian's once legendary silk industry. Fujian is no longer famed for silk, but it should be. Fujian has the climate, as well as the three kinds of mulberry trees that are useful for commercial raising of silkworms.

To appreciate the silk industry, I offer you quotes from Claude R. Kellogg's monograph[16], "The Silk Industry in Fukien" (presented to Fuzhou's Anti-Cobweb Society on May 22nd, 1931).

"One of the oldest and most fascinating industries, no matter from what angle it may be studied, is that of the production of silk. Ancient Chinese writings, themselves yellow with age, tell of an industry already well developed, with its beginnings some 5000 years ago. Four priceless scrolls, depicting the production of silk in detail, were for generations in the possession of the royal families of China but were so carefully guarded that no knowledge of the industry reached the outside world until the secret was stolen by some monks early in the sixth century...

"In the first century A.D. great caravans of snarling camels, laden with bales of silk stuffs, crept ceaselessly over the frozen wastes of the Pamirs so that the pampered aristocrats of the luxurious Roman court might be clothed in fine raiment. Some two thousand camels per day, on the average, were needed to carry the great bales of silk cloth to the

borderland of China, from where it was transported by nomad merchants to the Roman Empire…

"It is also interesting to note that no raw silk was sold to the western peoples. All silk was taken through Constantinople to the Island of Cos, in the Mediterranean Sea, in the form of woven fabrics and there unwoven, as this was the only way in which the Romans could get silk thread from which to reweave the costumes so desired by the few who could afford them. Silk at that time was worth its weight in gold. Until 550 A.D. no outsiders knew from what silk was procured.

"…Reports on Fujian silks made by the International Testing House, in Shanghai, showed that Fujian silk, if properly handled, would equal in quality that produced elsewhere. Any differences, then, would be due, not to the inherent quality of the silk itself, but to the methods used in its production.

"…The climate, though not of the best, offers no insurmountable difficulties, the mulberry trees of the necessary varieties grow readily and the land upon which they can be successfully grown is all about us, some of it not even being put to any use at the present time. Representatives of the American Silk Association, while in Foochow predicted that Fujian was capable of producing from 15 to 20 millions of dollars (Mex.) worth of silk per year. The pity of it is that not only are we not producing the silk as we should but we are even importing it from other parts of China. All that is needed is a careful painstaking following of the most approved modern methods of rearing silkworms and Fujian, who once sent out silks equal to the very best from any part of China, will again be enabled to export silks of the very highest quality, this time produced from silkworms reared on her own soil.

"…The Fujian silkworm (monovoltine) increases in weight 5,000 times, and 20 times in length. It then spins its cocoon, which is placed in hot water to kill the pupa and dissolve the cement holding the silk strands together. The cocoon is unwound, and the hapless pupa is dried, fried in peanut oil, and served up as snacks.

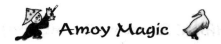
Supplement

The Filipino Hero from Quanzhou

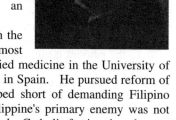

Jose Rizal was born June 19th in Calamba, Philippines, and died December 30th, 1896, in Manila. This patriot, physician and intellectual was an inspiration to many generations of Filipinos.

Rizal was the son of a wealthy landowner on the island of Luzon, and his mother was one of the most educated Filipino women at that time. Rizal studied medicine in the University of Madrid and became leader of the Filipino students in Spain. He pursued reform of Spanish rule in the Philippines, though he stopped short of demanding Filipino independence of Spain. In Rizal's eyes, the Philippine's primary enemy was not Spain, which was undergoing dramatic reform, but the Catholic faction that clung to power in Spain's impoverished colony.

Rizal continud his medical studies in Paris and Heidelberg, and in 1886 he published his first novel, in Spanish. "Noli e Tangere" exposed the evils' of the Catholic friars' ruleli much as Uncle Tom's Cabin brought to light the evils of America's slavery.

Rizal returned to the Philippines in 1892 to found a nonviolent reform society, La Liga Filipina, in Manila, but was deported to northwest to Mindanao, where during his four years of exile he continued scientific research and founded a school and hospital.

A nationalist secret society, the Katipunan, launched a revolt against Spain in 1896. Though Rizal had absolutely no connections with Katipunan, he was arrested, found guilty of sedition, and executed before a firing squad in Manila. i The evening before he was executed, he wrote the Spanish masterpiece, "Mi Ultimo Adios" (My Last Farewell"), which helped Filipinos realize that there was no alternative to independence from Spain.

Rizal International Shrine in Jinjiang In 2002, Jinjiang (a suburb of Quanzhou) invested 10 million Yuan to create the 5-hectare Rizal Memorial Park, with its 18.61 meter high statue of Rizal (much higher than the 12-meter statue of Rizal in Manial). Filipino business leaders invested an additional 2 million Yuan. \\ Filipino House Speaker Jose de Venecia said that China's park was a "great symbol of the 1,000-year-old friendship between our two nations," and, "This Rizal Park in China helps elevate the status of our Philippine national hero Dr. Jose Rizal as a hero for the whole Asian region."

The park will become a must-see for Filipino-Chinese, 80% of whom, like Rizal himself, trace their roots to Southern Fujian.

Quanzhou Specialties
While in Mystic Zaytun, stock up on these local specialties:

Dehua Porcelain—a limitless variety of fine China, as well as the ivory white porcelain figurines.

Dehua Famous Alcohol—brewed with herbs, it is "pure, mellow, fragrant, and "curative effect is prominent." Drink enough and you won't care if you're cured or not.

Hui'an Stone carvings and Shadow Carvings. Family portrait, perhaps!

Puppet Heads. The hand carved camphor wood heads are rapidly giving way to mass produced plastic puppets, so buy them while you can (and while you can afford them).

Old Fan Zhi Magic Lees—a concoction of corn, beans, and over 50 Chinese herbs, it is said to cure everything from stomach and spleen ailments to indigestion deng deng and perhaps dung dung.

Silk Flower Lanterns. Quanzhou Silk Lanterns are legendary. If possible, visit the city on Lantern Festival (15th day of the Chinese New Year).

Qingyuan Tea Cake , made from herbs and tea, has for a century been reputed to be just what the doctor ordered for increasing appetite, strengthening the spleen, (Chinese seem to have a thing about spleens!), helping digestion, etc.

Anxi Oolong Tea—the tea that sparked the American Revolution—we threw it overboard during the Boston Tea Party. I can see why that would have tea'd[17] the British off; I'd have been madder than the hatter[18] myself.

Anxi Rattan and Bamboo—several factories produce quality baskets, shelving and furniture; you can even get it made to order. Check the internet for sites.

Yongchun Preserved Vinegar, a black vinegar reputed to be one of China's "Four Famous Vinegars," has been a Quanzhou staple since the Song Dynasty. But I'd be careful with vinegar. "Drink vinegar" is a Chinese euphemism for "jealousy" and infers one's spouse is unfaithful.

Shishi Sweet Rice Cakes Dating from the Ming Dynasty, these are said to be some of the best rice cakes, but I wouldn't know. I prefer German chocolate cakes myself.

Laonei (老内) Notes

[1] Undies: underwear, lingerie (slang)
[2] Cantankerous: ill-tempered, disagreeable, hard to handle
[3] Blanc de Chine: French term for white, usually undecorated porcelain produced in Quanzhou's Dehua (technically, it refers only to that of the 17th & 18th centuries, though it was produced as far back as the Song Dynasty).
[4] Hindu "Star of David": an ancient symbol, the Satkona Yantra is a six-pointed star with the Tamil "Om" (primordial sound) in the center, and surrounded by a circle of fire. The "Star of David" did not become distinctly 'Jewish' until the 17th century.
[5] Spread a little e thick: exaggerate
[6] Holey: holy (a bad pun; sorry)
[7] Rub the wrong way: vex, annoy, anger
[8] Puppets in parliament: puppet, in this context, refers to a person under someone else's control. "Who's pulling his strings?" means "Who's controlling him?"
[9] Use the Force: from the Stars Wars movies
[10] Bombed out: exhausted, depressed
[11] Tie the knot: euphemism for "get married" (another is 'get hitched')
[12] Take for granite: a play on the phrase "take for granted"
[13] Incensed: angry, furious
[14] See red: angry, furious (as in, "The bull saw red.")
[15] Philips quote from Journal of the North China Branch of the Royal Asiatic Society, v. 28-29.
[16] Monograph: scholarly essay on a specific subject
[17] Tea'd: teed (to make angry; slang)
[18] Madder than the hatter: reference to the "Mad Hatter" in Lewis Carroll's classic, "Alice in Wonderland."

Chapter 11
Zhangzhou

Zhangzhou, on the "9 Dragon River"

"Chiang-chiu is a large city of 200,000 inhabitants, situated on a wide river, 30 miles west of Amoy... The scenery, it seemed to me, was the most beautiful I had ever witnessed. Within the circle of our vision lay that immense city with its extensive walls, its temples and pagoda, its river, bridges and boats, its gardens, its trees and shrubbery, and its densely crowded streets... Still further on, in every direction, our view was bounded by lofty hills whose cloud capped tops seemed as pillars on which the heavens rested. Nature had done her best to make this region a terrestrial paradise... Through the centre of this scene may be traced the course of the river with its numberless canals, like the Nile of Egypt, giving fertility wherever nature or the art of man conducts its waters...

"The same good feeling towards foreigners seems to extend far into the interior. At least we go from, village to village wherever we please without hindrance, and are always treated with kindness."
Diary of Rev. Talmage (Sept. 23, 1847)

"The city itself, when viewed from the walls, was one of the most beautiful that I have ever seen in China. Looking over it, it seemed like a huge forest. The Chinese have a passionate love for trees and flowers, and consequently every householder had planted some kind of a tree in his courtyard. These, during years of undisturbed prosperity, had grown large and spreading, until at length the city seemed to lie beneath the shadow of a mighty forest. Lines of streets could here and there be distinguished through the foliage, but it was difficult to realize that down below, a hundred thousand people lived, that great busy streets, crowded with buyers and sellers, stretched far away into the distance, or that the river beyond was lined with craft of all kinds, in which thousands of people passed their lives, and had no home besides them.

..."The people of Chiang-Chiu were proud and haughty. They were prosperous and well-to-to... They were proud, too, because of the exquisite silks and satin stuffs they could produce. Their looms were famous, and their designs were rare, and beautifully executed."
Rev. Macgowan, *The Story of the Amoy Mission* 1889

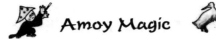
Zhangzhou (漳州)
—Home of Narcissus

Zhangzhou was the home of flower children centuries before Bob Dylan was blowing in the wind.[1] Settled by the Minyue people 5,012 years ago, Zhangzhou prefecture was established in 686. Today, Zhangzhou administers nine counties and a district, with a population of over 4 million spread out over 12,607 sq. km.

Officially, Zhangzhou has 33 scenic spots. I'd pass on some, but I highly recommend the ancient Song

Zhangzhou Narcissus

Dynasty fortress, Xiangcheng (the city of flowers and fruits"), delightful Dongshan Island, the beautiful beaches of Longhai Crater, China's kayaking capital, Changtai, and the "100 Flower Village," where residents have more plants[2] than the FBI.

100 Flower Village

For centuries, Zhangzhou people have grown an unimaginable variety of potted flowers, plants, and miniature Chinese landscapes (which go for as little as $10 or so). A brochure claims that "100 Flower Village" boasts 20,000 species of flowers, and over 10,000 potted flowers and miniature trees, but it has to be less than that because Susan Marie has bought more than her share of them.

Zhangzhou's most famous floral claim to fame is the Narcissus, which Chinese call "Water Sprite Flower." Secrets for its cultivation have been handed down from one generation to the next for centuries.

Zhangzhou had such a glorious past that many scholars argue Zhangzhou, and not Quanzhou, was Marco Polo's ancient port of Zaytun. Though I doubt this, it is true that archaeologists have unearthed enough foreign artefacts to suggest that this "Plain of Plenty" was, in its heyday[3], a major international port of call. Some of the findings have included Islamic carvings and Nestorian Christian crosses. And as Rev. Macgowan noted, Zhangzhou was famous for its quality silk (and Rev. Macgowan should know, since he was a "man of the cloth[4]"). Zhangzhou silk is sold even today in Hong Kong for upwards of $100 USD per yard!

Zhangzhou's giant cactus! Real... or fake? See for yourself!

Zhangzhou's 33 famous sites at home and abroad include:

Zhangzhou's Hongjian Village, just 1km. from Ciji Palace, is the

ancestral home of Corazon Aquino, former Philippine president (her great-grandfather, Xu Yuhuan, and other villagers sailed to the Philippines over 120 years ago). Corazon visited Hongjian in 1988, and donated money to rebuild their ancestral hall. Zhangzhou is also the ancestral home of Singapore's Prime Minister, Lee Kuan Yew, and Taiwan's Lee Teng-hui (though perhaps Zhangzhou does not belabor[5] the latter).

The Zhao Family Palace (赵家堡) Southeast of Zhangzhou and east

of Zhangpu, was built in 1279 by a member of the Song imperial family who fled invading troops from the north. The earthen Outer Wall was built upon a stone base, and is 6 meters high, 2 meters thick, and 1,200 meters in circumference.

An imitation of a Song dynasty imperial palace, the Outer City has five rows of houses and over 150 rooms, linked by walled courtyards.

The Inner City resembles the square Hakka structures in western Fujian, and is protected by a 20 meter high rammed earth wall. The complex boasts a flagstone courtyard and a lake with pavilions and arched bridges (including the excellent Bianpai Bridge), a primary school, stores to cater to the 500 resident families, a tourist museum, Jufo Pagoda, and Yu's granite stele[6] recounting Da Yu's achievements in river control, Jufo Pagoda, deng deng.

Zhangzhou's Nanshan Temple(南山寺) This temple was originally

the home of Chen Yong, a bigwig during the Kaiyuan Period of the Tang Dynasty (713-741). It was so grandiose that he was accused of upsetting the social order and putting on imperial airs. Chen's quick-witted daughter immediately became a nun and urged her father to donate the home as a temple.

Since ancient times, worshippers have flocked to pay homage to the 62 meter high stone Buddha, and in the rear Scripture Hall, the unique 2 meter, 2,000 kilogram white jade Buddha impresses even the most jaded tourist.

Longhai Old Crater (龙海古火

山口) lies on the shore of Niutou Mountain. A guidebook claims, "According to scientific records, its last eruption dates back to more than 22 millions years ago." Only Chinese could keep records 22 million years!

Better than the crater itself is the adjoining **White Beach**(龙海白滩)

"White Sands" beach

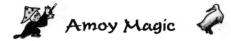

with beautiful white sand like silk between ones toes—and its one of the few places around with waves strong enough to beach your boogie board.

Zhangzhou City Hotels

Zhangzhou Guesthouse （漳州宾馆） Our long term favourite, with an excellent downtown location, garden setting, and excellent Chinese and Western cuisine (great sweet 'n sour, and jiaozis).
Address: 4 Shengli Road, Zhangzhou, Fujian 363000
Phone: 86 (596) 202-3322 Fax: 202-3431

Zhangzhou Overseas Chinese Hotel （漳州华侨饭店） Right beside the Guesthouse, it has Chinese & Western restaurants, a business center, coffee shop.
Address: 33 Xinhua Road North, Zhangzhou, Fujian 363000
Phone: 86 (596) 202-9988 Fax: 202-5201

Changtai （长泰） If you have a penchant for river rafting or kayaking, visit the home of China's kayaking team.
The Mayang River Kayak Center has hosted many domestic and international rafting and kayaking events. A brochure boasts of the 8 km course, "rip currents with blustering surges account for more than 50%. Soul-stirring, exciting and without danger, the place is the paradise for the braves."

Sue really flipped over kayaking!

If you're one of the braves, like Susan Marie (she flipped[7] over river rafting—literally!), and want your soul stirred with a river rafting adventure, phone: (596) 832-1001 or 136 0507-0871. And after you've flipped out[8], go take a hike![9]

www.fjdyp.com/English.htm

Take a hike! Changtai is a paradise for bushwalkers like Trish Boman. Endless trails wind through deep, verdant valleys, with pristine rivers foaming over polished granite boulders. There's also a lot of wildlife, like 100+-year-old giant tortoises, and pangolins (endangered armadillo-looking anteaters highly prized by Cantonese chefs).

Until just a few decades ago, Amoy Tigers also roamed the hillsides. Today about all you'll run across, if you're lucky, are wolves, wild boar, and mountain goats. And, of course, if you pay attention you might see snakes, but you have to keep a look out. While hiking with Chinese friends, they walked within two feet of this bamboo viper on the side of the path. It's silvery green blended right in with the leaves. When I pointed it out to them, they nearly fainted right on the spot!

Fortunately, we didn't run across any of Fujian's 33 foot reticulated pythons (better yet, they didn't run across us!).

Bamboo Viper

While in the area, visit the beautiful, 70m high Baizhangya Falls—but phone ahead to make sure its turned on! Neighboring Anxi county diverted the water for a power plant, so most of the time the Falls trickles like a Fujian mountain monkey with prostate problems.

Changtai beauty

Balancing Growing & Greening

Apart from debacles like Baizhangya Falls (which Changtai is helpless to do anything about), this area is something of a small development miracle. As you explore her, you'll find it hard to believe that just a decade ago, "Xiamen's Backyard" was an environmental nightmare.

Over 100 Years Old!

A few years ago, I spent an entire day hiking along the riverbank with county officials and investors for the proposed water rafting resort. The pristine river foamed over rocks and boulders flung across it like polished granite gems. But only 3 years earlier, that river had been a black, stygian stream of noxious industrial effluents that vomited forth to poison the valley. It's resurrection was due primarily to a visionary young county magistrate, Yang Ming-yuan, who told me, "It is pointless to prosper by destroying our environment. It is also senseless to go overboard environmentally and starve. So we emphasize both economic development and environmental protection."

Changtai Dairy Industry--on the *moove*...

One way that Changtai minimizes pollution and waste is with its closed cycle. The manure from Changtai's 30,000 cows fertilizes the grass they feed on, and tens of thousands of fruit trees, and over 2 million square meters of mushrooms (and the mushroom soil, after harvest, is also used for fertilizer). They've even found a use for the dairies' prodigious production of cow urine: it is converted into methane for cooking and lighting.

Changtai's environmental restrictions on have cost them tens of millions of dearly needed revenue, but the leadership is confident their policies will eventually attract both tourism developers and green industrialists. Magistrate Yang said, "We need to have a clean environment. We also need to eat!"

I hope Changtai can do both.

Lindun Town   I had visited Lindun (part of Changtai) half a dozen times without realizing that many of its ancient walls still stood.   The walled city was built over 400 years ago to keep out the invading Japanese pirates, who for centuries pillaged and raped and wreaked havoc on even these remote valleys.   Chinese called them wokou (a disparaging term meaning "midget barbarians").

Old Lindun was unique in that it had a wall down the middle of town, as well as around it.   I was told that the village had two factions who were forever fighting each other—at least when they weren't fighting together against the midget barbarians.

Lindun Village Wall (Changtai)

The old Opium Baron's manor also offers a fascinating glimpse into yesteryear.   It was built over 150 years ago by a Xiamen tobacco king—and built to last!   One of the granite slabs inside is 10 meters long.

Opium Baron's Manor

Before you leave Lindun, be sure and have a meal of the local mountain delicacies—rare wild veggies and critters.   Try the restaurant that has a hot springs attached.   It's run by Mr. Lin—which is no surprise, since virtually every one in the town is surnamed Lin.

Liudoushan Tropical Rainforest   This amazing rainforest, just 75 km from Zhangzhou city, is the perfect place for a wet walk (they average two meters of rainfall each year!).

This virgin rain forest has some of the rarest creatures and plant life on the planet, including over 700 'rare medicinal herbs' (not surprising, since it seems to me that Chinese find a medicinal use for anything edible, and for quite a few things that are not).

Tenfu Tea Depot and Museum.

When you see a mammoth teapot sitting on top of a hill south of Zhangzhou, don't worry! You're not going to pot. You're just getting close to a delightful oasis of tea. Tenfu Tea Depot has one of the best tea shops in the province—and the largest tea museum on the planet.

The museum, which enlightens tourists on tea's thousands of years of development, covers 80 mu. And no, "mu" is not the sound made by Changtai Chinese cows. It's a Chinese unit of measurement that Chinese persist in using in English material, even though no English dictionary says what it means. For the record, one mu is about 1/15th of a hectare (a hectare is about 2.471 acres).

If Tenfu starts pricing tea in taels (another ancient unit that Chinese persist in pawning off on Laowai), I'm boycotting the place.

The museum's 8,000 square meters of floor space is divided into four areas: Main Exhibition Hall, Tea Ceremony Classroom, Tianfu Painting and Calligraphy Hall, and Japanese Tea Ceremony Hall. The site also includes, I am told, ten major scenic spots, including "drinking vessels flowing on winding crook." Figure it out.

Address: Tianfu Museum Co. Ltd. Zhangzhou City, Zhangpu Industrial Dist. 天福茶博物院有限公司），漳州市漳浦县盘陀工业区　Postal Code: 350108
Phone: (0591) 288-2305　　Email: tenfu@mail.tenfu.com

Dongshan Island

is Fujian Province's Hawaii, with miles of beautiful beaches, and some of Fujian's best and cheapest seafood. It also has a rich history.

Supposedly, the last Ming emperor had a palace just offshore, and when he was killed by the Mongols on Hainan Island (the southernmost part of China, near Vietnam), the palace mysteriously sunk into the sea. Tongshan town has a large statue of the last Prime Minister of the Ming Dynasty. He was so mischievous as a child that his father put him on an island just offshore, where he lived and studied in a cave. It must have worked. I'm considering trying the same thing with my two sons.

Zhangzhou Seafood!

Copper Mountain Castle （铜山古城）and Guandian Temple are Dongshan's big attractions. I especially enjoyed the big crack in a rock, with an inscription below that proclaimed, "On May 31st, 1992, at 3:32 p.m., the rock cracked, smoke poured forth like a stone monkey, and an 80-pound python emerged."

A stone monkey of smoke? Sounds to me like someone was stoned[10] on some funny smoke![11]

There was also a Wind Rocking Stone, but we couldn't budge it even when we lay on our backs and pushed with our feet. Perhaps we could have used a few strong German sailors (Xiamen had a fine wind rocking stone until 1908, when German sailors teamed up and pushed it down the mountain).

Laonei （老内）Notes

[1] Bob Dylan: in the 60s, America's peace-loving hippies were called 'flower children,' and folk singer Bob Dylan became famous for his song, "Blowin' in the Wind." ("...the answer my friend, is blowin' in the wind...")

[2] More plants than the FBI: 'plant' could also mean 'microphone'

[3] Heyday: period of greatest success or popularity; prime

[4] Man of the cloth: minister, clergyman

[5] Belabor: discuss repeatedly or at length

[6] Stele: upright inscribed or sculptured commemorative stone tablet

[7] Flipped: turned over (the kayak turned over); to react strongly, or go crazy (slang)

[8] Flip out: go crazy (slang)

[9] Take a hike: get lost; get out of here; go away (slang)

[10] Stoned: intoxicated or drugged, usually from a substance like marijuana or opium

[11] Funny smoke: marijuana smoke

Chapter 12
Hakka Roundhouses

I have visited the down-to-earth, well-rounded folks in the earthen round houses at least two dozen times. While I prefer touring the castles that Hakka still dwell in, the official tourist traps also have their advantages. English speaking guides can explain the unique architecture, customs, history, deng deng. You can also spend the night in a roundhouse, and enjoy the local cuisine.

My favorite itinerary is to take the mountain road to Nanjing's roundhouses, then go on over the mountains to Yongding's tourist area, and return on the Longyan-Xiamen highway. It can be done in one killer 16 hour day, but the best bet is to spend the night (in a roundhouse, or nearby guesthouse).

Roundhouses supposedly were built in the round to keep out bandits, warlords and traveling salesmen, but I suspect the circular design is to prevent wives from getting their husbands in a corner. Though maybe the women are finally squaring off[1] with their elusive husbands. Nowadays, only 360 roundhouses are round, while 4,000 roundhouses are square.

Some of the square dwellings in Northern Fujian are over 1,000 years old (but don't look a day over 950).

Earthen fortresses house extended Hakka families up into the 100s. These massive structures are rammed into shape layer by layer, using an esoteric[2] mixture of raw earth, sand, lime, glutinous rice and brown sugar, all reinforced by "bones" of wood and bamboo.

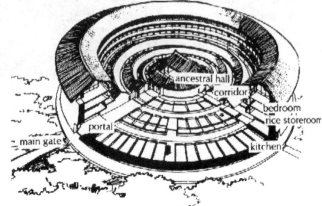

Roundhouses are generally 3 story affairs, with first floor for cooking, second for storing grains and grannies and grandpas, and third floor living quarters for the spryer younger folk.

As added protection from bandits, traveling salesmen, and Mormon missionaries, only the third floor has external windows.

All roundhouses boast a large courtyard in the middle where families socialize, work,

or eat, and usually have a well. All they need is a basketball court.

Archaeologists the world over have studied this unique Hakka architecture, and the culture behind it. Earthen architecture is relatively inexpensive, very durable, low maintenance, ecologically clean, aesthetically pleasing, and acoustically and thermally insulated. All in all, its no wonder Hobbits[3] like to live in holes.

The Pentagon

folks were sure shocked when roundhouses showed up on their satellite photographs! From space, they looked just like missile silos.

I asked one

B.B.

roundhouse dweller if the satellite dish on the roof was for their missile guidance system. He was shocked. "No! It's for television! We don't—"

"—I'm just joking!"

I guess that joke bombed.[4]

Hakka Earthen Castles

Zhengcheng Bldg.

Qingyun Bldg.

Guangyu Bldg.

Kuiju Bldg.

Shengheng Bldg.

"Well rounded, and down-to-earth folks!"

Yanglin Bldg.

Chaoyang Bldg.

Qingfu Bldg.

Lin Clan Ancestral Temple

Qingcheng Bldg. (Museum)

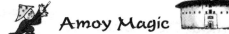
Prosperity Castle (福兴楼 Fuxing Lou), by far my favorite, was built in 1963 by the Xiao (肖) Clan. I asked them what it cost to build this magnificent three story castle and they said "Nothing! The earth and wood were all local. It just took a lot of labor." A lot of love, too, I could tell, judging from the care that had been spent on the fine wood doors, windows, and railings.

I like Prosperity Castle because it is a 'real' roundhouse, lived in by an extended family that greets foreign devils who show up unannounced with hearty laughter, smiles, and "Have some tea!"

I've packed Toy Ota with my MBA students probably a dozen times, and visited Prosperity Castle at least a dozen times, and even filmed a documentary of the place, because most Chinese have never seen these marvelous buildings either, and are as fascinated as we are. If you too visit the Xiao Clan, take a generous bag of sweets for the beautiful children! They'll of course politely refuse, so give it to the granny, who will pocket a bit to gum to death later, and distribute the rest to the kids.

Hanker[5] for more Hakka lore? Then make your way west to Changting, the "Little Red Shanghai," and to Shibi Village near the Jiangxi border, but before you do, pick up a copy of my "Fujian Adventure," still available at less discerning bookstores everywhere!

And now... on to Longyan and the X-rated[6] mountains of Liancheng!

Laonei (老内) Notes

[1] Square off: face each other for a challenge, dual, fight
[2] Esoteric: something unusual, understood only by a small group of people
[3] Hobbits: small people in J.R.R. Tolkien's classic "The Hobbit," and "The Lord of the Rings" trilogy. They lived in very nicely decorated holes (very much like the so-called cave dwellers of China's Shaanxi province).
[4] Bombed: fail miserably
[5] Hanker: strong, often restless desire (synonym for *yearn*)
[6] X-rated: sexually explicit content not suitable for children (you'll see why after you visit Guanzai mountain!)

Chapter 13
Longyan (Dragon Crag)

Longyan (龙岩), in Southwest Fujian, is where Mao began his Long March (followed by his Short April[1], which I explain in the footnotes, if I May).

West Fujian covers an area of over 19,000 square kilometers, and has a population of over 2.5 million. This enchanting corner of our province is home to over 200,000 Overseas Chinese, and boasts primordial mountains and forests, and rivers flowing through valleys planted in rich crops and fruits.

Amoy Tigers may have vanished from Amoy, but you can still find them in the Meihua Nature Preserve—a biological wonderland with over 1500 kinds of plants, and hundreds of insects and animals, including leopards, black bears and the Amoy Tiger, thanks to a 17.6 million USD tiger preservation project. Officials hope that the six protected tigers will have bred and expanded to 100 tigers by the year 2,010. That's a lot of breeding, but they're off to a good start. On July 20, 2001, Yuanyuan and Xiongxiong gave birth to Zhongzhong and Qiuqiu. Only 92 92 to to go go. To learn more, or to make contributions, visit,
http://www.savechinastigers.org/sct-adopt.htm

Longyan is a geological gold mine, boasting South China's largest deposit of iron, as well as gold, manganese, tungsten, and deng deng.

In addition to mining and agriculture (tobacco is the biggest crop, fertilized by lots of dung dung[2]), West Fujian is into electronics, metallurgy, machinery, forestry, building materials, chemicals, textiles, food, and light industries. The area exports handmade paper, rabbit fur, pepper, dried mushrooms, smoked plums, and peanuts. But the big claim to fame is Wuping County's dried pig gallbladder. The brochure claims,

> "Dried pig gallbladder contains various carbohydrates and vitamins, especially it is the best gift and delicious dish to be given or to entertain guests and friends with."

It would take a lot of gall[3] to dish that out to friends, but if you've the guts[4], go for it.

The **Chengang Wine** (沉缸酒) **Factory,** established in 1957 in Longyan, just off the 319 Highway, is well worth a visit. I've toured the place thrice, and while the speeches can be murder by monologue, the factory tour is fascinating. The Apostle Paul may have meant Chengang Wine when he urged young Timothy[5] to no longer drink water but take a little wine for his stomach's sake. The 200-year-old recipe for Chengang Wine has 31 Chinese medicines that cure anything that ails you, and a few things that don't.

The 500 employees and 96 technicians put out 10,000 tons of the sweet yellow wine each year. Address: #78 Shuangquan Rd., Xinluo District, Longyan. Phone: (0597)221-1222.

Gutian School

Gutian (古田), lies just north of Longyan city. Mao held his 1929 congress in a small school here (which is why we call Maoism a "school" of thought). Have friends photograph you behind Mao's old table-cum-desk, with ancient tattered posters of Lenin and Marx hanging in the background. To really capture the spirit of the era and place (it was in this area that Mao wrote *A single spark can start a prairie fire*), read this pulse-pounding paragraph from the official brochure!

> "Nowadays, step into Minxi this sacred land, tracing the footprint of revolution herald, and we still can feel the warm of kindling which set the prairie of ablaze and touch the pulse of revolution struggle which was blistering the heaven, boiling the mountains, and shaking heaven and earth and taste indeed that the revolution leader and the herald they rushed around, searched about and conquered numerous difficulties and endured all kinds of hardships and die for nations and natives with a generosity."

Well, I'm sold![6]

Yongfu Village of Flowers (永福) in Zhangping (漳平) County, at an elevation of 755 meters, is *the* place to feast your eyes on exotic orchids and your nose on camellia, and tantalize your taste buds with local teas and samples of the excellent pears, oranges, kumquats and tangerines. Try to arrange a visit during the annual Flower Fair, which is held on the 6th day of the first month of the Chinese New Year. Also check out their bamboo hats, rattan furniture, and unique paper cuts, and historical sites like Liuxiu Tower and Changqing Castle.

LianCheng （连城） resembles North Fujian's whimsical Wuyishan mountains but it is much closer — a mere hour north of Longyan (though with Fujian's new roads, even Wuyi is no longer that far away—a 9 hour drive today, compared to 35 hours in 1993!).

While Liancheng town is like many other modern Chinese towns (concrete cubism coated in bathroom tiles), the scenery is absolutely breathtaking. I thought ancient Chinese artists were high or drunk when they painted their surrealistic mountains rising through mists, but not so. Liancheng really looks like the paintings.

Root of Life
生命之根

Roots 'n Doors? That's Life!

Rental boats tour the 5 km Shimen Lake below Mount Lianfeng (Lotus Peak), cruising past strange jutting peaks and narrow clefts that bear an uncanny resemblance to various private parts of the human anatomy. Locals, of course, caught on real quick, and gave them names that leave little to the imagination. The brochure writes about the "Root of life" peak, and the tall narrow cave, "Door of Life":

> "Root of life （生命之根） about 60m high... and Life's Door （生命之门） of Shimen Lake are standing and facing each other, which can be rated as superb scenes of Guanzai scenic spot."

I suggest a **Liancheng Birds 'n Bees[7] Exhibit.** Better yet—put the whole place off limits at least until China's population problem is resolved.

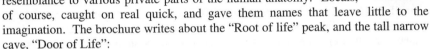

Sibao Printing. Liancheng was also one of the four great printing centers of ancient China, thanks to forests of camphor (to carve the printing blocks), pine (burned to produce soot for the ink), wild animal fur for brushes, and bamboo to produce the fine snow-white paper for which the area is still famous even today.

Bamboo Fujian's famous Anxi tea has figured in everything from the Mad Hatter's Tea Party to that even madder Tea Party in Boston, but the big money maker for Fujian folk, especially in Western Fujian, has been not tea but humble bamboo.

Bamboo is not a tree but a species of gigantic and graceful grass, and is so indispensable that Chinese artists portray it more frequently than anything else. As an ancient Chinese poet opined, "Better to live without meat than without bamboo."

Chinese ascribe to bamboo the attributes of a superman — chastity, honesty, gentleness, humbleness. The bamboo is strong,

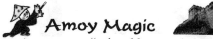

yet hollow and empty, even as "a humble man is not filled with his own importance".

Chinese claimed that bamboo is used to make a thousand products, and I believe it. A brief list includes: shirts, shoes, chairs, tables, dishes, shelves, scaffolds, bridge piers, houses, pens, hats, rakes, chairs, tables, stools, beds, musical instruments, dippers, pipes to blow the fire, strainers, steamers, chopsticks, kettle cleaners, dust pans, brooms, drain pipes, handles, smoking pipes, back scratchers (which Chinese aptly dub, "not call man"), pig baskets, cradles, toys, fences, gates, rope, screens, flour mills, hen coops, bird cages, tally sticks, lanterns, knitting needles, curtains, and umbrellas. To top it off, bamboo shoots, whether stir-fried or pickled, are delicacies of the first order. And finally, no plant panders to a panda's palate better than bamboo. (Now say that last line 3 times fast)

BAMBOO PAPER ... is treasured by artists because it is soft, absorbent, and snow white. The bamboo is felled in August and chopped into small chunks, and workers sing while rhythmically pounding it to pieces. They soak the pieces in a lime pond for half a month before removing and cleaning them, and boiling them for a week. Then more pounding and singing, after which the fibers are washed, and stirred to a pulp.

The most exacting of the 72 steps in bamboo papermaking is scooping the pulp onto a bamboo screen held by two people, who swing carefully, expertly, to spread the pulp out evenly. When the pulp has dried, they cut it into squares of smooth, white paper — provided that no one has cursed it with a slip of the tongue.

There are many superstitious customs associated with papermaking. Workers are fed white tofu so the paper will also be white. It is forbidden to speak the word "black" or "protrusion," lest the paper become spotted, or not be smooth. And papermakers cover their bases by worshipping Cai Lun, the legendary creator of paper and tutelary god of papermakers. Before Cai Lun came along, scholars wrote on tortoise shells, bones and metal, and later moved on to bamboo slips and wooden tablets. Silk was also used, but it was too dear for any but the Emperor. Eventually, Cai Lun discovered how to make paper from a pulp of hemp, bits of rope, rags and old fishing nets, and he has been worshipped ever since by papermakers and the bureaucratic devotees of the cult of triplication.

If you're sold on paper, buy some in Liancheng. This city's Xuan paper is, according to their report, "the best paper for calligraphy and drawing and it is an elegant gift for noted public figures".

Changting "Little Red Shanghai"

Changting

"China's two most beautiful small cities are Fenghuang in Henan and Changting in Fujian."
Rewi Alley

I could not agree more with Mr. Alley! And to think—I did not even mention Changting in the first issues of Amoy Magic! (But I gave the delightful little town 25 pages in *The Fujian Adventure*)

Just a couple of hours northwest of Longyan, on the Jiangxi Province border, Changting straddles the Ting River, mother river of the Hakka people. "Hakka" means "Guest People". They call themselves this because over 1,000 years ago they fled to Southern China from the central plains and settled down as "guests". Personally, I think that after 1,000+ years they'd drop the "guest" bit. I've had people wear out their welcome after a week, much less a millennium.

Hakka (architects of the earthen round houses), are a unique and headstrong people, but quick to point out that they are not a minority but bona fide[8]Han Chinese. They take **B.B.** great pains to trace their ancestry back dozens of generations, and in the town of Shibi (just north of Changting, in Sanming), the Hakka Ancestral Temple has thousands of records of lineages. When I visited Shibi, one fellow excitedly pointed out the ancestral records for my adopted name of Pan. He was shocked when the tour guide explained to him that I was a foreigner, not a real Pan (though he reluctantly admitted that my blond hair and blue eyes had aroused his suspicions).

Changting's attraction is three-fold: people, places, and fine Hakka Cuisine. While all Chinese are hospitable, greeting you with a "You're here! Come in and have some tea," Changting folk bend over backwards[9] to make you feel at home.

My host, the award-winning photographer Hu Xiaogang (胡 晓 钢 , nicknamed "Babushka" because he came from N.E. China and was blond as a child), led me right into people's homes without so much as a knock or how do you do.   Babushka said, "They don't mind. Their doors are open."

I learned that this was true in every sense of the word.

They served us tea, and showed us about the centuries old homes.   It seemed every family had a side business—making matches, or candles, or miniature paper umbrellas, or wooden handled brushes. No wonder their

Babushka and Family

overseas Hakka relatives are so successful. They are entrepreneurs of the first order.

They are also fine cooks!   Hakka food is some of the best I've had, and Changting's cuisine has won many a national award.   There is even a Chinese cookbook devoted entirely to Changting specialties, which include the mouth watering Hetian chicken.   I've had so-called Hetian chicken in many other places, but never anything to match what they serve up in Changting.

Changting sites are endless, ranging from the natural beauty at the mouth of the Ting River to the delightful walled Hakka villages like Tufang (about an hour southeast of the city). Here are some of my favorites:

Tingzhou Hakka Museum (汀洲客家博物馆) has Hakka exhibits in the hall on the left, revolutionary exhibits in the right hall, and the building in the back of the garden is the former revolutionary headquarters. All fascinating, but no Chinese subtitles below displays, so you'll need a guide, like the lovely Miss Hong who led me about. Changting people (like every one else in Fujian) boast the prettiest girls in the province, and the museum's Miss Hong was a runner up in a national beauty contest.

The pair of trees in the central courtyard, by the way, are 1,000 years old.

South Avenue (南大街) is a delightful old street with many old homes, and a restored Tang Dynasty gate and pavilion (三元阁 Sanyuan Ge) at the entrance. For a great look at yesteryear, check out the home at #105 South Street (and have them show you the loft where beautiful young Hakka maids were kept until they were married).

Carpenter Alley (唐宋古街) When I was in the U.S. Air Force in Taiwan, one of my favourite pastimes was to visit the woodcarving village. I spent a small fortune on furniture and carvings, most of which I sent home to my parents and sister. Alas, it is not so easy, for some reason, to find such bargains in the mainland, but I was happy to learn that Changting (and Xianyou, near Putian on the coast) has plenty of woodcarvers. As I talked to one craftsman, I learned why they are hard to find. The work is hard, the pay is relatively poor. He told me that he enjoyed the art, that it was more like a hobby than a job—but his son

had already left home to find better employ in Guangdong province, leaving his father behind to lumber along in the wood business.

Hakka Mother (客家母亲) Carpenter Alley ends

near the river; the statue in a small park across the river is the Hakka Mother, erected in 1995. Hakka never adopted foot binding, preferring instead the strong robust women who were as capable in the fields as in the home. It was the strength of Hakka women that made it possible for so many of the men to seek, and find, their fortunes abroad, and today, Hakka from all over the world return to West Fujian every October 28th to pay homage to the Hakka Mother.

Southern Meditation Temple (南 禅 寺

Nanchan Si)   Local Buddhists levelled an entire mountain to prepare the perfect fengshui for this mammoth temple complex. When completed in 2,010, this 50 million Yuan complex will be the largest in Jiangxi, Fujian and Guangdong provinces.

Three temples, on three different levels, each have their own idol, including a large Buddha carved from pure white jade. (We foreigners usually think of jade as green, but in fact it comes in many colors.)

The Buddhist Abbess asked me if Xiamen University had a religion department, and if I had interest in helping to start one. Given that Xiamen has China's oldest Protestant Church, and that Quanzhou is UNESCO's World Museum of Religion—maybe I should pass the plate for a collection!

B.B.

B.B.

Changting has a Confucian temple that, according to locals, has been miraculously free of cobwebs since it was built in 1133 A.D.. The city also has a massive temple complex for Mazu, goddess of the sea. The rationale for landlocked Changting folk to worship Mazu is that, until this century,

Miss Mazu's Boudoir

the Ting River was the only means of transportation. Like other Mazu temples, this Tianhou Palace has a beautiful apartment for the young goddess, complete with an ornate boudoir [10] and a dining room table with a vegetarian meal set for five.

Church of the Revolution

The London Missionary Society opened the Gospel Hospital (福音医院) on East Gate St. (东门街, Dongmen Jie) in 1908. In 1925 it became the Red Army hospital, and a foreign missionary doctor became a local hero because of his support of the Communist party—and became he delivered one Mao's sons. The church was, for a short period, 折 revolutionary headquarters, and Zhou Enlai had his office and bedroom in a small room upstairs in back. It's quite sobering to walk through the old rooms, which are now warehouses, and realize the historical of the meetings held in this little church 70 years ago. The elderly ladies who live in an apartment to the left of the church are delighted to have visitors and will happily show you around.

Hakka Hamlet of Tufang (涂坊)

I was delighted to learn that the model of a Hakka walled village in the Hakka Museum was based on a real village only an hour's drive East of Changting, so Babushka and I saddled up Toy Ota and we headed to Tufang village. I felt like I was blazing new trails for Laowai until Tufang's headman told me that an American businessman had opened a factory there. It turned out to be Bill Job—resident of Xiamen since 1987! (Ironically, Bill had invited me to visit his factory that day, but I had planned a trip to Changting, and so declined.)

Changting is more isolated and less populated than Yongding, so the Hakka did not need to build three story fortresses. Many villages are only one story high, and some are only partially enclosed (giving rise to the name "cow horn village").

Bill Job

I was surprised when Babushka had me stop at the Chuanxinzou Stables farmstead, (穿心走马楼) in Yang KengCun Hamlet (洋坑村). The photographer had discovered, only recently, that the walls inside the deserted buildings were covered with revolutionary slogans and political cartoons from the 20s or 30s. "These should be in museums!" he complained. "Vandals are destroying them and soon they'll be gone."

Chuanxinzou Stables

I tried to take photos, but it was too dim and I had no flash. I hope they're still there next time I visit. Or maybe I can get Bill Job to take photos, provided he knows how to use a camera. He and his wife Kitty are from Tennessee, so you never know… (That's why he went into business instead of teaching at Xiamen University. Just imagine Chinese students trying to speak English like they do in Tennessee!).

Hakka Hamlet of Tufang

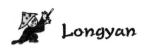
Other Changting Sites....

Xiamen University's Former Campus (厦门大学校本部旧址) When the Sino-Japanese war during the 30s and 40s, Xiamen University hid out in Changting for 8 years. (This is when the lady at the Protestant church moved to Changting).

Xiamen University Former Campus

Tingzhou Hakka Research Institute (中国汀洲客家研究中心 Zhongguo Tingzhou Kejia Yanjiu Zhongxin)

Tingzhou Ancient City Wall (汀洲古城墙 Tingzhou Gucheng Qiang) Tang Dynasty, at least 1200 years old.

Dragon Hill against White Clouds (龙山白云—Longshan Baiyun) – the Jin Sha Temple.

Zhongshan Park and the Qiu Bai Pavilion (秋白亭 Qiubai Ting). Every two-ox town in China has a Zhongshan Park (named after Sun Yat-sen, but called Lenin Park during the Soviet Chinese days). The Qiu Bai Pavilion is named after Qiu Bai, the young revolutionary martyr. To the rear of the Hakka Museum you can see where he was imprisoned, and where he was shot.

Hakka Girls. They're everywhere. But I didn't look *that* close, Susan Marie!

Ancient Well (老古井 Laogu Jing) Changting's oldest well, considered a miracle because it never dries up, whatever the conditions. On top of that, while Mao ZeDong lived in Changting, every morning he used the well to wash his face, brush his teeth, and clean his clothes (not necessarily in that order). And to make the well healthier, he brought in a well specialist, which I thought was a well-meaning gesture.

Chaodou Rock's Shuiyun Temple. The Buddha is said to have his back to tourists because he's piqued that so few people repent and begin life anew.

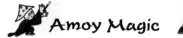
Goodbye Little Red Shanghai. There's so much to see in Changting, I could easily spend a month there. The covered wooden bridges, for one thing, or the site of the ancient dragon kiln, or the hot springs of Hetian (home of the delectable Hetian chicken). Give them a visit—and drop in on my old friend Babushka, and his wife and daughter.

And now… on to our Provincial capital, Fuzhou!

Laonei (老内) Notes

---

[1] Long March, Short April: the month of March, with 31 days, is 'long'; April, with only 30 days, is 'short.'

[2] Dung: animal manure (sounds the same as deng, for 等等)

[3] Take a lot of gall: nerve, boldness, outrageous insolence, effrontery, temerity

[4] Guts: intestines; courage, audacity (slang)

[5] Take wine for stomach's sake: The Bible, 1 Tim. 5:23 (圣经，提摩太前书, 5: 23 因你胃口不清，屡次患病，再不要照常喝水，可以稍微用点酒。)

[6] I'm sold: I'm convinced

[7] Birds 'n bees: euphemism for sex, propagation

[8] Bona fide: genuine, authentic (地道的)

[9] Bend over backwards: make great effort，exert oneself to the fullest

[10] Boudoir: a women's private bedroom, sitting room or dressing room

Chapter 14
Fuzhou

Fuzhou (福州) Fujian's capital since ancient times, Fuzhou used to be called Rongcheng because of the banyan trees planted all over the city during the Song Dynasty (960-1279). The scholar Zhang Boyu (张伯玉) started the trend by planting two banyans in front of the government building and encouraging others to do the same. Within decades the practice was firmly rooted and by the time Marco Polo showed up a few centuries later, the whole city was up a tree[1]—but a good tree. Banyans are known as "Fengshui trees" because they supposedly only grow where the Fengshui is good.

Fuzhou was settled by Neolithic folks about 5,015 years ago, and in the year 202 A.D. the city was named Yecheng (Smelting City). In 725 it was rechristened Fuzhou because someone said a mountain on the outskirts resembled 福 (Fu), the Chinese character for happiness. Personally, I've not seen any Fu-shaped mountains, and I suspect the real name of the mountain's discoverer was Fuling Yu.[2]

Fuzhou lies at the mouth of the mighty Min River, which has a greater flow than the Yangtze itself, and has wrecked many a ship, both Chinese and Western. In spite of the Min (or because of it), Fuzhou has been an important seaport for over 2,000 years, and a mere 1000 years ago (yesterday by Chinese standards) the Fu Ship, with its tall masts and powerful weapons, was one of the most advanced in the world.

Throughout the Ming Dynasty (1368-1644), Fuzhou was a center of commerce with Southeast Asian countries, and shared with Xiamen the dubious honor of becoming one of China's 5 treaty ports after the humiliating defeat in the first Opium War. It was from Fuzhou that majestic tea clippers like the Ariel and Cutty Sark sailed to New York and London.

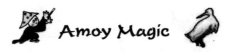

Pagoda Island (now Mawei, just east of Fuzhou) was China's great producer of ships for 2,000 years—right up until the 20th century.

Remote Pagoda Island was considered a harsh posting for Western consulate officials. Quite a few went crazy during their terms of office there. And I could see why. When I visited there wasn't a cheeseburger or pizza place in sight.

Fuzhou, and all of Fujian Province, were China's showcases for trade — until the 1950s. Then the entire province was transformed into a frontline defense against Taiwan. By the mid 70s, once prosperous Fujian was ranked as almost the poorest province in China (23 out of 29). It was a bitter pill to swallow, but they've swallowed worse medicine before and made a comeback. Over the past 20 years, Fujian has had an annual growth in GDP of 13.7%, and now ranks 11th, up from 23rd (GDP per capita is 6th, and import/export volume is 4th!).

By the end of 1998, 24,800 foreign-funded enterprises, with an investment of USD 54.6 billion, had been approved, and for the past 5 years, Fujian's foreign capital input has amounted to 10% of the country's total.

Fujian's fast recovery is not surprising. With 2,000 years of foreign trade behind them, Fuzhou folk are well known for both their risk-taking entrepreneurial spirit and their appreciation of traditional culture and values, which helps explain Fujian's present prosperity, and her determination to modernize without losing the charm of her ancient traditional architecture.

The "3 lanes & 7 alleys" (San Fang, Qi Xiang) section of Fuzhou retains many ancient homes, with whitewashed walls and greenish blue tiled roofs dating from the Ming and Qing Dynasties. I visited the home of Opium commissioner Lin Zexu's mother, and the home of the last emperor's tutor. Behind the plain walls, the homes and courtyards are a maze. Paper lanterns hanging from eves add to the charm, especially on hot summer evenings when old folk lounge about drinking tea and playing Chinese chess—and young folk scan newspaper ads for suitable spouses.

Meet Your Match? [3] While the traditional matchmaker still plays a role in China, Fuzhou also boasts a matchmaking center where shy souls (like myself) can read or write ads. One famous matchmaker's book on writing marriage advertisements became a top seller in China and overseas. Increased trade has also led to "Taiwan Straits Mandarin Ducks" as hundreds of Chinese from both Fujian and Taiwan have tied the knot.

Popular Fuzhou Tourist Spots

West Lake (西湖) Tourists have been enamored of picturesque West Lake's islets, pavilions, and towers since the Tang Dynasty (618-907), though its history goes back to the year 282 A.D, when Governor Yan Gao had the lake dug as an irrigation project. Over 700 years later, Wang Sheng zhi's second son built a royal park near the lake and dubbed it the Crystal Palace (probably influenced by a Buddhist Robert Schuller).

Popular attractions include the Guizhai Study (where the patriot Lin Zexu once burned the midnight oil), the Tang Dynasty Kaihua Temple, the Ming Dynasty Wanzai Hall, a museum, a flower garden, a zoo, and clean W.C.s. Also check out the Panda exhibition!

Gushan Mountain (鼓山) to the east of Fuzhou towers 900 meters above sea level (at high tide or low tide?). Gushan (Drum Mountain) is named after a drum shaped rock on the summit (though some say the name comes from the caves, which echo like drumbeats when storms whip the mountainsides).

Of Gushan's over 160 scenic spots, the most popular is the 1,100-year-old Yongquan Temple. Considered Fujian's most important temple, it has an extensive library of Buddhist scriptures. Take a gander at the various halls and towers, the Sutra Library (including some written in human blood), the ancient two-ton "Scripture Bell", (named after the 6,372 characters of Buddhist scriptures cast on the surface), and the copper pot that supposedly can be used to prepare meals for 1,000 people. Frequent buses run from downtown Fujian to Gushan. The statue on the highway below, by the way, is of the great philosopher and translator, Yan Fu 严复.

Min Lord Hall (闽王祠) was the residence of Wang Shengzhi (862-925 A.D.). Wang came to Fujian as a young soldier, and later the Emperor appointed him Min Lord (Lord of Fujian). He transformed Fujian during his 29 years of enlightened rule. He reduced taxes and cut the budget, moderated punishments, instituted water conservation projects, and opened the coastal ports to encourage foreign trade. His most far-reaching move, however, was his emphasis upon education, which earned Fujian the title "Home of Culture".

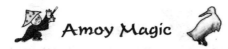
Luoxing Pagoda (罗星塔 "Catch a Star Pagoda") on Luoxing Hill in Mawei (Pagoda Island), has long served as a navigation landmark for laowai and laonei alike. Legend has it that the 31m high pagoda was built by Liu Qiniang, a rare Guangdong beauty whose husband was exiled to Fujian as a slave laborer because she refused the advances of a local despot. After her husband died, she sold the land and property and built the stone tower to beg the gods' blessing upon her husband and to condemn injustice in the world. During the Ming Dynasty, Laowai gave the pagoda the extremely imaginative name, "China Pagoda".

Luoxing Pagoda

Memorial Hall of Majiang River Naval Battle Built in 1884 as The Hall of Loyalty, this museum and memorial commemorates the French attack upon Fuzhou in August 1884. The attack was in retaliation for China's opposition to French actions in Vietnam. The Chinese fleet was destroyed in about half an hour, the shipyard was blasted to pieces, and for days afterwards, the bodies of men, women and children floated down the river. The museum's exhibits are in Chinese, but the photographs and sculptures, and the mass mausoleum containing the bodies of hundreds of Chinese seamen, speak eloquently for themselves.

> "How well I remember reaching Sharp Peak on the 28th day of April, 1887! It was a perfect day and the journey up the river was most fascinating, for it was only three years before this that the French Bombardment had occurred, and there were still evidences of it in the battered forts and derelicts at Pagoda Anchorage. Also to be seen were the graves of the large number of Chinese who lost their lives in that one-sided battle.
> H. Shelley Brand (Fuzhou, January 23rd, 1932)

Mawei shipyard after France's attack

 **Fuzhou**

Kaiyuan Temple （开元寺） Fuzhou, like Quanzhou, has a Kai Yuan Temple—but Fuzhou's is older, built in 548 A.D. . The temple is located in downtown Fuzhou on Jingyuan lane (a back street, not far from the government offices). Kaiyuan has 3 claims to fame. One, it has China's largest cast iron Buddha. The 50-ton 5.3 meter statue was created by wax casting almost 1,000 years ago! Two, Japanese revere Kaiyuan because Kukai, the founder of Japanese Esoteric Buddhism, stayed here before heading north in search of enlightenment. And three, the masters of Kaiyuan's "Fujian Buddhist Association Clinic" have long been reputed to be able to cure anything that ails you. (The association has now moved to #184-1 on the #2 Ring Road).

Iron Buddha

Shizhu Temple （石竹寺）(Stone Bamboo Temple), is on the picturesque Stone Bamboo Mountain, out past the Dongzhang Reservoir. The temple was founded in 847 A.D. in memory of the Taoist He brothers who "cultivated themselves into immortals and saved people from evil forces". The mountain and reservoir are beautiful, and as the Fuzhou tourbook says, "renders a view that will purify one's mind and fill his heart with boundless happiness."

While you're still basking in boundless happiness, head south to Xuefeng.

Xuefeng Temple （雪峰寺）is 77 kilometers from Fuzhou City, in Dahu Village, Minhou County. The temple was built during the Tang Dynasty, in 870 A.D., and is one of Fuzhou's five major temples, and the home of Singapore's Donglian, Xiaozhu, Fahai and Shengquan temples.

Shengshui (Holy Water) **Temple** （圣水寺）sprawls across the Lian Hua (Lotus Flower) Mountain in the south of Luoyuan County, and was built in the third year of Shaosheng's reign in the Song Dynasty (1096 A.D.). It was named after the clear sweet water of the mountain's pond. Tourists enjoy the Xiyun Cave, Brush and Ink Peak, and the stone statue of Guanyin.

Tai Hill Park （台山公园）is on the south side of the Min River, in Mingqing County, and boasts a Tang Dynasty stone pagoda. Wander about the park's 27 wooded acres, and relax by the Plum Stream.

Shengshou Pagoda(圣寿塔) on top of the South Mountain, was built during the Song Dynasty, in 1117 A.D. . The seven story octagonal pagoda is 27.4 meters high, with over 200 Buddhas in various shapes and postures carved into each story. The pagoda is in a park that also has a Memorial Hall to Zhenghe, the famed Chinese navigator who helped provide funds for the restoration of the pagoda back in 1413. This hall's a stone tablet, "the Oration of the Power of Tianfei's Spirit", the only record of Zheng's epic voyage to the west.

Zheng was a great man—but Fuzhou's favorite son was Lin Zexu.

*   *   *   *   *   *   *

Lin Zexu was the great Chinese Commissioner who tried to stop the West's opium trade. After China's humiliating defeat during the first opium war, Lin Zexu was shafted by foreigners and Chinese alike, but today he is hailed as hero and patriot, and I learned why when I played the part of Admiral Elliot in a TV miniseries about the Opium War.

Lin Zexu was born August 30, 1785. His father was a teacher and, like teachers today, poor — but determined that Lin should receive the education in Confucian Classics that would help him pass the Imperial Examinations and land a civil service job. He far exceeded his father's expectations.

Lin passed his initial exams in 1804 and became the Fujian governor's aide. In 1811, he passed the highest of examinations and joined the Hanlin Academy, which

Dr. Bill as Admiral Elliott!
--but binoculars in 1843?

advised the emperor himself. From 1820 on, Lin rose through the ranks of bureaucracy. He began with the salt monopoly and worked his way up through water-control, tax collection, and a term as a judge. His integrity, which earned him the name of "Lin the Clear Sky" , gained him the respect of his colleagues and subjects—and the enmity of the Western powers.

Lin condemned all suggestions to legalize the opium trade, and cited how he had eradicated the trade in the provinces which he controlled. The Chinese emperors had tried for decades to end the traffic, so Lin was appointed imperial commissioner in late 1838.

Lin appealed, in vain, to Western trader's sense of honor and morality, and eventually he confiscated tons of opium and burned it (apologizing to the very sea for polluting it with the drug). Britain declared war on China, attacked and razed defenseless cities up and down the China coast, and the

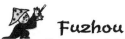
emperor, who had personally commended Lin's tough policies, dismissed him and exiled him to the Northwest, where he continued his loyal service. Eventually he was recalled from exile, but he died in 1850, on his way to help suppress the Taiping Rebellion. He has been hailed as a hero ever since, even though he utterly failed to halt the West's opium trafficking.

*   *   *   *   *   *   *

Nantai Island is of special interest for foreigners. The Opium Wars forced Fuzhou open for Laowai, but Laonei didn't want us barbarians living within the city, so they had foreign devils live on Nantai Island, which Chinese didn't want because it was supposedly haunted. Many of the beautiful colonial buildings are now gone. The British consulate was razed to make way for an army officer retirement home, and the adjacent Rotary Club is a shambles.

Old Stone Church Then 'n now

The beautiful Trinity College, modelled after the original in Dublin, was torn down to make way for a typical bathroom tile covered new school (though the Irish Tower still stands in the courtyard, right beside the former Russian consulate). But a few of the old churches still stand, my favourite being the beautiful stone church, which looks like it was transplanted right out of Celtic legend (it is now an army printing press).

The former American Consulate is now the library at a nursing school, and the Navy has taken over the former French Consulate (revenge, at last, for France's humiliating defeat of the Chinese navy in 1884?)

British Consulate (now gone)

Irish Tower (Trinity College)

Fuzhou Foods!

Fuzhou cuisine is a real treat, and not to be missed. Begin your culinary conquest at the Heart of Fuzhou, the East Gate Intersection (Dongjie Kou, 东街口). This is where East Street (东路, Dong Lu) crosses August 17th St (八一七路, Ba Yi Qi Lu). It has a KFC and two McDonalds, but what Chinese intersection doesn't? More importantly, it has the Juchunyuan Hotel (聚春园酒店—right above the KFC on the corner). It was a Juchunyuan chef that wowed judges during a culinary competition in Beijing, and won respect for Fujian Cuisine.

佛跳墙！

An Off the Wall Soup! [4]

Juchunyuan Hotel is where I met the master of Fuzhou's most famous dish, the ancient "**Buddha Jumps the Wall**" soup (佛跳墙). Supposedly, in ancient days some one boiled a lot of ingredients together for a long time to keep them from spoiling, and the aroma was so good that a monk cast his vegetarian scruples to the wind[5] and jumped a wall to get a bowlful.

Today, imitations are common, and even supermarkets sell cheap kits, but the Real McCoy[6] costs upwards of 1,000 Yuan a pot—and is well worth it if you can afford it (which I can't, and since I have more sense than cents, the only time I've jumped the wall is when Uncle Song[7] has picked up the tab). The ingredients, far from being run-of-the-mill things boiled up to keep from spoiling, include choice (and highly expensive) sea foods. I can't even begin to describe how it tastes, but its something you have to try at least once in your life.

Also in the Dongjie Kou area are the Qingjing Mosque (with the Ming Dynasty stele claiming Mohammed sent two disciples to Quanzhou), the Kaiyuan Temple, and the Black Pagoda. And no, it's not your eyes. The Black Pagoda is leaning. I think Pizza Hut should open a branch right below it and call the ancient pagoda the "Leaning Tower of Pizza."[8]

Leaning Tower of Pizza?

Fuzhou Hotels

Fuzhou Lakeside Hotel (福州西湖大酒店)　Henry Kissinger did time here! With 427 rooms and suites, Lakeside is reputedly Fujian's finest Five Star hotel—at least according to the beautiful color brochure which extols Lakeside with lines like, "Heart and eyes are soaked and moistened by the sudden appearance of the lake," and, "Pushing off the window, one can see the lake water and the mountain scene, gentle and quiet like a Chinese painting to make one's heart moistened to the bottom and become a lot of quietness…"

I'm sold. Let Lakeside Hotel moisten your heart to the bottom!

Address: 158 Hubin Road, Fuzhou, Fujian 350003

Phone: 86 (591) 783-9888　Fax: 783-9752

Business center, pool, dance hall (great breakfast buffet); 5 km. from train.

Golden Resources Int'l, a Five Star right downtown, is absolutely incredible (and incredibly expensive, unless Uncle Song or Uncle Sam is paying). It's worth a stay there just to enjoy the food in Macao Street Food Court (try the eggplant!). Address: # 59 Wenquan Gongyuan Rd. (Hot Springs Park Rd.—温泉公园路).

Golden Resources Int'l

Yushan Hotel (玉山宾馆) is one of my favorites.　It's rather plain, but clean, very affordable, and has an unbeatable location -- smack between FJTV station and Gutian Park, within walking distance to downtown.

Address: Gutian Rd, Fuzhou, Fujian, 350001　Phone: 86 (591) 355-1668

Hot Spring Hotel (温泉大酒店) has Chinese and Western restaurants, a pool, a conference room, and a business center.

Address: Wusi Road, Fuzhou, Fujian 350003 Phone: 86 (591) 785-1818

Minjiang Hotel (闽江饭店) Chinese and Western restaurants, conference rooms and business center, hot spring bathrooms, only 3km from train.

Address: Wusi Road, Fuzhou, Fujian 350001　Phone: 86 (591) 755-7895

Yongtai (永泰), just west of Fuzhou an hour or so, was one of Fujian's best kept secrets until Mr. Brian Hodges, manager of Rocky Mountain (Fuzhou) Drug Co. Ltd., spilled the beans![9] When he told us the place was so beautiful that he spent every weekend there, we saddled up Toy Ota and headed to Yongtai the very next day. We've yearned for Yongtai ever since, because in sheer beauty these beautiful mountains, valleys, waterfalls and high mountain meadows give Wuyi Mountain or even Guilin a run for their money.[10]

B.B.

While few Laowai know about Yongtai, it's time we stake our claim on the place—and I don't think I'm biased. Quite a few American college students read my praises of the place in the previous Amoy Magic, spent a weekend there, and came back raving about the natural beauty.

Yongtai has been populated since the Stone Age, and was established as a county in 766 A.D. . The 2241 square km area has over 77 peaks exceeding 1,000 meters, most of them blanketed in lush forests of pine and bamboo that are nurtured by waterfalls that cascade down the rocky cliffs year round. One of my favorites has two streams cascading down each side of a rock. Locals call it (no joking!), "The waterfall of the runny nose."

Runny Nose WaterFall

On the heights of Qingyun mountain are Crater Lake, and the vast "Million-Mu Grassland". And spelunkers will delight in the caves that honeycomb the mountains—all graced with names like "As You Wish It Cave," "White Cloud Cave", "Ever Joy Cave", "Successful Candidate Cave", and "Immortal Beings Cave".

There are at least 13 hot springs in Yongtai, and the city itself has a nice little 3 star hotel that boasts piped in hot spring water in the tubs. Pipes from this spring, which plummet over 400 feet below ground, also serve the mammoth swimming pool, so you can take a dip anytime of the year. Even in mid-winter, they can keep

the pool at 98 degrees.

There should be plenty to do in Yongtai. According to local officials, there are 116 cultural relics and historic sites – modest indeed, given that Quanzhou claims over 2,000 (or 1999, after we axe Yang Amiao's Former Home).

Visit the Yuan Dynasty Mo'ai cliff inscriptions if you're into ancient graffiti, or Fangguang Palace, which is a Buddhist temple built on a cliffside (reminds me of the ancient Indian cliff dwellings in New Mexico).

Locals enjoy the frequent performances of Min Opera, folk dances on stilts, dragon dances and lion dances, dragon boat races, and wushu (martial arts) exhibitions. Yongtai is considered one of the hometowns of Chinese martial arts, with over 30 wushu stadiums and 60,000 wushu practioners.

Yongtai appeals to businessmen as well as tourists. The county is rich in resources, from gold, silver and copper to peat, pearlite and pyrophyllite (whatever that is!). Over 30 foreign enterprises have gone into production in agricultural products, clothing, machinery, tourism, deng deng.

Yongtai has much to see and do. It is also the perfect place to do absolutely nothing, so plan on 3 or 4 days there.

The newest hotel is the Electrical Hotel, right downtown (of course, the whole town is within a block or two of downtown), but you might also want to try the Hot Spring Hotel. Or better yet, stay in the Bai Ma (White Horse) Mountain Villa, about half an hour South of Yongtai. Their beautifully appointed rooms will set you back less than 200 Yuan a night. (Info below).

If you tire of Chinese food (it does happen), Yongtai has several nice little bakeries, as well as the delightful (and cheap) "Candor Fire Chicken" . Right outside the hot spring swimming pool, it serves up great chicken burgers, fries, and chocolate mint ice cream.

Friendly crowds surround young Laowai

After dinner, stroll about the town and meet some of the locals. They've seen few Laowai, so of course they'll surround you every time you pause for a breath, or sit down—but they're kind, friendly souls, and bound to invite you home for tea!

One of the shops had a great selection of fireworks, and we bought enough to bomb the Taiwan military out of Jinmen island and set them off on the mountain side overlooking the town. I'd have had to sold my firstborn to have afforded such a display in America!

While you're in the neighbourhood, drop by the "Handicraft Company" (工 艺产品), on the north of town, just down from the bowling alley. They churn out beautiful wooden products for gardeners (antique-look half-barrel planters, for example). Most products are exported to Japan, but they could always use some more markets. But for an even better selection of fine wooden products and furniture, visit Xianyou (next chapter!).

YongTai Hotels

Hot Springs Hotel (天宇温泉酒店)   Downtown location, right next door to the hot springs swimming pool and the renowned Candor Fire Chicken!

Phone: 86 (591) 485-1548 Pager: 192 553-3588, or 139 050-21939

White Horse Villa.   These beautiful rooms set right in Yongtai's mountains are quite reasonable, and range from 180 for singles and doubles to 210 for triples. For reservations, phone 86 (591) 450-1148, 332-0922, or 1375096259.

Supplement
Love of Lacquer!

The Chinese character for lacquer (Qi 漆)
tells a story. The left three strokes and the
bottom right signify 'liquid', and the top right
(mu 木) means "tree." Lacquer, for all its
beauty, is simply glorified sap.

Archaeologists claim that Chinese
discovered the sap in varnish trees as early as 7,000 years ago (7,012 by now),
and began using it to create the beautiful and durable lacquer products that are
still valued even today. In 1955, several lacquer-painted pieces of pottery were
unearthed in Jiangsu Province's Tuanjie Village and Meiyan Township. They
dated from the Neolithic Age, when Chinese used lacquer to coat bowls,
ornaments and sacrificial implements. Between the 8th and 3rd centuries B.C.,
lacquer techniques made a quantum leap forward, and overnight lacquer became
the rage among the upper-class who demanded lacquer writing pens, furniture,
funerary articles, musical instruments, bowls and cups—even lacquer sedans for
traveling. These lacquer creations were ornamented with paintings of dragons
and birds, phoenixes and snakes, hunting and gardening scenes, as well as scenes
of court life, nightlife, and karaoke. (Just kidding—no karaoke). Before some
Chinese bureaucrat with a penchant for paperwork invented ink, they even used
lacquer for writing.

Lacquer techniques continued to advance from the 8th century B.C. until the
3rd century A.D., but in the 18th century we Laowai did a number on the lacquer
industry by introducing oil-based paints to China. Oil paints were cheaper than
lacquer, and easier and cheaper to apply, and quickly supplanted the use of
Chinese lacquer on daily utensils. Today, the use of chemical-based paints far
exceeds that of lacquer—though lacquer seems to be making a comeback now
because 1), it is beautiful, and 2), it outlasts any modern paints. Lacquer is
moisture-proof, retains its color and luster, and resists heat, acid, alkali and angry
pot-smashing housewives. It lasts for hundreds of years, whereas oil and
chemical based paints deteriorate in decades (which is long enough for me, but
not for Chinese who use the same plates and pots for generations). In addition,
one can apply dozens of coats of lacquer to an object and carve it; paint would
peel right off.

China's primary lacquerware production centers are Beijing, Yangzhou, and
our own provincial capital, Fuzhou, and they all get their lacquer sap primarily
from five provinces—Shanxi, Hubei, Sichuan, Guizhou and Yunnan. A tree
begins producing sap 3 to 5 years after planting, and tree tappers can get the

precious liquid only in June and July, during the early predawn hours before the sun dries the air and stops the flow.

Beijing lacquerware uses a brass or wooden body that is coated with up to several hundred layers of lacquer, which is then carved into landscapes, people, flowers, animals and birds. This layer technique is employed on everything from chairs and tea tables to vases and screens. Emperor Qianlong so loved lacquerware that he was dying to get some: he had his coffin decorated with carved lacquer.

Yangzhou lacquerware is carved with inlaid gems, gold, ivory, and mother of pearl. Exquisite stuff—but it pales beside China's "Three Treasures": Beijing cloisonne, Jingdezhen porcelain, and Fuzhou's famous "bodiless lacquerware".

(For even more bodiless favorites, try watching the stick figure models in Shanghai fashion shows).

Bodiless lacquerware, unlike the bodiless fashion models, has been created for ages in much the same way as modern craftsmen use fiberglass and resin: lacquer and silk are layered around a mold of clay, plastic, or wood, and dried, the body is removed and the piece is polished and embellished. Bodiless lacquerware won gold prizes in World Expos from 1898 to 1936, and Fuzhou artisans continue today to innovate upon and improve this ancient technique.

Other popular lacquer products include Xianyou's lacquer bowls, Yongchun's lacquer baskets, lacquer paintings, and lacquer thread carvings.

Laonei （老内）Notes

[1] Up a tree: in a predicament (as in a cat chased up a tree by a dog)

[2] Fuling Yu: sounds like "fooling you"

[3] Meet your match: can refer to a potential spouse, or to someone who is your equal in some skill or ability ("He met his match when he played chess with Tom").

[4] Off the Wall: unusual, extremely unconventional (slang)

[5] Cast… to the winds: throw away, discard

[6] Real McCoy: genuine, bona fide, the real thing.

[7] Uncle Song: the government (my version of "Uncle Sam" for China)

[8] Leaning Tower of Pizza: sounds like "Leaning Tower of Pisa" (in Italy)

[9] Spilled the beans: divulged a secret

[10] Run for their money: very strong competition

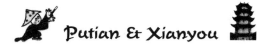

Chapter 15
Putian
and Xianyou

Putian (莆田), the most northern city of Minnan, was settled in 686 A.D.. It is known as "Lichee City" because of the delectable fruit that has given Chinese Emperors more headaches than the apple gave Adam.   During the Thang Dynasty in Chang 'An (the capital near modern Xi'an), an Emperor's concubine demanded fresh Lichees. The desperate monarch, after days of "Not tonight dear, I have a headache", established a relay of the fastest horses and riders between Guangdong, far to the South, and Chang'An. And thus the cantankerous concubine got her just desserts, daily.

Another Emperor's concubine was from Putian, and she too craved lichees, and she too got them fresh, daily—via Imperial Pony Express. thanked his lucky stars that she wasn't from Hui'an. "Not this year, dear…"

Guanghua Temple's 1 km. Wall

But the Emperor probably

Guanghua Temple is probably Putian's biggest attraction.   One of Fujian's largest monasteries, it was built in 558 A.D. and rebuilt in 1875.   This sprawling 16,000 square meter complex's most off the wall feature is a stone wall that is over one kilometer long.

Sakya Buddhist Pagoda, a five-story, 36 meter high pagoda built in 1165, has one of the wildest assortments of carvings you'll ever find— everything from Buddha and his disciples to playful lions.   It looks like its sinking but in fact it is just the build up of soil that has washed down from the hills around it.

Sakya Pagoda

The Venice of China is Putian's quaint little Hanjiang Township, where townfolk navigate their " streets " in small rowboats that just barely fit beneath the ancient granite arched bridges that cross the canals.

Venice of China

With a little imagination, locals could really lure in the honeymooners and tourists with Chinese gondolas!

To the northwest of Putian, perched in the mountains between Xianyou and Yongtai, is **Nine-Carp Falls**, with its picturesque lake, springs, forests—and of course the nine waterfalls. Visiting spelunkers won't have anything to carp about either. Nine-Carp Falls has over 100 caves to explore. Calligraphers enjoy the ancient graffiti engraved on the cliffs and rocks. Even East Los Angeles' spray-can generation can appreciate the latest additions, which are mostly of the "Pan ♥ Hong" variety.

The fastest route to Nine-Carp Falls is the bus from neighboring Xianyou County town. The fastest return trip is to jump.

If you find you've fallen for China's waterfalls, you might also want to visit Yongtai, just 90 minutes drive north of Nine-Carp Falls, or visit the 13 waterfalls of Jiulongji in Fujian's Northeast corner. Although Guizhou's Huang Guo Shu Falls is China's largest single falls, our own Jiulongji's 13 falls make up China's largest falls complex.

I hope this revelation doesn't give the Guizhou folks a complex.

Xianyou （仙游） to the southwest of Putian, is most famous for its magnificent Nine Carp Waterfalls. Why it's always nine dragons, or nine carp[1], I don't know. Chinese have something about the number nine. But I won't carp about it.

We also enjoy Xianyou's many craftsmen, particularly the woodworkers of near and in Arts and Crafts Town.

Founded in 1993 with an investment of over 40 million Yuan, the Town was

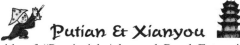

awarded the title of "Provincial Advanced Rural Enterprise in 1995", and won many prizes from the Fujian Forestry department. Marvelous products, great prices. As they write in their brochure,

> "... the Xianyou Arts & Crafts Town actively explores essence of traditional folk technology, traces the tendency of the times, blazes new trails audaciously and leads a solitary excellence...
> "...is now devoting to catch up with the international trend of art and craft with the spirit of constantly improving, being realistic, unity and exertion; to boom the Chinese and craft undertakings."

That's no small undertaking!

The Arts and Crafts center sells exquisite carved mahogany bedroom sets that would give Marie Antoinette the green eyes[2], or wooden friezes, carved water buffalo and deities and ancient heroes.   How about an imposing mahogany and brass grandfather clock?   Or maybe some ceramic Christmas and Halloween figurines, or colorful Grimm's Fairy Tale teakettles, or faux antique brass photo frames? Or what better represents China today than an intricately detailed miniature wooden bicycle, with everything from gears to brake cables?

Arrange a tour by phoning the Vice-Director, Mr. Chen Ren Hai (陈仁海), at 86 (594) 829-5483, or FAX: 86 (594) 829-8288. Or beep him: 129 200-1284.

Arts & Crafts Town may well be China's Wal-Mart of crafts, with everything under one roof, but to really appreciate Xianyou artisans, visit those who march to a different beat — like the drum makers.

Drumming up[3] Business

Master drum maker Ke Hongjin (柯洪金) works his magic on the right side of the road between Xianyou and Crafts Town.   While you wait, Master Ke will use tools & techniques unchanged for centuries to stretch rawhide over a beautifully crafted wooden barrel, and fasten it with hundreds of hand carved bamboo slivers (more durable than nails, and they don't rust).

Master Ke will drum up any size you can handle, from a handheld model to one of those Brobdingnagian[4] Buddhist boomers used in temples to scare off Chinese demons and foreign devils.

Master Ke's drums are no cheaper (200 Yuan and up) than if you bought them in stores, but at least you'll know who made them.

Ke Hongjin's phone: 86 (594) 839-1063.

Master Drum-maker, He Kong Jin

Rakish[5] Bamboo Products   A fellow right next door to Mr. Ke rakes in the profits with beautifully handcrafted bamboo benches, chairs, and rakes. Actually, he can't make much of a profit, considering he sells the finely crafted bamboo rakes for a paltry 2.50 Yuan each! They're almost too nice to use in dirt; I'd hang one on the wall if Susan Marie would let me, but she'd rake me over the coals[6] if I tried.

Further up the road you'll pass craftsman carving wooden statues, and 10 km. north in Xianyou town is a family that takes bamboo poles and churns out, daily, dozens of bamboo stools, chairs, rockers. I felt guilty paying only 4 Yuan for a beautifully crafted stool, or 10 Yuan for a high-backed chair. I'd have gladly paid that much just to watch them work!

Where've All The Craftsman Gone? Gone to plastic, every one.

For years, Xiamen had a master bamboo craftsman on Siming Rd., just outside Xiamen's Holiday Inn. We bought many a child's bamboo bike seat from the man, but plastic and progress sent him packing. It's a pity. The city has lost a tourist resource, and China is losing many traditional arts and crafts.

A **Hot Tip** for our city planners! They could boost tourism by following the lead of historical places like Williamsburg, Virginia, or Monticello, and hire craftsmen to wear traditional attire and produce their crafts in model shops. Tourists could photograph them at work, and purchase crafts directly from those who make them. (Though who knows? In Arizona, I saw genuine American Indian dreamcatchers that were stamped "Made in China".)

Meizhou Island （湄洲岛） Just off Fujian's coast, between Quanzhou and Putian, lies Meizhou Island, the Mecca for Mazu worshippers.

Legend has it that Mazu was called Mo (silence) because she never cried until one month old (when she let loose, "Enough already! Feed me!").

Mo could understand and interpret Buddhist scriptures by the tender age of eight when, according to a guidebook, "she began to worship gods and recite texts, with an intention to salvate [sic] poor people."

When she was 16, a celestial being gave her a bronze talisman, and from then on she grew in supernatural powers and wisdom. She went about doing good deeds, healing the sick with herbs, teaching how to prevent disease, and reading the sea

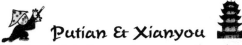

and stars and weather to help farmers know when they should fish and when they should stay home and tell fish stories. So far so good—but then she was credited with riding the clouds, and using her power to turn the tide and to save ships, and people began calling her "The Goddess" or the "Daughter of the Dragon". And her fate was sealed.

Mazu Worship

As Marilyn Monroe learned 2,000 years later, goddesses lead a lonely life, and Lin Mo ended hers at age 27, when she told her family, "I feel peace, but don't want to live this life anymore. I want to ascend the mountain and travel far." Lin Mo climbed Mount Meifeng, where mysterious clouds and music appeared. She hopped up on the clouds and sailed away with the wind, and has been salvating folks to this day.

Her spirit began appearing to ships in distress and guiding them to safe haven, and grateful fishermen started worshipping her as the goddess of the sea. Even the Imperial Court, thankful for an uninterrupted supply of fish and chips[7], granted her 28 royal titles, including "Holy Queen", "Holy Lady", and "Holy Mother". (I wonder if Hindus call their goddesses "Holy Cow"?[8]).

A tour book claims, "Mazu now becomes a tie linking the mainland and Taiwan, and has aroused the interest of the world." (How about a joint venture between the "Holy Lady" and "Our Lady of Fatima"?[9]).

Hundreds of thousands of pilgrims from around the world flock to Mazu Island each year to visit the temple and worship small statues of the goddess. They hold a special ceremony to invoke Mazu to live in the idol, and then invited the idol to return with them to their homes in Taiwan or Singapore, or Los Angeles.

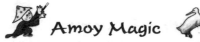
China held an International Mazu Cultural Tour Festival from April 29th to May 6th, 2002. In addition to religious services and Mazu arts and cultural displays, her devotees angled[10] to get more participants by holding fishing contests and kite flying competitions.

While on Mazu Island, you may notice that women's hair is coiled in the shape of a ship's sail on the back of their heads. This is to honor Mazu, and to invoke their husbands' safe return from the sea. Meizhou women also wear half-red, half-blue baggy pants in memory of Mazu's red-trousers. Only half of their trousers are red because they believe they are unworthy of all-red trousers like Mo.

Red tape[11], I suppose.

And now we head *North to Ningde!*

Laonei (老内) Notes

[1] Carp: to complain
[2] Green eyes: envy, jealousy
[3] Drum up: to create, to find
[4] Brobdingnagian: gigantic, extremely large (from Jonathan Swift's tale of Gulliver's travel to Brobdingnagia, the land of giants).
[5] Rakish: stylish, jaunty
[6] Rake over the coals: criticize, complain, punish
[7] Chips: french fries (炸薯条)
[8] Holy cow!: an English exclamation, or ejaculation (like "天!")
[9] Our Lady of Fatima: Virgin Mary supposedly appeared to 3 children in the village of Fatima, in Portugal, 1917. Pilgrimages for worship and healing have been made to Fatima ever since.
[10] Angle: to fish; to try to obtain something by scheming or tricky means
[11] Red tape: bureaucracy, paperwork, bureaucratic regulations

 Ningǒe

Chapter 16
Ningǒe

Ningǒe, Fujian's ortheast corner, only got one page in the previous Amoy Magic—but *eighty five pages* in the new *Fujian Adventure* because it has turned out to be one of my favourite places in the province. I could spend months exploring the incredibly beauty and ancient culture of Ningde, the "birthplace of South China civilization"

A new Ningde highway

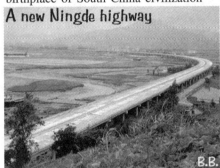

places like flat Shandong. But today, Fujian has some of China's best roads!

Fujian has forked out[1] billions blasting tunnels through mountains, and building bridges and elevated highways that arch high across deep valleys and ravines, or coastal mud flats. Where a drive from Xiamen to Wuyi Mountain used to take me 35 hours, it now takes nine!

Ningde is home of the She minority, and of strapping[2] souls like the Kung Fu fighting, carp worshipping highlanders of Zhouning. The surrealistic scenery of Taimu mountain looks like something God might have subcontracted out to Dr.

Traditional "She" minority architecture (or so they say). Fortunately, Ningde is a lot closer than it used to be!

When we drove Toy Ota around China in 1994, from Xiamen to the Gobi Desert, Tibet, and back, we found that Fujian had some of the worst roads in China—but no wonder! Fujian is mostly mountains, and one km of road costs many times what it would in

Tunnels are shrinking our province!

Seuss[3], with its weird hills and hoodoos[4] (yes, I had to look it up too). Ningde has the largest waterfalls complex in China, and to the southwest of Nine Dragon Falls is Baishuiyang—a gigantic lake where even mortals like myself can walk on water (though being a humble guy, I usually walk on water in private).

Years ago, Xiamen ABB's resident Englishman Scott Ballantyne raved to me about the beauty of Ningde (and its girls!), and he averred[5] they had the best seafood on the planet. He's probably right. (About the food, I didn't sample the girls, Susan Marie). It's worth a trip to Ningde just for the seafood alone (though I'm still not keen on dried minnow heads in my breakfast porridge).

All in all, Ningde is a delight, and I wish that Amoy Magic could give her the credit she deserves. So pick up a copy of Fujian Adventure and learn why Scott and I have fallen in love with the places and peoples of Ningde.

But for now, here's a quick summary.

Sandu'ao Island (三都岛)

Floating Assets   B.B.

is Kevin Costner's Water World come to life! The people who live on the floating fishing villages need never set foot on land. They have floating houses, stores, gas stations. They even have their own 911 (or 119, as they dial it in China—backwards just for the sheer principal, I suspect).

Though remote, this area of Fujian offers great hope for prosperity. Ningde has 1/3 of Fujian's coastline (878 km!) and one of the best natural harbors in the world. In Sun Yat-sen's Plan for National Reconstruction, he claimed this was the world's deepest ice-free harbour, and today the harbour can berth fifty 10,000 to 100,000 ton ships, and the harbor's narrow mouth keeps it calm even when the open seas are raging.

But Dr. Sun's dreams for Sandu'ao, like those for the "Oriental Mega-port" of Haicang, were stillborn (and for the same reason). In 1898, Sandu'ao became one of China's five open trading ports, and 13 foreign countries, including Britain, the U.S., Russia, and Germany, established consulates and trading companies. Sandu'ao was an overnight international success story until 3 Japanese bombing raids during World War II razed the place to the ground. And thanks to Taiwan's bombing campaigns, in the

B.B.
Catholic Church (Spanish architecture)

1950s Sandu'ao was transformed into an off-limits naval base. But today it is once again opening up to tourists and traders.

Take a motor boat to the island, enjoy a great seafood lunch, and tour the Spanish style Catholic church and old American nunnery—then head to the Japanese Holy Land of Xiapu.

Temple to Kukai   B.B.

Xiapu （霞浦） to the north is where the Japanese Kukai landed when he came to China in 804 to seek the Buddhist scriptures. He was actually bound for Chang'an but an accident forced his ship to land in Xiapu, where locals rescued his party, wined and dined them for 50 days, then sent them on to Chang'an (China's capital at the time), via Fuzhou. After studying in Chang'an with a Taoist master, Kukai returned to Japan to found the Shingon Sect.

430,000 Yuan!

Kukai, a "man of the people", would probably roll over in his grave[6] if he knew how much has been spent on him. His wooden statue cost 430,000 Yuan. The embroidered pieces on either side cost 200,000 Yuan each. The gold-plated copper chandelier cost 210,000 Yuan. It's a good thing that Japanese pilgrims are the temple's primary patrons.

River Rafting （杨家溪） is just a short drive north of Kukai's Cove. While the scenery is delightful, the

B.B.

people make the place. The children are natural hams, and happy to climb the giant banyans and pose for photos.

I also enjoy the old folks, like Mr. Chen, who still ferries the river even though he's in his 70s.

B.B.

www.yangjiaxi.com.cn

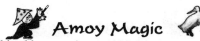

I was fascinated by his old water pipe, and his hand woven palm fiber rain cape. Check their website: **www.yangjiaxi.com.cn.**

Taimu Mountain Resort (太 姥山) just to the north of Xiapu, is called Fujian's "Fairyland on the Sea". Of course, Chinese name everything after fairies. It's no wonder there's such a big Chinatown in San Francisco, America's fairy capital. Taimu's hoodoos really do look like they were lifted from a Dr. Seuss book—or perhaps like some geological voodoo[7] hoodoo.

Who do you think likes Hoodoos? We do!

I guess you would get quite a view from a voodoo hoodoo.

Each hoodoo is named, of course. Over the past 5,015 years, Chinese have named every rock and hill in the country, and given special attention to Taimu hoodoos. Here are a few hoodoo handles[8]:

Some Hoodoo Handles

Husband and Wife, Nine Carps Facing the Sky (I counted eleven), Gods Sawing a Plate (I saw it too), Two Buddhas Arguing Scripture, Jade Monkey Looking at a Mirror, Bare-bellied Maitreya, Two Gods Playing Chess, Godmother Flying Toward Heaven, Rock for Seeing God, Cow's Backside (does that hoodoo moo?), deng deng.

Guoxing Temple, near the Taimu Park entrance, was once a massive place, with 360 granite columns supporting the roof! They've since been used to make walkways, bridges, etc. Quoxing is an archaeological treasure trove, with shards of Tang Dynasty pottery littering the grounds. Just after my first visit, archaeologists unearthed a magnificent

Guoxing Temple

granite courtyard.

Monks offer tea and tall tales—some of which I took with a grain of salt[9]. For example, one claimed the swastika that adorns Buddha's chest came from China. I didn't argue the point, but that's one of the few things that the Chinese did *not* invent.

The abbott was a colourful character. He even donned his robes for me and posed!

B.B.

 **Ningde**

Blue Creek at 9 AM! Or said the guide and locals. For 1,000 years, this creek supposedly has turned blue at exactly 9 AM every morning, and even a white cloth dipped in it will remain blue for a few seconds. "TV crews have even filmed it!" I was told. "What if your watch is off?" I asked.

Thread of Sky. Every Chinese mountain resort worth its salt[10] boasts the

best and tightest "Thread of Sky". Taimu was no exception. I dutifully navigated the extremely narrow defile, but I didn't think the crack was all it was cracked up[11] to be.

Miraculous 9 A.M. Blue Creek!

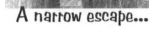

A narrow escape...

Stone Age Escalator?

Mountaintop Experience [12] Near Taimu's peak is a gate built in the year 2,543 (you'll have to visit yourself to figure that out—or read "The Fujian Adventure"). Behind the gate is a mysterious old temple built in 725 A.D.. They offer excellent vegetarian fare, and a room for the night if you need it. One of my friends actually spent his honeymoon there (probably much to the celibate monks' dismay). I was exhausted by the time I reached the temple—but my spirits were lifted by a happy young monk who traipsed up the mountain toting 50 pounds of tofu (which an hour later I happily devoured). "How can you lug 50 pounds up here?" I asked.

"Oh, usually it's 100 pounds," he said, smiling. "Today's a light day!"

My day was much lighter after meeting him.

Tofu Totin' Monk

Mountaintop Mani I wasn't surprised that Manicheans reached Quanzhou. After all, that great port of the Middle Ages was also the Jerusalem of Asia. But I was surprised to learn of an ancient Mani shrine on the peak of remote Moxiao Mountain. The Persian prophet's disciples sure got around! Today, though, the small stone shrine is dedicated to the goddess Taimu.

A Taimu/Mani joint venture, perhaps?

1,000-year-old Manichean Shrine

Mr. Chen Qingjun (陈清军) Before we leave Taimu, I must commend to you the services of the fellow who brought Taimu to life—the poetry-spouting camera-toting guide Mr. Chen. A Taimu native, he knows the lore of the land, and he allowed me to use in "The Fujian Adventure", free of charge, his beautiful photos of Taimu. You can find him in his shop at the entrance to the park, or phone him at: 1350 957 5718

Chen Qingjun's shop

Taimu Mountain
(by Mr. Chen Qingjun)

Zhouning, at an altitude of 888 meters, is Fujian's "Naturally Air-conditioned city". Home of the carp-worshipping, Kung Fu fighting highlanders, the mountain town has its own distinct traditions and culture, some of China's most beautiful scenery (including the largest waterfall complex), and some awesome mountain cuisine. The locals are delightfully hospitable—and some of the most entrepreneurial folk you'll ever find. At least 30,000 of the 190,000 population work elsewhere (over 20,000 in the Shanghai Pudong area alone), they said they recognized the opportunity before the Shanghai people themselves!

Wood 'n Stone

Check in to the Zhouning Guesthouse, and have a meal of mountain veggies and critters, and pounded pork. Like every other town, they claim to have the best pounded pork in Fujian. They said the granite bowl and wooden mallet preserve the taste of wood and stone. I said I'd never eaten wooden or stone but I'd take their word for it. And it was indeed excellent, as was the Buddha's Fist (a gourd that looks like hands folded in prayer—though the prayer didn't do the gourd much good because it still got stewed).

Stroll the gaily lit streets at night—especially West Street (Xi Jie 西街), which looks ancient but is just a few decades old. I enjoyed watching the blacksmiths, barbers, and checking out the strange herbs in the apothecary shop.

Next morning, visit the magnificent Nine Dragon (九龙) Falls. Be sure to go in the mornings but it pours in the afternoons. I asked the guide if it always rained so much in Zhouning. She looked at me as if it had finally dawned on her why some animals eat their young, and she said, "Of course it rains a lot. That's why we have China's biggest waterfalls." Duh.

Jiulongji Waterfalls

It's hard to believe China's largest waterfalls complex could go undiscovered until the 1970s, given that billions of Chinese have been traipsing about the countryside for eons naming every rock, nook, cranny and hoodoo. Nevertheless, it wasn't until 1978 that "9 Dragon Falls", only 10 km east of Zhouning, was discovered by a wood cutter.

9 Dragon Falls

He told the village elders, and the rest is history!

Nine Dragons has 13 levels of falls (but they of course name it Nine dragons anyway). The second fall is 67 meters high and 52 meters wide, and sends foam 20 meters high, and the mists raise 200 meters.

Liyu (Carp) Creek, which meanders through Zhouning's Puyuan Village, is home to 8,000 colorful carp, weighing as much as 30 pounds. The fearless rascals swim right up to the shore to be fed and even petted because for 800 years the local villagers have worshipped them as gods. Even during famine, the village forbids killing carp, and when one dies, it is buried in the village Carp Grave, and villagers offer sacrifices to it as if it were an ancestor.

Carp Village -- Where Carp is King

Village children sell round cakes baked specially for the carp (but they're pretty tasty, and I ate a few myself).

Also of interest is the ship-shape temple. It's shaped like a ship because an ancient slept there under a tree, had a dream of a treasure ship, and promptly collected lots of money to build a temple (and, in the process, probably collected quite a lot of gold). On the large tree that forms the temple's mast is a small iron bow and arrow. These are placed by a child's bed to spear nightmares (a use similar to North American Indian's "dreamcatchers").

Big Foot meets Bound Feet! It's getting harder to find the elderly ladies with the tiny bound feet so prized by centuries of Chinese men, but Carp Village still has a few. Old Granny Zheng has had a hard life, hobbling about

Big Foot meets Bound Foot!

on her tiny 4" feet, which were broken in childhood and bound tightly. But she says life has been better for her since 1949. Before then, she was lucky to have rice, much less veggies or meat, so she's happy that her fellow villagers, while still poor, aren't starving to death nowadays.

She used to be able to buy her tiny slippers, but there isn't enough demand for them now, so she makes her own, and gave me a pair as a keepsake. She laughed when I compared her feet with my own, and happily let me take a photo of the two of us together—and another photo of her feet beside the clodhopper shoes of a fashionable young Chinese girl.

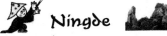

Bound Feet, Bound Bodies

Westerners penned indignant treatises against foot binding, and with good reason. But while Chinese bound women's feet, we Westerners bound women's entire bodies! To achieve the highly prized 17-18 inch waist, and thus land a husband, whale-bone corsets wreaked havoc on Western women's rib cages and internal organs. They could not bend over, or lift their arms over their heads. No wonder Victorian women fainted so often.

Foot binding was indeed barbaric, but we too have done some fairly barbarian things for the sake of fashion. In fact, we still do. Nowadays, of course, whale-bone corsets have given way to fashionable anorexia. Personally, skin-covered skeletons don't turn me on. I'll take Susan Marie's generous proportions any day—and her large shoes as well! At least my wife won't get blown over during a typhoon!. ☺

(If Susan Marie read this I'll be spending the rest of my life sleeping on the couch).

Bound feet, Bound bodies

S. Shaolin Kung Fu

Fujian was the home of Southern Shaolin Kung fu, and like all other villages, Zhouning has its own distinct style. Carp Village's Zheng style is passed down only to those with the surname of Zheng, and they must wait until their late teens to learn it because it requires such contortions of the muscles that it is feared it would stunt a younger person's growth.

One of the temples is to an ancient who killed a man-eat tiger—bare-handed!

Several Kung Fu masters, all named Zheng, of course, gave me demonstrations. The heavy wooden staff on one master's Kung Fu fork had been broken. The man, in his 60s, said, "I broke it on my elderly neighbour when we were practicing." He saw my shock and added, "Not to worry. I'm a doctor."

Master of Shaolin Shovel!

B.B.

I hammed it up in a mock battle, but the Carp Village headman is quite a ham himself, and gave me a demonstration of Kung Fu shovel technique.

Walking on Water

Being an extremely humble fellow, I usually don't make waves[13] by walking on water in public, but in Baishuiyang I made an exception.

I summoned the powers within me, and waltzed right across the vast 40,000 square meter lake. Of course, it wasn't that hard because the entire 40,000 square meter lake rests upon a massive flat rock just inches below the surface of the water!

Dr. Bill Walks on Water!

One of Fujian's seven national level scenic spots, and home to Mandarin ducks in the winter, and Rhesus monkeys year round, Baishuiyang attracts not just tourists but sportsmen who participate in events like track or bike races on the lake.

The local mountain cuisine is delightful. "Everything is all natural, and free of pollution," I was told. But when I was given a noodle made from an inedible plant by 18 steps, I said, "You said everything was all natural, but this is processed 18 steps."

"But all 18 steps are natural," they said.

I was also initiated into the heady[14] joys of eating fish heads. "Eighteen flavours!" they said, "and guest of honor gets to eat them!" I protested that I had no honor but in the end I ate the fish head, though I never made it through all 18 flavors. After

Baishuiyang Cabins

munching fish lips and chewing cheeks and brains and eyeballs I'd had enough. After all, I've always wanted to get ahead in life, but not that kind of head.

Baishuiyang has small cabins, as well as a restaurant—a perfect place for a weekend retreat. And after Baishuiyang, visit the old wooden covered bridge an hour south. It's incredible the structure has stood for 700 years!

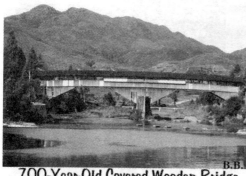

700-Year-Old Covered Wooden Bridge

The Mysterious She Folk live in Fujian's more remote mountain areas, and are hard to find. Most are in Ningde, but a few villages are scattered around the rest of the province as well (Changtai, west of Xiamen, has a *She* village).

Nowadays *She* usually wear their distinct costumes only on holidays. As one *She* girl told me, "Why spend an hour dressing when I can throw on jeans and shirt, and put my hair in a ponytail?"

She worship ancestral pictures that they keep secret from outsiders, but that reveal their ancestor was the Chinese unicorn Panhu, who evolved from a golden worm. Panhu married a princess and sired three sons named Pan, Lan, and Lei, who with Panhu's son-in-law, Zhong, became the ancestors of the *She*.

Every year, hundreds of *She* join a procession carrying wooden memorial tablets and ancestral pictures and head off for Liu Keng, a *She* village in the mountainous forests of Luoyuan County. Some hold wooden plaques inscribed with "Make Way", or "Silence" — which seems rather futile given that half of them are banging drums and cymbals.

And if you think Chongwu weddings are tough[15], try a *She* ceremony! The bridegroom

dresses like a Qing dynasty official and kowtows to heaven and earth and his ancestors, while the bride stands by silently (a good beginning). Then she is escorted to the nuptial chamber while the groom stays behind to drink wine with 7 bachelors chosen according to their horoscopes. They drink for 3 days and nights, without sleeping — with good reason.

Newlyweds used to not be allowed to sleep together for 3 years, but that was shortened to 3 days. So the groom cools his heels[16] and ardor[17] with wine, while the bride waits patiently (one hopes) for consummation of the marriage. Though after 3 days of drinking and no sleep, I can't imagine the groom would be up for anything but the sandman[18].

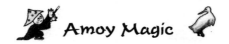

Laonei （老内） Notes

[1] Forked out: spent. paid (informal)
[2] Strapping: strong physique, muscular
[3] Dr. Seuss: popular American children's author and illustrator who drew strange cartoon mountains in his books
[4] Hoodoo: strangely shaped column of rock produced by weathering.
[5] Aver: affirm positively, declare as a fact. Scott B. frequently makes averments about food, as well as those about those of the feminine persuasion
[6] Roll over in his grave: be very upset
[7] Voodoo: a Caribbean religion concocted from Catholicism, animism and magic.
[8] Handle: person's name (slang)
[9] With a grain of salt: with reservations, skepticism, doubt
[10] Worth its salt: worthwhile, useful,
[11] Crack up: praise highly (informal)
[12] Mountaintop experience: very pleasant or enlightening experience (from the biblical story of Moses meeting God on top of Mount Sinai).
[13] Make waves: attract lots of attention, cause an uproar, make trouble
[14] Heady: intoxicating, stupefying, exhilarating, upsetting the balance of the mind or senses
[15] Chongwu weddings: you may remember from the Quanzhou chapter that, traditionally, Chongwu bride and groom could spend only three nights a year together until a child was born
[16] Cools his heels: to wait, or to be kept waiting (the heels are 'hot' because of the impatient pacing back and forth as they wait).
[17] Ardor: passion, fiery intensity of feeling
[18] Sandman: character in Western folk tales who makes children go to sleep by sprinkling sand in their eyes. But I've had sand in my eyes before and it's not pleasant, much less soporific (sleep-inducing). Sandman, no—but sand*wich*, perhaps?

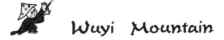
Chapter 17
Wuyi Mountain

Wuyi Mountains (武夷山) , a geological, biological and historical wonderland in Fujian's Northwest corner, derives its name from the legendary Qian Keng who lived during the Shang Dynasty (16th century-11th century BC) and was supposedly the 8th generation descendant of Huangdi, the Yellow Emperor. After earning the title of lord of Pengcheng, and the surname Peng, he escaped the wars by fleeing with his sons Peng Wu and Peng Yi to mountainous northern Fujian, where he settled down to a peaceful life of farming. The area was named after his sons, Wu and Yi, and for the past 2,000 years, every Emperor has offered sacrifices to Master Wuyi.

A mere 2,000 years ago, the King of Min had a magnificent palace just southeast of Wuyi City. Today, it is in ruins, and Wuyi is a rather backwater place because, even with better roads, it is still rather remote. But with its own airport, and train service, Wuyi is starting to come into its own once again, especially since UNESCO designated it as a World Heritage Center.

Within Wuyi's forests, which cover 92% of the area, live 475 vertebrate species of animals, 100 species of mammals, 300 species of birds, and 32 insect orders with 4,557 species. Wuyi has 2,466 higher plant species and 840 lower plant species (including 50 or so found almost nowhere else, like the strange "square, black bamboo (Fangzhu 方竹)), which the famous poet Guo Mou Ruo wrote of in a poem. Wuyi has a diversity that probably rivals the Garden of Eden[1]. Another similarity with Eden is serpents—62 kinds of them!

Snake in the Grass [2]

Wuyi, the self-proclaimed "Serpent Kingdom of the World", has more than its share of king cobras, bamboo vipers, and ten meter reticulated pythons. No wonder the ancients worshipped snakes.

2,000-year-old snake carving

Wuyi's 6,000 square meter Snake Garden (Dazhu Gang Sheyuan, 大竹岗 蛇园) claims to have more than 10,000 snakes! (Entrance fee cheerfully refunded if you die from snakebite)

Snake Doctors, not surprisingly, are well thought of in Wuyi, and the services of Xiamei Village's Master Wang are in great demand.

Master Wang, is illiterate, so he had to memorize the herbal cures in his ancestors' compilation. He told me that he has not only never lost a patient but that his patients have never lost a limb, though had they gone to a hospital, many would have lost at least an arm or a leg.

"That's nothing," I said. "American hospitals routinely charge patients both an arm *and* a leg.[3]"

B.B.

Master Wang
Snake Doctor

Wuyi snakes bring in big bucks! In addition to eating snake flesh, Chinese use the bile, poison and blood for various medicinal purposes, and items made of snakeskin are increasingly popular,

蛇血	蛇毒	蛇胆
Snake Blood	Snake Poison	Snake Gall Bladder

though I draw the line at snakeskin belts. I saw one coiled up; it nearly scared me out of my own skin.

When I was in the Air Force in Taiwan, villagers in remote mountains milked the venom from a cobra, added rice wine, and offered it to me. "Makes you virile!" they said.

"No thanks," I said. "I don't need it!" But guest of honor and all that... In the end I said some quick prayers, drank it, and survived. Never again! Though maybe it did work. I've got two great sons. ☺

Surrealistic landscapes, not serpents, are my favourite feature of Wuyi. Chinese have praised and painted and eulogized Wuyi's peaks for over 1,000 years. Ancient Taoist scriptures call Wuyi "16 Cave Fairyland" (there's those fairies again!), and it is from the heights of Wuyi's Huanggan Peak (at 2,168 meters, South China's highest mountain), that the mighty Min river begins its course to the sea at Pagoda Island.

The strange mountains could be passed off as life-sized Chinese paintings, or scenes from a George Lucas' movie (no Ewoks[4], but the town has plenty of woks; if they did find any Ewoks, they'd stir-fry them). These mountains have inspired great philosophers. Zhuxi lived here when he developed his neoConfucianism, which transformed stagnant Confucianism and dominated Asian thought and politics for centuries.

Nine Bend Stream (Jiuqu Xi 九曲溪风景区) is Wuyi's chief drawing card. At 80 Yuan a person, the 2 ½ hour 7.5 km bamboo raft ride isn't cheap, but it's well worth it, as you meander down the river through narrow gorges, past the ancient "boat coffins" suspended high on the cliffs, towards Wuyi's trademark[5] Jade Maiden Peak (玉女峰, Yunu Feng).

Shannon poling towards Jade Maiden Peak

Heavenly Tour Peak (Tianyou Feng, 天游峰) offers a bird's eye view of Wuyi, but it's a long haul, and on holidays the trail is packed solid with tourists. Chinese call the peak "The End of the Earth", and it feels like it.

Red Robe Tea After visiting the ends of the earth,

go check out the planet's most expensive tea—Big Red Robe! In an auction at the 2nd Canton Tea Fair, in 2002, 20 grams were sold for 180,000 Yuan! Big Red Robe is so expensive because it only comes from three wizened little tea bushes growing halfway up a cliff in a narrow Wuyi valley.

Wuyi is perfect for tea growing. It has just the right humidity, nutrients in the soil, and amount of sunlight (restricted by the narrow valleys' walls). In fact, Westerners used to call tea "Wuyi" before we adopted a variation of the Minnan word "dei".

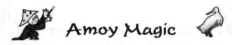

Wuyi Wildlife Preserve （武夷山自然

保护区） After visiting Big Red Robe, Water Curtain Falls, and "The Scenic Spots Civilized Pretty Gifts Travelling Route", check out Huanggan Mountain's wildlife. Buses make the trip each morning from the Wuyi Long Distance bus station. Be sure and take your passports, because this is a UNESCO restricted area and they will check your I.D. .

As buses pull in, wild monkeys scramble down from the hillsides for handouts. The Wuyi Nature Museum has displays of the seemingly limitless varieties of local animals and insects. There is also a site where injured animals are cared for, and next door is a restaurant. I'm not sure if the two are connected or not.

A Wuyi Family

B.B.

Yulingting Dragon Kiln

YulingTing Song Dynasty Dragon Kiln

Dragon kilns originated in South China about 2,000 years ago, and this 2m x 113m kiln, which snakes down a hillside West of Wuyi City, is a fine example. Craftsman in the gift shop will demonstrate the potter's wheel, and you can buy replicas of the black porcelain that was so prized by the Japanese many centuries ago.

B.B.

Xiamei Village （下梅）, just east of Wuyi City, has many well preserved centuries old houses, with ornately carved wooden beams and latticework, and stone carvings. The picturesque village has a small creek running down the center, and as we toured the village we passed a husband and wife blacksmith team. "I work iron just like my ancestors," the man said, proudly.

"Just like my ancestors!" said Xiamei's blacksmith.

Some Chinese gents[6] playing poker were proof that Chinese not only invented playing cards but the poker face as well (the color original of the hilarious photo below is in "Fujian Adventure"). They stared each other down with priceless expressions, so intent on their game that they totally ignored the foreigner snapping photos of them!

Gone to Pot We paid the Snake Doctor a visit, and his father shoed off his antiques and ancient family heirlooms. I was careful to avoid admiring their treasures too closely, lest they give them to me. Chinese are that way. Betray the slightest interest

Snake Doctor's Antique Collection

and Chinese will give you the shirt right off their back[7]. As it was, I left Wuyi two days later with four pieces of pottery—one from the Tang Dynasty, two from the Song, and a Qing Dynasty blue and white piece.

I don't see how they can give away all their porcelain without going to pot[8].

Min Yue Kingdom Museum

(Chengcun Hancheng Yizhi, 城村汉城遗址) is about 35 km. south of Wuyi City, just east of the 101 highway's 341 km. marker (near the railroad track). The 10,000 sq. meter palace ruins remind me of a Mayan temple. Among other things, the palace had a 10m×5m bathing pool. The 2,000

Remain's of King of Min's Palace

year old well still has water, and my companions filled up their empty mineral water bottles. "It's very clean, Professor Pan!" they said. But only minutes earlier a tourist had dropped their eyeglasses in the well—and who knows what else had dropped down it over the past 2,015 years! So I passed.

The Min Yue Museum, just a few hundred meters south, has a fine painting of a crowd of folks admiring the Min King's dress, a statue of the great man, and a mock[9] archaeological dig.

King of Min

Just north of the museum is an ancient village with exceptionally well preserved old homes, and a tea house in a 400-year-old home. The young proprietor showed me his ancestral records. He is 37th generation in that village!

The village was once quite important because of the river ferry in back, and the ferry is still in use. The riverside temple to Mazu, goddess of the sea, was built to insure the ferry's prosperity and safety.

Folks in this ancient

Ancient Ferry

village live much the same as their forebears—except they have pool tables, television, electric freezers with ice cream…. Okay, much has changed. But what probably hasn't changed is the Chinese spirit of hospitality. Here, like almost everywhere I've been, I was greeted over and over with, "Have some tea!" And when I entered a courtyard and saw crowds of young and old alike sitting around tables, meticulously sorting tea leaves, and appreciated how much labor is behind each cup of this Chinese beverage, I determined that I won't take either the tea or the hospitality for granted!

B.B.

Sorting Tea

B.B.

Getting There   The cheapest route from Xiamen to Wuyi Mountain is overnight train, but if you're strapped for time, fly directly to Wuyi Mountain's new airport.

Or if you fancy suicide, take a bus.

Mr. Wu Guangmin (吴光民) In Wuyi, as elsewhere, it is people who bring the place to life—passionate people like *Wuyi Mtn. Daily*'s photographer Mr. Wu Guangmin.

Like Changting photographer Babushka, Guangmin is set on capturing China's vanishing cultural heritage on film. "In a few years," he said, "all that will be left are photographs. Old architecture, ancient farm implements, unusual customs—they're all disappearing."

He spends most weekends traipsing around rural villages or mountains, taking 3 or 4 rolls of black and white photos of old architecture, and color photos of nature—like duelling king cobras!

Mr. Wu Guangmin

Guangmin almost stepped right on top of a pair of king cobras who were faced off in a clearing. He froze, and finally got the nerve to snap a photo (the one to the right!). They both faced Guanmin, and his heart stopped! But inveterate[10] photographer, he snapped another photo. Flash! The king cobras took off one way, and Guangmin took off another!

Guangmin photographs everything from monks and monkeys to monarchs (the Dutch queen visited Wuyi), and he has passed on his infectious enthusiasm for culture, history and nature to his wife and daughter—and to me!

If you're in Wuyi, look them up.

Wu Guangmin's Wife and Daughter

Wu Guangmin's daughter learning classical Chinese music

Wuyi Mountain Hotels

Wuyi now has literally dozens of fine hotels and guest houses. Check the Jnternet for the latest. But I *must* recommend one of China's finest retreats…

Wuyi Mountain Villa (武夷山庄) hosted the Queen of the Netherlands when she visited Wuyi. This delightful mountain getaway's architecture blends so harmoniously with the natural setting that it has been written up in a book on outstanding international architecture. The villa has both Western and Chinese restaurants (great local dishes, like mountain taro[11]), a banquet hall, and a coffee shop. Best of all is Wuyi Villa's service. When they heard I needed tape recorder batteries, two different maids rushed off to different stores to buy some—and both refused payment.

Address: Wuyi Palace, Wuyishan, Fujian 354302 Tel: 86 (599) 525-1888

Main Street (Gucheng)

Elegant old Xiamei architecture

Laonei （老内） Notes

[1] Garden of Eden: the Biblical garden （伊甸园） in which God placed the first man and woman, Adam and Eve（亚当, 夏娃）

[2] Snake in the grass: euphemism for "bad person," "evil doer," "deceitful person"

[3] Arm and a leg: very expensive; 贵的

[4] Ewok: little bear-like creatures in George Lucas' Star Wars movie.

[5] Trademark: most representative; what Wuyi is best known for

[6] Gents: gentlemen (informal)

[7] Give the shirt off your back: extremely generous

[8] Go to pot: fall apart; go bankrupt

[9] Mock: replica, reproduction; 假的, 伪造的, 模拟的

[10] Inveterate: determined, persistent, long-established, deeply-rooted, habitual, . 根深的, 成癖的, 积习的!

[11] Taro: tuber that forms the main staple of Polynesian islanders （芋头）

Chapter 18
Scenic Sanming

Scenic Sanming!

Lansing, Michigan (U.S.A.) knew what it was doing when choosing Sanming as a sister city. For sheer scenic beauty, Sanming is unsurpassed in Fujian. And fortunately, new roads are making it more accessible.

Sanming, in the very west of Fujian, bordering Jiangxi Province, was so remote that even the Japanese could not reach it. Mountain passes were too narrow to fly

Sanming by night...

through safely (locals should shoot planes out of the sky from the comfort of their front porch rocking chairs!), and it took days to lug a boat up the river, using ropes pulled from the shore. But thanks to new highways, it is only a five-hour drive from Xiamen to Sanming—and another half hour to that culinary oasis of Shaxian, and "Shaxian Snack Street (沙县小吃街, Shaxian Xiaochi Jie)".

Shaxian Snacks (沙县

小吃) are famous throughout China, but the so-called Shaxian cuisine sold anywhere else is a poor substitute for the 100+ dishes offered in this unique melting pot of menus!

About 1,000 years ago, people began flocking to Shaxian from all over China, and they brought with them their unique foods and

Shaxian Snacks

cooking methods. Over the centuries, the styles have mellowed and blended to create the over 100 "Shaxian snacks". Who needs an entrée when you can enjoy a meal of one hors d'oeuvre after another? And ordering is no problem even for

B.B.
Shaxian 'Snacks' -- Heavenly!

illiterate Laowai. Many "Snack Street" shops have menus with photos. Just point, eat, and hand over your wallet. (Actually, the dishes are very reasonable).

By the way, our favourite dish, by far, is Xiao Mai Wan (小麦丸)!

Siesta Goddess?

B.B.

Goddess of Siestas? [1]

China's largest reclining Buddha lies on a hillside West of Shaxian. We got there late, but the gatekeeper wanted ten Yuan apiece anyway—which I thought was a bit steep, given that the display room was closed, and the giant idol was asleep anyway.

Malinqiao Zoology Fairyland,

between Sanming City and Shaxian, has a kayaker on the sign—but this zoology fairyland has no kayaks, no zoos, and no fairies (that I could see, anyway).

But they do have nice rubber rafting though—provided they first turn on the

river. No joke! We had to wait for them to turn the river on, and flush it clean, before we could go river rafting. Only in China!

But it was fun, and lifeguards posted along the river keep it safe— and probably turn the river down or off if it gets out of hand. The owner has invested 100,000 USD in the little resort, and plans on adding go-karts on the mountainside. If he gets that going, he'll really be on a roll.

"Help! Turn the river off!"

Mingxi Town, Fujian's gem capital, has 20 kinds of gemstones, including rubies, and is China's fourth largest producer of sapphires. In addition to jewelry, some local firms are on the cutting edge[2] with their elegant gem-studded knives and swords. I bought one that looked for the world like something elves would have used in "Lord of the Rings[3]".

Mingxi Jewelled Dagger (Cutting edge technology!)

B.B.

Taining—City of Gold! During the Song Dynasty, about 820,000 folks flocked to Taining—in part to mine for gold. The gold is pretty much gone now (though I found a pretty nice chunk of gold ore!), but Taining has struck gold again with tourism!

Gold Lake, created when the Gold River was dammed, attracted over 50,000 tourists in 2002. Every weekend, thousands fish along the

Cruising Gold Lake

B.B.

lake's shores, or take the half-day boat cruises through the winding valleys—or go parasailing. Prices are strictly regulated to avoid rip-offs of tourists, be they Laowai, Laonei, or folks like me who no longer know just what kind of Lao they are.

Gold Lake -- a Sportsman's Paradise

Taining shares the same mountain range as Wuyi, and so has the same biological diversity—meaning, plenty of wild critters and snakes! Wuyi's main advantage has been that it was better promoted, and more accessible. But when the Fuzhou—Beijing highway is completed in 2007, Gold Lake will really shine. They are also working on a "Fuzhou—Shaowu Gold Lake Tourist Train". (I had something to write about that, but lost my train of thought[4])

The Ming Dynasty Village in Taining has been meticulously reconstructed, thanks to a 600,000 Yuan investment by Mr. Huang Shuang An, an Overseas Chinese. Over 6,000 square meters has been completed, and another 4,000 square meters is on the way.

One very unique attraction is the dozens of animated wax figures going

Ming Dynasty architecture (Taining City)

about life as it must have been a few centuries ago (and as it is today, in some places). Drop a coin in the wooden box and they will sing, perform the dragon dance, grind wheat, or pour tea to dignified Chinese gentlemen.

Animated figurines (Taining)

Yuhua Cave (玉华洞, Jade Flower), just East of Taining in Jiangle, is Fujian's largest limestone cave, and one of the top four karst[5] caves in China. Over 200,000 visitors annually explore Jade Flower Cave's three subterranean rivers, two passageways, and six halls, and marvel over the 100 stalagmites[6] and the 2,000-year-old stone carvings. The caves extend over five kilometers, and the main cave is 2.5 kilometers long. Carlsbad Caverns "Big Room", by comparison, is but 610 meters long.

Yuhua Cave needs **investors for expansion**! For info, phone Liao Yuhui, at (0598) 232-3977.

Shibi Village (石壁, Stone Wall), some 25 km from Ninghua County seat, was home to Li Shimin (Emperor Tai Zong of the Tang Dynasty), Jiang Ziya (Prime Minister during the Zhou Dynasty), deng deng. Their ancestors still live in Shibi, and carefully tend the family trees and family temples. The area is so remote that no war has hit Hakka territory since the Tang Dynasty. Even the Japanese missed it!

Hakka Ancestral Temple (Shibi Village)

 **Scenic Sanming**  271

Shibi once boasted 200 villages, but because of the exodus of its youth, only 2,000 people, sharing 6 surnames, remain in 20 villages. But every year, Hakka from all over the world return to worship their ancestors and trace their lineage in the Hakka Temple.

Visit nearby Ninghua's Hakka Folk Custom Museum, and while you're in Hakka heaven, snap some shots of the picturesque covered wooden bridges. You'd think you were in Vermont, were it not for the distinctly Chinese upturned wooden eaves.

Anzhen Fortress is off the beaten path but well worth a visit. Built just over a century ago, the walls around the 10,000 sq. meter compound are 9 meters high and 4 meters thick. The walls and towers complement each other in such a way that those

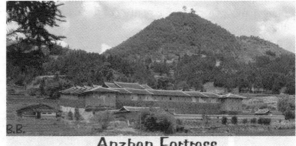

Anzhen Fortress

within could safely shoot the enemy (barbarians, warlords, insurance salesmen), no matter what direction they attacked from.

The fortress had 12 kitchens, six on each side, with "alligator" vents above. Second floor granaries had trap doors leading directly to the kitchens below.

The fortress is in excellent shape, but much of the fine wooden and stone ornamentation was destroyed during the Cultural Revolution, and the furniture hauled off. The caretakers of Anzhen Fortress are now seeking funds to repair the site, and buy back the stolen furniture and art work.

Sanming sites are far too numerous to cover in *Amoy Magic*, or even in *The Fujian Adventure*. Your best bet is to explore Sanming yourself—places like the delightful 1.21 sq. km. Linying Stone Forest—and then share your discoveries with me and other Laowai by dropping me an e-mail at **bbrown@public.xm.fj.cn**

Also, check for updates on Susan Marie's site: **http://www.amoymagic.com.**

Finally, a final and totally shameless plug for the 431 page full-color *The Fujian Adventure* (published by Lujiang Publishers, in Xiamen, but they've survived it so far).

And after you've explored Fujian, tackle[7] the rest of this wonderful country!

Beyond Fujian...

Endlessly fascinating Fujian has something to offer everyone, from Zhangzhou's annual flower festivals and narcissus celebrations to Quanzhou's annual puppet shows. So keep your eyes and ears open for special happenings around our province. But eventually you'll want to see the rest of the country, and Xiamen is the perfect base for travel in every direction but down (because we're already at sea level—though you could try scuba diving). Oddly, no trains go south from Xiamen, but you can head west and hop[8] a southbound train in Nanchang. Or if you've really got the wanderlust[9], wander west to the Roof of the World...

Tibet or Bust   How does one take in a nation as vast as China? The same as one eats an elephant: one bite at a time! In 1993, we bought a van, christened her Toy Ota, and set off around Fujian Province and the rest of Southeast China. Encouraged by our survival, we then embarked on a 40,000 km., 3-month drive to Tibet and back.

Tibet
Aug.'94
B.B.

We drove Toy Ota up China's east coast through Hangzhou, Suzhou, Qingdao, Jinnan, and Beijing. Then we cut across to Mongolia, and plowed[10] south through the Gobi Desert, where we had a run in with the swashbuckling[11] descendants of Dambin Jansang, the Avenger Lama. We tackled part of the Silk Road, which wasn't really all that silky, and pressed on[12] to the Himalayan heights of the Qinghai-Tibet Highway, pushing poor Toy Ota across the permafrost[13] of 17,000 foot mountain passes. After we'd paid our respects to Lhasa, we returned home through Sichuan, Yunnan, Guizhou, Guanxi, and Guangdong.

It took us three months to make it to Tibet and back to Xiamen University, and we had

Toy Ota ...Lhasa at last!
B.B.

just barely scratched the surface[14] of this marvelous country.

Six years later, we're still itching[15], and still scratching.

China has too much to see in one lifetime, but give it a go anyway! To the **North** of Fujian Province are the famous Yellow Mountains (but never eat yellow snow!), the ancient silk capital of Hangzhou, Qingdao (China's Bavaria), the Great Wall, Manchuria, Mongolia, and Starbuck's Coffee in Beijing. To the **South** lies Guangzhou and China's Hawaii, Hainan Island. To the East is Taiwan Province, if you don't mind a long swim.

To the **West** is historic Jiangxi Province of Long March and Short April fame, the surrealistic[16] scenery, caverns and waterfalls of Guizhou, the stone forests of Yunnan, the frozen heights of Tibet—and the otherworldly scenery of Guilin and **YangShuo**!

A Yen[17] for Yangshuo Guilin has gotten rave reviews for centuries, but our *favorite hangout in China* is Yangshuo, just 66 km south of Guilin!

If you've ever seen a Chinese painting of stark peaks in a sea of mist— you've seen Yangshuo! The subterranean scenery is just as breathtaking as that above ground (the area has the largest caverns in Asia).

After soaking up[18] the scenery, chow down on a two-fisted "No Name Burger at the No Name Café" (无名咖啡, #97 West St.), or try some dishes at Minnie Mao's Café, MeiYou Restaurant, Drifter's, or Red Star Café (they boast a real pizza oven). These little cafes serve up the best Chinese Western food in China. For breakfast—steak, eggs, hashbrowns, and banana pancakes. Lunch— burgers and fries, or pizza. Dinner—hot Wienerschnitzel, or chicken steak with country gravy. And of course, Laowai's favorite Chinese food: sweet 'n sour pork, lemon chicken, beef 'n green peppers, mushu pork—everything but the fortune cookies!

Getting Around... No Name Café not only has great food but invaluable advice on what to see (Silver Caves, for instance) or what to do (cross-country cycling, or a boat ride from Xingping to Yangdi). Ask for Lilian, or phone: (0773) 882-1304.

Meet Mr. Mok! A good guide is invaluable, and the best around is the world famous (well, almost!) Mr. JiangMing Mo, manager of the Sunny Travel Agency. Jiangming (aka "**Mok**",) knows Yangshuo like the back of his hand[19], and the rest of China like the front. He's happy to guide you from Muslim Xinjiang to the Gobi Desert and anywhere in between.

Address: #9-11 Shen Shan Road, Yangshuo, Guilin, China
Phone: 86 (773) 882-0102 Fax: 882-2060 Pager: 126-1602870
E-mail: jiangmingmo@hotmail.com

Paradise Resort (阳朔百乐来度假饭店) was, at least on our last visit, Yangshuo's premier hotel. Tour groups pay up to $100 U.S. per night, but they'll give discounts if you ask nicely. (Get a family suite: Two bedrooms, two baths, kitchen, and living room).

Address: # 102 West Street, Yangshuo, Guilin, China

For reservations, call: 86 (773) 882-2109. Fax: 882-2106.

Laonei (老内) Notes

---

[1] Siesta: Spanish for "afternoon nap, or rest" (xiuxi, 休息)

[2] Cutting edge: forefront, most advanced, position of greatest importance

[3] Lord of the Rings: a fantasy trilogy (series of 3 books) written by Englishman J.R.R. Tolkien, and made in to a movie series

[4] Train of thought: line of thinking (forgot what I was thinking)

[5] Karst: irregular limestone formations created by erosion; 石灰岩地区常见的地形

[6] Stalagmite: 石笋, a mineral deposit, usually of calcite (方解石) or aragonite (霰石), on a cavern floor, formed by dripping water

[7] Tackle: attempt, take on, wrestle with (as with a problem, or an opponent); 固定, 处理, 抓住

[8] hop: board, 上车

[9] Wanderlust: urge to wander, travel, explore; restlessness; 旅行热潮, 流浪癖

[10] Plowed: we drove through desert sands like a plow through fields (literally, sometimes!)

[11] Swashbuckling: flamboyant (辉耀的, 华丽的, 火焰似的) swordsman or adventurer; 恃强凌弱的, 虚张声势的

[12] Pressed on: continued, persisted (in the face of obstacles)

[13] Permafrost: permanently frozen subsoil; 永久冻结带

[14] Scratch the surface: explore or understand only a small amount; superficial

[15] Itching: desiring to travel further ("I had an itch to travel")

[16] Surrealistic: oddly dreamlike, or unreal quality; 超现实主义的

[17] Yen: a strong desire, inclination, yearning, craving; 渴望

[18] Soaking up: enjoying fully (as if immersing oneself)

[19] Like the back of his hand: intimately familiar

Chapter 19
Chinese FoodFest!

One should eat to live, not live to eat.

Molière (1622—1673)

Moliere never had Chinese food.
Bill Brown (1956—?)

Salutations and Salivations! And welcome to a subject dear to my heart—and stomach. For as Americans say, "The way to a man's heart is through his stomach." Which is true, mostly.

An earnest Beijing reporter asked me, "Why'd you move to China?"

I earnestly responded, "Because Chinese food is too expensive in America."

It wasn't entirely a jest.

People the world over love Chinese food, and where better to get it than China, where 1.3 billion people are living proof that Eve was not Chinese (for had Eve been Chinese, she'd have tossed the apple and eaten the snake).

Chinese greet one another not with, "How are you?" but with, "Have you eaten yet?" Americans may eat to live, but Chinese live to eat, and if we could sum up China in a nutshell[1], we could engrave the nut with "Food"—provided we got to the nut before some Chinese gastronome stir-fried and ate it.

China has always had a love affair with food, but only recently have peasants even in remote villages begun to share the **Horn 'O Relative Plenty**[2]. A few years back, I visited a remote mountain hamlet, which I reached after a rocky boat crossing, a torturous bus ride, a jaunt on a 3-wheel tractor, and a two-mile hike. Villagers who had never seen a foreigner kept their aplomb[3] and greeted me with their cheery, "You've come!" A farmer invited me in, and apologized for an impromptu lunch that included fresh fish, duck, pork, tofu, stir-fried rice noodles, and various vegetables. Their "simple" fare would have set me back a small fortune in Los Angeles' Chinatown.

Chinese Cuisines

Food has been China's avocation ever since the first mythical hero, the hunter and fisherman Fu Xi, invented the kitchen and cooking. At least 3,015 years before Christ, villagers in Banpo, near Xi'an, feasted on steamed chicken, carp and elephant. And in 700 B.C., Chinese chefs wowed emperors with exotic bitter melon soup, and lamb stewed with sugar cane.

The Han Dynasty (206 B.C. to 220 A.D.) gave China flourmills, noodles and tofu, and the Tang Dynasty (618-907 A.D.) saw the advent of the wok and stir-frying. But it was the Song Dynasty's overabundance of food that fueled the great explosion of culinary innovation.

Even Laowai had a hand in influencing Chinese cuisine. The Manchus left behind the winter hot pot now popular throughout China, but adapted in Xiamen to feature seafood instead of mutton. And chili peppers introduced through Portuguese Macao helped ignite Sichuan's fiery fare.

A few millennia of culinary evolution has given Chinese cuisine a diversity unimaginable for a simple American soul like myself, for whom variety is a baked potato instead of mashed, or a side of canned peas – never such common but delectable Chinese delicacies as pea plant leaves or spinach roots. But for all its infinite diversity, most Chinese food fits roughly in five (some say "eight") basic schools: Beijing, Sichuan, Shanghai, Fujian and Guangdong (most popular abroad).

There are also hundreds of local styles. Our Fujian cuisine is sweeter in the south, saltier in the north, and heavy on sweet potato, rice flour noodles, taro and peanuts in the west. (Warning: never eat taro with beef. It's taro-bull).

Beijing Cuisine (北京菜) Tofu and wheat, rather than rice, are staples in Beijing, where vendors sell steamed breads, buns stuffed with pork and vegetables, and Chinese dumplings stuffed with garlic, cabbage, pork, onions and MSG. One popular Northern dish is "Beggar's Chicken". The hallowed recipe begins, "First, steal a chicken".

The famous Winter Hotput helps benumbed Beijingers survive frigid winter evenings, but they feast on Beijing Duck year round.

Diners adopt a live duck for life by painting a number on its side. But it's a very short life. The hapless duck is promptly murdered, stripped to its skivvies[4], and sewn up tightly so it can hold the boiling water that ensures the roasted carcass will be juicy and flavorful inside. The first course is the crisp skin, basted with sweet Hoisin sauce and served with scallions wrapped in small, thin pancakes. For the second course, the leavings are cooked and served with bean sprouts or slices of bamboo. Nothing is wasted. Even the bones are crushed and cooked with water, ginger and onion, and then boiled with cabbage and sugar to form a soup.

Beijing Duck used to be hard to come by in Xiamen, but no more. Try the Marco Polo's Chinese restaurant, on the second floor (Cantonese style Beijing Duck, but tasty!).

Sichuan Cuisine (川菜) Sichuan's fiery fare is a perfect antidote to the sultry summers of this remote but most populous province. Chefs combine ginger, red peppers, onions and soy sauce to create dishes that will ream a Mexican cowpoke's sinuses. But not all Sichuan food is hot; they also serve up sweet, sour, salty, fragrant, and bitter — in every combination possible and some that are not possible but come off anyway.

Xiamen's best Sichuan food is found not in a restaurant but in the home of Xiada's famous art professor, Tang Shaoyun. He and his wife and daughters whip up the tastiest (and fieriest) food imaginable. But if you can't wangle an invite to their home, you can still get decent Sichuan cuisine in most of the major hotel restaurants, as well as many hole-in-the-walls[5] (like those in the 'wet market' facing Nanputuo Monastery). Look for the characters 川菜 (Chuancai).

Shanghai Cuisine (上海菜) In coastal Shanghai, crowds throng about vendors hawking rolls stuffed with pork and beef, and gourmands from all over Asia fly in to sample Shanghai hairy crabs, four-gill carp, and meats spiced with Shaoxing wine, often arranged in beautiful floral designs on delicate china. But where's the beef? Beef is still rare, in Shanghai and elsewhere, for grazing land is scarce in this populous nation. Even if it were not, peasants see it as poor form to reward an ox's faithful service by eating him. So the pig remains the perennial king with Chinese chefs, who use everything from offal to oink.

You've had Shanghai Cuisine! The American favorite, Sweet'n Sour Pork (*tangcu rou* 糖醋肉) is not Cantonese (as many think), but Shanghai. Good Sweet'n Sour used to be hard to find in Xiamen (the local variety tastes like spiced ketchup). For now, the best is at Lujiang Hotel's rooftop restaurant, the "Jade Garden Restaurant" (6th floor, behind the Donghai Department Store), or blue door.

Lujiang Restaurant's awesome Sweet 'n Sour Pork

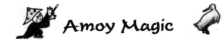

Cantonese Cuisine (广东菜)

Question. What's the difference between a Cantonese zoo and a Cantonese restaurant?

Answer: not much...

The Venetian vagabond Marco Polo wrote of his Chinese hosts, "They eat all sorts of flesh, including that of dogs and other brute beasts and animals of every kind which Christians would not touch for anything in the world."

Evidently, Laowai still don't touch them. A Chinese restaurateur complained of meat and potato Canadians, "They don't want real Cantonese cuisine. It's always sweet 'n sour pork, lemon chicken, beef and green peppers, fried rice, spring rolls, fortune cookies (which aren't even Chinese)."

While Laowai may prefer Mrs. Paul's[6] fish sticks over fricasseed fish lips, Chinese still devour anything that won't eat them first. And if they can't eat it, they call it medicine and ingest it anyway. But Cantonese take the tofu. Even other Chinese say of them, "They eat anything that flies but planes, and anything with four legs but the table and chairs."

Cantonese menus include live monkey brains, sparrows, wild ducks, snails, snakes, eels, frogs, turtles, deer penis soup, and the latest in canine cuisine. (In 1990, an MBA student asked me to invest $10,000 in his scheme to export canned dog meat to America. I asked him if he'd ever heard of market surveys).

Cantonese restaurants abound in Xiamen, but some of the more popular restaurants seem to be in Bailu Zhou (along the lake) and on North Hubin Road, past the Sports Arena. They must be good because they're always packed to the gills[7], and the fins, and the flippers, deng deng.

Xiamen Cuisine (厦门菜)

Canton, though renowned its seafood, comes nowhere close to Xiamen's offerings. Off magical Amoy's contorted coastline, if it swims, crawls, wiggles, or squirms, some enterprising soul will wrest it from the sea and serve it up with Minnan rice noodles, taro dishes and five-spice meat rolls, salty and peppery roast chicken, abalone, duck webs with glutinous rice, scented pork kidney, stuffed cucumbers, braised frogs. We enjoy everything from shark, crab, mussels and oysters (stir-fried with eggs), to sea urchins, mineral-rich seaweed, and sea cucumber. But I still pass on Xiamen's #1 specialty – boiled seaworm embedded in cold jellyfish.

For authentic Xiamen cuisine (a cross between Cantonese and Fuzhou styles), try the Xiamen Guesthouse, near Zhongshan Park, or the Overseas Chinese Hotel, near the Cultural Palace.

But some of it is still too froggy[8] for my taste...

Never try to catch two frogs with one hand.
Chinese Proverb

Froggy Food A Chinese friend removed from his kitchen cabinet a plastic baggie of about four ounces of a grayish, stringy dried matter, rather like a finely shredded spoge. "Only 210 RMB," he said, beaming delightedly. "My brother brought it straight from the mountains!"

This expensive gray stuff was a rare Chinese medicine and cooking ingredient, second in efficacy only to bird's nests (made from dry swallow spit). It was dry frog spit. Not just any frog spit, mind. It was that of a rare mountain frog, and collected only during a very brief season in the spring.

It seemed that everyone had frogs on the brain[9]. A few days later our MBA Center invited me to lunch with a group of Provincial leaders who were taking my night courses. They complimented me on my lectures, though one confessed he wasn't sure if I was contributing to China's modernization or sabotaging it. Halfway through the meal, the waitress set in front of me a shot glass full of a bright, evil looking ruby liquid. It was redder than the inside lining of Dracula's[10] cape, and shimmered with a life of its own. I suspected it wasn't V-8 Juice.[11]

"What is this?" I asked.

"Oh, that's the blood of a rare mountain frog. It is second in potency only to the blood of …"

"No thanks, I'll pass."

"But Professor Pan, you're the guest of honor!"

"I have no honor. You drink it!"

Eventually the rankest person present took the small cup in both hands, ceremonially offered it to each diner, then downed it in one gulp and smacked his lips.

The waitress then handed me a cup of pale yellow liquid. "What's this?" I demanded. "Frog pee? Second only to—"

"—Of course not," she said in disgust. "It's beer."

Frog blood, beer, cobra venom (I've had it).

I wish they'd stick to tea…

Tea Time

Our trouble is that we drink too much tea. I see in this the slow revenge of the Orient, which has diverted the Yellow River down our throats.

J. B. Priestley

According to tradition, tea cures bad eyesight, eases rheumatism and impotence, and was an ingredient in the Taoist's elixir of immortality. It also tastes good, which is why the Portuguese and Dutch and British flooded into Xiamen. Tea fanned the flames of independence in Boston. Tea made the Hatter Mad.[12] And the major pastime in Xiamen is once again becoming the Minnan tea Ceremony...

Minnan Tea Ceremony

Okakura wrote in his timeless classic, *The Book of Tea*:
"To the latter-day Chinese tea is a delicious beverage, but not an ideal. The long woes of his country have robbed him of the zest for the meaning of life. He has become modern, that is to say, old and disenchanted. He has lost that sublime faith in illusions which constitutes the eternal youth and vigour of the poets and ancients...His Leaf-tea is often wonderful with its flower-like aroma, but the romance of the Tang and Sung ceremonials are not to be found in his cup."

The problem was never ideals but economics. Until the early 1990s, even in Anxi, the tea capital of the world, my tea-growing peasant friends could not afford to drink their own tea. While Anxi's Oolong and Tiekuanyin graced tables from Boston to Bali, Anxi farmers brewed choice weeds and grass. But a decade of rapid economic reform has helped rekindle the romance of the Tang and Sung ceremonials. Once again, the cult of Teaism is flourishing.

The teashops lining Xiamen streets sell specialty teas from all over China, ranging in price from pennies a pound to hundreds of dollars an ounce, depending on the type and size of leaves, when and where they were picked, and how they were prepared.

Minnan lasses in minty green mini-skirts lure pedestrians with samples from the Heavenly Blessing Tea Shop, and I once succumbed (to the tea, not to the minty green mini-skirts).

I perched inside the doorway of the tiny shop on a wooden stool before the thickly lacquered oblong cross section of a tree trunk that served as a table. A

girl rinsed the tiny Minnan cups, which are so small they resemble thimbles with handles. She measured out half a swallow of Moli Hua Cha (Jasmine Tea) and used two hands to carefully present the miniscule cup to me.

Tea connoisseurs eye the color, delicately sniff the bouquet, roll the tea on the tongue, swallow, and compliment the host. But I'm a teatotalling coffee drinker used to ½ liter plastic mugs from Arco Gas Stations. I downed the hatch, smacked my lips like a bona fide barbarian, and said, "Good stuff. How much?"

In truth, it was marvelous tea—nothing like the Laonei's Notes that we make palatable only by adulterating[13] with shovels of sugar and cream—a sacrilege to Chinese who add naught but pure water—though Chinese were not always such purists. 1500 years ago they poured on not just cream and sugar but rice, ginger, salt, orange peel, spices, and even onions. They eventually abandoned most of these. Salt was the last to go, during the Song dynasty, but Tibetans still consume copious amounts of salted tea flavored with rancid yak butter. Yum.

A few sips of pure, Chinese black tea (which Chinese call "red tea") is enough to help even an American coffee fiend appreciate why ancient Chinese raised Teaism to cult status—and why Japanese still worship what are essentially just glorified Camellia leaves. But as Solomon said, there's a time for everything. I concur with Wendell Holmes, Sr., who wrote, "The morning cup of coffee has an exhilaration about it which the cheering influence of the afternoon or evening cup of tea cannot be expected to reproduce."

We Told You So... Chinese, you will soon learn, are indefatigable proselytizers, especially of Chinese medicine and tea. Every single one of my friends has argued, "Coffee's bad for you but tea is healthy."

And how a hate a smug, "I told you so" — especially 1.3 billion of them.

On September 11, 1997, the University of Kansas issued a news release, "More Proof that Green Tea May Postpone Cancer, Heart Disease." The study claimed that green tea was twice as effective as red wine, 35 times more effective than vitamin E, and 100 times more effective than vitamin C at protecting cells and their DNA.

Ok, so tea's healthy. But as a wise man (Redd Fox[14]) once said, "Someday all those health nuts are going to feel pretty stupid lying in hospitals dying of nothing."

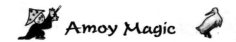
The Book of Tea

Kakuzo Okakura's *The Book of Tea* not only affords marvelous insights into the influence of tea on the culture of Asia, but also highlights the differences between East and West—and why we should try to narrow them:

"[Teaism influences] our home and habits, costume and cuisine, porcelain, lacquer, painting—our very literature...the initiated may touch the sweet reticence of Confucius, the piquancy of Laotse, and the ethereal aroma of Sakyamuni himself.

"The average Westerner, in his sleek complacency, will see in the tea ceremony but another instance of the thousand and one oddities which constitute the quaintness and childishness of the East to him.... When will the West understand, or try to understand, the East? We Asiatics are often appalled by the curious web of facts and fancies which has been woven concerning us. We are pictured as living on the perfume of the lotus, if not on mice and cockroaches. It is either impotent fanaticism or else abject voluptuousness. Indian spirituality has been derided as ignorance, Chinese sobriety as stupidity, Japanese patriotism as the result of fatalism. It has been said that we are less sensible to pain and wounds on account of the callousness of our nervous organization!

"Why not amuse yourselves at our expense? Asia returns the compliment. There would be further food for merriment if you were to know all that we have imagined and written about you. All the glamour of the perspective is there, all the unconscious homage of wonder, all the silent resentment of the new and undefined. You have been loaded with virtues too refined to be envied, and accused of crimes too picturesque to be condemned. Our writers in the past—the wise men who knew— informed us that you had bushy tails somewhere hidden in your garments, and often dined off a fricassee of newborn babes! Nay, we had something worse against you: we used to think you the most impracticable people on the earth, for you were said to preach what you never practiced.

"Such misconceptions are fast vanishing amongst us. Commerce has forced the European tongues on many an Eastern port. Asiatic youths are flocking to Western colleges for the equipment of modern education. Our insight does not penetrate your culture deeply, but at least we are willing to learn. Some of my compatriots have adopted too

much of your customs and too much of your etiquette, in the delusion that the acquisition of stiff collars and tall silk hats comprised the attainment of your civilization. Pathetic and deplorable as such affectations are, they evince our willingness to approach the West on our knees. Unfortunately the Western attitude is unfavorable to the understanding of the East.

"Perhaps I betray my own ignorance of the Tea Cult by being so outspoken. Its very spirit of politeness exacts that you say what you are expected to say, and no more. But I am not to be a polite Teaist. So much harm has been done already by the mutual misunderstanding of the New World and the Old, that one need not apologise for contributing his tithe to the furtherance of a better understanding.

"Let us stop the continents from hurling epigrams at each other, and be sadder if not wiser by the mutual gain of half a hemisphere. We have developed along different lines, but there is no reason why one should not supplement the other."

Perhaps the supplementing has begun with **McChina™** ...

McChina (麦中国) A Hong Kong McDonalds' TV advertisement boasted, "It's not a place, it's an experience." And it's a quite common experience nowadays. Hong Kong has dozens of McDonalds, including 8 of the world's 10 most profitable outlets, and Xiamen is close on its heels.

Hundreds of cheeseless Laowai were thrilled to hear that Uncle Ronald was coming to Xiamen during the Mid-Autumn Festival. Cheeseburgers and mooncakes! But the grand opening was postponed until Christmas, then New Year, then Chinese New Year. We finally **Just what the doctor ordered!** figured it was like the Second Coming[15] — no man knoweth the day nor the hour. Though it turned out that local bigwigs[16] knew both. On the long awaited opening day, we raced to the Zhongshan Rd. McDonalds and were stopped at the door by two guards. Invitation only.

Forget McDonalds! But two weeks later, Sue and I were strolling down Zhongshan Rd. on our weekly date, and it was hard to ignore the bright paper posters and menus plastered on the giant plate glass windows. We succumbed, ordered burgers and fries, and were told, "Electricity's out. Nothing but drinks."

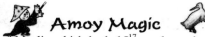
(To the vast delight of Muslim shish-ka-bobI[17] vendors whose charcoal braziers were planted right on McDonald's doorstep).

Sue ordered a coke and I a coffee, and I contemplated devouring the photo of a cheeseburger on the colorful paper place mat.

After our liquid feast I sought out the bathroom, which as expected was spotless. Or I think it was. With no lights, windows, or power, it was pitch dark. I hope I found the urinal and not the sink.

We finally landed our Big Macs a week later. I still prefer Lin Duck House's 5 Yuan pork rice special (排骨饭), but McDs is a nice break from routine — and has the hottest (and cheapest) coffee in town.

Cheeseburger, Hold the Cheese   Better than *eating* burgers is *watching* others eat them!   I've seen folks two soda straws as makeshift chopsticks to eat burgers piece by piece.   Speaking of straws, I cringe at the memory of the granny who tried sipping her boiling hot tea through a plastic straw. I can still hear her blood curdling scream.

I'm sure that was the last straw[18].   Had she been in America, she could have sued McDonald's and retired her entire extended family for life, and soda straws, which are too small for warnings, would now come equipped with instruction manuals.

Thanks to street-side Ronald McDonald performances and weekly offerings of "Collect Them All!" plastic burger men, fry folk, and plastic Snoopy dolls, Xiamen may become like Japan, where children think Big Macs are as indigenous as sushi.   But Ronald McDonald is no longer the only player on the field.   At Xiada the demilitarized zone between McDonalds and KFC is only 100 meters or so.   Several times I've seen the Chinese Ronald McDonald (who looks more like a Japanese Opera star) wooing kiddies away from KFC's magician.

Burgers and pizza and fried chicken are nice for a break – but one of the nicest aspects of life in China is **Chinese** food.   For ½ the price of a Big Mac, I can have Lin Duck's Pork Special—rice, vegetables, tea egg and meat.   But mom and pop shops are having a tough time holding out against Uncle Ronald. With golden arches around every corner, the day may come when Xiamen tourists can find nothing but burgers and chicken McNuggets, or perhaps McSweet 'n Sour™[19], McFried Rice,™ and McLemon Chicken Nuggets™.

But contrary to doomsayers' dire predictions, McDonalds and KFC et al. have not monopolized the fast food market, but helped create and expand it.   As Pepsi (the perennial number two of soft drinks) discovered, wherever Coke goes, the overall soft drink market expands, allowing Pepsi to make billions in Coke's wake.   Likewise, rather than transforming the Celestial Kingdom into McDragon™, McDonalds has created new opportunities for domestic and foreign enterprises alike — and taught some valuable lessons on quality, cleanliness, and consistency.

In closing…

KF China Matt has lived in China since he was six months old, so we make allowances for questions like the one he asked when we drove around America in 1995. "Dad, do they have Kentucky Fried Chicken in America?"

Supplement
There *is* an American Cuisine!

"I don't like American food," some Chinese have told me.

"That's because you've never eaten it!" I respond.

The stuff in fast food chains is as much like real American cooking as instant noodles compares to a dish of Anxi's famous noodles. Not even close! Or take Hakka cuisine, for instance. I thought I'd died and gone to heaven when I ate Hetian

Sunday meal at the Brown's
(Xiamen University)

B.B.

chicken in Longyan's Hetian Village, but when I ate the same dish in Sanming, just a few hours away, I was bitterly disappointed. Fortunately, I still sing the praises of Hakka cuisine and Hetian chicken because I know what the dish is *supposed* to taste like.

Of course, others claim that American food is just a mix of other countries' cuisines. That's true—but that's what makes it so American. America is as much a melting pot of menus as of men. In fact, American reminds me of a much larger (but much younger) version of —West Fujian's little Shaxian Town.

About 1,000 years ago, people from all over China moved to remote Shaxian and brought with them their own unique cooking styles. Over the centuries, the extremities of tastes mellowed, and today the 100+ distinct dishes that make up the 'middle of the road' Shaxian style are popular all over China.

Similarly, as Americans come in all colors, so American food come in all tastes, and those who think we lack variety need to look at my wife's vast library of cookbooks, which have literally tens of thousands of recipes for American food. (Pick up your own copy of the excellent *Joy of Cooking* at Book City, SM Mall 3/F; Amoy Magic also has some American recipes).

Like China, each region of America has specialties. Kentucky Fried Chicken came from the South, where fried foods are popular. Texans enjoy Tex-Mex cuisine, a unique adaptation of Mexican food. (There's nothing like chili con carne, or breakfast burritos!). French cuisine influenced Louisiana's Cajun cooking. Midwest American barbeques are heavenly, and Boston baked beans can be a meal in themselves.

Americans adapted Italian cooking to create pizza, which was fair enough since Italians stole the idea for spaghetti from Chinese noodles. Even our American staple, potatoes, came from abroad. The Spanish introduced potatoes from Peru to Europe in the 16th century, and eventually they made it back to America (largely via Ireland). Turkey and corn are genuine native American foods (we got them from the Native Americans).

Americans also have inventive salads, like the Waldorf and Caesar, and endless desserts like chocolate brownies and pumpkin pie. American food is

A 2-Fisted American Cheeseburger!

not yet recognized as a distinct 'cuisine' because it is too new, but give us a few centuries and our food will be as legitimately "American" as Sichuan cuisine is Chinese (Sichuan food is hot because, centuries ago, they got hot peppers from Portuguese traders).

Those who turn up their nose[20] at American cheeseburgers might change their tune if those noses got a whiff of a real burger: a thick, juicy, ground beef patty (shaped by hand, not stamped out by machine the same way we make leather shoe soles), bedded between two fresh buns with slices of tasty real cheddar cheese (not processed imitation cheese), fresh lettuce, tomatoes, pickles, grilled onions, and slathered in a rich sauce or dressing. Burger marking can be such an art that Los Angeles actually has a five star burger shop.

Amoy's 1ˢᵗ American Café!

Everyone knows I love Chinese food. In fact, I joke that I moved to China solely because Chinese food is too expensive in America. But the fact is, I also love good American home cooking. Fortunately, Father and son team, B.J. and Isaac Gingrich, have now opened Xiamen's first American coffee house— The White Rose!(see page 293)

"The White Rose" Xiamen's 1st American Restaurant!

B.J. 'n Isaac (his son)

B.J. and Isaac have two goals: First, to give Chinese a place to make friends and practice English with foreigners. Second, to serve Chinese and foreigners real American food (many of the dishes are Isaac's grandpa's time-tested recipes)   Two-fisted burgers are juicy and come with a generous side of fries, and I could make a meal of the potato salads. Hearty breakfasts have French toast, eggs, and hash brown potatoes. We also enjoy their homemade pizza, pasta, T-bone steak, or grilled cod, followed by heavenly homemade apple, and washed down by some of the best gourmet coffees in Xiamen.

America *does* have a cuisine, and you can try it at the White Rose. Drop in on B.J. and Isaac, improve your English, and enjoy some real American home cooking!

Laonei (老内) Notes

---

[1] In a nutshell: summarize very concisely, completely
[2] Horn O' Relative Plenty: adapted from "Horn of Plenty"; cornucopia, 聚宝盆
[3] Aplomb: poise, self-confidence; 沉着, 泰然 自若, 垂直
[4] Skivvies: underwear (technically, a trademark for underwear)
[5] Hole-in-the-wall: very plain, unpretentious place

[6] Mrs. Paul's: famous brand of frozen convenient foods like "fish sticks" (breaded, boneless strips of fish).

[7] Packed to the gills: very full; (after eating too much, we often say, "I'm stuffed to the gills").

[8] Froggy: related to frogs

[9] Frogs on the brain: could think or talk about nothing but frogs

[10] Dracula: vampire (吸血鬼) from Bram Stoker's classic novel, *Dracula*

[11] V-8 Juice: trademarked blood red vegetable juice blend, made from 8 vegetables, primarily tomato

[12] Mad Hatter: character in Lewis Carroll's classic tale, *Alice in Wonderland*

[13] Adulterate: add other ingredients (often used negatively); 搀杂, 搀兑; *a.* 通奸的; 搀假的, 伪造的

[14] Redd Fox: a black American comedian

[15] Second Coming: Jesus Christ's future return to earth

[16] Bigwig: V.I.P., important person (in the West, those of higher status wore larger wigs)

[17] Shish-ka-bob: barbequed meat on a stick; 烤肉串

[18] The last straw: last of a series of disappointments or problems that leads to loss of temper or hope—from the Proverb, "It's the last straw that breaks a camel's back."

[19] TM;: Trademark (just joking, of course; my names for McDonald's foods are not trademarked)

[20] Turn up ones nose: show disdain, arrogance

Chapter 20
Our Favorite Eateries[1]

With over 250 hotels and 1,000s of restaurants, Xiamen's offerings are diverse and, nearer to my heart, cheap. We have Chinese, Western, Middle Eastern, African…keep abreast of local Laowai's latest favorites at **http://www.Amoymagic.com**. And don't weasel out[2] by always settling for Western fast food chains. When you're in the typical Westerner's hurry, try some Chinese fast food chains like the Eternal Great King of Soy Milk--or our all time favorite, Lin Duck House.

#1! Lin Duck House (林家鸭庄),

right outside Xiamen University's old gate and facing NanPutuo, is run by a Taiwanese family now PR in Fujian. Lin Duck's extensive **English-Chinese menu** has over 100 items, all at reasonable prices. For the budget-conscious, (Susan Marie says "cheap!"), I suggest the 5 RMB special, "Specialty pork with rice (排骨肉饭)". At least once a week, for 15 years, I've had this bowl of rice, tea egg, vegetables and Japanese tonkatsu (breaded pork cutlet), with a side bowl of broth—all for only 60 cents U.S.!

Lin Duck House! Our family favorite since 1988!

思明南路418号 (418 S. Siming Rd) （厦大一条街）☎ 2086666

#2 Shop 思明南路412号之2 ☎ 2096509 （厦大一条街下街）

Our favorites include chicken in a fried potato-string nest, deep-fried squid, mapuo doufu (Szechuan style beancurd), doufu with brown sauce (Hongshao Toufu), eggs and tomato, Xiamen style fried clams or oysters with egg, french fries, deng deng. Give Lin Duck a try! Phone in advance for take-out. Phone: 208-6666

Yiyuan Hotel, on the Island Ring Road just past Celebrity Villa and before Zeng Cuo 'An Village, serves up excellent (and inexpensive) Western food, as well as delightful Chinese dishes. Try **Chef Matt**'s chicken cordon bleu, gourmet burgers, hot dogs and pizza, or fine seafood. They also offer a nice 38 Yuan buffet on Friday and Saturday nights.

Chef Matt's creations are as much a feast for the eyes as for the stomach Here are photos of some of the amazing sculptures he and his team created from radishes and other vegetables.

Chef Matt 'n Crew

厦门驿缘酒店
XIAMEN YIYUAN HOTEL

B.B.

Yiyuan Hotel's Vegetable Art...

B.B.

Too Beautiful To Eat!

Amoymagic.com

Lujiang Hotel, (鹭江宾馆)
is on the harbor at #54 Lu Jiang
Rd., (鹭江道 54 号) right across
from the Gulangyu Ferry Terminal.
To borrow a pet phrase here,
Lujiang is "famous at home and
broad"—but in this case it's true.
The Lujiang has even been featured
in culinary programs on American
television.

Rooftop Dining on Lujiang Restaurant

Amoymagic.com

B.B.

Lujiang Restaurant's awesome Sweet 'n Sour Pork

Try Lujiang's "Deep-fried
stuffed crab" , "Lobster and Chinese
wolfberry" , "Ginseng and chicken".
They also have some of the best
sweet 'n sour pork in town. Good
food, and open air rooftop dining
offers a prize view of scenic Amoy
harbor. Also check out their
morning dimsum.

Dimsum (for dim sums)
Dimsum supposedly from the
Chinese word dianxin, but I
think it has to do with the
accounting. They bring
around carts full of trays and
small bamboo steamers
loaded with all kinds of
delightful little snacks—
chicken feet, dumplings,
various meats and veggies,
rice congee, etc. Pick what

B.B.

Amoymagic.com   Lujiang Dimsum

you want, and they'll make marks or stamps on what looks like a Chinese
Bingo card. "How much is this?" you ask, and they'll give you a dim sum
(or else they think you're too dim to sum it).

Hence the name dimsum.

But seriously, Lujiang has some of the best dimsum in town, and for a few
dollars you can enjoy what would cost $50 back home in California.

Serve it Again, Sam!   Sam's Barbecue, near Marco Polo Hotel and right around the corner from Lifeline Medical Clinic, offers a mouth watering marriage of Singaporean and Filipino cuisines. Try Sam Chan's pineapple fried rice (served in a pineapple!), coconut chicken (served in a coconut), and savory shish-ke-babs (served on a stick, of course).

Sam started his barbeque as a way for him and his Singapore movie star/pop singer wife to meet more people, and he's so serious about quality food that he even has a farm in Tong 'An to raise his herbs.

When Sam's not serving up mouth watering cuisine, he's running his many other businesses— like the Sony Digital Workshop in the World Trade Center Mall (near the train station), or mining for minerals in Xinjiang, or printing Mabuhay, the official magazine of Philippine Airlines.

Mr. and Mrs. Sam Chan

Sam's Bamboo Rice

Sam's Coconut Chicken

Sam's Pineapple Rice

Amoy's 1st American Restaurant—The White Rose Café. B.J. & Isaac Gingrich, a father-son team, serve up awesome burgers, sirloin, steaks, pizzas, including some of grandpa Gingrich's recipes—and the best gourmet coffees in town. Ph: 202-7298(see page 287)

WESTERN & CHINESE CUISINE

ENGLISH & CHINESE SERVICE

拜伦·金里奇 B.J. Gingrich

手机：8 9 2 0 6 3 1

11AM to Midnight Daily

86-88 Wen Xing Yuan Building, 2nd floor, Wen Yuan Rd, XiaMen
Tel:0592-2027298 Fax:0592-2026258
厦门市文园路86-88号文馨园二楼 361004

中西美食 中英文服务

Mongolian Munchies?

In Lianhua Garden's Mongolian Restaurant (草原城, Caoyuan Cheng), near the Philippine Consulate, you can pretend you're Ghengis Khan as you sit in a Mongolian yurt and lasses in Mongolian garb serve up roasted leg of lamb. Wrap the lamb in thin pancakes with scallions and plum sauce and it's rather like Beijing

Amoymagic.com

B.B. Mongolian Restaurant

Duck without the Duck. If you're not sheepish, order a whole roasted sheep! Two girls bear it on a large wooden platter. It stands upright, eyes bandaged, staring at you, jaw grimacing like a Holocaust victim.
Nice.
Be sure and try the Feibing cakes (飞饼). Phone 24 hours ahead if you want the whole roasted lamb.
Address: 嘉莲里嘉莲花园 3 号
Phone: 555-3318.

B.B.

Jared had a little lamb. Yum.

Havana, behind the Philippine Consulate, offers nice Cuban (or Spanish?) cuisine in a rustic décor with plenty of wood and wrought iron (everything but the black velvet Elvis).

I especially like the "Bravo Potatoes" , and the shrimp and ham croquettes, but so far I've not found anything that I did not enjoy.

    Shannon especially liked the minced beef with rice.

"Havana" (Spanish Cuisine)
--behind Philippine Consulate

SM Mall Food Court   After browsing in Fujian's largest bookstore (3/F), sample some of the diverse offerings of SM's Food Court.   I enjoyed the Muslim food, as well as some of the Japanese cuisine.

    There's an even larger food court, with outdoor dining, on the 5th flood of the World Trade Center Mall, beside the Train Station.

Beef-rice special (Havana)
Amoymagic.com

Muslim Restaurant, SM Mall Food Court

Tea Break! (SM Mall Book City)

World Trade Center Mall

World Trade Center Mall (by train station) not only has plenty of shopping but also a delightful rooftop food court with a broad array of ethnic cuisines from all around China (and earth as well). Pretty lasses in costume offer Yunnan delicacies, or you can have Japanese sushi, Chinese dumplings—even burgers! The Anderson Bakery had a large full-color poster depicting 8 or 10 beautiful loaves of specialty breads.

Open Air Dining (World Trade Center Mall 5/F Food Court--Beside Train Station)

I was in hog heaven—until they told me Anderson did not have even one of the many kinds of bread on the poster.

"What's the point of the poster?" I asked.

"Oh," the girl said brightly. "These are photos of the ones we don't have."

Muslim Restaurant, 5/F Food Court
World Trade Center Mall (beside Train Station)

The Xinjiang stall (hidden in a back corner), offers barbeque mutton—and the best Muslim flat breads in town. Because they're baked, not fried, they're not oily, and are the perfect base for a pizza that you can slap together in minutes. Just throw on some Maling Brand tomato sauce, spices (basil, oregano), ground pork, grated Chinese (from the Olive Oil Stores), and you're ready to take on Pizza Hut for the Nobel Pizza Prize.

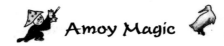

The Eternal Great King of Soy Milk(永和豆浆大王) chain offers Chinese food with the fast service, cleanliness and bright atmosphere of Western food chains.

For years, Susan and I wished that Xiamen had the sesame bread, youtiao (deep fried bread sticks) and hot soybean milk that we used to enjoy for breakfasts in Taiwan — maybe a nice little chain called Dunkin' Doughsticks™. Happily, the Eternal Great King of Soy Milk comes close.

We thought there was yet another KFC across from the Holiday Inn until we looked closer. Instead of the familiar red and white vertical stripes, it sported elongated red and white triangles, like a giant backgammon board. And the Colonel Sanders, on closer inspection, turned out to be a grandfatherly Chinese gentleman beaming at a sign that said, "Eternal Great King of Soy Milk." (The old gentleman logo has since been removed).

"Let's try it, Bill!" Sue said excitedly.

Sue's always up for something new, while her deadbeat husband could eat Lin Duck House's Tonkatsu special until it came out his ears. But the Eternal Great King of Soy Milk was a hit with Laowai and Laonei alike, serving up all our favorites—hot soy milk, Taiwan-style sesame breads, deep fried dough sticks, onion breads, Chinese dumplings, deng deng.

Now other entrepreneurs are milking soymilk for all its worth. In Shenzhen, the sprawling metropolis bordering Hong Kong, I saw half a dozen versions of Great Soy Milk King, all with red and white backgammon motifs — "The Spring Great King of Soybean Milk", "The Forever King of Soybean Milk", "The Eternal King of Soybean Milk." While many Chinese chicken and burger shops flop in months, Chinese seem to really have a handle on Chinese fast food. But the best are still the old standbys, like Lin Duck House.

The Jade Garden, on top of the hotel behind the Dong Hai department store, offers excellent sweet and sour pork, as well as sizzling beef, lemon chicken — all the great dishes you'd get back home in Chinatown or Panda Express. It's a great break from the locals' run of the mill salted jellied seaworms, and cashews and chicken feet. Great food, excellent prices.

Shuyou Seafood Restaurant (舒友海鲜酒楼), on North Hubin Road (湖滨北路), is a marriage of Sea World and Red Lobster. Select your favorite eel, fish, octopussies, squid, seaworms, sea urchins, shellfish, deng deng, from rows of fish tanks on the first floor, then ascend to the second floor dining rooms and wait for your victims to be served. Top quality food (top prices too).

Xiamen Hotel （厦门宾馆）, near Zhongshan Park, is famous for such local dishes as Monk Climbing the Wall ("Fotiao Qiang" 佛跳墙), a tasty combination of shark's fin, abalone, sea cucumber, scallop, tendons, *deng deng*. Also try the "Sun rising from the east mountain" (日出东山), "Phoenix tailed prawn bowl", "Deviled clam", "Eastern Ocean Lobster", (东海龙虾), "Deep-fried taro", "Snail breaking into nest," "Steamed scallop with onion", "Baked fan scallop", and "Steamed perch lined with crab yolk". Address: Xiamen Binguan, Huyuan Rd, # 16, 厦门市虎园路 16 号

The Blue Door is a favorite with Laowai, though I've no idea why it's called the Blue Door when there are no blue doors, blue windows or blue anything else! Their English menu  offers all the westerners favorites. We especially like the pinecone fish (a fish cut to resemble a pinecone, in sweet 'n sour sauce), the sweet 'n sour pork, the cucumber salads, and the deep fried battered apples or bananas (which you dip immediately in cold water so they don't stick together).

    The Blue Door (or whatever color it is) is on a major intersection on Hubin N. Rd. past the XMTV building.

Hao Qing Xiang Restaurant （好清香酒楼） has delighted gastronomes from all over South-east Asia since 1940 with its Southern Fujian snacks, including my wife's favorite zongzi's (the pyramidal bamboo wrapped glutinous rice and meat dumplings), as well as garlic cake and meat onion dumplings, taro cake, and jelly fish (no peanut butter fish yet). Menu favorites include "High quality chicken stewed with Ginseng", (if you're on a budget, maybe you can ask for "Low quality chicken boiled with dandelions?"), Braised squid and straw mushrooms," "Lucky and sweet dew prawn ball", "Glutinous rice porridge with sea crab", "Deep-fried five-flavor rolls" (one of Xiamen's most famous delicacies), "Steamed crayfish", "Deep-fried fish in squirrel shape" (I'm nuts about that one), "Deviled lion's head" (Chinese meatball – excellent!), and "Deviled duck in dipper shape".

    Address: No. 22-34 Da Yuan Road; 厦门市大元路 22 到 34 号

Lu Fa Gourmet Grand Garden Restaurant has a magnificent gate
in front, but the restaurant itself is quite
impressive as well. The 38 million Yuan place
covers 8,000m^2! With 1,500 seats, 22 rooms,
and 10 luxurious VIP rooms, the place is so long
that if you sit at the south end you just about
need to hail a cab to reach the bathroom on the
north side. Even so, Lu Fa is often packed to
capacity. What's there to eat? Just about
anything you can think of, from local Minnan
cuisine to Chaozhou clay pot and Shanghai hairy
crabs. It's no wonder this has become Susan
Marie's favorite restaurant.

Their specialty is Taiwanese,
Minnan and Guangdong cuisines,
including Australian and South
African abalone—which according
to Lu Fa cures virtually everything!

"Abalone has a function of
nourishing yin, balancing blood
pressure and tonifying the skin.
Chinese traditional medicine
believes that abalone can

Lufa Gourmet Rest. (Cashew chicken, Teppan beef)

replenish vital essence and relieve dryness, improve the function of liver and
eyes and can cure the deficiency of vital essence of the liver and kidney,
consumptive fever, deficiency of blood of the liver and blur sight.

"Modern medicine considers abalone full of nourishments with plenty of
protein, fat, iodine, calcium, phosphor and vitamin A and a very good tonic.
Cooked in clay pot in an ancient way abalone is the best dish for diners."

If abalone doesn't cure what ails you, try Shark's fin:

"For a long time, shark fin is regarded as a rare table food and is well known
for its function of improving health and delaying aging. Shark fin has
abundant organic gelatin which can improve the blood circulation and energy.
When done, the soft and melting shark fin in excellent sauce is the best select
for distinctive people to treat their friends."

Well, folks, at 198 Yuan per person I don't think I'm distinctive enough to treat
anyone to shark's fin. Bring on the sweet 'n sour.

Celebrity Villa Restaurant, a 4,500 m^2 place on the Island Ring Road, just past Xiamen University, is run by the same firm as Lu Fa. The parent restaurant, in Shanghai, is 18,000 m^2!

BeachComber's Cuisine. Outside of Xiada's beach gate are small restaurants offering Chinese and Japanese dining with a great harbor view. A laowai favorite: french fries topped with braised pork. (malingshu he rou).

Trek further down the beautiful ring road, past Huli Shan Fortress, and you'll come to more restaurants and snack shops. Sip tea, read, take a swim, or just vegetate and enjoy the site of marvelous two masted Chinese junks gliding gracefully through the waters between Xiamen and Taiwan-occupied Jimei Island (with binoculars you can watch KMT soldiers patrolling Jinmen Island).

Xiamen Mandarin (悦华酒店) back in '88 won its way into Laowai hearts and wallets with its Western Café's "Macaroni 'n cheese" because it was the only authentic western food in Xiamen. Nowadays, we get better western food elsewhere, but it's still hard to beat the Mandarin's excellent Chinese cuisine, or the ambience—or the prices. Specialties include "Dragon attending banquet" (fried lobster), "Deep-fried crab legs" , "Monk Jumps the Wall" , "Coin-shaped crab cake" , "Abalone embellished with radish ball" , "Flock of birds (prawn) exposing to the sun" (exhibitionists?), and "Deviled roast eel". Address: Huli Foreigner Residential Area 厦门湖里外商住宅区

Mandarin Seaview

Mandarin Seaview, adjacent to the Exhibition Center, offers an extensive breakfast, lunch and dinner buffet. Check out some of their special promotions, like the recent Hakka Cuisine Festival.

Hakka Cuisine Festival
(Mandarin Seaview Hotel, April 2003)

The Overseas Chinese Building (华侨大厦), just off the north end of Zhongshan Rd., serves up some of the best local cuisine in Xiamen. Try the "Beancurd braised with cucumber", "Crescent crisp fragrant-flowered garlic cake", "Xiamen pancakes", or "Chicken roll in lotus shape".

Address: 厦门市新华路70-74号　No. 70-74 Xinhua Road, Xiamen

Gulangyu Hotel (鼓浪屿宾馆), with its classic Western colonial architecture, may attract as many film-makers (and diplomats, like Nixon) as diners. The hotel offers both Western and Chinese cuisine. Favorites: "Steamed prawn in flower shape", "Baked crab with garlic", and "Gu Bin pancake". Address: No. 25 Huangyan Road, Gulangyu Island 晃岩路 25 号，鼓浪屿

South Seas Seafood Restaurant

Soups Up!

South Seas (南海) **Restaurant** has four branches in Xiamen. The one at the harbor, on the end of Xiahe Rd., has a couple dozen brightly colored paper lanterns at the entrance, and a fellow making seafood soups in the biggest soup pots I have ever seen. The place seems to sprawl forever, and serves everything imaginable. They even had a plastic basin full of savory scorpions scurrying about! Choose your victims, then choose indoor or outdoor seating.

Xin Qiao Hotel's (新侨商店) brochure says,

"To welcome all people at home and abroad, 'Chun Hui Yuan' Chinese Restaurant would like to recommend you 'Xin Qiao' delicacies — Cold Spicy Pork Intestines, Iced Crab Meat in Chicken Soup, Drunk Pigeon w/Bear, Egg Roll in Laver, Jellyfish Salad w/Minced Chicken, together with dishes of Guang Dong typical, South China typical and hundreds of Xin Qiao morning teas."

Yum. But these dishes certainly merit a go: "Shrimp w/Minced Taro", "Wrapped Thin Pancake", "Two flavor lobster", "Dumpling stuffed with prawn".

Address: No. 444 Zhongshan Rd., Xiamen 厦门中山路444号

Singapore Hotel (新加坡酒店), right behind Zhongshan Park, has a British Pub, Western Coffee Shop, deng deng, but Chinese food's the ticket here. Try their "Deviled chicken shish-ka-bob", "Ba dong prawn", "Singapore-styled fried pigeon", "Roast free eel", "Deep fried prawn cake with sesame", and "Multi-flavored vegetable roll".

Address: #113-121 Xi'an Road, Xiamen 厦门溪岸路113-121 号

Xin Nan Xuan Restaurant (新南轩酒家), on South Siming Road, is one of Xiamen's oldest restaurants, established in 1911. The place can seat 700 people and serve 10,000 tourists in a single day. Some items to try: "Steamed grouper in Kylin shape", "Sea cucumber", "Fried tripe in butterfly shape", "Lobster on vegetable", "Spiced snail", "Crisp fried prawn ball" (heavenly!), "Dark green scallop", "Crisp fried fish flesh", "Baked crab", and "Butterfly shaped prawn".

Address: South Siming Road, Xiamen 厦门市思明南路

Huang Ze He Peanut Soup Shop (黄则和花生汤店), founded the same month as New China (October, 1949), would thrill Jimmy Carter with its more than 20 kinds of snacks and drinks made from peanuts. And the prices are peanuts. Feast on "Fried dough with egg and sesame seeds", "Peanut soup", "Dumpling soup", "Deep-fried jujube", "Seasoned millet mush", "Deep fried glutinous rice", and for a real breath of fresh air, try "Deep-fried garlic".

Address: #22-24 Zhongshan Rd. Xiamen 厦门市中山路 22-24 号

Wu Zai Tian Snack Shop (吴再添小吃点) is the locals' idea of McDonalds. The place boasts 300 seats, usually packed to the gills with guests feasting on such Xiamen delicacies as "Scallion cake", "Taro cake", "Fried onion dough", "Zongzis", "Noodles with prawn", "Deviled noodles", "Jelly fish", "Octopus", (my favorite), and "Braised pig's feet and trotter in soy sauce" (after trying the trotters, I was trotting too).

Address: #49 Datong Rd., Xiamen 厦门市大同路49号

Uncle Walt goes to hotpot

Xia Da Campus Restaurant (aka, International Academic Exchange Center) boasts an English menu and good food (though a bit oily and salty for my taste, or lack of it). Favorites include spicy prawns (eat shell and all) and deep fried squid! Check out their self-serve individual hotpots (in wintertime).

Veggie Tales One of the nicest Vegetarian Restaurants around is across from NanPutuo Temple (南普陀), just down from Lin Duck House. The menu is limited, but it's a nice break from burgers, pizza and sweet 'n sour. Better yet, try Nanputuo Temple's restaurant, for when it comes to a mess of veggies, Nanputuo's denizens don't mess around.　A set price will land you a vegetarian meal that's as much a feast for the eyes as for the stomach (and why not, for as the Japanese say, "The eyes eat, as well as the stomach").　Try Nanputuo's "Diced mushroom & gluten soup in half moon shape" , "Steamed beancurd and vegetarian" , "Fried strawmushrooms" , "Beancurd in lotus shape" (fried, then steamed), "Putuo rice noodles" , and "Drizzling and mushroom shape cloud".

　　Address: Nanputuo Temple, # 515, S. Siming Rd. Xiamen

　　南普陀，思明南路 515 号，厦门

Xiamen Plaza—the first place in Xiamen to offer iced water—a real treat in those days!　(It's bad enough being in hot water[4] all the time without having to drink it too).　Xiamen Plaza is beside the train station, across from the Friendship Store.　For a little afternoon delight, try the afternoon buffet.

Harbour Café (**Holiday Inn**) offers generous (but pricey) Western buffets morning, noon and night.　Check out their special buffets at Christmas and Thanksgiving.　Also check out their Chinese, Japanese and Italian restaurants.

Knife-Shaved Noodles!　Around Xiamen you can find folks deftly shaving long strips off a big ball of dough.　They fly straight into bowling water, and are then scooped out and fried with meat, veggies, and seasonings.　You won't find fresher noodles anywhere, and at only 3 or 4 Yuan a bowl you can't beat the price!

Knife-Shaved Noodles

Knife-shaved noodles

Muslim Noodle Shops (西北拉面) are scattered all over Xiamen.　Look for the swarthy fellows with white linen beanies on their head.　Like all good Muslims, they serve only beef, no pork.　Try the beef soup and beef dumplings (jiaozi), or the hand drawn noodles and beef.　Cheap, and filling, but a bit salty.

They will cut back on salt and oil if you ask—but sometimes it gets a bit tricky communicating with Xinjiang noodle makers if you don't use your noodle[5]...

Use Your Noodle

We Laowai aren't the only ones who murder Mandarin's tones!   So do some of Northwest China's Muslims.

Longterm Xiamen resident Bill Job visited a Zhongshan Rd. Muslim noodle shop.   He asked for hand--pulled (La) noodles, and requested that no hot peppers (La) be added. The La for "Pepper" is 4th tone; the La for "pull" is 1st tone, and they both sounded the same to the young Muslim waiter, who protested, "How can I make hand-pulled noodles without pulling them?"

Mynmar Restaurant, around the corner from the 1st Department Store has fine Burmese food.   Tutto Bene, near Marco Polo, has excellent Italian cuisine, and for some of the best French cuisine in Fujian, try **Sarah's**, which has nice lunch buffets as well (though the barbequed octopus look more Chinese than French to me, but who knows what snail-snacking French cook up?).

Bi Gong Hotel (碧宫酒店) offers excellent Guangdong cuisine, prepared by well known chefs under the guidance of Chinese dieticians.   Try their morning tea (dimsum), and such items as "Green & gold crab in lotus shape" , "Wild chicken in Phoenix-tail shape" , and "Lobster flakes in lamp shape".

Address: Hubin Middle Rd. , Tobacco Bldg 湖滨中路烟草大厦

Japanese Food Try Marco Polo Hotel's "Shogun Restaurant", the Holiday Inn's Japanese restaurant, and the Xiamen Mandarin Hotel's "Goza Japanese Restaurant."   Better yet, sample the marvelous cuisine and ambiance of "Dosun Japanese Restaurant" at 844 Xiahe Road (厦禾路 844 号). Phone: 517 0656. The World Trade Center Mall Food Court also has a nice Japanese sushi bar.

KFC (肯德基—Kendeji). The Colonel has already staked out four locations, including one on each end of ZhongShan Rd. The other two KFCs are in the LianHua area, and across from NanPutuo Temple (within fighting distance of Uncle Ronald's place). (Don't confuse KFC with take-offs like Kenrocky Fried Chicken House!).

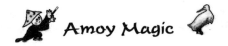

Yes, Pizza Hut offers two outlets — one out in Lianhua, past the choo-choo station, and one on the Harbor on the 24th floor of the Seaview Building (the best salad bar and best view in town!). Order the marvelous Seafood Supreme, and try your hand at building the tallest salad using a one-trip-only wooden salad bowl. Chinese salad experts use sliced cucumbers and onions, cemented with salad dressing, to enlarge the bowl, and construct a tower of veggies that resembles the Leaning Tower of Pizza.

Shannon Brown crafts the all-American salad!

McDonalds (麦当劳 — MaiDangLao)

has at least a dozen outlets around Xiamen: Zhongshan Rd., Xiamen University Xiada (across from Nanputuo Temple), two flanking the train station (a few hundred yards up the road both direcdtions), and the Lianhua and Huli branches.

Dining Tips!

Famished at the Feast. Many Americans prefer to eat their meat and vegetables together with their rice, but when Chinese eat out, they often don't order rice at all, preferring to fill up on things they don't get at home, like jellyfish and seaworms, pickled piggy toes, deng deng. But while these exotic delicacies may tantalize the taste buds, they don't stick to the ribs, and you can easily find yourself famished at the end of a 20 course feast. You should order some fried rice or noodles, or even plain white rice. But beware that unless you hound the waitresses, the rice is likely to be served at the end of the meal, when you're ringing up the tab. Plain, dry white rice is not terribly appealing (and doesn't make for a dessert either). Ask the waiter, clearly, to bring the rice first. Once they agree, hound them because they aren't used to serving rice and will forget. The Holiday Inn's waitresses agreed three times to bring out the rice and still didn't bring it until we'd paid the tab.

MSG. If you're one of the 10% of Americans allergic to MSG, see the Gulangyu Catholic priest about last rites. In the meantime, ask the waitresses, "Qing buyao Weijin (Please—no MSG)." Some cooks refuse to believe anyone can be allergic to

this all purpose culinary chemical and shovel it in anyway. You'll know when your tongue tingles and your face flushes.

The best way to avoid MSG is to cook Chinese food at home... so here are a few Xiamen favorites.

Food and Culture
(or the lack thereof)

Chinese are eating well nowadays. And they're eating slowly...

Not What We Eat, but How

It is almost as hard for Laowai to get used to *how* Chinese eat as to *what* they eat. While Americans urge waitresses to hurry, Chinese are apt to scold, "Slow down. Let us enjoy our food." Our son Shannon once remarked halfway through a three hour banquet, "This sure isn't fast food, its slow food."

I've been in China a full decade, but my Chinese colleagues still jest that I swallow my food whole and chew it later. Chinese prefer to chew their food, not their cud. They zealously fish the flesh from pencil-thin crab legs, and pick excitedly over moist but minuscule bits of chicken or fish that I would not bother picking from my teeth with the splintery scraps of lumber they pass off as toothpicks. I'm still too American, I fear, and tend to emphasize quantity, not quality. Supersize it, and eat on the run. Literally.

No wonder the two most bestselling kinds of books in America are cookbooks and diet books.

Chinese food has given me some food for thought, and I'm trying to slow down and smell the radishes, and heed the advice of grandma who punctuated mealtimes with such pearls of wisdom as, "You're not a cow; chew before you swallow!" and, "Last one up from the table lives the longest."

It appears that grandma's "family meal" had more merit than she imagined, psychologically as well as physically. Research has shown that families who eat together have less incidence of juvenile delinquency.

So the ancient Chinese were right after all. We are not just *what* we eat but *how* we eat.

Nothing more rapidly inclines a person to go into a monastery than reading a book on etiquette. There are so many trivial ways in which it is possible to commit some social sin.

Quentin Crisp

Nights of the Round Table We spent our first New Year feast with our dean. Chinese rice wine and Tsingdao beer flowed like water, and we were urged to partake of the choicest delicacies — boiled seaworms embedded in a grayish round mold of cold jellyfish, giant platters of local crab, fish, shrimp, squid and octopus (my favorite, especially the suctions cups, which are chewy, rather like rubber grapes), red braised chicken, beef and peppers, pastries, soups, vegetables you've never dreamed of (like bitter melon and spinach roots), and of course the desserts: tiny individual egg custard pies, cakes stuffed with black beans, white fungus broth.

We were used to American dining, where the host lays all their cards on the table[6], and we stuffed ourselves on the first 4 courses. We had no idea they had 16 more courses up their sleeves. By the 12th course I was stuffed to the gills[7]. By the 20th, I never wanted to see Chinese food again in my life.

Chinese spend days shopping and preparing, and when they eat, they eat slowly (not like Americans who gulp their Thanksgiving turkey whole so they can retreat to the couch and the football game). Chinese serve their painstakingly prepared dishes almost reverently, one at a time, placing them in the center of the Round Table.

Chinese use round tables because they don't have individual servings or pass food. They serve the food on large lazy susans in the middle of the table and chopstick wielding diners dig right in. The hosts often fish out choice morsels of chicken for us, using the same chopsticks they've been eating with. Though we've not been sick from it yet, it makes us uneasy. And our hosts invariably interpret our hesitation as keqi' (ceremonial politeness) and stab us a few more crab legs, or chunks of beef or chicken.

It sounds distasteful, but it is done with great grace, and increasingly Chinese are familiar with foreigners' scruples, and set aside a set of chopsticks used solely for serving rice and cai.

Cai? Good question. When Matthew was five, he asked during a meal, "Daddy, how do you say cai in Chinese?"

"Cai *is* Chinese."

He looked confused, then said, "Oh. Then how do you say it in English?"

Chinese have two main words for food — fan, for grains and rice, and cai, for vegetables and meat (just about everything but fan). Chinese revere rice, which is

the focal point of ordinary meals. Rice three times a day still goes against my grain, but I sure crave it at banquets, where just a spoonful of rice would help the jellied pig tendons go down. But bona fide banquets are allowed only those choice delicacies that stick to your wallet but not to your ribs. It is all too common to go 18 rounds of fried fish lips, sauteed sow ears, jellied seaworms, deng deng, and return home famished from the feast.

But whether hosting a banquet or a simple lunch, Chinese are masters of etiquette, ceremony, and presentation, making dishes as much a feast for the eyes as for the stomach. Even common radishes and carrots are carved and laid out like phoenixes and dragons, and humble watermelons become dragon boats and pagodas.

Though Chinese are a race of convention and protocol, at the board they let their hair down, because the paramount purpose of Chinese dining is eating — and they are delightfully free from the bonds of etiquette that ensnare Western gastronomes.

After 17 years of marriage, I still can't remember how to place the four spoons, 3 knives, and 4 forks, and in what order to use them. Even my dear mother-in-law has sought to exorcise her savage son-in-law's innate inelegance with such delicate dissuasions as, "Work from the outside to the inside, Bill."

Yes, but from which side of the outside, pray tell?

Dorothy Parker got it right when she wrote, "Those who have mastered etiquette, who are entirely, impeccably right, would seem to arrive at a point of exquisite dullness."

There is seldom exquisite dullness at a Chinese table. They don't use different pairs of chopsticks for meat and vegetables and desserts and rice or noodles. They wield but one pair, usually fashioned from humble bamboo, though more sophisticated Socialists are now opting for plastic, wooden or even bone chopsticks. And unused chopsticks may reside either side of the bowl — though fishermen never place them across the top, lest their boat run aground, and no Chinese jams their chopsticks upright in the rice, for that resembles incense in the rice bowls sacrificed to demons and ancestors, and is a sure way to court unwanted spiritual attention.

Wits and Half-Wits   Chinese newspapers have reported that researchers suggest Chinese are more intelligent than us knife and fork wielding barbarians because chopsticks require more dexterity. My response is that knife and fork take two hands, so we use both sides of the brain, whereas those who use but one hand use only half the brain — half their wit, in other words. But I too have begun to doubt our barbarian intelligence, given the panoply[8] of epicurean[9] protocol beneath which we labor.

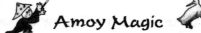

Consider the simple soupspoon. Sue forever intones, "Circular, Bill, away from you and up." Her dear mother adds, as if to a slow child, "So you don't spill soup in your lap, Bill."

Chinese often don't even bother with soupspoons. It is proper, even expected, for one to eat the soup solids with chopsticks, hold the bowl to ones lips, and down the hatch[10] with rest. Simple, and elegant.

But I suggest an innovation: **ChopStraws**™, or hollow chopsticks. Then one could suck the broth without slurping. Though don't follow the granny in McDonald's example and use them for piping hot soup.

Laonei (老内) Notes

[1] Eatery: restaurant (informal)
[2] Weasel out: take easy way out
[3] Serve it again, Sam!: variation of the famous line, "Play it again, Sam!" from the movie from the classic 1942 movie, *Casablanca*, with Humphrey Bogart and Swedish heartthrob actress Ingrid Bergman
[4] In hot water: in trouble
[5] Use your noodle: use your brain ("noodle" is slang for brain)
[6] Lay all cards on the table: be open, frank, honest (from poker)
[7] Stuffed to the gills: could not eat one bite more
[8] Panoply: splendid or striking array or collection; 全套披甲
[9] Epicurean: devoted to pursuit of pleasure, good food, comfort and luxury; 享乐主义者, 美食家, 信奉伊比鸠鲁学说者
[10] Down the hatch: swallow, or guzzle (refers to a ship's hatch)

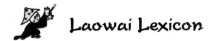
Chapter 21
Laowai Lexicon of
Chinese Cuisine

Getting a Handle[1] on Chinese Food

It is a sad truth, but we have lost the faculty of giving lovely names to things. Names are everything. I never quarrel with actions. My one quarrel is with words. . . . The man who could call a spade a spade[2] should be compelled to use one. It is the only thing he is fit for. Oscar Wilde

Chinese prefer strange and exotic foods, but failing that, they give common foods strange and exotic names. They pass off[3] plain chicken as "Phoenix Breast" , or duck eggs as "Lotus Eggs". And the famous "Monk Climbing the Wall" soup has neither monk nor wall. I hope.

The playwright who quarreled with words would have appreciated these offerings from Chinese menus:

Silver Fish Wrapped in Snow, from Beijing, is neither winter precipitation nor the ornery bugs[4] that ate holes in my wool Scottish tie. It is simply cooked macaroni fried in whipped egg white.

Chicken in a Lantern, also from Beijing, is cooked chicken and vegetables wrapped in clear cellophane and tied with a ribbon.

Phoenix Breast, from Sichuan, is not the legendary Egyptian fowl but plain old chicken breast, like you get for 69 cents a pound at Safeway[5].

Lotus Eggs are not the lotus' source; they're just chicken eggs.

Dragon and Phoenix Ham, from Sichuan, is naught but duck, pork, water chestnuts, chicken wing bones, ham and white bread – mixed and fried. (So who was the dragon?).

Steamed Dragon's Eye rolls, from Sichuan, are strips of pork rolled around red bean paste, topped with a cherry, and served on glutinous rice.

By the time I've worked my way to a menu's soup section and come across, "Bright Moon in a River" and "Buddhist Monk Climbing the Wall" , I'm ready to climb the wall myself.[6] But it's worth the climb. The elegantly named dishes are invariably just as elegantly prepared and served, and well worth the wait.

To make your life easier, we offer the Laowai's Lexicon of Chinese Cuisine.

If you can't pronounce any of the dishes, **just point!**

Chinese Cuisine

中餐 (ZHONGCAN) Chinese Food 西餐 (XI CAN) Western Food

PORK 猪肉(ZHU ROU)
青椒肉丁（QING JIAO ROU DING）Stir-fried Pork & Green Peppers
青椒塞肉（QING JIAO SAI ROU）Steamed Green Peppers Stuffed
      with Minced Pork
炒肉片（CHAO ROU PIAN）Stir-Fried Pork Slices
木须肉（MU XU ROU）Stir-fried Pork Slices & Eggs
糖醋里脊 (TANG CU LI JI) Sweet & Sour Pork (Boneless)
糖醋排骨 (TANG CU PAI GU) Sweet & Sour Pork Rib
红烧猪肉(HONG SHAO ZHU ROU) Braised Pork with Brown Sauce
栗子红烧肉(LI ZI HONG SHAO ROU) Braised Pork with Chestnuts
冬笋肉丝(DONG SUN ROU SI) Stir-fried Shredded Pork & Bamboo Shoots
炸丸子(ZHA WAN ZI) Fried Pork Balls

BEEF 牛肉 (NIU ROU)
咖喱牛肉 (GA LI NIU ROU) Beef & Curry
炒牛肉片 (CHAO NIU ROU PIAN) Stir-fried Sliced Beef
红焖牛肉 (HONG MEN NIU ROU) Braised Beef in Soy Sauce
蚝油牛肉 (HAO YOU NIU ROU) Braised Beef in Oyster Sauce
红烧牛腩(HONG SHAO NIU NAN)Braised Beef Tenderloin Chunks
    in Soy Sauce
青椒牛肉(QING JIAO NIU ROU) Beef & Green Peppers

CHICKEN 鸡 (JI)
果仁鸡丁(GUO REN JI DING) Stir-Fied Diced Chicken and Peanuts
青椒鸡丁 (QING JIAO JI DING) Stir-Fried Chicken with Green Peppers
炒鸡片 (CHAO JI PIAN) Fried Chicken Slices
冬笋鸡片(DONG SUN JI PIAN) Stir-fried Chicken and Bamboo Shoots
糖醋鸡条 (TANG CU JI TIAO) Sweet 'n Sour Chicken Strips
双冬鸡条 (SHUANG DONG JI TIAO) Braised Chicken with Mushrooms
      & Bamboo Shoots
栗子鸡 (LI ZI JI) Stewed Chicken and Chestnuts
油豆腐鸡 (YOU DOU FU JI) Stewed Chicken with Fried Bean Curd (Toufu)

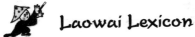 

油酥鸡 (YOU SU JI) Crispy Fried Chicken
蚝油手撕鸡 (HAO YOU SHOU SI JI) Fried Shredded Chicken in Oyster Sauce
炸鸡 (ZHA JI) Fried Chicken
炸纸包鸡 (ZHA ZHI BAO JI) Paper Wrapped Fried Chicken
炸鸡肉串 (ZHA JI ROU CHUAN) Fried Chicken Shish–ka–bob
烤鸡 (KAO JI) Roast Chicken
冬笋门膑 (DONG SUN MEN ZHEN) Stewed Gizzards & Bamboo Shoots
草菇蒸鸡 (CAO GU ZHENG JI) Steamed Chicken & Straw Mushrooms
荷包栗子鸡 (HE BAO LI ZI JI) Steamed Chicken Stuffed & Mushrooms
芝麻鸡 (ZHI MA JI) Sesame Chicken
咖喱鸡 (GA LI JI) Curried Chicken
红烧鸡翼 (HONG SHAO JI YI) Braised Chicken Wings with Brown Sauce

DUCK 鸭 (YA)
烤鸭 (KAO YA) Roast Duck
北京烤鸭 (BEIJING KAO YA) Beijing Duck
蚝油扒鸭 (HAO YOU PA YA) Braised Duck with Oyster Sauce
红烧全鸭 (HONG SHAO QUAN YA) Whole Braised Duck in Soy Sauce

EGG DISHES 蛋 (DAN)
炸象眼鸽蛋 (ZHA XIANG YAN GE DAN) Fried Pigeon Eggs & Minced Meat
火腿蒸蛋 (HUO TUI ZHENG DAN) Steamed Ham and Eggs
肉末鸡蛋 (ROU MO JI DAN) Minced Pork Omelette

OTHER FOWL PLAY
核桃禾花雀(HE TAO HE HUA QUE) Spicy Sparrow & Walnuts
炒鸽松 (CHAO GE SONG) Fried Minced Pigeon Meat
烤酿禾花雀 (KAO NIANG HE HUA QUE) Baked Stuffed Sparrow
鸡 茸燕窝 (JI RONG YAN WO) Braised Bird's Nest with Minced Chicken

MUTTON 羊肉 (YANG ROU)
红烧羊肉 (HONG SHAO YANG ROU) Braised Beef with Soy Sauce
烤羊肉 (KAO YANG ROU) Roast Mutton
烤 羊排 (KAO YANG PAI) Roast Mutton Chops
芝麻羊肉 (ZHI MA YANG ROU) Fried Mutton with Sesame

MISCELLANEOUS CARCASSES
(Thumper, Bambi, Yogi & Kermit).
炒兔片 (CHAO TU PIAN) Stir–Fried Rabbit
红烧鹿肉 (HONG SHAO LU ROU) Braised Deer with Brown Sauce
红烧熊掌 (HONG SHAO XIONG ZHANG) Braised Bear Paw in Soy Sauce

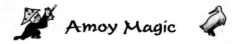

炸田鸡腿 (ZHA TIAN JI TUI) Fried Frog Legs

SEAFOOD 鱼 (YU)

糖醋鱼片 (TANG CU YU PIAN) Sweet and Sour Fish
糖醋石斑鱼 (TANG CU SHI BAN YU) Sweet 'n Sour Garoupa
炒鱼片 (CHAO YU PIAN) Stir–Fried Fish Strips
炸鱼条 (ZHA YU TIAO) Deep Fried Fish Strips
酥炸鱼条 (SU ZHA YU TIAO) Crispy Fried Garoupa Slices
炸鱼 (ZHA YU) Deep–Fried Fish
炸桂鱼 (ZHA GUI YU) Deep–Fried Mandarin Fish
蒸鲜鱼 (ZHENG XIAN YU) Steamed Fresh Fish
蒸桂鱼 (ZHENG GUI YU) Steamed Mandarin Fish
红烧鱼 (HONG SHAO YU) Braised Fish with Soy Sauce
红烧鳗鱼 (HONG SHAO MAN YU) Braised Eel with Soy Sauce
红烧鲤鱼 (HONG SHAO LI YU) Braised Carp with Soy Sauce
清炖甲鱼 (QING DUN JIA YU) Braised Turtle in Clear Broth
炒鱿鱼 (CHAO YOU YU) Stir–Fried Squid
炸鱿鱼 (ZHA YOU YU) Deep–Fried Squid
蚝油鱼唇 (HAO YOU YU CHUN) Braised Fish Lips in Oyster Sauce

SHRIMP 虾 (XIA)

盐水虾 (YAN SHUI XIA) Boiled Shrimp
清炒虾仁 (QING CHAO XIA REN) Stir–fried Shelled Shrimp
油炸虾丸 (YOU ZHA XIA WAN) Deep–Fried Shrimp Balls
红烧大虾 (HONG SHAO DA XIA) Braised Prawns in Brown Sauce
炸大虾 (ZHA DA XIA) Deep–fried Prawns
炸烹大虾 (ZHA PENG DA XIA) Fried King Prawns
炸虾串 (ZHA XIA CHUAN) Fried Prawn Shish–ka–bob
炸虾饼 (ZHA XIA BING) Fried Prawn Cutlets
箭酿大明虾 (JIAN NIANG DA MING XIA) Fried King Prawns in Soy &
     Ginger Sauce
炸竹笋脆虾 (ZHA ZHU SUN CUI XIA) Fried Prawns & Bamboo Shoots
炸虾球 (ZHA XIA QIU) Fried Prawn Balls

CRAB 蟹 (XIE)

蒸螃蟹 (ZHENG PANG XIE) Steamed Crab
炒蟹肉 (CHAO XIE ROU) Stir–Fried Crab Meat
奶汁蟹肉 (NAI ZHI XIE ROU) Stir-Fried Minced Crab & Cream Sauce

OTHER SEA CRITTERS

红烧海参(HONG SHAO HAI SHEN) Braised Sea Cucumbers in Brown Sauce

虾仁海参 (XIA REN HAI SHEN) Stewed Sea Cucumbers with Shrimp

油爆干贝 (YOU BAO GAN BEI) Fried Dried Scallops with Vegetables

白汁干贝 (BAI ZHI GAN BEI) Stewed Dried Scallops in White Sauce

面拖牡蛎 (MIAN TUO MU LI) Fried Oysters

蚝油焖鲍鱼 (HAO YOU MEN BAO YU) Stewed Sliced Abalone in Oyster Sauce

红烧鲍鱼 (HONG SHAO BAO YU) Braised Abalone in Brown Sauce

冬菇鲍鱼 (DONG GU BAO YU) Braised Abalone & Black Mushrooms

VEGGIES 蔬菜 (SHU CAI)

炒素菜 (CHAO SU CAI) Stir–Fried Mixed Vegetables

菜心扒鲜菇 (CAI XIN PA XIAN GU) Stir–Fried Vegetables & Mushrooms

炸茄盒肉 (ZHA QIE HE ROU) Fried Eggplant Stuffed with Pork

醋熘白菜 (CU LIU BAI CAI) Stir–Fried Chinese Cabbage

油焖笋 (YOU MEN SUN) Braised Bamboo Shoots

烩鲜菇蔬菜 (HUI XIAN GU SHU CAI) Stewed Fresh Mushrooms & Vegetables

炒香菇笋片(CHAO XIANG GU SUN PIAN) Stir-Fried Mushrooms & Bamboo Shoots

TOFU (BEANCURD) 豆腐 (DOU FU)

炒豆腐 (CHAO DOU FU) Stir–Fried Tofu

炸豆腐 (ZHA DOU FU) Deep–Fried Tofu

红烧豆腐 (HONG SHAO DOU FU) Braised Tofu in Brown Sauce

素什锦豆腐 (SU SHI JIN DOU FU) Braised Tofu with Mixed Vegetables

红烧什肉虾仁豆腐 (HONG SHAO SHI ROU XIA REN DOU FU) Braised Bean Curd, with Shrimp, Meat & Brown Sauce

鱼脊肉酿豆腐 (YU JI ROU NIANG DOU FU) Steamed Tofu Stuffed with Minced Fish

猪肉酿豆腐 (ZHU ROU NIANG DOU FU) Steamed Tofu Stuffed & Minced Pork

油豆腐嵌肉 (YOU DOU FU QIAN ROU) Fried Tofu Stuffed 'n Minced Pork

蚝油豆腐 (HAO YOU DOU FU) Tofu in Oyster Sauce

SOUPS 汤 (TANG)

鸡茸玉米汤 (JI RONG YU MI TANG) Chicken Corn Soup

牛肉汤 (NIU ROU TANG) Beef Soup

鸭汤 (YA TANG) Duck Soup

三鲜汤 (SAN XIAN TANG) Fish, Shrimp & Pork Ball Soup
鲍鱼鸡片汤 (BAO YU JI PIAN TANG) Abalone & Chicken Soup
酸辣汤 (SUAN LA TANG) Hot & Sour Soup
燕窝汤 (YAN WO TANG) Bird's Nest Soup
豆腐汤 (DOU FU TANG) Tofu Soup
蛋豆腐汤 (DAN DOU FU TANG) Tofu & Egg Flower Soup
鸡蛋汤 (JI DAN TANG) Egg Drop Soup
锅巴口蘑汤 (GUO BA KOU MO TANG) Mushroom & Crispy Rice Soup
干贝汤 (GAN BEI TANG) Dried Scallop Soup

ON A ROLL

馒头 (MAN TOU) Steamed Bun
素菜包子 (SU CAI BAO ZI) Steamed Bun Stuffed with Vegetable
肉包子 (ROU BAO ZI) Steamed Bun Stuffed with Minced Pork
饺子 (JIAO ZI) or 水饺 (SHUI JIAO) Boiled Stuffed Chinese Dumpling
蒸饺 (ZHENG JIAO) Steamed Jiaozi (Dumpling)
三鲜蒸饺 (SAN XIAN ZHENG JIAO) Steamed Seafood Jiaozi
锅贴 (GUO TIE) Lightly Fried Jiaozi
小笼包 (XIAO LONG BAO) Small Dumplings in Bamboo Steamer
春卷 (CHUN JUAN) Deep Fried Spring Roll
葱花饼 (CONG HUA BING) Pancake with Green Chinese Onion
肉饼 (ROU BING) Fried Meat Pie
烧饼 (SHAO BING) Baked Sesame-Seed Cake
米糕 (MI GAO) Steamed Rice Cake
油条 (YOU TIAO) Deep-Fried Dough Sticks (breakfast food)

NOODLES 面条 (MIAN TIAO)

拉面 (LA MIAN) Hand pulled noodles (usually Muslim)
炒面 (CHAO MIAN) Fried Noodles
牛肉炒面 (NIU ROU CHAO MIAN) Beef Fried Noodles
虾炒面 (XIA CHAO MIAN) Shrimp Fried Noodles
海鲜炒面 (HAI XIAN CHAO MIAN) Seafood Fried Noodles
蔬菜炒面 (SHU CAI CHAO MIAN) Fried Noodles and Vegetables
方便面 (FANG BIAN MIAN) Instant Noodles
米粉条 (MI FEN TIAO) Rice-Flour Noodles
肉丝拌面 (ROU SI BAN MIAN) Noodles with Shredded Pork
汤面 (TANG MIAN) Noodle Soup
三鲜汤面 (SAN XIAN TANG MIAN) Seafood Noodle Soup

FRIED RICE 炒饭 (CHAO FAN)

猪肉炒饭 (ZHU ROU CHAO FAN) Pork Fried Rice
牛肉炒饭 (NIU ROU CHAO FAN) Beef Fried Rice
鸡炒饭 (JI CHAO FAN) Chicken Fried Rice
鸡蛋炒饭 (JI DAN CHAO FAN) Egg Fried Rice
什锦炒饭 (SHIJIN CHAO FAN) Fried Rice With Shrimp, Mushroom & Chicken
蔬菜炒饭 (SHU CAI CHAO FAN) Vegetable Fried Rice
蘑菇炒饭 (MO GU CHAO FAN) Mushroom Fried Rice

SWEET TOOTH 饭后甜食 (FAN HOU TIAN SHI)

拔丝苹果 (BA SI PING GUO) Apple Fritters
拔丝香蕉 (BA SI XIANG JIAO) Banana Fritters
核桃酪 (HE TAO LAO) Sweet Almond Paste

MISC. SURVIVAL

请不要味精 (QING BU YAO WEI JING) Please, NO **MSG**!

菜单 (CAI DAN) Menu

账单 (ZHANG DAN) Bill

我没有钱! (WO MEI YOU QIAN!) I don't have any money!

后门在哪里? (HOU MEN ZAI NA LI?) Where's the back door?

等等 (DENG DENG) Etcetera, etcetera, etcetera.

Laonei (老内) Notes

---

[1] Get a handle on: understand ("handle" is also slang for "name")
[2] Call a spade a spade: to be frank, blunt; to not mince words (like calling a "garbage collector" a "sanitation engineer").
[3] Pass off chicken: to pretend chicken is something more exotic
[4] Ornery bugs: an insect called "silverfish" eats clothes
[5] Safeway: large American grocery chain
[6] Climb the wall: anxious, going mad

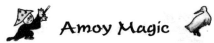
Chapter 22

Home Cooking
—Chinese & Western

Eating out is fun and, dear to my heart, cheap. But so is home cooking, thanks to Xiamen's abundance of great markets. Old Amy is the cornucopia[1] that suckled Zeus himself, with an unimaginable variety of vegetables, fruits, of fish, fowl and fungi. You name it, Xiamen has it—and much fresher and cheaper than you'll find back home.

In earlier editions of Amoy Magic I included local recipes, as well as Western recipes for Laowai who forgot to bring their cookbooks. Nowadays, you can go on the Internet and find just about any recipe you want. Still, here are some of our favorites—beginning with local Xiamen Cuisine.

(Of course, all recipes call for MSG, but we survive without it).

Xiamen Specialties

Spicy Fried Rolls Wrap these ingredients in a round sheet of dried tofu: cubed pork, fish meat, onions, water chestnuts, soy sauce, five spices, sweet potato starch. Deep fry, cut in slices, serve.

Spring Rolls These delightful delicacies are like a Minnan version of a Mexican burrito. Buy spring roll wrappers at the market, and for the filling, make a mixture of shredded carrots and bamboo shoots, green peas, shredded meats and shrimp, tofu, and anything else that strikes your fancy or wanders in off the street. Cook it well, add salt and soy sauce, and wrap in spring roll wrappers, along with a little mustard, chili sauce, plum sauce, scrambled eggs, leeks, and Chinese parsley (coriander). Enjoy.

Oil-Scallion Cake Add fish meat to diced pork and water chestnuts, then add a little sweet potato starch, some scallions, a dash of Five Spice, and some sugar and salt. Form into balls and coat with rice starch in bowls and steam. Let cool, and sprinkle with your favorite Chinese condiments (chili paste, pickled radish, deng deng).

Tosun (Jelly Fish and Sea Worm) This is Xiamen's number one specialty. It's also the one thing I can't handle—but you haven't lived until you at least try. These culinary delights are dug from the mud on the beach. Enough said there. Wash the Tosun (jelly fish) clean and stew over a slow fire until the gelatine dissolves. Pour soup into cups and allow to cool into a jello-like substance. (Somewhere along the line you should add the seaworms, I guess). Force down with Chinese chili sauce, mustard sauce, vinegar.

Fried Squid Our favorite! Clean squid thoroughly and soak in clear water for a couple of hours, then cut it into thin slices and score with intersecting diagonal cuts. Fry the squid with bamboo shoots, scallions, tomato, sugar and vinegar until they roll up into a tube shape. (Don't overcook or they'll have the texture of rubber grapes).

Fried Oysters (sort of an oyster-egg pancake) Dip oysters in sweet potato starch, add soy sauce, and fry. Pour beaten eggs on the mixture and continue to fry until done. Add Chinese parsley (coriander); eat with mustard or chili sauce.

Stir-Fried Rice Noodles Deep fry rice noodles (a vermicelli type noodle) until golden, then rinse in boiled water to remove grease. Stir-fry shredded pork, fish, mushrooms and bamboo shoots in **A fowl way to get a head in life...** peanut oil and add chicken bouillon[2], Shaoxing wine, and salt. Add the noodles and serve hot. Awesome.

Zongzi My wife's favorite! These are pyramid-shaped dumplings of glutinous rice and other ingredients, wrapped in bamboo leaves. Originally served on the Dragon Boat Festival, nowadays they are found year round. Make your own by stir frying glutinous rice, pork, chestnuts, mushrooms and shrimp (or some use red beans), and wrap them with bamboo leaves into a pyramid shape, and tie them, then braise them in a soup until well done.

Want more recipes? **The Chinese Garden** has more great recipes from all over China. Download beautiful color photographs and recipes, in either Chinese or English, from http://www.chinese-garden.com

Laowai Survival Recipes

Chinese food is fresher, more varied, and healthier than most Western food, and eating out is fun and, dearer to my heart, cheap—especially if you live on Chinese fast food specials at Lin Duck House. Day or night, stalls offer such choice delicacies as Chinese rolls, breads, bean curds, dried mushrooms, fricasseed fish lips.

But when a bout of homesickness lays you low (and it happens), a little home-cooking is in order. Fortunately, Xiamen now has almost anything you need to whip up[3] a nice Western meal.

For **Breakfast**, eggs, milk and bread are readily available. (Toasters aren't always easy to find though). Chinese oatmeal (mai pian, or 麦片) is cheap, and makes great porridge, muesli (or granola in America), muffins, or pancakes (use local yogurt in the batter, and add sliced bananas).

For **Lunch**, canned Chinese luncheon meat (wucanrou, or 午餐肉), or the excellent frozen "Dragon Island" ham from Guangzhou, makes a good sandwich, especially with Pringles Chips (or some tasty local potato chips).

For **Dinner**, use Chinese noodles for spaghetti, and make a sauce from Ma Ling Brand tomato paste, ground pork, a little basil, pepper, and salt. Slap the same sauce on a 2.50 rmb round Muslim bread and you've a nice little pizza.

Or take the easy way out with take-out pizza from Pizza Hut, or frozen chicken pot pies from Beatrice (unfortunately, seldom in stock).

Homemaking Tip from Susan Marie

You can bake cakes or roast small fowl in the small Japanese or Chinese toaster ovens, but Sue finally bought a good 'ole Sears oven in Pasadena and shipped it back (even with shipping, it was cheaper than our little Italian oven that we bought in Hong Kong and didn't work from day one).

If you're going to hang your hat here awhile, make life simpler with a decent oven and a good food processor. The best investment you can make is a decent rice cooker (150 Yuan models are as good as the 800 Yuan electronic gizmos[4]).

With a rice cooker, just add 1 cup of cleaned rice, two cups of water, push the button, and wait ½ an hour or so for practically perfect rice. Even I can manage a rice cooker, and I've been known to burn water.

Lastly, get a Chinese freezer to stock up on those veggies and meats that are here today and gone tomorrow.

E-Z Western Entrees from Taiwan's Laowai!

Laowai who forgot their cookbook, as well as Laonei Pengyou who want to try Western cooking, will enjoy our most asked for idiot-proof, time-tempered recipes. And you can do your part in improving Cross-Straits relations by serving these to your Chinese friends, because many recipes are from the cookbook/handbook *Tips 'N Treats on Taiwan*, written by Taiwan's Laowai (Grab a copy if you're ever in Taipei, or swim across to Jinmen Island).

     Tip: try Xiamen's own **BB Brand Worcestershire sauce**! (free advertising) ☺

Captain's Chicken (5 Stars!)

3 lbs. chicken breasts	3-4 tsp. curry powder	seasoned flour
1 ½ tsp. salt	½ cup oil	1 tsp. thyme
2 chopped onions	½ tsp. white pepper	2 cans tomatoes
2 chopped green peppers	1 minced garlic clove	1 Tbsp. chopped parsley
¼ cup currants or raisins	¼ cup toasted almond slivers (optional)	
6 cups hot cooked rice (use a rice cooker)	*Continued on next page...*	

Remove skin from chicken. Roll breasts in seasoned flour. Fry in oil until browned. Remove chicken—keep warm. Cook onions, peppers, and garlic in remaining fat in pan until tender. Stir in curry powder, salt, pepper and thyme. Mix well. Add tomatoes and parsley. Place breasts in large casserole. Pour sauce over chicken. Bake in **preheated** oven at 325°. When tender, place chicken on rice and cover with currants and almond slivers.

Tuna Burgers

1 can tuna	1 cup chopped celery	1 cup cut up cheese
1 small chopped onion	¼ cup mayonnaise	salt and pepper

Mix all ingredients together. Fill 6 hamburger buns (from Beatrice) and bake for 15 minutes. **Shopping tip**: get tuna and cheese from the Olive Oil Store or Xiada's "Cheese Store". Beatrice has cheese, but it's costlier. (See Chapter 23, Laowai Life).

Swedish Cabbage Rolls

12 large cabbage leaves	1 pound hamburger	1 beaten egg
1 cup cooked rice	¼ cup chopped onion	18 oz. can tomato sauce
1 tsp. salt	1 tsp. lemon juice	¼ tsp. pepper
¼ cup milk	1 tsp. Worcestershire	1 tsp. brown sugar

Immerse cabbage leaves in boiling water for 3 minutes or until limp; don't boil too long or they fall apart. Drain. Make meat mixture—egg, milk, onion, salt, pepper, hamburger, and rice. Place ¼ cup in middle of cabbage leaf and roll up. Make tomato sauce mixture—remaining ingredients. Pour over rolls. Cook

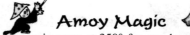
in crock pot 6 hours on low or in oven at 350° for one hour. Chinese cabbage works very well too. Serves 6 (unless you have teenagers![5]).

Tamale Pie

1 cup corn meal	1 tsp. salt	¼ cup milk powder
½ tsp. salt	¼ tsp. pepper	2 tsp. chili powder
3 cup hot water	¼ cup chopped onions	1 cup water
¼ lb. grated cheese	2 cans tomato paste	1 1b. hamburger

Mix corn meal, milk powder and salt together in sauce pan. Slowly add <u>hot</u> water while stirring. Cook in double boiler or over low heat stirring often for 30 minutes until fairly stiff. Brown meat, add tomato paste, salt, pepper, onion, chili powder and simmer for 15 minutes. In 1 quart casserole, layer cheese, cornmeal mixture and meat mixture. Place in preheated oven at 350° for 20 minutes. May be made ahead of time and heated later. Makes 3 servings.

Homemade Barbecue Sauce

2 tsp. tomato sauce　　½ cup ketchup　　salt & pepper　　onion　　bacon
lemon juice　　little honey　　2 Tbsp. brown sugar　　2 Tbsp. Worcestershire
　　Add ingredients to taste; mix well. Baste chicken, wrap in foil, and barbecue. Delicious!

Last but never least...

Susan Marie's Sauteed Shark 鲨鱼(Sha Yu) Steaks!

Sue landed some beautiful shark steaks for only 15 Yuan a jin (about 1.1 pounds), but they're hard to come by, so if you find them, stock up! (They freeze well) And Sue's shark recipe is a winner!

Rub a few drops of lemon juice and olive oil on shark steaks. Sprinkle with seasoned salt, like Lawry's. Dip steaks in seasoned flour and sautee in hot olive oil. Fry for about 2-3 minutes on each side. Serve with tartar sauce (Real mayonnaise mixed with hot dog relish or chopped sweet pickles).

And now it's time for your **just desserts...**[6]

Just Desserts

Taiwan's Laowai cook these recipes in rice cookers, but Susan Marie says mainland rice cookers don't work the same way, so use an oven.

Pineapple-Upside-Down Cake

½ cup butter	1 cup brown sugar, packed	3 cups flour
2 cups sugar	1 can sliced pineapple	4 t. baking powder
1 tbsp. salt	2 eggs　　1 1/3 cups milk	2 tbsp. vanilla

Melt butter in 9 × 13 pan in oven.   Sprinkle brown sugar evenly over butter, then attractively arrange pineapple slices over this.

Measure flour and all dry ingredients in bowl, add all other ingredients and stir until smooth.   Pour batter over fruit.   Bake in **preheated** oven at 350° for 40~50 minutes until toothpick stuck in center comes out clean[7].   Cool 5 minutes then turn upside-down onto serving plate.   Serve warm.   Add a spicy touch with 1 tsp. cinnamon, 1 tsp. nutmeg.   Raisins, nuts and cherries optional.

Banana Cake

¼ cup oil   ¾ cup sugar   1 t. soda   2 large or 3 small bananas, mashed
2 cups flour   2 eggs   1/8 t. salt   ¼ cup sour milk (add vinegar to milk)

Stir ingredients together and bake in a loaf pan in a **preheated** oven at 375° for one hour. (A fun and E-Z recipe for Laonei friends to try).

Goofproof Goofy Cake

Laowai & Laonei alike have begged for this idiot-proof chocolate cake recipe that *never* fails!

3 cups flour   2 cups sugar   6 Tbsp. cocoa
1 tsp. salt   ¾ cup oil   2 tsp. baking soda
2 tsp. vanilla   2 cups cold water   2 Tbsp. vinegar

Sift dry ingredients together, then add remaining and stir until smooth.   Bake in a 9 × 13 pan in a gas oven at 350° for 30 to 35 minutes.   If you use a small counter-top toaster oven, like Dr. Jan's National, it takes an hour at 180~200℃, and Susan Marie says two small loaves are better than one big loaf because the middle cooks faster.

Speaking of loaves… I like to loaf around on Sunday but we usually have visitors for half the day.   Oh well. Half a loaf is better than none.

Fluffy White Frosting (for goofy cake)

1 ½ cups sugar   ½ cup water   2 egg whites
½ tsp. vanilla   ½ tsp. cream of tartar

Stir and dissolve sugar and water in pan over low heat.   Cover pan and bring to boil.   Boil 5 minutes.   Uncover pan and continue cooking without stirring until mixture reaches thread stage.   Beat egg whites until frothy, add cream of tartar, and beat until stiff.   Then add the syrup in a steady thin stream while beating.   After all the syrup is added, continue beating 2 minutes.   Fold in vanilla or peppermint extract.

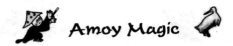

Blonde Brownies (awesome!)

2/3 cup butter	2 cups brown sugar, packed	2 beaten eggs
2 cups flour	1 tsp. vanilla	1 tsp. baking powder
1 tsp. salt	¼ tsp. baking soda	1~2 cups chocolate chips

Melt butter and add brown sugar. Cool, then add eggs and vanilla. Sift together flour, baking powder, soda and salt. Mix well and place in 9×13 inch pan. Add chips on top. Bake in **preheated** oven at 350° for about 25 minutes. Avoid over-baking. They puff up when done.

Fudge Brownies

2 cups sugar	4 eggs	1 1/3 cups oil	1 tsp. baking powder
½ tsp. salt	2 cups flour	½ cup coca	½ tsp. vanilla

Beat sugar, eggs and oil; add sifted dry ingredients. Mix together. Bake in 10 ×15 pan (use black oven pan) for 15 minutes in **preheated** oven at 350°.

E-Z Apple Pie

Crust... Put 2 cups flour and 1 tsp. salt in a Food Processor. Add: ½ cup oil and ¼ cup cold water. Roll between two sheets of wax paper. Produces 2 crusts.

Apple Filling... Slice apples (in food processor), place in unbaked pie shell, sprinkle a few spoonfuls of lemon juice, two spoons of flour, and two Tbsp. of sugar, cover with top crust, make slits in top for steam to escape, bake in **preheated** oven at 425° for 35~45 minutes. Serve with vanilla ice cream.

Soy Be It!

Sweet on Tofu? Tofu (豆腐) (Chinese bean curd) is not only highly nutritious but also an excellent substitute for Philadelphia Cream Cheese (available in the Olive Oil Store) in cheesecake, and ricotta cheese in lasagne! The following Tofu recipes are so tasty it's hard to believe they are good for you.

Tofu Cheesecake

E-Z 8" pie crust: finely crush your favorite cream-filled cookies, like Oreos, mix in a couple Tbsp. of margarine, use a large spoon to press this firmly into the bottom of a pie pan, and bake in **preheated** oven at 350° five or ten minutes, or until brown. Allow to cool before adding filling:

Filling

1 lb. tofu (2 cups)	2 Tbsp. lemon juice	½ cup brown sugar
¼ cup oil	1/3 cup honey	1 tsp. vanilla
pinch of salt	1 Tbsp. unbleached white flour	

Blend ingredients in food processor until smooth and creamy, then pour into the unbaked pie shell and bake for about 45 minutes in an oven preheated to 350°, or until cracks begin to form on the edges of the filling.

Tofu Cookie Pudding.

½ lb. tofu (1 cup)—steamed	1/3 cup sugar	
2 Tbsp. oil	1 tsp. vanilla	pinch of salt

Blend ingredients in blender or food processor until smooth and creamy, fold 8 Oreo cookies (broken into quarters) into the pudding, and chill from 2 hours to overnight.

And an excellent Tofu Entrée...

Two-Tofu Lasagne

Follow your favorite lasagne recipe, but substitute tofu for ricotta cheese, and use wonton wrappers (buy stacks of them in produce markets) for pasta. After you've tried wonton wrappers, try using dried tofu sheets instead (soaked until tender but don't fall apart) for a highly nutritious and exceptionally tasty lasagne.

Just in case you don't have a recipe, here is Susan Marie's:

Spaghetti Sauce   1-2 packages of tofu
1 ½ lbs. wonton wrappers *or* a stack of dried tofu sheets
Mozzarella and Parmesan cheeses (from Olive Oil store)

Prepare a spaghetti sauce with browned ground meat (add minced garlic if you like). Add sauteed minced onion cooked in chicken bouillon (the more onion the better).

Put a thin layer of spaghetti sauce with meat on the bottom of a 9 x 13 inch pan. Cover with 1~2 layers of wonton wrappers (or sheets of soaked, dried tofu), spoon on stirred tofu, layer with meat sauce, parmesan cheese and mozzarella cheese. Repeat layers until pan is full. The top should just be a thin layer of meat sauce, with a little mozzarella and parmesan.

Cover and bake at 350° for 45 minutes or until done.

Serves four adults or half a teenager.

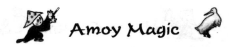

Mad about Oatmeal ☺

Many Xiamen shops offer one of our planet's most nutritious and versatile products: plain old oatmeal 麦片 (Maipian).   I use oatmeal for everything from fantastic fruit muesli (Granola, as we Americans say), to oatmeal muffins, oatmeal bread, oatmeal pancakes, oatmeal cookies—

Quality Chinese Oatmeals
Amoymagic.com

and plain old boiled oatmeal for breakfast, with a dash of cinnamon.

Xiamen shops offer brands imported from England, Australia and the U.S., but I've found that Chinese oatmeal is just as good, and ½ to 1/3 the price. (But rolled oats, which are best for Granola, aren't available yet; bring it from home).

Oatmeal Pancakes

Mix 1½ cups oatmeal with 2 cups sour milk (add 2 Tbsp. vinegar to 2 cups of milk), and let sit.   In another bowl, stir together ½ cup flour, 1 tsp. sugar, 1 tsp. soda (use finger to pinch so no lumps), 1 tsp. salt.   Add this to the oatmeal mixture, and stir in 2 beaten eggs.   Fry in hot greased griddle until golden brown. Top with Chinese honey.   **Optional**: add sliced bananas

Oatmeal Bread (Dr. Bill's own!) ☺

Combine in large bowl:
    2 cups oatmeal   ½ cup honey   1 Tbsp. salt   2 Tbsp. margarine
Add 2 cups boiling water.
Dissolve: 1 package (1 Tbsp.) dry yeast in ½ cup warm water.
Add yeast after batter cools, and stir in 5 to 6 cups of white flour.
Knead and add white flour until the dough is satiny and smooth.
Place in greased bowl, cover with cloth, let rise until doubled.
Punch down loaves, place in greased loaf pans, allow to double, brush with a
    beaten egg, then bake in **preheated** oven at 350° F. for 30~40 minutes.
Cool on rack, slice, and serve up with a hearty barley & cabbage soup.

Oatmeal Muesli (Granola)   I make a month's supply at a time!

Fill the biggest bowl you can find (washbasins work well) with oatmeal (rolled oats if you can find them).   Mix a spoon of salt through the dry mixture. Slowly dribble peanut oil over the mixture while stirring constantly (this keeps the muesli flaky, and prevents clumping). Add just enough to moisten the flakes. Repeat this dribble process with a cup or two of honey.   Stir in a couple spoons of vanilla, and a spoon of cinnamon.   Add raw peanuts and other nuts, and bake in **preheated** oven at 350° for 20 to 30 minutes, stirring every ten minutes or so to keep from burning.

After the mixture has cooled, add all the finely chopped dried fruits that you can find—and Xiamen has plenty! I add shredded coconut, banana chips, and dried papayas, mangoes, pineapple, apple, apricots, raisins, figs, deng deng!

For ultimate convenience, stir in a couple bags of powdered milk and store in a tightly sealed container. Then simply add ice water, stir, and serve.

Oatmeal Cookies (four dozen)

Put through a sieve:

1 ½ cups white sugar	1 ½ cups brown sugar	3 cups sifted flour
2 tsp. salt	2 tsp. soda	1 tsp. baking powder.

Cut in 2 cups shortening, and add 6 cups oatmeal.

Combine mixture in bowl with 2 beaten eggs and 2 tsp. vanilla.

Drop teaspoonfuls onto greased baking sheet, flatten with fork, and bake in **preheated** oven at 350° for 12 minutes or until well browned.

Oatmeal Muffins   (one dozen)

Stir in mixing bowl:

1 cup sifted flour   ¼ cup sugar   3 tsp. baking powder   ½ tsp. salt

Stir in: 1 cup oatmeal   ½ cup raisins

Add: 3 Tbsp. oil   1 egg, beaten   1 cup milk

Stir just until dry ingredients are moistened. Fill greased muffin cups 2/3 full, bake 15 minutes in oven **preheated** to 425°.

Veggie Tips Vegetables are often grown with nightsoil, so treat them properly, especially if eating them raw or in salads.

If eating them raw, wash thoroughly with soap and water, and peel – or dip in boiling water for 10 seconds.   Or—rinse vegetables in chlorine water (1 T. to a gallon), then rinse in boiled water.   Or… don't bother.   Just build a 19 Yuan salad at Pizza Hut.   Boil drinking water for ten minutes.

Babies under 3 months old should be bathed in drinking water.

In Season, & Out...

One of the nicest aspects of life in China, and particularly in Xiamen, is our great abundance of fresh fruits and vegetables. Because they're fresh, they also tend to be highly seasonable—though seasons are getting longer now that roads are better and we get shipments from all over the country (and we have more greenhouses now).

Canned and dried fruits are, of course, available year round.

Fruit lovers enjoy Zhangzhou's mandarin oranges and bananas,

B.B. The Sweet Potato Man

Putian's lichees, Changtai's pomelos (rather like a grapefruit), Longyan's pears, deng deng. As broad a selection as you'll find anywhere back home, though at much better prices—when in season…

Bananas	-	All year, especially summer
Cantaloupes	-	May, June
Coconut	-	All year
Grapes	-	July, August
Guavas	-	June
Kumquat	-	Dec., Jan.
Lemon	-	July, August (but increasingly common other times; we still bring in lemon juice)
Loquat	-	March, April
Mango	-	May, June
Oranges	-	October thru January
Papaya	-	May, June
Pear	-	August
Persimmon	-	August, Sept.
Pineapple	-	May, June
Plums	-	April, May
Pomelo	-	August through December
Star Fruit	-	March, April
Strawberries	-	April
Sugar Cane	-	January thru March
Tomatoes	-	All year
Watermelon	-	June-August

Substitutions

For	Use
1 cup sour milk	1 cup milk and 1 T. vinegar or lemon juice
1 cup sweet milk	½ cup evaporated milk, ½ cup water
1 T. cornstarch	2 T. flour
1 cup honey	¾ cup sugar, ¼ cup liquid
1 pt. whipping cream	1 pt. water and 2 cups dry nonfat milk solids; add 1 T. sugar and 1 T. lemon juice before whipping
1 cup nut meats	1/3 cup butter
1 egg (for leavening)	½ tsp. baking powder
1 cup granulated sugar	1 cup honey or syrup
1 teaspoon baking powder	1 tsp. cream of tartar & 1 tsp. baking soda
1 ½ cups corn syrup	1 cup sugar plus ½ cup water
1 cup canned tomatoes	1 1/3 cup chopped fresh tomatoes simmered for ten minutes
½ cup catsup or chili sauce	½ cup tomato sauce plus 2 T. sugar, 1 T. vinegar, 1/8 teaspoon cloves,
½ cup tartar sauce	6 T. mayonnaise plus 2 T chopped pickle relish
1 cup tomato juice	½ cup tomato sauce & ½ cup water
¼ cup cinnamon sugar	¼ cup granulated sugar plus 1 tsp. cinnamon
1 teaspoon allspice	½ tsp. cinnamon, 1/8 tsp. ground cloves
1 cup chicken broth	1 chicken bouillon dissolved in 1 cup boiling water

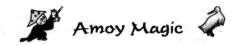

Supplement
In Toni's Kitchen!

Toni Mueller has been sharing her five generation family recipes with Laowai and Laonei alike through her articles in the Xiamen Daily's Saturday English Section, Common Talk, as well as in cooking classes at the local YMCA. Check out her latest recipes at Amoymagic.com.

Below is her five-generation recipe for Apple Bars.

Five-Generation Apple Bars

Pie Crust: 2 ½ cups flour, 1 tsp salt, 1 cup butter, 1 egg yolk with enough milk to make 1 cup, 1 beaten egg white

　　Mix pie crust. Spread ½ on cookie sheet.

Apples: 8-10 apples sliced, 1 cup sugar, 1 tsp cinnamon, 2 cups crushed cornflakes

　　Mix together the apples, sugar and cinnamon. Spread the cornflakes on top of the crust on the cookie sheet. Spread the apple, sugar and cinnamon mixture on top of the corn flakes. Cover with remaining dough. Crimp edges. Brush top with beaten egg white. Bake for 50 minutes at 175 degree Celcius.

Chef Toni and avid students

Frosting:
1 cup powdered sugar　1 tsp vanilla
1 Tablespoon milk
Mix together then dribble over top of warm apple bars.

5 Generation Apple Cake Recipe

Laonei (老内) Notes

---

[1] Cornucopia: endless supply of vast variety of food

[2] Bouillon: thin, clear broth made from simmering beef or chicken in water with seasonings.

[3] Whip up: prepare, create

[4] Gizmo: gadget: mechanical device whose name is forgotten or unknown

[5] Unless you have teenagers: teenagers eat a lot!

[6] Just desserts: idiom meaning "getting what one deserves" (usually negative)

[7] Toothpick comes out clean: if moist dough sticks to the toothpick, it has not baked long enough

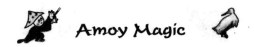

Chapter 23

LaoWai Life (Shopping)

When East Minces West
or
Minimizing Culture Shock

I hope that some of you are so enchanted by our magical Amoy that you'll make yourself at home here. The best way to make yourself at home is to bring a little home with you: photos of family and homeland, some wall hangings, your favorite music CDs or videotapes, a SW radio, and perhaps a board game or two. Such niceties will help you keep your sanity—and help your Chinese hosts learn more about you and your own homeland.

Good English reading material is scarce, so subscribe to your favorite magazines: *Newsweek* and *National Geographic* for you, *Sesame Street* and *Discover* for the kids. And bring a good travel guide. [If you lack reading material, you can always camp out in the business center of the Holiday Inn and read their magazines!].

Some Laowai have boasted, "I'm tough. I'll go native." And they've headed home, disillusioned, tail tucked between their legs.[1] While I love my Chinese home, I know I'm Laowai, not Chinese. When pressure mounts, it helps to retreat to familiarity. Otherwise, I take it out on family, or myself—or my bewildered Chinese hosts and friends. So make yourself at home by lugging a little bit of home in your luggage.

Bring from Home   Xiamen still lacks a few Laowai staples, so give your palate and psyche an occasional break by bringing things like cheese. (Xiamen now has cheese, but it is costly; try the great Beijing Cheese if you travel up north).

In addition to such spices as oregano, basil, cinnamon, and nutmeg, you might want to bring some packages of spaghetti seasoning or chili seasoning. Mexican food goes over big with Laowai and Laonei alike, and pizza is a cinch, especially if you use Muslim flat breads as a ready-made crust, and give it a dash of Parmesan (from the Olive Oil Store).

Pizza Tip: use spaghetti sauce mix with tomato paste and tomatoes to make pizza sauce. Take a simple dough, ground pork or beef, fresh mushrooms and green peppers, and some cheese, and you're in heaven. Share that heaven with your Chinese hosts and you might very well land the Nobel Pizza Prize.

Through the years we've compiled a sample **Wish List**:

Nobel Pizza Prize

Rubber spatula, serrated bread knife, cheeses, liquid smoke, maple flavoring, almond flavoring, peppermint extract, lemon juice, bay leaves, rosemary, pumpkin pie spice, allspice, chili powder, sage, thyme, marjoram, summer savory (the latter four for making great sausage), coriander leaves, red pepper, oregano, paprika, cayenne pepper, mace, celery seed, mustard, bacon bits, parsley, dill weed, wax paper, aluminum foil (now available in Xiamen, but pricey), angel food cake pan, and pie plates. (And why not – taco shells and tortillas.).

Medicines to Bring From Home Xiamen has many good hospitals (try Zhongshan Hospital's Laowai Ward, and the Lifeline Clinic for Laowai), as well as a very advanced eye hospital and a great dental clinic behind Zhongshan Park, on Douxi Rd. But pack a medicine bag for basic first aid and health care. It should include: thermometer, aspirin or tylenol for fever, a good medicine for diarrhea (like Lomitil), a box of rehydration salts, vitamins, a good cold medicine (Xiamen now sells Contact), a Bee Sting Kit, Pepto Bismol tablets, deng deng. It might also help to bone up on basic first aid. The main steps in most ailments—colds, flus, food poisoning—are stop fever, stop diarrhea, and drink plenty of water with rehydration salts.

Bring a CD-ROM Family Medical Guide, and the excellent book, Where There Is No Doctor.

Also beware that Xiamen has poisonous snakes (cobras, bamboo vipers). One American lady was bit by one right outside our apartment, though no foreigner has died from one yet. Locals have antivenoms and experience, and should that fail, Gulangyu Island's Catholic Church gives last rites.

Buy China!

Years ago, Wal-Mart got a lot of fanfare with its campaign to save American jobs by buying American products. Nowadays, China could use a similar strategy. It seems everyone is bent on buying imported products or services— even when local products of equal quality cost much less. That's

especially ironic when you consider that just about everything in America is stamped "Made in China".

But increasingly, we can buy quality Chinese products right here in China as well—like Ma Ling Ketchup, whole milk powder from Mongolia, Chinese corn flakes, boxed fruit juices from Beijing, and fruit jams from Shanghai—made not with chemicals and preservatives but with real fruit (in America they'd be labeled "All Natural!" and go for thrice the price!).

In the same vein… Wal-Mart and Metro aren't the only stores in town—or the cheapest. Many local shops, like the small shop on campus at the foot of the hill we live on, offer good selection, low price, and friendly service. Give them a try.

One Size Fits All!

My wife dug through a pile of sweaters displayed in a street side stall in Longyan city. She found one she liked, but it was too small. "Bu yao jin!" [No problem!] the lady said. "It stretches when you wear it!"

"I don't know," Sue said. She eventually found another sweater she liked, but it was far too large. "Bu yao jin!" the same lady said. "It shrinks when you wash it!"

"Shrinks when washed!"

"My Chinese women friends had taught me what to look for in embroidery: to pinch up the satin-stitched motifs which, they said, should bend smoothly and look as even as the silk itself, not showing a single loop; to look for fine tight Peking knot-stitch—the aristocrat of stitchery—and to examine the twist of the threads themselves. They showed me how to discover whether chopsticks were made of genuine ivory. Putting them side by side, they would lay a bamboo sliver horizontally across a drop of water placed on the sticks. If they were ivory the sliver would immediately come alive, swing round vertically and stop. On any other substance it would remain motionless. But the skill by which they could infallibly distinguish carved lacquer from veneered composition, good cloisonné from pieces lifted and assembled on modern bronzes by Japanese craftsmen, would, I knew, never be mine. It was their inheritance, compounded of discerning sight and the miraculously sensitive touch that, for them, made the incised mahjong tiles so easy to read with finger-tips alone.

"Our Chinese friends had taught us too the rudiments of judging jade. The women showed me how to look for transparency, texture, depth of colour and so brilliant a polish that the stone looked 'dipped in water'. But they themselves prized only the precious emerald jade as a jewel, while I preferred the variegated stone which lent itself so perfectly to imaginative carving."

Averil Mackenzie-Grieve, *A Race of Green Ginger*

These ladies were really egging Shannon on!

Xiamen Shopping A to Z

Xiamen shops offer almost everything a Laowai could long for, but the place changes daily, so as always, Caviar Empty! Or Caveat Emptor[2]. Or something to that effect. **Please e-mail me** your updates, corrections, or suggestions.

Airlines   Please see Chapter 9, Transportation.

Antiques   The best place to find antiques may be the shops in the Bailu Zhou shopping area on the Yundang Lake. If you bargain, you may cut the price by one half to two thirds. Also try the Gulangyu Island, and the small shops on Siming Rd. near the Holiday Inn.

Beware that some antiques, **particularly the old coins**, are fakes fresh from antique factories. One American bought 50 old silver coins. Every one turned out to be fake (they turn green when you rub them with detergent).

Personally, I prefer the "new" antiques, like the new foot-pumped black Singer sewing machines sold in department stores. They look like something out of a 1910 Sears Catalog—and they work great. But you can also find local tailors using 100 year old Min River sewing machines.

Appliances (家用电器 Jiayong Dianqi).   It's hard to believe that a decade ago not a shop in Xiamen sold microwaves and coffee pots. Nowadays you can find almost anything you need (except for frost-free upright freezers).

Most department stores (Hualian, # 1 Department Store, Friendship Store), offer everything from programmable rice cookers to electric ersatz fireplaces (and all stores that sell appliances can arrange delivery and installation).

For the largest selection, try these:

#1 Department Store's Appliance Division, on Zhongshan Rd. roughly across from the McDonalds.

Si Wen Appliance City (思文电器城), on Siming Rd. between Zhongshan Rd. and Xiahe Rd.

Li Min Appliances (利民电器商场), Douxi Rd. #38-46 (斗西路 38-46 号).

Art   Xiamen has many excellent art shops offering classical and modern Chinese paintings.   I'm perfectly happy with 10 Yuan poster reproductions, but you can also pay thousands for quality reproductions (as well as tens of thousands for 'originals' that are sometimes churned out by poorly paid university art students).

In Taiwan, a friend paid a Chinese artist to produce

awesome copies of Van Geoghs. You too can have local artists give you hand painted copies of Western and Eastern classics—or even order them from the internet's Great China Art Supermarket, at http://www.art-china.com/indexa.htm.

How about Renoir's "La Colazione Del Canottieri"? A machine-made copy runs $108 U.S., and hand painted will set you back $363. Or get a hand-painted copy of Van Geogh's "Sunflowers" for only $198.

Auto Rental http://use_car.com.cn. 365 days per year, 24 hrs. per day. Phone: 239-8459 厦门优卡汽车服务有限公司, 厦门市小学路 146 号 202 室

Auto Repair Shunlong Auto Center (厦门顺龙汽车维修中心) not only keeps Toy Ota in top shape but also handles all the bureaucracy for me—from insurance and traffic fines to taxes and annual inspections (I'm fairly certain this is called Red China because of all the Red Tape[3]). Shunlong is located right beside Xiamen University Hospital #172 University Road. 厦门市大学路 172 号. Phone: 208-5533, 219-1393, or 13906040676

Bread (面包 Mianbao) Chinese say all breads are either "sweet" or salty. You'll probably prefer so-called "salty," which is not salty at all; it's just not sweet.

For a morning treat, try sliced and toasted Chinese steamed breads (mantous). They are very similar to English muffins. And Chinese strawberry and apricot jams are cheap and tasty (and unlike imported Western jams, are made of real fruit, not chemicals and flavoring).

Bakeries

The first Western-style sliced bread in Xiamen is still on the shelves. It's a long loaf in a clear bag with blue lettering that says "**Bai Mian Bao**" 白面包 (white bread). It has a slightly unWestern flavor, but the small slices are great for tuna or egg salad sandwiches. The best bread, at present, is the whole-wheat sold at the chain of "Milky Way" bakeries. Also try Beatrice stores, Trust-Mart, or Andersen.

Andersen (安德鲁森面包店) has a broad selection of breads, cakes, cookies, ersatz croissants, deng deng, good whole wheat breads, as well as a variety of sliced white with green and purple streaks. (No, it's not mold). And check out their late-night ½ price specials.

Andersen will also make a wide variety of cakes (chocolate, pudding, coffee, fruit, peach) to order for you for any occasion.

Andersen's has locations all over Xiamen including,

Use Mind Food （优思麦食品） Someone was really using their head when they came up with that name. But they have cakes and cookies, mooncakes and Chinese pastries, and breads. Branches are throughout Xiamen.

Barbers and Beauty Parlors — everywhere. Sue & Shannon's favorite is **Winnie's**, near the Friendship Store (check Amoymagic.com for details). Ms. Coco runs a chain of quality beauty salons at the Yiyuan Hotel, Mandarin Hotel, and Marco Polo Hotel. Her prices, at present, are shampoo & blow dry: 18 Yuan; haircut: 28 Yuan; facial: 50-120 Yuan; manicure: 38 Yuan. Ph: 251-9888×3107

You'll also find plenty of old fashioned barber shops with chairs that would be nice museum displays. By the way… do you know why barber poles have red stripes? It's because barbers used to moonlight as surgeons, and the red hid the blood. But Chinese barbers have green stripes. Gangrene, perhaps?

Xiada barbers cut hair for only 5 Yuan, and the schools of Cosmetology do it for free. Of course, you get what you pay for, and it can be a hair-razing[4] experience.

Bicycles （自行车, Zixingche). Engineering studies of both animals and people have found that the most efficient means of transportation on earth is the bicycle. They're also good exercise and nonpolluting. "Forever" brand bikes are good (I've ridden the same one for 11 years), but Xiamen brands are cheaper (the quality is poorer, but adequate). And don't skimp on buying a strong chain and good lock (motorcycle lock and chains are 90 Yuan).

Several large bike shops are near the corner of South Hubin Rd. and East Hubin Rd. （湖滨北路 and 湖滨东路）

Books
Xiamen Book City（厦门图书文化城）, at SM Mart, 3/F, is Fujian's biggest bookstore! Its great selection includes imported English novels and classics, romances, westerns, Sci-fi novels, mysteries—even *Chicken Soup for the Soul* and *Joy of Cooking*! Address: 嘉禾路468 号 SM Mart 3/F. Phone: 553-8373

Also try Foreign Language Bookstore (外文书店) at 163 Zhongshan Road (中山路 163 号). Phone: 202-4059.

Xiamen International Book Center (厦门对外图书交流中心) is past the train station at 809 South Hubin Road. (湖滨南路 809 号)

Two **MUST BUY** books are the little red Oxford's and Barron's:

1) **Oxford's** *Concise English-Chinese Chinese-English Dictionary*《精选汉英英汉词典》. Informed Laowai lug this little red volume around with more zeal than Red Guards wielded Mao's little red book. It is *the best dictionary* available for daily use—small, so it's easy to whip out and wield on Laonei.

2) **Barron's** *Chinese at a Glance*, is a palm size *Phrase Book & Dictionary for Travelers*.

Oxford's Dictionary is usually available in the Foreign Language bookstore, but all of the above books are available in Hong Kong bookstores, the two biggest being Swindon's and Page One. Alternatively, order them from Amazon.com, though be aware that surface shipping takes 12 weeks (only 4 weeks to get here, but 8 more weeks to clear customs). If you can afford an extra $30 per order (on top of the normal $5.95 per book charge), Amazon will send them DHL and they'll get to you within 5 days or so.

Chinese history buffs should read *The Soong Dynasty*, about the Soong family which virtually owned China before Liberation. I also thoroughly enjoyed *The Stilwell Years*, about America's General Stilwell in China.

And read *The Hobbit*, to better appreciate Shaanxi's cave-dwellers.

Business Cards (名片 Mingpian) Many photo developing shops make business cards, and the quality is fairly uniform, now that they are created with computer instead of hand-aligned rubber blocks. For some really humdinger cards, try places like Xiamen Lucky Star Card Printing.

Address: 厦门市将军祠西边社 5 号 Phone: 212-1208 or 203-1208

Carpentry   For 15 years, we've turned to Mr. Chen Gengsheng (陈更生) for custom furniture, remodeling, or repairs. He works wonders with wood. You draw a picture and he'll make it!
Phone: 218-4496 Pager: 129 519-3615

Carpets & Tapestries (地毯 Ditan) galore, including Asian and Western style wall hangings, can be found at # 135 Gu Gong Road, in Xiamen. They also offer Persian-style carpets, and hand-embroidered relief wall hangings.
Address: 故宫路 135 号 Phone: 213-8291 And check out the fine carpet shops on Douxi Road (斗西路).

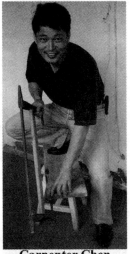

Carpenter Chen
--a real 'cut up!'

Cheese (干酪 Ganlao) Yes, Xiamen now has cheese. Try the Olive Oil Store (later in this chapter, under "Food Markets") for blocks of cheddar or mozzarella. But the cheapest New Zealand sliced cheese (17 Yuan for 12 slices) or butter is found in the little store on the corner next to the triangular park area by Nanputuo Temple and Xiamen University. (Their butter is 10 Yuan, versus 15 Yuan at Beatrice).
Name: 厦门市育城商场   Address: 演武路 15 号
Phone: 209-2238.   Also check out their tuna, mayo, and condiments.
(If you visit Beijing, try the excellent Beijing Cheese in the Friendship Store).

Christian Gift Shop   **Jehovah Nissi** (耶和华尼西), opened November, 2002, is the first Christian gift shop in Fujian Province. It was located on Siming Rd. between the train track and the Holiday Inn, and sold a broad selection of

Christian sculptures, paintings, magnets, stationary, calendars—about everything you can imagine. They have also applied for a book license. In the meantime, you can buy nice Bibles (including Chinese/English parallel versions) in the local churches bookstores.   Nissi has moved, but you can phone or check their website for the latest details. Contact: Ms. Chen at 876-7651 or 208-4818.
Website: http://www.xmnissi.com   E-mail: nissi@xmnissi.com

Clothes (衣服 Yifu, or 服装 Fuzhuang) Mao blue and gray may have been in vogue a decade ago, but no more. Chinese are not just following fashion but leading it. Zhongshan Road is lined with boutiques. Try the 2/F of the 1st Department Store, or the Donghai Building.   SM-Mart has a gigantic Laiya store, and all

over town, shops cater to name brands from around the world, but name brands don't necessarily imply quality or durability, so don't buy based on price—as folks learned on Gulangyu a few years back.

A youth sat on the sidewalk trying to hawk good quality cotton shirts—a steal at only 15 Yuan. After hours of no takers, he made a new sign: "Quality shirts—150 Yuan". He sold every shirt.

Computers(电脑, or. Diannao) shops are all over Xiamen, but Electronic City （电子城） has the most under one roof. Address: # 69 S. Hubin Rd. （湖滨南路 69 号） Also check out **Cybermart**, at SM Mart, 3/F, beside Book City.

Condiments   I saw a Minnan lass in a Shanghai store hawking **B.B. Brand** condiments. BB. Nice ring, eh? And no, I'm not making the stuff in my bathtub. BB's fine products are made right here in Xiamen, at #35 Zhenhai Rd. （镇海路 35 号） near the #1 hospital. Try them. They spent $3 million U.S. to import Taiwanese equipment to produce dozens of great sauces, including hot sauce, satay sauce, sweet 'n sour sauce, Worcestershire, sesame oil, BBQ chili oil, soy sauce, rice vinegar, deng deng. Buy them in stores throughout Xiamen.
B.B.'s phone: 205-1170; 502-4079. Fax: 205-7377.
The Olive Oil Store (later in this chapter) offers ketchup (I recommend good, cheap Maling brand Chinese ketchup), American and European mustards, mayonnaise, caviar, deng deng.

Cooking Oil （菜油 Caiyou）. Chinese usually use peanut oil, perhaps because we're so used to working for peanuts. Rapeseed oil is healthier but lacks that Jimmy Carter flavor. Olive oil is now available in the Dahua (United Bank Building) store, Beatrice, or the Restaurant Supply (address under "Food Markets").

Natural Rock, Minerals, Crystals

Crystals & Minerals I've collected minerals and crystals since I was seven, and our apartment is almost a museum. Xiamen has many gem shops, but I like the small shop in the basement of the SM Mart, near the exit.

陶　然　奇　石　轩
TAO　RAN　QI　SHI　XUAN

Li Kai Ping　　经理 Manager

地址: 厦门市思明南路188号定安商业广场1A12
　　　SM城市广场底下层WSO2　**SM Mart**
电话: 0592-2056760　　手机: 13950171117

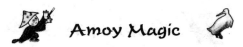

Dentist （牙医, Yayi） The Sino-Japanese joint venture behind Zhongshan Park offers excellent dental care—though at a cost. An American family in Xiamen discovered that military hospitals also offer excellent, but affordable, dental care.

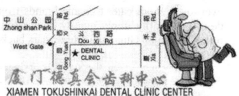

厦门德真会齿科中心
XIAMEN TOKUSHINKAI DENTAL CLINIC CENTER
Joint Venture with Japan's Largest Dental Group
Address: 2F, No. 2 Dou xi Rd. (Across Zhongshan Park's West gate)
Reservation: Tel: 2136688
Working Hours: Weekdays-8: 00-18: 00 Sunday&Holiday-8: 00-17: 00

Eggs. Duck eggs （鸭蛋 Yadan) are big and white, chicken eggs （鸡蛋 Jidan) are smaller and brown. Chinese doctors swear duck eggs are more nutritious, but I chicken out and go for tastier chicken eggs (though I'm not ducking the issue). Whichever, be sure they're fresh or they can get rather fowl.

Eggspress Mail Services
> **DHL**: 601-0503/4/5
> **EMS**: (Chinese Post Offices)
> **UPS**: 563-9828; 563-2835; 563-2765
> **Federal Express**: 510-1771, or (800) 830-2338
> **Pony Express**: Just neigh.

Home Electronics: Xiamen has dozens of places selling appliances, but

Yuxing Songbai Electronics （育兴松柏家电商场) has served Xiamen for *over two decades*, and offers both local ownership and local service.
Phone: 510-5611, 510-8585. Location: Diagonal across the intersection from SM-Mart in Songbai District. There is also a nice branch across from the XiaXi Market （霞溪市场) at #7 Siming Dong Rd. （思明东路 7 号）—a 3 minute walk from the ZhongshanRd./Siming Rd. intersection. Or—place orders online in English! Website:
http://www.xm-yuxing.com.cn/default_en.asp

Flour: Fine cake flour （精粉 Jingfen) gives best results in baking breads or cakes. Wholewheat flour is still hard to come by, but at least we no longer have to buy dry corn (used for pig feed) and grind it by hand with the 200 hundred pound granite mill I lugged home during a hair-raising and hernia-inducing trip to the countryside. Many shops like Beatrice sell a perfectly serviceable corn meal. Just ask for yumi fen (玉米粉).

The Olive Oil Store (look under Food Markets) offers excellent domestic cake flour in large quantity. Dr. Jan says that in winter months, non-white flour from Gansu Province is available. **Baking tip**: with bread, substitute 1/3 Chinese oatmeal to make tasty and nutritious oatmeal bread.

Flowers: the shops behind Zhongshan Park sell potted and cut flowers, as well as all you need to raise birds, fish, turtles...

For a marvelous selection of nursery items, including potted plants and flowers, fertilizers, miniature landscapes, pots and vases, try the gigantic nursery mall on Lianqian Road 莲前路 about halfway between the traffic circle across from the Exposition Center and the beach (it looks like a row of airplane hangers covered in plastic).

Forklifts: If you shop like Susan Marie, load your car with a forklift from the German firm Linde. Phone: 610-2990.

Furniture Xiamen furniture shops offer everything from 4 Yuan bamboo stools and inexpensive bamboo and rattan couches and bookshelves to mahogany dining room sets that should belong in a museum of Oriental art. Douxi Road (斗西路) has several shops. Susan even had rattan furniture custom made. For marvelous mahogany furniture from Yunnan,

Susan Marie and Bamboo Master Huang

in Southwest China, try Yunnan Province Dali City Furniture Company located at 399 Xiahe Rd. (厦禾路 399 号). Phone: 211-9898 or 138 606-6868

Hardware (五金店 Wujin Dian) Datong Rd and Jiangtou (near the Airport) have lots of hardware and construction shops, but my all-time favorite is near Xiamen University at #165 Univ. Rd.
Phone: 2191433

Honey (蜂蜜 Feng mi) We used to wangle our honey from a country doctor way out in the countryside because our local honey was always watered down with sugar water (to keep it from spoiling, we

My favorite hardware store
University Rd. #165 (大学路 165 号)

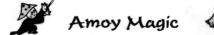
were told, but it always fermented, whereas pure honey keeps forever). Fortunately, Xiamen shops now offer many excellent honeys. To be sure it's pure, turn the bottle upside down; the slower the bubbles rise, the thicker and purer the honey.

Housekeeper (保姆 Baomu)   A good Chinese housekeeper/cook will make your stay much more enjoyable (read "Half the Sky"). One source is Mr. Hugh Bing at 1360 691-9006, or e-mail: Hughbing@hotmail.com.

Ice Cream (冰淇淋, Bingqilin) It was hard for me to believe that Chinese had invented ice cream when I first tasted Chinese ice cream in '88. Then a local firm began selling White Snow (which sure beats yellow snow.). Unfortunately, they only sold it for a few weeks a year, claiming it was too cold to eat in winter (though icebound Northern Chinese scarf ice cream year round). Then came Walls, a foreign firm that in one fell swoop installed ice cream freezers throughout China, Amoy included. Walls, offers a broad variety of ice cream bars, cones, fudgesicles—and year round.

Local firms have finally read the writing on the Wall and have come up with some winners, but they keep changing the brands' names, so you'll just have to experiment.

Leah Loves Ice Cream!

Internet Café (因特咖啡屋 Yinte Kafei Wu) How on earth or China did we ever survive without internet or e-mail (just 3 years ago.)? And our service is getting faster and cheaper all the time. You can even access the internet without an account. Yep—no user name, no password. Just dial 8163, type "8163" for the user name, and whatever phone you use will be charged (roughly 6 Yuan an hour). But folks in China Telecom's two Internet Café's are happy to help you set up your own internet account.   To get a DSL account, phone: 1000

If you don't have a computer, get a free e-mail account with Yahoo.com or Hotmail.com, and use the Internet Café's computers. You can also get a private VIP room

Jewelry Several Chinese friends have asked me to buy gold for them in Hong Kong because local gold jewelry is sometimes plated or filled. Buy gold from a reputable jewelry store. Zhongshan Rd. has several.

Language & **Management Training** Mandarin, English, Japanese, Management… learn them all at Emerge Corporate Training and Advisory Services! Ph: 581-1621 E-mail:vinnyho@starhub.net.sg

Malls Xiamen has many shopping centers but the largest are in the Zhongshan Road area, beside the train station—and the massive Philippine-based SM Mall.

Maps Bookstores and street hawkers sell great English maps of Xiamen and Gulangyu for only 10 Yuan or so (compared with 15 to 30 Yuan in local hotels for the same map). Bookshops also have dozens of map books covering all of China, as well as countries back on planet earth.

Margarine (黄油, Huangyou) like bread, comes as "salty" (咸, xian) or as "sweet" (甜, tian); get the so-called "salty". (Both are colored lard, not butter).

Massage—*Get rubbed the right way!* China has the best therapeutic masseurs on the planet! They might not feel as relaxing but their effects are long lasting. Our favorite is just across from the Overseas Chinese Museum, beside the bookstore. For 50 Yuan you get 90 minutes, plus drinks and food!
Also try the Holiday Inn (60 Yuan an hour, but you can watch cable TV).

Blind Body Massages (中医盲人保健推拿 中心) are a special treat that may be unique to China. I feel a lot less self-conscious knowing that the blind masseuse cannot see my contours! Our favorite, just around the corner from Lianban Pizza Hut, is a bargain at only 30 Yuan per hour. Phone: 513-3477

地址: 香江花园 2 号楼明珠阁 6 层 B 座 (全家福豆浆店对面)

Meat (肉 Rou). Pork (猪肉, or Zhurou) is cheap and plentiful, but buy it early in the day because it is often not refrigerated. And beware of frozen meats in small shops; because of power outages (increasingly rare nowadays), they have sometimes been thawed and refrozen many times.

Beef (牛肉 Niurou) is less popular than pork, and so a little more costly, but quality varies from imported Australian to domestic road kill.

The best beef is in the Xiaxi Rd. Market 霞溪路市场—at the #7 market (probably because of their proximity to the Muslim Mosque, which was relocated).   And **they deliver.**   Phone: 552-9513.

You can grind beef and pork in minutes with a good food processor, or spend 25 Yuan on a cheap metal grinder. Sometimes you can find ground meats in the Olive Oil Store, Beatrice, or the Donghai's food department, and the **Yikang Dried Produce and Fast Food Supply** (益康干果调味店), across from the #7 market, has frozen chicken and beef patties. (See "Food Markets")

Milk (牛奶 Niunai) "Dutch Lady" and "Anchor" brands of powdered milk are excellent, but getting hard to find. Domestic milk powders are half the price (and bags are half the price of canned), but make sure you buy the unsweetened milk. If you're a real milk lover, try the fresh whole milk in the plastic liter bottles from **I ♥ Milk.** Best of all, they deliver.   **I ♥ Milk's** Phone: 552-8828.

Music (音乐 Yinyue) The Donghai Department store's third flood music center has good prices on pianos and electronic keyboards,   acoustic and electric guitars, trumpets and clarinets, harmonicas,   as well as a broad variety of traditional Chinese instruments, like the shrill nuona horn, or the banjo looking pipa, or the erhu (the world's first violin. Though only two-strings, and often shrill to our ears, in the hands of a master it can sound as sweet as any violin).

Also, try the excellent Musical Instrument Store on 123 Zhongshan Rd.   For guitars, try the hip little guitar shop a few hundred feet from Xiamen University Hospital, on University Road. I think the hip proprietors give lessons.

For imported, and expensive, Japanese, American and European pianos and brass instruments, try the shop just down the street from the train station (about halfway between McDonalds and the station).

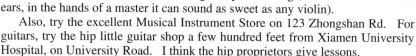

Music Performances One of Xiamen's many goals is to become the Music Center of Southeast China.   Not a month goes by that Xiamen doesn't have performances by visiting orchestras, ballet troupes, opera stars, deng deng. For   the   latest   offerings,   check   the   Internet   at www.xmec.cn/performance/

Pets

Jukou St. Aquarium（厦门局口水族馆） offers an excellent selection and good service, and they deliver. It's just off Zhongshan Road, down Jukou Rd., the little side road to the left of the foreign languages bookstore and the DVD shop. Address: #17 Jukou St. （局口街 17 号） Phone: 202-0880

Cats and Dogs For the best prices in town, call Mr.贺国强 . He will give you directions to his place on Hudong Rd. , near Hexiang W. Rd.
Address:厦门市湖东路 Phone:580-8553 or 868-2546

Pet Home（宠物之家）**(Supplies and Veterinary care).** It's a relief to find someone who can neuter a cat or spay a dog (we had to get a people doctor for our cat; poor thing was tied spread eagled to a chair while his manhood was diminished). But Pet Home has quality supplies for cats and dogs, and good vet care, in both Xiamen and Fuzhou. The Xiamen branch is just a five minute walk to the right of the Gulangyu Ferry (Xiamen side).
Address: Lujiang Blvd. Qianhao Market St. #7（鹭江道钱朝商业街 7 号）
Phone: 210-7891
Fuzhou Branch: 0591 335-8514
Website: www.wj-pethome.com

For birds and fish, and beautifully crafted bird cages, try the shop behind Zhongshan Park. Also check out the nice aquarium supply across the street.

Bird 'n Fish Shop
龙辉水族宠物店
白文龙
地址: 厦门市公园北路 3 号之 1、2 店面
电话: 0592-2020797 小灵通: 8975999
Gong Yuan Bei Lu, #3, Shop 1 and 2

Pharmacy (药 – Yao, or medicines). The most complete pharmacy around is right downtown on the corner of Zhongshan and Siming roads. They have a broad range of both Chinese and Western medicines, as well as vitamins, band-aids, ace bandages, deng deng. Zhongshan Rd. and SM-Mart 1/F also have Watson outlets (a HongKong-based store that sells prescription and nonprescription drugs, medicines, and health care products).

Plastics — pots, basins, chairs, plastic sheeting (everything plastic but credit cards.) can be had in a little shop one block south and across the street from the Olive Oil store. Prices run half that of similar items in department stores.

Plumbing, hardware, electrical, deng deng. (五金家电类) Datong Rd., (大同路) parallel to Zhongshan Rd. and two blocks north, has several hardware, plumbing and electrical stores. And try the many good shops around Douxi Rd. (斗西路) and Xiahe Rd.(厦禾路).

Real Estate. There are many agencies, including Century 21, but for private housing, I recommend Mr. Hugh Bing, who has distinctively Western tastes. He can also help you land reliable domestic help. Mobile Phone: 1360 691-9006
　　E-mail:Hughbing@hotmail.com

Ms. Eunice Chau (Huang Jiali, 黄嘉力), of Symphony Trading Co., Ltd., also helps with home searches, travel arrangements, education advice, orientations, etc.. Phone: 581-1621. E-mail: symphony@public.xm.fj.cn
　　Fax: 581-1718　　Address: Unit 1206 Haixia Building, Hubin E. Road □

Rice (米, or Mi) is a weighty topic for Chinese, who revere the grain almost as much as Cambodians (for whom it is a criminal offense to insult a rice plant). Don't skimp on it. Grades and prices are innumerable, but cheaper grades are prepared on roadsides and include, at no extra charge, white gravel masquerading as rice. After a few chipped teeth, I heeded my comrades' rice catechism and became a connoisseur of rice.
　　Rice comes long grained and short, polished and coarse, fat and thin, sticky and sweet or hard and chewy, deng deng. In addition to dozens of grades of domestic rice, we can also buy Japanese, Thai or American rice in local shops. Our favorite is the domestic "Dongbei" (Manchurian rice, or 东北大米), which is even cheaper than local rice.

There are dozens of ways to serve up the dozens of grades of humble rice. In Northern Fujian, the cooked rice is so dry it rasps your throat. In the South it's almost mushy, and Xiamenese prefer rice congee — a watery rice porridge livened up with salted and pickled vegetables, shredded pork, dried minnows (such sad little dried faces) and diced Thousand Day Old Eggs (which are purplish greenish, gelatinous, and smell of ammonia or horse pee).

For Chinese (in the South, at least), rice is life and they use it for everything — except weddings. No self-respecting Chinese would irreverently toss rice. When they hear of this, I suspect they'll seek revenge by tossing cheeseburgers at Chinese weddings.

2nd Hand Market has everything from drum sets to fridges & freezers. It's on a side street near the #1 Olive Oil Store, etc.   **Xiamen's "2nd Hand Market"**

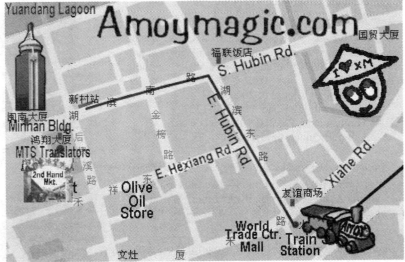

Spices of Life. （香料,or Xiangliao）. Chinese eat everything edible, and what isn't edible is called medicine and ingested anyway. Which makes it surprising that many of our common spices are nowhere to be found in Xiamen. It took me weeks to learn that nutmeg （肉豆蔻, or Roudoukou) and cinnamon （肉桂, or Rougui) were found only in Chinese medicine stores, and vanilla extract was sold in the paint store, between the enamel and the paint thinner. They argued this was because both paint and vanilla are chemically prepared. And I think they were right. I put a match to a spoon of vanilla and it exploded. It was the last time I used it, because after four months in China I'd lost a lot of weight and didn't need any *thinner*.

The broadest variety of spices can be found at the Yikang Dried Produce and Restaurant Supply across from the #7 Market (see "Food Markets" , top of page 201). Also try Beatrice. Some spices you'll still need to bring from home (see our "Wish List" at the beginning of this chapter). Also bring a few Lawry spice mixes—spaghetti seasoning, taco seasoning, chili seasoning, sloppy joe mix—to add a little spice to your life.

Sports Events Xiamen folk have sporting in the blood, and not a week passes without a game or competition. Buy tickets at these locations:
1. Sport Center West Gate: 506-4618 or 506-2107
2. Xiada Yuanwu Road # 18   209-3865
3. 4/No.2, Kaipin road, Siming District: 220-9846
4. Songbo Park: 512-5612
5. Lujiang Hotel Market: 202-2922, extension 713
6. Huli Park: 603-7092
7. Lianhua Crossroads: 512-4396

Subscriptions   Keep abreast on China with a few subscriptions to excellent Chinese magazines and newspapers.   Subscribe at your post office or these service centers:
　　#3 Zhongshan Road Ph: 202--1662
　　#47 South Siming Road Ph: 202-1227
　　#6 Huyuan Rd.   Ph: 210-9988
　　　　I particularly enjoy…

Fujian Pictorial（《福建画报》, Fujian Huabao) has great photos of Fujian—like this photo of Shannon and Matthew in the October '91 edition!
China Daily（《中国日报》 Zhongguo Ribao)
　　http://www.chindaily.com
Beijing Weekly（《北京周报》, Beijing Zhoubao)
China Today（《今日中国》, Jinri Zhongguo)
　　http://www.chinatoday.com
Women of China（《中国妇女杂志》, Zhongguo Funu Zazhi)
World of English（《英语世界》, Yingyu Shijie)—for English learners, but I
　　enjoy the broad selection of foreign articles

Theaters (影剧院 Yingjuyuan) include:
Siming St. Theater (思明电影院, Siming Dianying Yuan)
#2-14 N. Siming Rd.   Phone: 202-3412
Zhonghua Theater (中华电影院, Zhonghua Dianying Yuan)
#225 Zhongshan Rd.   Phone: 202-3861
Lianhua Theater (莲花影剧院 Lianhua Yingju Yuan)
#4-6 N. Lianhua Rd.   Phone: 506-4074   503-2891

Translation & Internet Services:
Frank Wei is the advisor and patron saint of Amoymagic.com! To enlist his able services, check out his Master Translation Services.
E-mail: frank@xmmaster.com

Utensils.   Xiamen shops sell Teflon skillets and pots, but rubber spatulas are still not easy to find, and steel ones rub Teflon the wrong way. So bring a rubber spatula.

"Bottled Water—Mineral, Purified..."

The Ancient Mariner[1] was probably in China, not at sea, when he cried, "Water, water everywhere, nor any drop to drink." And though bottled water companies are a dime a dozen nowadays, in China, as in America, quality is sometimes suspect.

Taps[2] for Tap Water. Some so-called 'mineral' water is little more than bottled tap water (aptly named, because in China its taps for anyone who drinks tap water). Though some companies guarantee their water is not only pure but cures every ill that ails you, that reassures me about as much as the sign that used to be on dining tables at Acapulco, Mexico's 5 Star Princess Hotel Resort. The sign said, "The manager has personally passed[3] all the water."

Health is wealth, and given that adult bodies are up to 65% water, it behooves us to choose bottled water wisely. We relied upon trial and error—severe error! We began to think that dysentery runs[4] in the family. Fortunately, we now have Yinlu Brand.

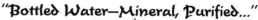

www.yinlu.com

For Delivery call: 581-1621 or 882-3208

Amoymagic.com

Yinlu is produced in a sprawling 500 acre complex in Tong An, and has such high standards that during a sustained draught in 2002, they recalled every bottle produced during a certain period because of suspected quality problems (even though most people would have never known the difference)!

Yinlu has received over 60 awards. Better yet—Susan Marie likes it, and that's saying something! Sue is a connoiseeur of water, more dscriminating than any wine or tea taster you're likely to meet—and much harder to please. During our travels, we now carry a case of Yinlu in the back of Toy Ota.

---

[1] Rime of the Ancient Mariner: epic ballad published by Coleridge in 1798
[2] Tap water: 自来水; Taps: bugle call sounded at military funerals
[3] Passed the water: the water passed inspection; "pass water" also means 小便
[4] Runs: (slang for "diarrhea"); runs in the family: hereditary

Yinlu sells mineral water (taste varies a little depending on weather) and purified water (which Sue prefers because it is pure, sweet, and never varies).

For Home or Corporate Delivery, phone: 581-1621, or 882-3208
Fax: (86-592) 5811718   Email: **symphony@public.xm.fj.cn**
Note: I am not paid for this recommendation, or any other in Amoy Magic!

Food Markets

Chinese Produce Markets are scattered all over Xiamen, and offer endless varieties of rice, eggs, beans, noodles, veggies, meat, tofu products, fish, deng deng.   But it takes a while to get a handle on their hours.   The market outside of Xiada's beach gate is a "morning market" , open from 6:30 until high noon.   Afternoon markets in other locations are usually open from around 4 to 6 p.m.

The #7 Market, aka Xiaxi Market (第七市场, or 霞溪市场) just off Zhongshan Road and E. Siming Rd., on Xiaxi Rd. is one of the best markets around.   Fight your way off a bus at the intersection of Zhongshan Rd and South Siming Rd, hang a right on Zhongshan Rd (away from the harbor) and take the road off to the left and walk to the "T" intersection. The market will be on your left, right across from the #2 Olive Oil Store (below).

Fresh Fish? Check out the morning offerings at the Ding An Rd. Market on Ding An Rd. #34-38—just across from the Min Ke Long market. (It's the little street just off Siming Rd. to the left (between Trust-Mart/KFC and Zhongshan Rd.). Ding An Rd. also has a bustling **night market!**

Across from the #7 market is **Yikang Dried Produce and Fast Food Supply** (益康干果调味店) at # 19 E. Siming Rd. (思明东路 19 号思东建行边).   They have reasonable prices on everything from dried fruit and meats to canned vegetables, McCormick spices, Miracle Whip (only 20 Yuan a jar), McCormick Grape Jelly (8.50 Yuan.), and Pizza Hut salad dressings. They also offer frozen hamburger patties, chicken filets, french fries, deng deng.   Phone: 212-9721.

Olive Oil Store! （厦门旭立贸易有限公司） **(Cheese, Bacon, Tuna, deng deng)** Now you can finally bring home the bacon, and the cheese as well. The first Xuli Restaurant Supply (loyal Laowai call it **the Olive Oil Store**) is only a ten minute walk from the train station, but a new one has opened right across from the #7 market, near the corner of Zhongshan and Siming Rds. (and prices are a little lower). They offer corn flakes, diet Coke, several kinds of cheeses (for less than $4 U.S. a pound.), Shanghai bacon, olive oil, pimentos, and dozens

of other products hard to find (or afford) anywhere else in Xiamen, like tuna [though Trust-Mart has the best prices in town for Century brand tuna in spring waterSusan Marie appreciates these Olive Oil store staples:

> frozen peas, whipping cream (on shelf next to boxed milk), Nestle baking chocolate (a 1 lb. brick that is the same as Toll House chocolate, but much cheaper), pudding powder (called "Custard Powder"—it's excellent with bits of Nestle chocolate sprinkled on top), fine cake flour, hot dogs, bacon, cream cheese, evaporated milk, evaporated water (just kidding), cold cereals, fine table salt, hot dog relish, tuna, frozen french fries, frozen uncooked shelled shrimp, deng deng.

Xiamen Xu li Restaurant Supply   厦门旭立贸易有限公司
Downtown Address: Xiaxi Rd. #142 霞溪路 142 号 or one near train station:
E. Hexiang Rd., Longxiang Garden #18-8 禾祥东路, 龙祥花园 18 号之八
Phone: (0592) 517-9188 or 517-7599 Mobile Phone: 13906000118

Another decent produce market is the Lianhua Market (莲花市场), on Lianhua North Rd. (莲花北路). You can also find a broad variety of fresh, frozen and dried produce at the various Trust-Marts, Wal-Marts, etc.

Friendship Store. Take a #1 bus to the end of the line—the train station. The 4 story Friendship Store is right across the street from the train station and the Xiamen Plaza. They offer a fairly good selection of everything from foodstuffs to handicrafts and pianos and toys.

Chinese Supermarkets. The best prices (almost wholesale) on canned or dried foods, coffee and oatmeal, cookies and candies, deng deng, are at the small warehouse type stores like Xiamen Harbor Foodstuffs Market (#66-68 University Road), near the corner of the street leading up to the Overseas Chinese Museum. Also try the large market in the building below the Big Egg Bowling Alley on Xiahe Lu (just up the street from Siming Beilu, or another one on the street parallel to Zhongshan Rd. roughly in front of the New China Bookstore). The Donghai Department Store also has a small selection of foodstuffs, as well as everything else.

Dr. Jan recommends the Minkelong warehouse store. When coming from Xiada on Siming Rd, turn left on the night market street just before and parallel to Zhongshan Rd. Walk up it a few hundred feet and it's on your right, down some steps.

And try **Xiamen Heyang Supermarket** (厦门和洋超市), in the United Bank Building, (Dahua Bank Building—大华银行) at #19 Hubin North Rd. (湖滨北路 19号)

Beatrice — "Your Friendly Community Store", with at least 6 Xiamen locations, is more convenient than Xu li Restaurant Supply, though costlier. Beatrice offers a good selection of baked breads, hamburger and hotdog buns, cakes and cookies, as well as various European cheeses and other items hard to find elsewhere (like Dragon Island Ham, and microwave frozen pizza). Some Beatrice's also have Sam's Snacks, a small concession area that offers whole roast chicken (20 Yuan), sweet Chinese buns (1 Yuan) and jumbo hot dogs (9 Yuan).

Since they're popping up like mushrooms I won't bother with locations. They're everywhere.

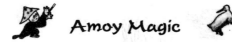
Foreign Chains Metro, the world's 3rd largest retailer (after Wal-Mart, and France's Carrefour), has an enormous store out near the airport. You must get a membership card (Chinese must show a business license, foreigners must present a passport). Prices aren't really any lower than anywhere else for most things, but they do have unique items you can't find elsewhere in Xiamen—cottage cheese and sour cream, for instance).

SM Mall

Wal-Mart has two locations in Xiamen—one in the World Trade Center Mall (by the train station, and the other in SM Mall's basement).

Flute tooter tutors tout flute tooting to tourists
(World Trade Center Mall, 5/F)

World Trade Center Mall (by train station)

Sony—by Sam!

While you're at the World Trade Center, check out Sam Chan's state-of-the-art Sony store and training center. It has every Sony item you could want, from MP3 players and notebook computers to robot dogs, and classes on how to use them.

If only he had a class on how to make the money to afford them…

Sony Training Center

Xiuxi—China's Siesta

Be aware that many official offices, small shops and stalls shut down for xiuxi (siesta). Last week we were shocked to find that Xiada Hospital even locks the elevators during xiuxi. Lord help the patient with an emergency.

Even university gate guards, who are sticklers for security, abandon their posts for their noon nap. I think xiuxi's are fine things, but if the PLA (People's Liberation Army) is following suit, they should bone up on history. Over a century ago, General Sam Houston's 700 men defeated General Santa Ana's (the "Napoleon of the West") 1,600 men in only 20 minutes. His secret strategy? General Sam attacked at 3:30 p.m., knowing that Santa Ana and his officers were taking their siesta.

Zhongshan Road (Sun Yat-sen Road), the heart of downtown Xiamen, offers great scenery (a harbor view of the Gulangyu Island, and nicely renovated colonial architecture), and a good variety of shops, boutiques, restaurants, and fast food outlets.

HuaLian Department Store (Donghai) (华联商厦) Zhongshan Rd. # 1-4. The "Hualian Store" says "Donghai Building" on the front so that's what the Laowai characters who can't read characters call it. Since 1987, the Donghai (let's call it Hualian and keep the locals happy) has offered excellent prices on a broad variety of products, including clothing, electronics & appliances, sports equipment, musical instruments, housewares, stationery, toys, wigs, deng deng. Hualian also boasted Xiamen's first escalator, which I dubbed **Stairway to Heaven** because of how it intimidated folks back before they became so cosmopolitan. We enjoyed watching people dare one another to step foot on it. One burley dock worker was jeered by his comrades when he took the stairs—after 3 year old Shannon skipped up the escalator two steps at a time.

Hualian Department Store's other locations include:

N. Lianhua (Lotus) Road #21-1 (莲花北路 21 号之一). Ph. 503-7045

N. Hubin Rd. #36-38-5,6 (湖滨北路 36-38 号之五, 六). Ph. 205-6337

Lianyue Rd. # 1-4 (莲岳路 1-4 号) Ph. 512-3730

Bailu Zhou Store (白鹭洲), just off Huzhong Rd (湖中路) Ph. 508-3686

Blue Hut is actually just off Zhongshan Rd., but I include it because it's one of Xiamen's more unique little gift shops. Blue Hut's unique blend of Western & Eastern sights, sounds and scents is more what I'd expect in Maui or California than Xiamen. Selections vary each time we visit, and the service is great. The 3 young proprietors will deftly gift wrap your purchases for free.

One of the partners also opened "Band" just around the corner.

Musical Instrument Store Zhongshan Rd. #123
This place used to have a monopoly on musical Instruments (pianos, guitars, classical Chinese instruments), music books, CD and cassette players, CDs, guitar strings, deng deng. Nowadays, music stores are a dime a dozen, but this one remains popular because it's convenient, and will probably be around a longtime so you're assured of good service.

#1 Department Store (第一百货商店), at #123 Zhongshan Rd., has a broad assortment of odds and ends on the first floor, and clothes and shoes on the upper two floors. Between the 1st and 2nd floor is a nice shop selling clocks and watches. Phone: 202-4538. They also have branches in Huli and Lianhua.

Fast Food Muslim hand-pulled noodle shops (西北拉面 Xibei Lamian), as well as the ubiquitous Pizza Hut, KFC, McDonalds, deng deng.

Postage Stamps You can win lots of friends by judicious distribution of canceled stamps from back home, but you might also enjoy collecting Chinese stamps, many of which have won international design awards.

The post office used to strictly regulated stamp sales to clamp down on the black market, but I never understood the fuss. Who would buy black stamps when colored ones are so much prettier?

The best selection of beautiful Chinese postage stamps is in the Post Office at the end of Zhongshan Road, across from the PSB. They charge the basic rates even for limited stamps. But for hardcore stamp enthusiasts, try the Philately Shop next door to the Donghai (Hualian) Department Store on the harbor.

Foreign Language Bookstore Zhongshan Rd. # 153-161

Excellent selection of Chinese books, and quite a few Western classics and biographies— and on the 3rd and 4th floors, Zhongshan Rd.'s cleanest restrooms. But for a great selection of imported English books, try the Xiamen Book City (Fujian's Largest!) at SM Mart.

Bank of China Across from the Donghai (Hualian) Department store, by the harbor. (I used to joke that it was located right under the giant Ronald McDonald sign's armpits, but the city fathers disarmed me when they removed the Ronald McDonald sign)

The easiest way to get money from home is to open a savings account in USD, and have money wired to it. (But note that they charge a service fee, and deduct an additional ½% when the money arrives). I wouldn't suggest trying to cash a personal check. It takes a couple of weeks, and then you are required to deposit it in a 30 day CD before withdrawing it.

Zhongshan Map

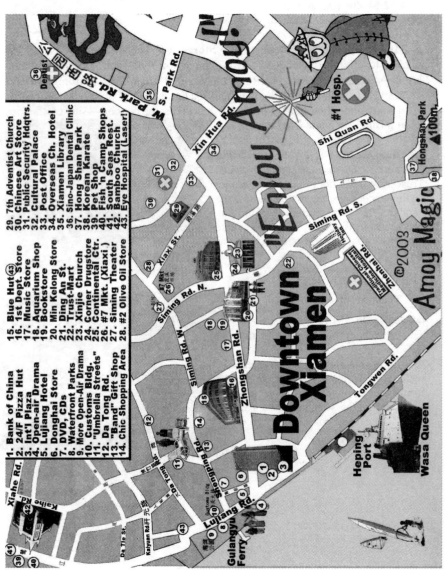

1. Bank of China
2. 24/F Pizza Hut
3. Int'l Plaza
4. Open-air Drama
5. Lujiang Hotel
6. Donghai Store
7. DVD, CDs
8. Waterfront Parks
9. More Open-Air Drama
10. Customs Bldg.
11. "Umbrella Streets"
12. Da Tong Rd.
13. "Band" Gift Shop
14. Chic Shopping Area

15. Blue Hut(43)
16. 1st Dept. Store
17. Music Store
18. Aquarium Shop
19. Bookstore
20. Min Kelong Store
21. Ding An St.
22. Trust-Mart
23. Xinjie Church
24. Corner Drugstore
25. Continental Ctr.
26. #7 Mkt. (Xiaxi)
27. Siming Theater
28. #2 Olive Oil Store

29. 7th Adventist Church
30. Chinese Art Store
31. Public Security Hdqtrs.
32. Cultural Palace
33. Post Office
34. Overseas Ch. Hotel
35. Xiamen Library
36. Sino-Japan Dental Clinic
37. Hong Shan Park
38. Korean Karate
39. Pet Shop
40. Fish 'n Camp Shops
41. South Seas Rest.
42. Bamboo Church
43. Eye Hospital (Laser)

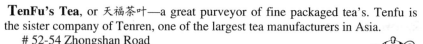
TenFu's Tea, or 天福茶叶—a great purveyor of fine packaged tea's. Tenfu is the sister company of Tenren, one of the largest tea manufacturers in Asia.
52-54 Zhongshan Road
Phone: 202-2318

Minkelong （闽客隆）**Department Stores** was one of the first chains in Xiamen to offer big selections and low prices on foods and household items. Try the store at 34-38 Ding An Rd, （定安路 34-38 号）just across from the Ding An Market （定安市场）. It's on the small road to the left of Siming Rd, between Trust-Mart and Zhongshan Rd. (headed towards the harbor)—site of the rip roaring Ding An. Night Market!

Ding An Rd. （定安路夜市场）**Night Market!** On the little road between Trust-Mart and Zhongshan Rd., it's a lot of fun—and leads to great finds like the bamboo shop and factory. But you don't have to wait until dark. Folks like this bird map throng the streets by day as well.

Trust-Mart—(Chengda Gouwu, 诚达购物) on Siming Road, between Zhongshan Road and the Holiday Inn, is a Taiwan-based version of a Wal-mart Supercenter, with good prices on everything from home appliances to groceries. But you might want to take ear plugs; the canned pop music is loud!

Trust Mart (Between Holiday Inn Zhongshan Rd.)

Amoy Hotels

Home Sweet Home
— DaHua

Amoy's Laowai have plenty of options for long-term residence. One popular hangout is **Plaza Pacific's** efficiency apartments behind the **Dahua** bank building (United Bank Building). *Photo at right.*

Dahua is home to dozens of families with such firms as Kodak, Nokia, Fluor Daniel, and G.E., and also houses the offices of many firms, including American Line, Evergreen, and Maersk Sealand.

Dahua is a popular Laowai hangout, but Overseas Chinese are also hanging about now that the Singapore Consulate is located on the 9th floor (Dahua also hosts Fujian's Singapore Club).

I toured the apartments, and talked to a manager. He said, "Our emphasis is providing a home environment—friendly and caring services, English speaking personnel, security, cleanliness, good food."

The "good food" part went straight to my heart—especially the Western breakfast buffet, which is free to residents. Omelettes to order, pancakes and bacon and eggs, cold cereals—a far cry from the rice porridge we lived on for our first few years.

(**Note**: Plaza Pacific also offers short-term accommodations).

Address: #19 N. Hubin Rd （湖滨北路 19 号） Phone: 511-3888

E-mail: ppsaxmgm@public.xm.fj.cn   Home page: www.ppsaxmn.com.cn

Other options for longterm residence include **Marco Polo Hotel**, the **Taiwan Villas**, or the **Celebrity Villas** (near Xiamen University on the beach road).

For those of us on a mere mortal's budget, check with a Chinese real estate agent, who can probably land you a marvelous little 2 or 3 story home for only $300 to $400 U.S. monthly.   Mr. Hugh Bing has helped several Laowai get great homes at very reasonable prices. Phone: 1360 691-9006, or e-mail him at: Hughbing@hotmail.com

Xiamen also has hundreds of quality hotels for longtermers, or shorterm guests. Consult your phone book for the best selection, but here's a start:

Xiamen Hotels

Best Western Hotel of Xiamen as of this writing is Fujian's largest 4-star hotel, with 500 rooms and suites. Opened August, 1997, it was the first Best Western in China—proving that East can meet West (or at least that Western can meet Eastern). Of special interest to parents is the International Children's Club. Location: North of Changqing Rd. (长青北路)
Phone: 512-3333 Website: **http://bwxm.com/eg_main.html**

Dahua — see description on previous page under "Home Sweet Home". Dahua offers special rates for short stays.

East Ocean Hotel Phone: 202-1111 Fax: 203-3264 Renovated in 2,000, the East Ocean Hotel is at #1 Zhongshan Road, behind Donghai Department Store and a two minute walk to the Gulanyu Islet Ferry. We love the 6/F Jade Garden Restaurant; great food, and prices.

Holiday Inn Phone: 202-3333 (Siming Rd. & Zhenhai Rd.). Best downtown location; excellent Western buffets, Italian food, and Japanese and Chinese cuisines.

Jimei Guesthouse Phone: 606-8560

JinBao Hotel Phone: 601-3888 (#124-126 Dongdu Road)

Lujiang Hotel Phone: 202-2922 #54 Lujiang Road (On the harbor facing Gulangyu; excellent restaurant).

Mandarin Hotel Phone: 602-3333 #101 Yuehua Rd. Huli District, Xiamen 361006 Our only 5 Star! E-mail: mandarin@public.xm.fj.cn，http://www.xmmandarin.com

Mandarin Seaside The Mandarin's Seaside branch, adjoining the trade center, is a bit remote, but offers a delightful seaview, peace and quiet, and some of the best buffets in Xiamen. Phone: 595-9999 **http://www.xmmandarin-seaside.com/**

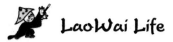

Marco Polo Hotel Phone: 509-1888 Fax: 509-2888   Located on the bank of Yundang Lagoon, next to City Hall. Hubin North Road, #8 Jianye Road.   E-mail: xiamen@marcopolohotels.com http://www.marcopolo.xm.fj.cn

Minnan Hotel Phone: 518-1188   Fax: 518-0460   #26, Yili, Hubin South Rd. Xiamen,   361004   (Revolving restaurant)

Overseas Chinese Hotel   Phone: 202-5602   #70-74 Xinhua Rd., facing the Cultural Palace. Famous for Xiamen Cuisine.

United Hotel Xiamen Phone: 505-5888   # 469 S. Hubin Road. Chinese and Japanese Cuisine

Xiamen Guesthouse   Phone: 202-2265 Just down from Zhongshan Park; across from the Martyr/s Memorial. Famous for authentic Xiamen Cuisine.

Yiyuan Hotel （驿缘酒店）Last but not least，a family favorite (named after the inns that riders on the ancient Chinese Pony Express used to stay in). Accredited 3-stars in only one year, Yiyuan is a 3 minute walk to the beach—and we love Chef Matt's Western cooking. Address: #5-6 Cangli, Zengcuo'an Village
   Phone: 251-9888 FAX: 251-9189

厦门驿缘酒店

Gulangyu

Beautiful Island Hotel   Phone 206-3309 206-3409   133 Longtou Road, Gulangyu Islet.   Nice rooms, reasonable rates.

Gulangyu Guesthouse Phone: 206-3856   #25 Sunlight Rock Road (The site of many movies, colonial architecture gives it an Old World ambience).

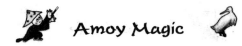
Supplement

Half the Sky
—Get a Baomu.

A woman is like a teabag—only in hot water do you realize how strong she is.

Nancy Reagan

Half the Sky

After seven years in Los Angeles, life in China seemed to proceed at a snail's pace. But even so, we had little free time, because our everyday chores took all day—until we hired a baomu (housekeeper/cook).

Unless you have a baomu, the head of the house, or her husband, must spend hours each morning haggling over every onion, carrot, head of cabbage, or block of tofu with merchants who point to enigmatic scratches on bamboo scales that haven't changed in 5,012 years, and proclaim that 4 eggs weigh a pound and a half. And once back home, the cleaning, chopping, cooking and dishwashing takes hours. No wonder that a baomu is a top priority for even poor professors.

We eventually heeded our colleagues' urges to hire a baomu. Our first candidate was a grandmother who crossed our threshold and crossed my wife in one fell swoop by instructing Susan on the errors of her ways in cooking, cleaning, studying, and raising kids.

She did not last a week. Our next time around we tried our hand with students, who were thrilled at getting paid for learning English (which is what they interpreted their job to be). Xiao Hong and Melanie did little but read our English books and watch TV.

At long last a Chinese professor suggested, "Why not hire a baomu from the countryside? They are honest, hard-working, dependable, and cheap."

"Cheap" went straight to my heart, and the next day we met Lixi, a cook's wife, never imagining that froward, silent soul would become like family.

It was an oppressively hot and muggy October day, but Lixi sported her entire wardrobe: long johns and striped naval undershirt beneath cotton pants and long-sleeved shirt; over that, a vintage, frayed exercise suit, topped off with a ratty gray sweater buttoned to the neck, and olive drab canvas regulation army tennis-shoes that were probably handed down from the Long March.

Lixi contemplated her navel while her husband, wise to the "honest, hardworking peasant" lore, extolled her virtues. The few times I addressed Lixi

directly, she peered furtively through thick, disheveled bangs, then resumed picking her frayed cuffs with calloused fingers.

"Can she speak?" I inquired.

"Not Mandarin, just the Minnan dialect," her husband confessed. "But she's smart. Just show her what to do."

"Can she cook?"

"No, but I'll teach her."

I suspected this sullen apparition was incapable of motion, either physically or mentally, but just as I sought to tactfully end the interview—she moved. Matthew was edging towards the doorway and the dangerous street beyond, and Lixi flew to her feet, snatched him to her breast with practiced swoop, and face aglow, bustled him off to his room. Then she retreated to her chair, donned her practiced frown, and picked at her frayed cuffs.

Inspired, her husband cried, "She's great with children."

Enough said. Sue hired her on the spot—to my immediate regret.

If the way to a man's heart is through his stomach, Lixi ought never to have landed a man. No wok wizard, she was more of an alchemist than a cook. She transmuted the choicest slices of fish into blackened slabs of charcoal, and fresh vegetables, baptized in oil and pickled in salt, became mush

And how to communicate with her? Her Mandarin was worse than ours, and she could not read. Even sign language failed. I suggested to Sue that we dismiss her, but Lixi's desperation defused my anger, and I consoled myself that man does not live by rice alone.

Though incommunicado with us, Lixi was telepathic with tots—especially Matthew, whom she bore on her back from dawn to dusk. But no wonder she understood children: she had four of her own before begging the doctor to tie things off down below.

Mark Twain wrote,

> "There was never yet an uninteresting life. Such a thing is an impossibility. Inside of the dullest exterior there is a drama, a comedy, and a tragedy."

Twain must have meant Lixi, whose plebeian dust jacket does no justice to her contents.

Lixi raised four children single-handedly by working the fields until her staunch Buddhist family drove her from home after she became a Christian. She trekked over the mountains to Xiamen and became a day laborer, lugging baskets of granite slung across her brawny shoulders. After two years in the school of hard rocks, she graduated and became our brawny baomu, lugging towheads with heads lighter but harder than the granite she was used to hauling around.

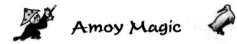
Lixi applied her diehard spirit to becoming a capable member of our household.   She learned Mandarin and, to my chagrin, taught herself to read some of the characters that still eluded me. She even taught herself to cook both Chinese and Western food. By watching Susan she learned how to whip up a pizza, sandwiches, burgers and fries, Irish stew. Even Chinese guests begged for her recipes.

After Lixi had been with us for two years, we moved her four children to Xiamen to help educate them and to fatten them up a bit, for they were skin and bone. Her oldest son eventually took up computers, her sister opened a small shop, and Lixi used her limited income to help those even poorer than herself, both in Xiamen and back home in Anxi, proving that investments in the poor reap compound interest.

Give and it shall be given…

Chairman Mao claimed, "Women hold up half the sky," but I think that was an understatement. Chinese women, even with hands bound by lack of education, hold up a lot more than half.

Hire a baomu!

Laonei (老内) Notes

[1] Tail between legs: defeated (as a dog slinks off, cowering with tail between legs.
[2] Caveat Emptor: Let the buyer beware (Latin)
[3] Red tape: excessive bureaucratic procedures and paperwork
[4] Hair-razing: variation of hair-raising (thrilling, exciting)

Chapter 24

Chinese Festivals & Culture

Happy Holidays! Which ones? Take your pick! Over the past 5,015 years (I was told China is 5,000 years old, and that was 15 years ago), Chinese have created so many holidays that I would not be surprised if they didn't declare the rare nonholiday a unique event, and celebrate it as well. And to add to Chinese New Year, Moon Festival, Lantern Festival, Kitchen God Day, deng deng (Chinese for "etc."). Just a few weeks ago, in the countryside, we passed them celebrating some festival in which they carried children on a miniature bamboo Ferris wheel! It just proves, *"what goes around comes around."*

To add to the merry mayhem (and to fill in the few days that aren't already Chinese holidays), they've adopted Western holidays!

Our first Chinese Christmas, in 1988, was a disappointment, but now they celebrate it as much as we do. Even the post office had a Christmas tree, and local churches broadcast over loudspeakers such traditional hymns as Silent Night, We Three Kings, Frosty the Snowman and Jingle Bells.

Chinese have taken to Valentine's Day with a passion (literally!). A girl gas station attendant in a remote town asked me, "Did you buy your wife flowers? It's that day, you know!" Shops and stalls are full of roses. Kids sell them on street sides. And stores have Valentine's cards, and cute little sweetheart figurines—with a Chinese slant to them!

One student said, "We Chinese learned all about Valentines from the West." I said, "With 1.3 billion population, I doubt it!"

Bill's Birthday was again celebrated by millions of Chinese this year! Though Chinese, of course, prefer to call it "Grave Sweeping Day".

Every April 5th, folks flock to the hillsides, tidy up and sweep their extinguished ancestors' resting places, and burn sacrifices of "Hell Money". They burn stacks of fake billion dollar bills, the idea being that demons down below can't tell real from fake. Thus the dearly deceased can spend more money than Bill Gates—but it must create some hellish inflation down there...

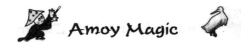

Foreign Holidays in Amoy!

(We've 'stolen' the
Mooncake Game!)

Easter Egg Hunt
(Island Ring Rd.)

Master
of
Mooncake Game!

Amoymagic.com

Xiamen
Nov. '95
B.B.

Amoy Thanksgiving

Amoymagic.com

Christmas is a Gas in Amoy!

Amoy is most magical and merry on Chinese Holidays—and China has certainly accumulated her share of them over the past 5,012 years!

Your hospitable Chinese hosts are bound to invite you to celebrate these festivities with them. Go for it! But also note that some customs and taboos differ from ours.

For example, in China red is the color for luck, so a piece of red paper is often placed on top of a gift, wedding cars are decorated with red ribbons, and children are given New Year gifts of cash stuffed red envelopes (Hongbao, or 红包). And don't be surprised when brides wear bright red (which we associate with prostitution) instead of white. Chinese wear white at funerals because white, black and blue symbolize grief.

A few **local taboos** include:

1. Never point at people with the middle finger.
2. Don't sweep the floor in front of guests; they'll think you are shooing them out.
3. To break a bowl or utensil at a wedding feast is seen as an augury of great misfortune.
4. Never serve a guest six dishes of cooked food. A Qing Dynasty rule dictated that only death row prisoners were fed six dishes right before execution.
5. Don't lay chopsticks across a bowl, lest fishermen's boats run aground.
6. Never turn a fish over to get the meat on the bottom side of the skeleton, or a fishing boat will sink. (Dr. Jan says, "Lift the skeleton out.").
7. Don't jam chopsticks upright in rice: they resemble sacrificial incense sticks.
8. Never pat a Chinese adult on the head.
9. Always give and receive gifts with **two hands**! And when receiving business cards, don't just stuff them in your pocket. Read them for at least 15 or 20 seconds, compliment the design of the card, then set in on a table (or place it carefully in your wallet).
10. A person who hasn't "settled down" (married) can receive HongBao's (cash-stuffed red envelopes) but can't give them.
11. Mentioning monkeys in the presence of babies may cause the babies to get sick.

And speaking of monkeys...

Monkey Business

According to a Xiamen University professor, Chinese legend has it that we Laowai are the fruit of an unseemly union between an ancient Chinese maid and a monkey! When I protested, he pointed to my arm, smiled, and said, "You foreigners are hairier than us Chinese!"

Tibetans, by the way, are proud of such monkey business. They boast that all Tibetans are descended from a union between the monkey God Chenrezi and the mountain goddess who seduced him.

Darwin would be gratified.

Two monkeys ➔

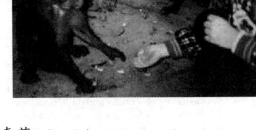

Chinese New Year (春节 Chunjie), aka Spring Festival, is to Chinese what Christmas is to Westerners. It falls on the first day of the first month of the Luny Calendar, and so changes each year, but usually is in January or February.

As the New Year approaches, don't even think of using public transportation. We were once stuck in Beijing for two weeks because every bus, plane, truck and boat was packed with gift-laden passengers headed home for the holidays.

In the countryside, shiny new bicycles groan under the weight of parents and children returning to their ancestral home with bundles of gifts, and baskets of live ducks, geese, chickens and piglets. Even in the remotest hinterlands, mountain paths teem with families making the long but joyful trek home, possessions slung over parents' shoulders, children skipping and laughing in anticipation of grandma's cooking and grandpa's tall tales of the Japanese invasion, and of the revolution.

A New Year's celebration has always been a very intimate affair, family only. But either times are changing or we now have a very big family. When the MBA Center's Dean learned, to his horror, that we had not prepared our own Chinese New Year feast, he invited us to share his family's 20 course banquet.

And every year since, some Chinese family has shared their intimate meal with this family of homeless Americans.

All around Xiamen you will see traditional sayings in gold letters on red paper (some with Mickey and Minnie Mouse on them) pasted up on both sides of doors. They are to insure good luck in the New Year, and a typical couplet might read:

"May there be lots of things to sell, and lots of money."
"May the marketplace be crowded, with noisy business people."

When only one character is posted, it is usually for Spring (春 Chun), Long Life (长寿 Changshou), or Fortune (福 Fu).   They are often placed upside down so demons can't read them and give them the opposite! (It is also a play on the Chinese words "fu" and "dao", meaning "fortune will come".).

You'll also see round mirrors above some doors, because demons are so ugly that when they see themselves they are frightened away. And it might work—at least on Foreign Devils. I've scared myself a few times before my morning shave.

Red paper is never used if an elderly person has died in the household within the last three years. Instead, they use green paper if the deceased was a man, and yellow if they were a woman, and the sayings are calculated to placate the recently extinquished personage:

"Remember to be reverent for three years."
"Cherish the memory of your parents like a cloud rising to the sky."
"Wholeheartedly remember the past."
"Where'd you hide the safe's key, dear departed Dad?"

The night before New Year's Eve, families prepare sweets like cooked dates, Chinese melons, cakes and candied peanuts.   In the countryside and those cities where it is not banned, people set off firecrackers to ward off demons and the dreaded man-devouring Nian that stalks the land every New Year's Day.

Lantern Festival (元宵 or Yuanxiao) falls on the 15th day of the Luny Calendar. Be sure to take in the shows at Zhongshan Park, and buy your kids (or yourself!) one of the little battery-operated brightly colored plastic lanterns, and parade down Zhongshan Rd. with everyone else.

According to tradition, young girls prowl about on this night, hanging around the lanterns, or pulling up people's onions and vegetables, all in the hopes of getting married. (I've never understood what pulling up veggies has to do with matrimony, unless she wants to land a husband with a higher celery?).

Another practice is for the eligible lass to cast divining blocks, and then to walk in the direction they tell her until she meets someone.   She memorizes the

first word that person speaks, and then a fortune tellers divines whether the word is lucky or not, and thus whether she will marry or not that year.

National Day (国庆节, Guoqingjie). It is ironic that our planet's oldest nation is also one of the youngest. We celebrate New China's birthday on October 1st, and usually get 3 or 4 days off for National Day festivities. Most likely you'll be invited out by colleagues or friends to celebrate with a meal, and an evening of entertainment that may include fireworks, special performances of ballet or orchestras, or Minnan Opera. Or you can hibernate at home and watch the gala specials on CCTV, Shanghai TV, or our own XMTV.

The Dragon Boat (龙船) **Festival**, on the 5th day of the 5th lunar month, is called the Double 5th Day Festival in Taiwan, and the 5th Day Festival in Xiamen. Some people still insert Chinese mugwort in the doorway, poor wine on the floor, and pin charms on the children to keep evil spirits away. It's also a great day to air out clothes, clean the house, eat zongzis (pyramid-shaped dumplings of glutinous rice and meat in bamboo leaves), and to watch the annual International Dragon-Boat Race held in Jimei's Dragon-boat Pool. (Some dragon boats in the countryside are so long they require 80 rowers!)

The Dragon Boat Festival, or Double 5th, is one of 3 traditional days for settling accounts with both the living and the dead. Various deities are responsible for success in health, wealth and warfare, and with lakes and rivers

numerous in the south of China, many Southern deities live underwater. This explains why some people throw rice and zongzis into the water—to feed the hungry deities, demons, ghosts, and dragons (the chief water creature being the dragon). Yet another tradition says the zongzis are thrown to an ancient poet who drowned himself.

Zongzis supposedly originated with Qu Yuan (屈原), a Minister in the State of Chu back during the 4th century B.C. He gave detailed instructions on how to wrap rice in silk, with threads of five colors. They eventually came to be wrapped in leaves, in triangular shape, and bound with leaf fibers or string.

Susan Marie loves Zongzis, and Double Fifth is the time to find them—both the sweet ones and the meaty ones. Give them a try.

Qingming Festival (清明节) or Grave-Sweeping Day, falls on the 105th day after the Winter solstice, or April 5th (which, lest you've forgotten, is also my birthday). On this festive occasion, folks eat "spring cakes, " go for strolls in the countryside, and show respect to ancestors by sweeping their graves. While some people still burn "hell money" to ease the dearly departeds' debts down below, nowadays more people are just leaving flowers, at both ancestors' graves and the cemetery of revolutionary martyrs.

The willow has long been used to celebrate Easter because it is one of the first flowers to bloom in spring. Likewise, Chinese use it for Qingming Jie. In fact, tradition has it that women must wear a sprig or risk being reborn as dogs! This tradition began back during the Tang Dynasty when Emperor Gao Cong (650 to 683 A.D.) plucked sprigs of willow and ordered his retinue to wear them in their caps to protect them from scorpion stings.

Oddly enough, another name for Qingming Jie is Zhishujie (植树节), or "Tree Planting Festival" , and it falls at the same time as the West's Arbor Day (which is also set aside for planting trees).

On grave sweeping day, a meal and 3 glasses of wine are offered to ancestors, candles are lighted, and 3 sticks of incense smolder while the family prostrates itself before the dead. And as a precaution against evil spirits stealing the sacrifices, they often make a separate sacrifice of Hell Money (called 外随纸 Wai Sui Zhi, or Outside Following Paper), which the demons scramble after.

If someone can't make it to the ancestral tomb, they worship by correspondence. They put the Hell Money in large square bags, address it to the deceased recipient, prepare a smaller package for the evil demons, place them on the bed, light candles, kneel and worship. The parcels are then taken

outside, wine is poured on them, and they are set afire. Hence the origin of **"dead letter mail?"**

Cold Food Festival on April 4th is yet another cool festival. Fire and smoke are forbidden because some official was burned to death on that day a few thousand years ago. In remembrance of this man, Chinese used to forego fire for an entire month, but they cut it back to 3 days, and now it's only one day, if even that, and people eat only cold spring rolls, cold noodles, and cold take-out cheeseburgers and KFC.

So why not just use a microwave?

Mid-Autumn Festival (中秋节 or Zhongqiujie), also known as **Moon Festival**, falls on the 15th day of the 8th Luny month.

Contrary to popular opinion, Neil Armstrong was not the first person on the moon. It was Chang-O, a beautiful lady who fled to the moon back during the Xia Dynasty (2205—1766 B.C.). During Moon Festival, worshippers of this Moon Goddess offer her moon-cakes, tea and fruit, and Hell money.

Just before the Moon Festival, people present mooncakes to family, friends, co-workers and bosses. In Taiwan's private schools, teachers traditionally give mooncakes to students, and students reciprocate with a nice cash-stuffed Hongbao (Red Envelope).

I wouldn't mind starting that tradition in Xiamen University.

One tradition has it that on Moon Festival Eve, the later a girl goes to sleep, the longer her mother will live—so many girls stay up the entire night.

And once upon a time, on mid autumn festival, unmarried but wealthy girls past their prime would throw an embroidered ball out her window to a crowd of unmarried men below. She could throw the ball to any man she chose, and the one who caught it had to marry her, and they lived happily ever after, or at least had a ball.

In the evening, families are reunited to eat mooncakes, drink wine, and guess riddles, and in Southern Fujian and Taiwan, we play Koxinga's "mooncake gambling game".

Moon-Cake Gambling, like Minnan Opera, is found only in Southern Fujian and parts of Taiwan. The game was invented by pirate-cum-patriot Koxinga to keep his homesick troops occupied.

Every mid-autumn festival, quiet evenings are punctuated by the ringing of dice in large porcelain bowls as families and work unit members gather around tables to compete for mooncakes. They take turns tossing 6 mahjong dice into the bowl, taking care that no dice bounces out (for then they lose a turn).

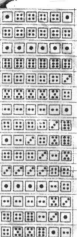

Prizes range from tiny cookies to medium and large mooncakes, with one grand prize — the Zhuangyuan cake. The different sizes represent different official positions won in taking the imperial examinations of yesteryear. The Grand Prize, called Zhuangyuan, represents #1 scholar, Duitang is #2 scholar, Sanhong is #3 scholar, deng deng.

Few people actually enjoy the green bean and egg and fruit stuffed pastries, but who's going to mess with tradition? Mooncakes probably fill much the same niche as fruitcake back home. Fortunately, many families (and work units) are now replacing mooncakes with fruits, food, or practical things like towels, toothpaste, and laundry detergent. Our family usually

wins enough toothpaste from Foreign Affair's annual game to last the year. If we ever miss out on Moon Festival, our Dentist will be the first to know about it.

For more precise directions on Mooncake Gambling, just stick around. Your hospitable hosts will either teach you the ropes or hang you with them.

But worry not. 'Tis a piece of cake! So much so that our boys have made a board game out of it, battling year round over hand-drawn cardboard cakes.

Possible Mooncake Game Combinations

One red is Yixiu, and lands the smallest cookie.

Two fours, Ligu, gets you a larger cookie.

Higher combinations land larger mooncakes, until eventually you get the grandprize, or Zhuangyuan — which is four fours or above.

But **beware!** If you throw Zhuangyuan, don't eat the cake yet. If someone throws a higher one later, they can take it away from you.

Which just goes to show you can't always have your cake and eat it too.

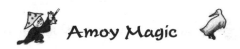

Winter Festival (冬至, or Dongzhi) falls on the shortest day of the year, the Winter solstice, and according to custom is the best day for buying, selling, and signing contracts. On this day, eating a plate of Winter Festival dumplings will supposedly add a year to your life.

Sending off the Gods Day is the 24th day of the 12th Luny month. On this day, the gods down here on earth report to the heavenly emperor on who's been naughty and who's been nice. To get on their good side, people offer them sacrifices, and burn spirit money, and give out New Year cakes to friends and family. This is also the only day they dare to clean house.

According to ancient custom, every single object in a house has a god living in it, so people who still follow old customs (especially in Taiwan) are very careful about how they clean house, lest they jostle and anger the deities resident in the couch or teapot or porta-potty. But on Sending off the Gods Day, the gods have all left to make their reports to the Emperor upstairs.

This is also a good day to marry. Fortune tellers aren't needed to determine if it's a propitious day because the trouble-making deities have all skipped town.

On Weddings & Funerals...

Weddings have been a festive occasion in China ever since they were instituted about 3,012 years ago by Fuxi, whose sister complained to him about the promiscuous way that people were living together. Fuxi acted on her advice, drew up marriage regulations, instituted match-making, and the redoubtable Hans have been henpecked ever since.

Early on it was ruled that people with the same surname could not marry, but given that 1.3 billion Chinese share only 400 surnames, it's fortunate that this rule was abolished, lest some bride be force to marry the wang husband.

Traditionally, Chinese had 8 considerations in selecting a mate: 1) different surname, 2) not related, 3) rich, 4) social position, 5) behavior, 6) health, 7) appearance, 8) lucky or unlucky.

Speaking for myself, I possess # 8, good luck: I'm lucky my wife didn't belabor the other seven.

Wedding dates are carefully chosen according to the Chinese horoscope, and presided over by seniors in both families. Traditionally, the day before the marriage, the bride's family sends the dowry to the groom's family and decorates the bridal chamber. Early on the wedding day, the bridegroom fetches the bride

in a wedding car, and holds a banquet for guests that evening. After the feast, guests can go to the bridal chamber to joke with and tease the bride and groom.

On the third day, the bride and groom return to the bride's family, where a feast is held to celebrate their survival of the first 3 days.

But nowadays, many lovebirds forego the feasting and teasing and head straight for the honeymoon.

Wedding gifts should always be given well before the wedding day, never on or after it. But if your friend hands you a sack of sweets and says they've just been married, no gift is expected.

Wedding gifts used to be practical, like Double Happiness Brand thermoses, blankets, electric rice cookers, electric fans, deng deng. But to avoid getting five rice cookers and four fans and thirteen thermoses, many now prefer the increasingly ubiquitous cash-stuffed Hongbao.

Though Hell Money may be best for dearly departed newlyweds...

Till Death Do Us Marry   Even with divorce rates sailing past 50%, Americans still staunchly vow, "Till death do us part." But not even death unties the knot for Chinese. In fact, some don't even marry until after they're dead.

In Chinese communities worldwide (though rarer in the mainland), spiritualists sometimes inform bereaved families that their dead child cannot rest until married to some other dearly departed soul. Both families then spend a small fortune to wed the dead, who attend by proxy (often in the form of engraved wooden "spirit boards", to which sacrifices are offered).

I suspect some girls end up with some real deadbeat husbands.

And speaking of dead folks... China not only has the largest population of living, but the most dying as well, so you may be invited to a funeral. Funerals, even more than weddings, have brought home to me just how alike, in the end at least, are we Laowai and Laonei.

Filming a Buddhist Funeral

The village square facing the ancient Buddhist temple was crowded with old and young alike, and a few dogs and chickens as well. I walked up and down with my video camera, filming the funeral of my student's father. Per his request, I filmed everything. I panned the gifts of blankets draped over bamboo poles, and the rickety table covered with food offerings to the deceased, whose photo was propped up on the table so he could oversee the proceedings.

As I filmed, everyone who saw me shouted "Laowai!" This shouting and pointing gets to some Laowai, but look at the other side of the Yuan. Laowai zip about snapping shots of old men in PJs brushing their teeth on the roadside, or of fishermen mending nets, or babies in split pants, as if they all were Smithsonian cultural exhibits. I'm not sure which is worse, "Laowai!" or "Flash!"

Yankee Doodle Dirge Mourners and curious onlookers watched the deceased's family bustle about preparing food for the growing crowd. Shaven headed, saffron robed Buddhist priests bustled about preparing for the service. And three bands played simultaneously. A white uniformed brass ensemble played Western music, ranging from Sousa's marches to Camptown Races. An ancient trio played classic Chinese instruments like the suona (a brass horn shrill enough to wake the dead or exorcise them), and the two-stringed erhu (Chinese violin), which is often high pitched and shrill but in the hands of a master is as sweet as any Western violin. A third ensemble played Spanish flamenco on guitars. The icing on the corpse's cake was a Chinese ghetto blaster blaring a funeral dirge that cast a mournful pall that no one could bear (except, perhaps, the pallbearers).

Just about the time I felt like joining the mourners myself, the brass band broke into a rousing rendition of "Yankee Doodle Dandy".

Chinese funeral music appears to emphasize volume, not quality. Perhaps it's like the 100 million dollar hell notes, and false bottomed baskets—the dead don't know any better. Besides, funerals (like weddings) can bankrupt you, so why waste money on good music for the deceased when their ear for music is dead anyway?

Farewell Forever After an hour of solemnities, the relatives led a procession out of the village common and down the dusty path into the countryside, marching to the three bands' merrily mournful music. Behind the bands came the pallbearers, followed by the sons, more family, professional mourners, a solo guitarist playing Spanish music, hundreds of friends and curious onlookers, children, dogs, and one lone water buffalo, who must have known what he was about because everyone ignored him.

And I ran back and forth filming the entire procession.

The sons' devastating wails reached new heights when we passed a beautiful 3-story partially completed home on the outskirts of town. It was to have been the father's retirement home.

After marching far out into the countryside, the mourners took a left fork in the road back to town and the male family members continued on with the coffin towards a small copse in the middle of a dusty field. We passed into the shadows of gnarled, ancient oaks, and approached a dark, musty cave piled high with moldy urns and bones, a few leg bones here, a thigh bone there, a pile of skulls on a shelf.

The place had obviously seen its share of skullduggery.

The sons lifted the blanket and I nearly dropped my camera in shock. I had thought the father lay in state in a coffin, but under the red blanket was naught but a small porcelain urn of ashes.

(Given how much he smoked, I think the extinguished gentlemen would have preferred a lacquer ashtray to an urn).

The sons placed the 8 x 10 and the urn on a shelf dug into the damp cave wall, I shot one last scene, and we returned to the village courtyard, which was already cleared out and deserted, as if the funeral had never taken place.

Life goes on.

Weddings and funerals. Life and death. We Laowai and Laonei really do have a lot in common. As someone said, "Life is tough, and then you die." But Chinese are certainly no strangers to suffering, and I increasingly appreciate their love of life, and even their ability to laugh at death, as in these ancient Ming Dynasty (1368-1644) tales:

Live to Tell About It—a Ming Dynasty Tale   On his sickbed, retired prime minister Ye Heng asked a visitor, "I am dying. Is death a desirable state?"

"Yes, of course it is!"

"But how do you know that?" Ye Heng asked him.

"If it were so bad," the visitor said, "they would have all come back by now, but since none have returned, they must be happy over there!"

Red Sorghum—a Ming Dynasty Tale   A man complained to his friend, "Your mother has just died and instead of mourning you are eating red steamed sorghum!"

The friend replied, "Then I suppose those who eat white rice every day are in mourning?"

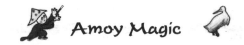
These Are the Magi
(Gift-giving in China)

He who gives when he is asked has waited too long.
Chinese Proverb

The Art of Chinese Gift-giving   It is written that the wise men who brought gifts to the Christ child came from the East. I suspect they meant China, because 1) you can't get any further East than China, and 2) Chinese have raised giving to an art form.

Our first Christmas in China, our elderly dean gave our two sons a toy electric car that set him back at least a week's wages.   Two months later, on Chinese New Year, a teacher gave each of our sons a Hongbao (Red Envelope) stuffed with 100 rmb—a small fortune by that teacher's standards.   Any doubts on the importance of gifts in China vanished when I read Lesson 38 in, *Modern Chinese Beginner's Course.*   The correct response to an impromptu invitation to a Chinese friend's home was, "But we haven't brought any gift."

Gift giving rituals vary around China. Tibetans give a white silk scarf, while Hainan Islanders place a lei of flowers over guests' shoulders.   In Xiamen, the most common gifts are bags of fruit or packages of our local Oolong tea.

Xiamen folk avoid giving odd numbers of gifts. It must be two bottles of Chenggang medicinal wine, not one or three bottles, or 4 boxes of Tiekuanyin tea, never three or five.   The gifts must be proffered respectfully with two hands, and accepted with two hands.

Americans have no qualms in giving an inexpensive gift or card to convey a sentiment because it's the thought that counts. But not in China, where face is everything, and a small or trifling gift may be worse than no gift at all. Conversely and perversely, the larger the gift, the more face for both parties. Over the years, our face has been lifted more times than Elizabeth Taylor's.

Guests have materialized on our threadbare astroturf welcome mat with 50 bananas, or 30 pounds of roasted Longyan peanuts, or 15 pounds of freshly caught fish, or 4 dozen freshly fried home-made spring rolls. We've protested, futilely, that 50 pounds of bananas will rot before we can finish them off. In the end, we either go on banana binges or make a quick pilgrimage to a Chinese colleague's home with a second-hand gift of bananas, tea, dried mushrooms or fresh fish. They probably pass them off too, but somewhere down the line some soul has to get 50 pounds of bananas down the hatch.

Where's the Beef?   We had some knotty experiences until we learned the ropes of Chinese gift giving.   Shortly after we moved into Chinese professor's housing, Susan baked chocolate cake, which at that time few Xiamen folk had tried. She gave our neighbor a couple of slices to sample, and the astonished granny thanked her profusely and shut her door slowly, politely. Next morning, bright and early, she rapped on our door, and thrust a plate full of beef in Sue's face. She said, "For you," and beat a hasty retreat, ignoring Susan's protests.

"This is terrible, Bill," Sue said. "She should not have done that."

"This is great, Sue." I retorted. "Two pounds of beef costs a lot more than two slices of cake. Think how much we'll save on meat if we give cake to all our neighbors."

Now I know why Marie Antoinette gave everyone cake.

It is Cheaper to Give Than to Receive   Nowadays, we are more careful (though not paranoid!) with gift-giving, because it can be costly for all concerned. Those whom we give gifts feel compelled to reciprocate, whether they can afford it or not.   As for receiving gifts... they sometimes have more strings than ribbons.   But all things considered, I still think Chinese are the Magi— particularly where family and homeland are concerned.

Giving to the Motherland   When overseas Chinese labored in abject poverty in the mines and fields of Africa and Colonial Asia, or to build American railroads, they invariably sent a large portion of their meager earnings home to family. It was these pittances, multiplied a million fold, that kept China afloat when we were bleeding her dry through the opium trade.

Some laborers became industrial magnates, like Tan Kak Kee, and donated millions to China.   Even today, regardless of political persuasions, overseas Chinese continue to remit millions annually not only to their mainland relatives but to local governments to build schools, colleges, orphanages, and roads.

Chinese, rich and poor alike, are a generous people.   A lowly mason who lives in a shack nearby gave me 5 pounds of freshly netted fish because he heard my in-laws were visiting from America.   A disabled, retired campus laborer shows up occasionally with fresh greens from his garden, or new flowers for our yard.   When word got around that I wanted a stone mill to grind wheat, several peasants headed to the rural stone quarries, and we were blessed with not one mill but three (never again will I take wheat for granite).

The mason, the disabled laborer, the peasants, sought nothing in return. They gave because we were friends—like the poor bicycle repairman who repeatedly insists, "It's a small thing. Pay me when you have a real problem to fix." The man's entire world is but a tiny, dusty shop only 8 feet wide and 4 feet deep. Greased bike chains and sprockets, rims and tires and tubes, bike seats and pedals hang from nails on the walls. His furniture consists of two bamboo stools, one for himself and one for customers, and a bamboo footstool that doubles as a table for his cheap tea set, which he sets up every time I stop by.

He has spent more serving me tea than he will ever make from fixing my battered bicycle.

Chinese have always given sacrificially to family and their immediate community, but charity beyond that was rare, for it was seen as depriving family and local community of scarce resources. But times are better now, and Beijing is seeking to widen the scope of giving.

Half a dozen programs encourage wealthier urbanites to help their less fortunate and far more numerous comrades in the countryside. Every year, "Project Hope" (希望工程) allows millions of urban Chinese to help fund poor rural children's education. And "Helping Hand" pairs up city kids and country kids, who write to each other and exchange gifts.

Get involved!　　　Many foreign firms and individuals have participated in campaigns like Project Hope. For details on how to get involved, contact your Chinese colleagues or the municipal government. You can even arrange with local governments to help sponsor schools or poorer students. Opportunities are limited only by your imagination and your purse.

Project Hope Online: http://www.project-hope.org/english/eindex.htm

Gold Rats and Oxen — A Ming Dynasty Tale (1368—1644)
On his birthday, an official's subordinates chipped in to give him a life-sized solid gold rat, since he was born in the year of the rat (each year of a twelve year cycle has a different animal). The official thanked them, then asked, "Did you know that my wife's birthday is coming up? She was born in the year of the ox."

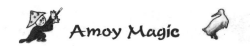

Chapter 25

Mad About Mandarin

"Translation is always a treason, and as a Ming author observes, can at its best be only the reverse side of a brocade—all the threads are there, but not the subtlety of color or design."   Okakura, *The Book of Tea*

If you're staying in Xiamen awhile, I recommend you try to pick up a little Mandarin. Xiamen University's Overseas Correspondence College offers full and part-time courses — or hire a tutor (though the tutor route takes lots of discipline, and the tutor may be more interested in learning English than teaching Chinese).

I'm still hoping to get Mandarin down myself. Years before coming to China, I took college Mandarin courses. I memorized stacks of flash cards bought in Taipei and Los Angeles' China Town. I tried the course advertised in flight magazines — the one that promises native level proficiency and a high post in the Diplomatic Corp within 90 days or double your money back. In desperation, I even paid $500 per month for a year of private tutoring, and a year later and $6,000 poorer could barely tell our tutor zaijian (goodbye). Xiamen was my last hope. I could just see those enigmatic squiggly characters coming to life — if I could just survive the enigmatic enrolment.

Our college administrators had good hearts, but I suspected some were but simple souls hauled in from the countryside and handed a pen, an official chop and a blotter, and told to go manage—just like hundreds of thousands of city folk were carted off to the countryside, handed a hoe, and told to go farm; getting enrolled was certainly a long roe to how.

The administrator began day one of our beginner's class by handing out a pile of Chinese forms and explaining rapidly, in Chinese, that we were to fill out the forms, in Chinese. When we just sat there, lost, he said, "What is wrong? Please fill out the forms now."

In my haltered Chinese I said, "Teacher, if we could already read and write Chinese, we would not be in this beginner's Chinese course."

He stalked out and returned with a translator.

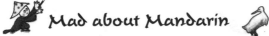

Shanghaid on Shibboleths

Not to worry. Chinese are exceptionally patient, and good humored. Just talk with everyone you meet and you'll pick it up eventually — with a southern accent!

The Book of Judges (Bible) recounts how the Israelites found out who was friend or foe by making them say Shibboleth. The foe could not pronounce the "sh" and invariably said "Sibboleth." And lost their tongue and head with it.

Southern Chinese can't pronounce "sh" either, so Shanghai is Sanghai. They also can't tell *f* from *h*, or *l* from *r* and *n*, or the long *e* and the short *e*. To further complicate matters, they hear no difference between *t* and *th*, or *c* and *ch* or *z* and *zh*, deng deng. And it does make a difference, especially in business, because it is impossible to tell "4" from "10" or "eat" (yes, the tone is different, but they mix that up too).

If Southerners can't get the sounds out in Chinese, it stands to reason they trip over the same ones in English. No matter how hard most Xiamen people try, my name "Bill" invariably comes out "Beer". One Christmas, my hapless Southern students threw in the towel and their tongue and presented me with a Christmas card made out to, "Professor Beer" , and a nicely wrapped bottle of Chinese Tsingdao beer (the most enduring legacy of Germany's occupation of Shandong Province up North).

Inevitably, I too have acquired a slight Southern Chinese accent, to Northerners' endless amusement. That's why many Chinese experts recommend learning the language in the North, but I'll take a few shibboleths over frostbite any day.

So, *Ni Hao*, y'all!

A Word's Worth 1,000 Pictures

I often preface proverbs with, "Confucius said" , because it's a safe bet that either he or some other ancient Chinese did — and probably in 4 words or less.

Most of the planet says, "A picture is worth a 1,000 words," but for Chinese, a word may be worth a thousand pictures, for over the aeons they have distilled their wisdom and experience into concise proverbs that strike to the heart of any matter, and strike fear into the heart of foreign language learners.

Even after memorizing the 3 to 4,000 characters of a minimal vocabulary, we've no guarantee we have any idea what they mean when they are used against us. No dictionary can convey the full nuances of a character, and 3 or 4 strung together in one of China's tens of thousands of proverbs conjure up ancient historical incidents, or classic poems, or paintings, or deep philosophical notions. My favorite ancient Chinese book is *The Art of War*, which has influenced military, business, and diplomacy—and the entire classic is only 5,000 characters. That's like fitting *War and Peace* between the covers of Dr. Seuss's *The Cat in the Hat*.

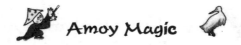

Chinese have a proverb for every occasion. A Chinese businessman who squanders his capital "drains the pond to catch the fish". A public figure who thinks he can hide an immoral private life, "Covers his own ears while stealing the bell." Impatient people are "rice pullers" — like the foolish farmer who killed his rice plants when he tugged on them to make them grow faster.

"Contradiction" in Chinese is maodun, or "spear-shield". It refers to the ancient fable of the weapon salesman who marketed both impenetrable shields and unstoppable spears. Inappropriate public policies are like "using wood to put out a fire". People with unrealistic fears see, "a soldier in every tree and bush." A persistent person is like the old granny determined to "grind an iron rod into a needle." The fawning sycophant capitalizing on others' power is the "fox exploiting the tiger's prestige".

Every saying makes a point, but also stirs up images of the story behind it. Lao Tzu, founder of Taoism (The Way), used only 4 words to preach an entire sermon on the power of gentleness and softness over inflexibility and hardness. He said, "Teeth fall, tongue remains." (hard teeth fall out, soft tongue and gums remain into old age). Translation: "Go with the flow!"

Mandarin is both fascinating but frustrating, yet I'm drawn to it.

Perhaps because I like drawing.

Drawn to Chinese

Drawn to Chinese The Chinese have a saying or a solution for everything except how to teach foreigners the ABCs of Chinese. That's mainly because there aren't any ABCs. No alphabet at all—just 40 to 50,000 characters to memorize.

Chinese characters are pictographs—drawings of objects or ideas. So in a sense, all literate Chinese are artists. And pictographs have a great advantage over alphabets. They aren't abstract representations but concrete drawings, so any Chinese can 'read' their meaning, even though they are pronounced completely differently in Cantonese, Sichuanese, Pekinese, deng deng. Even Japanese can read them, for Japan's language, like much of her culture and religion, evolved centuries ago from ancient China.

Some Chinese pictographs so closely resemble their object that even illiterate foreign friends can figure them out. 凹 is obviously "concave" , and 凸 is "convex". And if you know that "man" is written as 人, then 大, a man with outstretched arms, easily suggests "big" or "great".

刀, or "knife" , looks like Yan's Chinese cleaver. Add a dot to signify a drop of blood and you get 刃 "knife's edge" or "to kill with a cleaver" , and the plot of Julia Child's upcoming bestseller, "Yan Can Kill."

"Mountain" is 山 , which resembles 3 peaks, and "river" is 川 , which suggests a flowing river.

If all Chinese characters were so easily deciphered, beginning Chinese students would have no problem filling out Chinese enrollment forms. Yet no doubt to frustrate foreign friends, for the past 5,012 years Chinese have stylized their pictographs until today only Vincent Van Geogh could possibly see "star" in 星 . And why all this:香蕉, for a banana, when this would do 🐟 ?

And why mess with 16 strokes for apple,苹果, when you can whip it out with two strokes and a flick:ひ ?

Nothing is fishier than the evolution of "fish" , which started out well but floundered:

First century Christian's did it well enough with:

Change is afoot, though. (Speaking of which, people ask, "Is there a lot of change in China?" I answer, "None! Taxi drivers don't have change, stores don't have change; postal clerks don't have change…)

But characters are changing. After must post-Liberation deliberation, New China decided to fight illiteracy by simplifying characters. For example, that most fundamental of New Chinese characters "hui" (or "meeting" , for Chinese spend many of their waking hours in meetings) was simplified from 13 strokes to 6—much easier to memorize and to write. But the art of simplification can go too far. On bus signs, for example, "Xia" , (from Xiamen) is often written with three strokes instead of twelve, as 下 instead of 厦. Taken this far, simplification robs characters of much of their beauty and meaning. Think of how we would react if Uncle Sam fought illiteracy by simplifying English. How *wud we lik it if our govurnmint tride too improov literasee and speling bi geting rid ov awl unesesaree leterz and xsepshuns in speling*?

A Modest Proposal Aesthetics aside, it was courageous of Beijing to tamper with the ancient language of the most tradition-bound people on earth, and strike a mighty blow against illiteracy. But illiteracy might be vanquished forever if Beijing finished the job of simplification by using a few of my suggestions:

Triangle: instead of the patently ungeometrical 三角形, just use ∇

Ear: who but Mike Tyson's opponents have ears like 耳朵? Just use 𝄪 !

Eye: the ancient's 👁 for "eye" made more sense than 眼睛.

Fast Food: last but least, why defeat the point of fast food (saving time) by wasting half a day writing the 20 odd strokes of 快餐 for "fast food"? Just read the writing on the wall and use ⅯⅯ
Deng Deng.

Ups
Chinese and Downs

To further brutalize us barbarians, Chinese tones play havoc with our ears (see Dr. PinYin's unPatented PinYin Guide at the end of this chapter). Grammar and word order are different too. "Please buy me a coke" becomes, in Chinese, "Please give me buy a coke." And Chinese change a sentence's meaning, tense, or intensity by tacking on little sounds like *le*, and *ma*, and *ee*, which is why Chinese who speak English often say changee instead of change, and lookee instead of look.

There is no end to the mistakes, some quite embarrassing, that Chinese coaxes out of Americans.

About a century ago, an American missionary asked his Chinese maid to prepare chicken for dinner. The maid returned 3 days later and said, "I'm sorry, Pastor, but I couldn't find anyone willing to marry a foreigner."

"Chicken" sounds similar to "wife" , but even said correctly in another context, "eating chicken" can mean dallying with a prostitute, much to Colonel Sander's dismay.

Then there's the matter of knowing one's left from one's right. While English is written from left to right, and Hebrew is written from right to left, Chinese goes with the flow — left to right, or right to left, or even top to bottom. All are equally acceptable. I've even seen diagonal (but so far no bottom to top), and I've come across sentences going two or three directions on the same page. Only by context do you know the direction, and short sentences are a bear.

I once told a Chinese friend, "Xiamen University has buildings all over China and Hong Kong!" I pointed to a sign with the two characters for "Xiamen University": 厦大.

My friend laughed. "You're reading it backwards!" Sure enough, Xiamen University backwards (大厦) was Dasha, or hotel (from Russian "dacha").

An excess of courtesy is discourtesy.   Chinese Proverb

Titled Gentleman   Even if you can talk to your Chinese friend, how do you address them?   Chinese honorifics are legion and lethal. Even common laborers have titles. They are called "Master," and they are, and they know it.   Try to get a carpenter who is just lumbering along to finish a job on schedule and you'll see just who is master in Socialist China.

I have at least 8 licit titles and a few I'd rather not discuss.   I have been called "Professor Pan" , "Teacher Pan" , "Master Pan" and "Mr. Pan".   My Chinese elders may call me Xiao Pan (Xiao means little, or young), but people younger than me say Lao Pan (Lao is old, or venerable).   Some Chinese children like to call me uncle—but which kind of uncle?   I'm either Bobo or Shushu, depending on whether I am older or younger than the child's father.   When the child doesn't know an elder's age, then he really cries uncle.

But it all Pans out in the end.   Besides, aunties and uncles are on their way out, thanks to the one child policy.   With no aunts and uncles and nieces and nephews, traditional family structures are undergoing greater simplification than the language.   Happily, in my wife's home I use only two titles: "son", and "your highness".

But in all seriousness (wow!), Mandarin is a beautiful language, and spending a little time on it will make your stay a lot more pleasant and profitable.

Dictionaries, Diction, and Deng Deng   Whether you master Mandarin or not, a good phrasebook and dictionary are essential.   The absolutely best dictionary around **is Oxford University Press's** *Concise English-Chinese Chinese-English Dictionary*.   It is one of the very few that use Pinyin throughout, so you can make a semblance of pronouncing those pictographs—and so you can look both English and Chinese words up alphabetically.   Otherwise, given that Chinese doesn't have an alphabet, how do you look things up?   You can use pinyin, but if you don't know the character, then you can't even pronounce it to spell out the pinyin.

There are several methods of searching Chinese dictionaries, but none are foolproof, even for Chinese.

Some arrange by number of strokes: characters with 1 stroke, 2 strokes, 三 strokes, 四 strokes, 五 strokes, deng deng.   This is broken down further (and I do mean broken) by arranging them according to which stroke is first (vertical, horizontal, slanting down and left, or up to the right, deng deng).   But I've come across characters that even Chinese professors could not find in this way.   One professor who was a real character rifled the pages of my dictionary for 15 minutes, then said, "It's no problem looking this up because we know it anyway."

Well, different strokes for different folks.

A good phrasebook is the palm size *Barron's Chinese at a Glance*. It's a marvelous work that covers basic grammar and pronunciation, and gives enough phrases to get you in trouble in almost any situation imaginable.

The little red *Oxford Dictionary* is usually sold in the Foreign Language Bookstore on Zhongshan Road, but you'll have to pick up your Barron's before coming to China (back home, or in H.K.'s Swindon's Book Store, or Page One Bookstore). Or…order it from Amazon.com!

A *Chinese-English Dictionary*, produced by Beijing's Foreign Language Institute, is another excellent tool—and plain fun to read! I read it through twice in four months just because I enjoyed the sample English sentences!

Bear in mind, of course, that it was printed in 1988—scarcely a decade after the unCultural Revolution, so it's not surprising that every sentence had a revolutionary bent.

My favorites include:

Suppose: I *suppose* she's gone to practice grenade throwing again.

Anew, afresh: launch a *fresh* offensive.

Barely: When I joined the 8th Army route, I was *barely* the height of a rifle.

Be: I want to *be* a PLA man when I grow up.

Armed with such a vocabulary, imagine the conversations that students used to strike up in Friday night English Corners!

But jesting aside, it's a very comprehensive little dictionary.

Mandarin Chinese—a marvelous language! And it would behoove you to learn a little. After all, it's the official language of 1/5 of the planet's people. But if 40,000 pictographic characters intimidate you, start with China's official romanization scheme, PinYin. It's simple, and useful—and I tell you how in "Dr. Bill's unPatented PinYin Guide."

Dr. Bill's unPatented Pinyin Guide

Make the magic of Amoy come alive by spending a few minutes mastering China's official romanization system, Pinyin. Some sounds are similar to English, but others are otherworldly. For example, how on earth do you pronounce "Xiamen?"

All Chinese words come in 3 parts: initials, finals, and tone. In "Xiamen", "X" is the initial and "ia" the final, and the "Xia" is pronounced with the 4th tone. Pinyin's "X" sounds like "sh," so Xiamen is pronounced like "Sh-Yah Men," (with Sh and Yah crammed together so that Xiamen has only two syllables—something like "shaman with a yah after the sh").

With only 400 or so distinct sounds, Mandarin is a haven for homonyms, but the 4 tones (plus context) help us decipher them:

1st tone is level, and at the top of one's normal vocal range for speaking.

2nd tone rises from the middle of one's range to the top.

3rd tone starts in the middle, drops to the bottom, and rises at the end (Susan Marie says that if your chin hits your chest on the low note, you've got it right).

4th tone starts high and ends low, as if you were scolding someone.

The four tones (sounds like a 60s Pop Group!) sound like this:

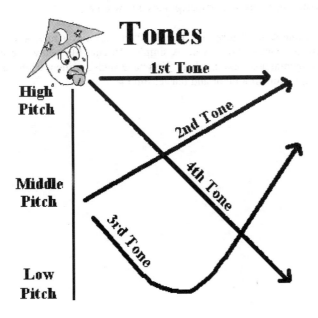

Tones

1st Tone

2nd Tone

4th Tone

3rd Tone

High Pitch

Middle Pitch

Low Pitch

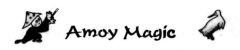
Tones completely change the meaning of words. Take *ma*, for example. With 1st, 2nd, 3rd, and 4th tones, *ma* means "mother" , "hemp" , "horse" , and "to curse". Get it wrong and you might call someone's mother a horse!

Intimidated? Don't be! And don't cop out with the "I'm tone deaf" ploy because you've been using tones since you were a toddler…

"Tone Deaf…"
…and other Lame Laowai Myths

Frustrated Laowai often excuse their poor Mandarin with, "I'm tone deaf!" Sheer nonsense. All English speakers use tones—especially us married ones. I've heard all four of Mandarin's tones, and a few dozen more, from Susan Marie.

When Susan yells, "Bill!" with the 1st tone, she means, "Come here!" The 2nd tone "Bill" asks, "Where are you?" or "Is that you?" The 3rd tone "Bill" is reserved for giving me the third degree and means, "Do you expect me to swallow that?" The 4th tone "Bill," a sharp, barking descent, means I'm in hot water. But when my sweetheart drops my nickname altogether and intones with the dead calm of a Taiwan typhoon's eye, "William" , it is the neutral 5th tone, a portent of dire peril, and I am not long for this world.

Americans, particularly us domestipated ones, know tones.

Fortunately, Chinese are a forgiving people, even when you massacre your Mandarin and create tones of your own. A simple "Ni Hao Ma" (how are you) will have your congenial hosts exclaiming, "You have such excellent Chinese!"

But do them and yourself a favor and master PinYin.

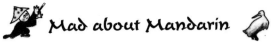

Pinyin Initials

Pinyin	English	Examples	Pronunciation
b,m,m,f,d, n,l,g,k,j,s, y,ch,sh,t,w	about the same as in English	dou gan shu	dough gone shoe
c	Like *ts* in *rats*	cai can	tseye tsahn
h	Guttural *h*, like German *ch* in *ach*	hao hu	how who
q	Like *ch* in *chick*	qu qin	chew cheen
r	Between *j* & *r*	ru	roo
x	Like *sh*	xia	shee-yah
z	Like *ds* sound in *kids*	zai zong	dzye dzong

Pinyin Finals

Pinyin	English	Examples	Pronunciation
a	*ah* in *ah!*	ba ta	bah tah
ai	Like *y* in *my*	lai hai	lye hi
an	*ahn* (lawn)	can	tsahn

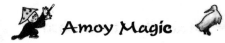

ang	*ahng* (angst)	mang	mahng
ao	*ow* in *cow*	zao	zow
ar	*ar* in *are*	nar	nar
e	*u* in *bush*	re	ruh
ei	*a* in *day*	gei	gay
en	*un* in *pun*	wen	wun
eng	*ung* in *rung*	leng	lung
er	*ur* in *purr*	mer	mur
i	Like *ee* in *wee* (after b,p,m,d,t,n,,j,q,x)	qi mi	chee mee
	Like *z* after z,c,s	ci zi	cz dz
	Like *r* after ch, sh, and r	shi chi	shir chir (*chir*p)
ia	*ee-ya*, in one syllable	xia	sheeyah
ian	*yen*	tian	tyen
iang	*yahng*	jiang	jyahng
iao	ee-yow (meow, in one syllable)	piao tiao	pee-yow tee-yow
ie	*yeh*	tie	tyeh
in	*een* in *preen*	pin	peen
ing	*ing* in *sing*	ming	ming

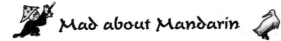

iong	*eeyong* (long o)	xiong	sheeyong
iu	*eo* in *Leo*	liu	leo
o	roughly like a long *o* and short *u* run together, with a *w* in front	mo / po	mwo-uh / pwo-uh
ong	Like *ong* in *gong*, but with long O sound.	tong	tong
ou	*o* in *toe*	zhou	joe
u	like *oo* in *boo*, except after j,q,x,y, and then like the French *eu*	du / lu / yu	doo / loo / yeu
ua	*wah* (*ua* in *guava*)	gua	gwah
uai	*wye* (as in *rye*)	guai	gwye
uan	*wahn* (*swan*) except after j,q,x or y, when it is *wen* (*when*)	duan / yuan	dwahn / ywen
uang	*wahng* (as in *angst*)	kuang	kwahng
ue	*oo* and *yeh* (yeah) said in one syllable	xue	shooeh
ui	like *way*	chui	chway
un	like *woon* with the *oo* of *book*	jun	jwun
uo	like *o* (*oh*) and *u* (*uh*) in one syllable	duo	dwo-uh

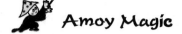

Supplement

Uncle Beard's Sandwich Stories

www.unclebeard.com

My study of Chinese characters began with Xiamen University's famous Chinese character[i], Professor Ji Yuahua. His self-taught English was perfect even back in '88, so it's no wonder that today 'Uncle Beard' is famous for his language learning methods—especially sandwich stories.

Sandwich stories use words or phrases of a 2nd language sandwiched within a story in one's mother tongue. The 2nd language words are repeated throughout the story, not mechanically but naturally, so learning is easy and fun. As students progress, 2nd language content increases until eventually the language learner is reading entertaining stories entirely in their new tongue.

While Uncle Beard did not invent sandwich stories, he was first to use them in China, and over the years has written over 60 sandwich story books with tapes and VCDs, papers in four international journals, and he has lectured in several countries.

Grab a sandwich today! (The top headings of **www.unclebeard.com** are in Chinese, so you'll have to experiment with them until Uncle Beard gets around to sandwiching in some English headings for Laowai sandwich lovers!).

The Sandwich Story of Happy Pig
(does that make this a pork sandwich?)

Long ago，有一只 little pig。He was very happy.人们都叫他 Happy Pig。Happy Pig lived in a little house。His house 前面有一个 garden。Every morning, Happy Pig 总是很早就 got up，然后就 worked in his garden。In his garden，Happy Pig 种了 a lot of vegetables— 有 tomatoes, potatoes, cabbages, turnips, and onions。

In the afternoon, Happy Pig went to the market to sell his vegetables. His vegetables were very good. 大家都抢着买。人人都说："Happy Pig's vegetables are very good. His potatoes, cabbages, turnips, and onions are very big. His tomatoes are big and red and sweet. We all like Happy Pig's vegetables."

But one day, suddenly, Happy Pig was unhappy. 他嘟嘟囔囔地说："Every morning, I have to get up and work in my garden. Every afternoon, I have to go to the market to sell my vegetables. I have to work all the time. My life is not interesting. I am tired. I am unhappy. My name should not be Happy Pig. My name should be Unhappy Pig. I want to change my life. I want to live a new life. 从现在起，谁也不要叫我 Happy Pig. 应该叫我 Unhappy Pig." 说完，Unhappy Pig 就离开了 his little house. He went looking for a new life. ......

---

[i] Character: a colorful personality or person

Chapter 26
Lords of Opium

Every time history repeats itself, the price goes up.
Anonymous

He who sacrifices his conscience to ambition burns a picture to obtain the ashes.
Chinese Proverb

Nobel Laureate Elie Wiesel wrote in *A Personal Response*:
"My goal is always the same: to invoke the past as a shield for the future, to show the invisible world of yesterday and through it, perhaps on it, erect a moral world where men are not victims and children never starve and never run in fear."

Why "Lords of Opium?"

If you've waded this far through *Amoy Magic* you'll understand why Susan Marie complains, "Bill is never serious!" My study of the Opium Era sobered me—and yet most Westerners know so little about it. An American professor in Xiamen actually asked me, "Didn't the West fight the Opium Wars to prevent China from exporting opium?"

I love magical Amoy's beaches and hills, and colonial architecture, and Sundays in the oldest Protestant church in China. But sadly, it was a different kind of magic, a dark sorcery, that opened magical Amoy to the West.

Western nations speak loud and long of justice and morality, but for an entire century they trafficked in opium on a scale that dwarfs any modern Colombian multi billion dollar drug empire. Even though most Westerners opposed the trade, by the 1920s, fully half of Europe's Asian profits derived from opium!

Just Say No? China, not America, started the first "Just Say No!" anti-drug program. Chinese leaders appealed to our sense of morality and justice, and the "Way of Heaven". The West responded with a "Just Say Yes!" campaign and

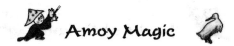
two wars to implement it, and America's ex-President Adams made our first complaint against China's human rights by declaring that her refusal to import opium was a violation of "the rights of men and nations".

I'm thankful that Amoy's true magic lies not in her architecture or geography or climate, but in her people—a forgiving people!

The Opium Den
(Macgowan, *The Story of the Amoy Mission*, 1889, p. 180)

"The shops today are all busy, for customers crowd into them during the busiest hours of the fair. But how is it that, interspersed amongst them, there are so many houses with bamboo screens hanging in front of the open doors? Let us enter one, for it is not a private house. It is an opium den. We put the screen aside, and come into a dimly lighted room, with a broad bench running round the sides of it. Little lamps are placed at various intervals, and men are reclining beside them. Some are asleep, and most ghastly do they look with their haggard, opium-hued faces. They are stretched on their backs, and they seem as if they were corpses. They don't appear like men whose spirits are wandering in fairy land, and are entranced with gorgeous scenes of beauty, such as the opium smoker is said to enjoy… One man smiles at me [and says], 'This comes from your country, doesn't it?' I feel distressed, for I know he does but express the common opinion that all opium comes from England. But this opium den is an unsavoury place to be in. The close, horrid smell, the ghastly figures ranged along the benches, and the sense of being in the midst of some of the very lowest of the population, are oppressive. We hear the sounds of voices outside, and we see the rays of the bright sun shining upon the bamboo mat, and we rush out of the dim, fetid place, with a sense of deliverance, into the open air."

"But there was no deliverance for those inside."

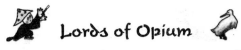

Birth of the Opium Trade   European opium smugglers flirted with China's death penalty as early as 1729, for opium's immense profits were more addictive than the poppy.   The only problem was supply, which Britain solved in 1756 by conquering Calcutta.

Clive marveled at India, the "rich and flourishing kingdom".   Within decades that rich kingdom was pauperized as farmers were forced to abandon traditional crops and to grow what became the Crown's primary cash crop, and China's main import—opium.

Warren Hastings, India's first governor-general, wrested control of the Dutch opium trade, rapidly expanded poppy production, and dispatched two opium-laden ships to Canton on a trial run.   One was shipwrecked, but the other evaded Chinese officials and sold 200,000 pounds of opium in Huangbo.

After an English census of China revealed 300 million potential "clients", the Crown awarded the Honorable East India Company a monopoly on the "trade", carefully avoiding the use of the word "opium"—a face-saving subterfuge employed right into the 20th century.   (For the record, the majority of British merchants and missionaries protested against Britain's foray into drug trafficking, but to little avail).

On Dec. 2, 1799, a distraught emperor penned an anti-opium edict, noting:
"The infirm and weak perish gradually from want and hunger, while the strong and vigorous become thieves and robbers, the ultimate ruin of all being thus equally certain and inevitable."

But Britain saw not ultimate ruin but a 2,000% profit on each 130 pound chest.   The Company sold 3,000 chests in 1790 and 30,000 chests in 1836.   Between 1820 and 1835 alone, China's addict population grew 50 fold.

Lord Hastings maintained that Britain's opium smuggling was carried out 'in compassion to mankind', but the Emperor wrote that foreigners,
"smuggle in prohibited opium, which flows and poisons the land. When this conduct is referred to the heart, it must be disquieting; when referred to reason, it is contrary to it."

After the Dao Guang emperor's 3 sons, including his heir, died of opium addiction, he ordered the viceroy at Canton to tighten up controls.   He lambasted Britain as "a Christian nation devoid of four out of the five Virtues".   Indignant opium smugglers demanded that Britain redeem her honor, but parliament urged patience, reasoning that the Emperor would give in when he saw the magnitude of the profits to be made.   But the Emperor refused the part of Judas.   He wrote,
"It is true that I cannot prevent the introduction of the poison; gainseeking corrupt men will, for profit and sensuality, defeat my wishes; but nothing will induce me to derive a revenue from the vice and misery of my people."

As the stakes grew, so did the smugglers' audacity.   In Feb. 1832, Lord Amherst sailed up the coast from Canton to seek opium markets.   In a Fujian harbor he assured Chinese officials that his ship was actually on its way to Japan from Calcutta and had been driven ashore by the storm. It was harder for him to explain away his crates of Chinese leaflets advertising for coastal trade outlets.

Chinese protests in Canton were fruitless. The indignant British protested they'd never heard of such a ship — technically true, since Lord Amherst had used a fake name on the vessel. Arthur Waley, in *The Opium War Through Chinese Eyes*, concluded, "It is not surprising that during his Canton days Lin worked on the hypothesis that nothing the English said could be relied upon."

Lord Amherst's escapade was lauded in London, where the House of Commons sanctioned the production and sale of opium. Lord Shaftsbury later testified that the government not only encouraged the use of the drug but carefully studied the tastes of Chinese addicts to "inflame the temptation so as to ensure an ample demand."

In 1836, the angry Emperor issued yet another edict ending in "Tremble". An indignant Lord Napier ended his reply with, "Therefore tremble, Governor Lu, intensely tremble."

Governor Lu reluctantly dispensed with diplomacy and blockaded the river above and below the foreign merchants' ships, and a humiliated Lord Napier conceded defeat. When Napier fell ill, Governor Lu sent him to Macao, where he died, becoming a martyr to the opium cause.

Furious Westerners demanded revenge for Napier's death. Matheson, the premier opium merchant, lambasted the unwavering Chinese mandarins as "imbecile, avaricious and obstinate", and demanded that Britain force open more ports for free trade. Jardine and Matheson built sleek teak ships, armed them to the teeth, and sailed the coast, plying what Matheson persisted in calling the harmless 'merchandise China needs'.

Even as Britain promoted opium in China, she passed several laws forbidding its use in England. Western medical experts supported such dual standards by arguing that for Chinese, opium was "a harmless social family luxury", on a par with tea. The Deputy-Surgeon-General of Bombay would later claim that Chinese find in opium "a source of enjoyment, of comfort, of necessity, and of even a blessing." He added, "Opium is especially suited to the Chinese constitution, habits, and to the small pecuniary means of the masses."

A Western writer in the *Chinese Repository* (Nov. 1836, vol. V., p. 300) had different views. He accused traffickers of murder and,

"the perpetuating and encouraging and engaging in a trade which promotes idleness, disease, poverty, misery, crime, madness, despair, and death."

An Assam tea plantation superintendent wrote that to obtain opium, addicts "will steal, sell his property, children, the mother of his children; and finally even commit murder". Walter Medhurst, the London Missionary Society's tireless opponent of the opium trade, described the "harmless" drug's effects:

"In proportion as the wretched victim comes under the power of the infatuating drug, so his ability to resist temptation is less strong; and debilitated in body as well as in mind he is unable to earn his usual pittance. Shut out

from his own dwellings, either by angry relatives or ruthless creditors, they die in the streets, unpitied and despised."

Britain was unmoved. In fact, she transformed her sordid traffic into a moral crusade, arguing that opium was China's salvation, for without it the over-populated Chinese would grow poppies instead of food.

The Way of Heaven In a poignant letter to Queen Victoria, Imperial High Commissioner Lin Zexu wrote,
> "I am told that in your own country opium smoking is forbidden under severe penalties. This means that you are aware of how harmful it is. So long as you do not take it yourselves, but continue to make it and tempt the people of China to buy it, such conduct is repugnant to human feeling and at variance with the Way of Heaven."

"The Way of Heaven," Lin argued, was,
> "...fairness to all; it does not suffer us to harm others in order to benefit ourselves. Men are alike in this all the world over: that they cherish life and hate what endangers life. Your country lies 20,000 leagues away; but for all that the Way of Heaven holds good for you as for us, and your instincts are not different from ours; for nowhere are there men so blind as not to distinguish what brings profit and what does harm..."

But for Britain, the profit justified the harm. On April 6, 1843, the *Times* would sum up Prime Minister Robert Peel's position:
> "Morality and religion, and the happiness of mankind, and friendly relations with China, and new markets for British manufactures were all very fine things in their way; but that the opium trade was worth to the Indian government £1,200,000..."

Reluctantly, Commissioner Lin gave the British a 3-day ultimatum, and after waiting a full week for a response, he blockaded the harbor. During the foreigners' confinement, Cohong merchants carefully preserved the Westerners' property from harm, and insured that their foreign prisoners wined and dined in comfort. Lin reasoned that if he treated his foreign prisoners with respect and courtesy, they would recognize the error of their ways, abandon the opium trade, and turn to legitimate pursuits. But Western newspapers trumpeted China's barbarous treatment of Europeans, and stoked up the war propaganda machine.

Up in Smoke A sullen Captain Elliott surrendered 20,283 chests of opium, valued at £2 million. It took Lin six weeks to destroy it, and as gray smoke clouded Canton's sky, he noted of foreign observers, "I should judge from their attitudes that they have the decency to feel heartily ashamed."

But anger, not shame, reddened their faces. In July 1839, the British destroyed and scattered 29 Chinese war junks. Unsuspecting peasants rushed to

greet British ships off TingHai on July 5ᵗʰ. In *Six Months with the Chinese Expedition* (1841), Lord Jocelyn described the British greeting:

"The ships opened their broadsides upon the town, and the crashing of timber, falling houses, and groans of men resounded from the shore...We landed on a deserted beach, a few dead bodies, bows and arrows, broken spears and guns remaining the sole occupants of the fields."

Rather than submit, city officials committed suicide, for as Waley wrote,

"It had not from the first any chance of withstanding the concentrated fire of fifteen warships; as well might one expect Hiroshima to have hit back at its attackers."

British troops immediately launched a protection racket ("security placards") by which families purchased immunity from plunder if they voluntarily surrendered their livestock. *The Chinese Repository* (1840) recorded:

"They [the Chinese] have in a thousand instances received great injustice at our hands. While we have been issuing proclamations, talking sweet words...our soldiers and sailors have been plundering them and forcibly carrying off their poultry and cattle..."

On October 10, 1841, British forces captured Chen-hai, on the mainland opposite Ting-Hai. Ningpo was taken 3 days later. Cao Sheng recorded his experiences upon returning home during the attack on Shanghai:

"I found several foreigners there, beating it down with their muskets. I thought of my wife still hidden within and determined that if death was to be her fate, I would share it. I rushed up and attempted to thrust myself between them and the gate, but was seized and held. They then went into the house and ransacked all the chests and boxes, taking money, headdresses, trinkets—everything they could lay hands on. When this plundering was over they held a knife to my throat, threatening to kill me unless I showed them where I had hidden my other valuables...I did my best to make clear to them by gestures that we were not rich people, and at last they let me go...

"During the day several large bands of them came, and the same performance was repeated..."

A friend helped Cao get a chicken to buy a "protection placard" , and then he and his wife, who had not eaten in 3 days, ventured outside. Cao wrote,

"At supper that night, chicken-bone in hand and cup between my lips, glancing back at my two sons who were waiting upon me just as usual, I stretched out my hand and stroked their heads...I did not know whether to laugh or weep."

On June 22ⁿᵈ, Cao Sheng wrote, "The foreigners have contented themselves with loot and rape, but as the city fell without resistance, there has been no general slaughter." The "general slaughter" came July 9ᵗʰ, in Chinkiang, where the poet Chu Shiyun recorded in his diary:

"Corpses litter the town…is the horror ever going to end?   Will our family
ever be reunited…For days women have been raped or carried off."

The soldiers consoled their victims by plastering the town with proclamations
encouraging the survivors to flock to Sui-Shan, where "opium is on sale very
cheap—an opportunity not to be missed."

Surrender   A devastated China surrendered.   Under the *Nanking Treaty*
(June 26, 1843), China agreed to pay an indemnity of £6,000,000 for the
destroyed opium (three times its value) and cede Hong Kong to Britain. This
settlement infuriated Lord Palmerston, who complained that six million did not
cover the cost of the destroyed opium or the punitive expedition.   The *Times*
ridiculed this claim, arguing that Britain owed China compensation for "pillaging
her towns and slaughtering her citizens in a quarrel which would never have
arisen if we had not been guilty of an international crime" .

The Crown countered critics by arguing that the war was over free trade, not
opium.   And Sir John Davis, who became governor of Hong Kong in 1844,
declared that the Chinese weren't sincere about prohibiting opium, and that
Britain had never forced the issue.   He protested that Britain "only supplied the
poison, which the Chinese were not obliged to take" .

Since the Nanking Treaty studiously avoided the word "opium" , the drug
technically remained illegal.   Britain even promised in a supplementary treaty
that British officers would end the smuggling entirely.   Empty words.   When
Captain Hope of the H.M.S. Thalia prevented several opium-laden ships from
proceeding past Shanghai, he was criticized for interfering with British subjects
in the course of their "trade" , relieved of duty, and packed off to India.

When a large vessel has opened a way it is easy for a small one to follow.

Chinese Proverb

Hitchhiking Imperialism   Western   nations   unanimously   applauded
Britain's victory.   Ex-U.S. President Adams declared the war was caused solely
by China's 'insulting and degrading' attitude towards foreigners, and averred:
"The fundamental principle of the Chinese Empire is anti-commercial. It
admits no obligation to hold commercial intercourse… it is time that this
outrage upon the rights of human nature, and upon the first principles of
the rights of nations, should cease."

America rushed envoy Caleb Cushing to China, where he announced
America's intent to conclude a treaty of "everlasting friendship".   He took three
gunboats to help underscore America's friendliness, and Cushing reminded the
humiliated Chinese,
"The late war with England was caused by the conduct of the authorities at
Canton, in disregarding the rights of public officers who represented the
English Government."

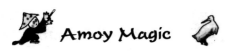

Cushing added that if China had not learned her lesson, "it can be regarded in no other light than evidence that she invites and desires [war with] the other Western powers [America]."

A French diplomat followed on Cushing's heels with seven French warships in tow and similar demands for everlasting friendship and trading rights. This "hitchhiking imperialism' lasted right up until Liberation in 1949.

Though Britain had fought a war to protect her opium trafficking, opium was opposed by most merchants, manufacturers, government leaders and missionaries, on economic as well as moral grounds. One merchant proved statistically that the opium trade had destroyed legal commerce and that in "supplying the Chinese with an intoxicating drug, we are drying up their natural capacity to consume our manufactures."

Pottinger coined a stock answer: "If India does not produce it, other countries will." He added smugly that if the Chinese were truly such a virtuous people, they "would neither use the opium nor permit it to be smuggled".

China continued to resist the opium trade, and in the 1850s, Lord Palmerston warned, "The time is fast approaching when we shall be obliged to strike another blow in China." He explained, 'these half-civilized governments such as those of China, Portugal, Spanish America...require a dressing down every eight or ten years to keep them in order."

Dressing Down China — The Arrow War   The excuse for China's "dressing down" came from Hong Kong, which teemed with Chinese criminals and pirates luxuriating under the protection of the Crown. Commissioner Yeh seized the Chinese ship "Arrow", and convicted twelve of its notorious Chinese pirates. The British furiously demanded the criminals' release, arguing they had been taken from a British ship entitled to British protection. Lord Derby ridiculed the charge:

> "Chinese built, Chinese captured, Chinese sold, Chinese bought and manned, and Chinese owned. And that is the British vessel which is said to be entitled to claim the protection of a treaty by which British ships are exempted from the visits of the Chinese authorities."

Commissioner Yeh surrendered the pirates, but refused Sir John Bowring's demand for an apology. Britain now had her excuse for China's "dressing down". With characteristic hyberbole, Palmerston denounced Commissioner Yeh as "one of the most inhuman monsters that ever disgraced a nation." On Feb. 3, 1857, Britain declared war because of China's "acts of violence, insults to the flag and infraction of treaty rights".

Parliament unanimously opposed the second Opium War, agreeing with Lord Derby's sentiment that the war was "the shedding of the blood of unwarlike and innocent people without warrant of law and without the warrant of moral justification". Lord Palmerston furiously accused the dissidents of disloyalty to the Crown, dissolved Parliament, and went to war anyway.

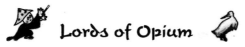 **Lords of Opium** 405

When the Chinese refused to ratify the Treaty of Tiantsien, British and French forces attacked Beijing and burned the Summer Palace to the ground. Besieged from all sides, China succumbed, ending a full century of resistance. Opium was finally legalized, and imported at a lower duty than England, the proponent of "free trade", levied on Chinese silk and tea.

Scapegoat   The English now intensified a two-decade effort to convince Western public opinion that Britain had never forced opium on China. Mr. Gladstone, in the opium debate in Parliament on May 10, 1870, argued that the Chinese government had 'wisely' decided to deal with opium as a commercial commodity. He praised the opium trade as not only a source of revenue but of great benefit to China and India:

> "This is one of the most remarkable cases which the whole fiscal history of the world presents. I do not suppose there is, or ever has been, a country...in which £6,000,000 of its revenue has been derived from a particular article [he still evades the word 'opium'], of which you could say with so close an approximation to the truth, without any violation whatever of political justice, that the 6 million was virtually and substantially paid by the inhabitants of another country who did not complain of the burden."

The *London Times* (Oct. 22, 1880) claimed that "the Chinese government admitted opium as a legal article of import, not under constraint, but of their own free will, deliberately". Lord Curzon, later Under Secretary for India, "denied that England had ever forced opium upon China; no historian of any repute, and no diplomatist who knew anything of the matter, would support the proposition that England coerced China in this respect."

Born and Bred to the Opium Pipe   Westerners had long held the vast, ancient kingdom of Cathay in awe, but by the end of the Opium Wars, Chinese were beneath contempt, mere creatures born and bred to the opium pipe. It is ever thus, for gross atrocities, whether in China or Auschwitz or South Africa or Nicaragua or the antebellum South, can be sustained only by dehumanizing our prey and by canonizing ourselves. Britain argued that not only did the Chinese want opium but that their physical constitution required it, and that the British opium monopolies throughout Asia were a humanitarian service for the Chinese.

As the dragon sank into opium dreams, Shaftbury's prophecy was fulfilled: easy money killed honest money. In 1877, Mr. Samuel S. Mander wrote that of China's £12 million in imports from India, the 85,000 chests of opium counted for £10.5 million, leaving £1.5 million for legitimate trade." Legitimate merchants suffered as China's moral and economic foundation foundered, and private bankers in London warned, "The purchasing power of China seems paralyzed by the opium trade." Sir Arthur Cotton, a well known authority on India, argued in a letter to the Anti-Opium Society (May 6, 1882), "...there is not a shadow of excuse for our continuing this trade..." He affirmed,

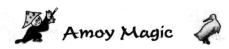
"the astonishing fact that we are perfectly independent of the opium revenue, having a clear surplus of £3.5 million without it, and that revenue increasing at the rate of £500,000 a year!"

Opium apologists argued that Indian farmers needed opium profits, but Sir Cotton proved that the farmer could make 4 times as much profit from an acre of sugar as he could from an acre of poppies.   But like Chinese opium addicts, Britain's Indian poppy farmers were expendable. And expended they were.

Britain's mandatory substitution of poppies for traditional food crops ended with Indian mothers feeding their emaciated children opium to ease the gnawing hunger that plagued them from their beleaguered birth to their premature death.

In 1838, 800,000 Indians died in the Agra famine. Over 500,000 starved in 1860 in the Northwest, and in 1865-1867, one million perished in the Orissa Famine – 1/3 of that area's population. In 1868-1870, 1/3 of the Rajputana population perished of hunger.

Embarrassed by the public outcry in Europe, Britain adopted a simple famine relief program. Only 28 died in the Bihar Famine of 1873-4, but at one dollar per life, Britain abandoned the program as too costly. Two years later, India's British masters idly watched the South India Famine destroy 5.25 million people in British territory alone.   Another 750,000 starved in the 1896-1897 famine, and in 1899, 2.5 million perished.   But the poppy prospered.

On Deadly Statistics   "When the officer inquired whether after the war people would not ask what happened to the millions of Jews, Eichmann [Hitler's right hand man] replied: 'A hundred dead is a catastrophe. A million dead is a statistic.'"
Nuremburg war crimes trial witness

Fighting Fire With Fire   China reluctantly decided to destroy the Western opium trade by flooding the market with domestic opium.   It was a painful decision, for Chinese rulers held that production of opium, for any reason, would "provoke the judgment of Heaven and the condemnation of men".

It certainly provoked Britain's condemnation, which resented China's infringement upon her private opium monopoly. By 1876, China was earning over 1.5 million annually from opium, but Sir R. Alcock told the House of Commons that China would gladly abandon the trade if Britain stopped her own trafficking.

Five years later, Sir R. Alcock, the stalwart anti-opium crusader, sold out.

Turncoat   In December 1881, Sir Alcock shocked anti-opium advocates with his article *Opium and the Common Sense*. He claimed that opium was no more harmful than alcohol and insisted:

1) "In early years, the Chinese were insincere in prohibition..."

2) "The British government never had forced opium on China; the Chinese were always eager to take more than India could supply."

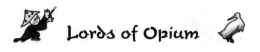 **Lords of Opium**
Mr. B. Fosset Lock explained Sir Alcock's betrayal in his article *The Opium Trade and Sir Rutherford Alcock* (*Contemporary Review*, April, 1882). It turned out that only one month before publishing *Opium and the Common Sense*, Sir Alcock had been made a director of the British North Borneo Company, an affiliate of Dent, the premier opium trading firm. Alcock proved to be an even better opium trafficker than moral crusader. By the 1920s, fully 100% of Britain's income from North Borneo came from the opium trade.

China's Death Rattle   The ranks of addicts now swelled with women and children. In 1889, Mr. Samuel Smith declared before the House of Commons, "one thing is certain: unless the vice is combated, China will commit something like national suicide and her population will succumb to pauperism, famine and death." He asked Britain to make a sacrifice by ending the trade, for "nothing ennobles a nation more than to make sacrifices for a great cause."

Britain's ennobling response was the Royal Opium Commission's 2,556 page report, which concluded that opium was no worse than alcohol and, furthermore, "there is no evidence from China of any popular desire that the import of Indian opium should be stopped."

China's Viceroy, Chang Chih-Tung, begged to differ. In 1896, he wrote in *China's Only Hope*:

"Cast out the poison! The foreign drug is debasing the homes and sweeping away the lives of our people.

"It is not foreign intercourse that is ruining China, but this dreadful poison. Oh, the grief and desolation it has wrought to our people! Opium has spread with frightful rapidity and heartrending results through the provinces. Millions upon millions have been struck down by the plague...The ruin of the mind is the most woeful of its many deleterious effects. The poison enfeebles the will, saps the strength of the body, renders the consumer incapable of performing his regular duties, and unfit for travel from one place to another. It consumes his substance and reduces the miserable wretch to poverty, barrenness, and senility...Many thoughtful Chinese are apprehensive that opium will finally extirpate the race..."

In 1901, French writer and Naval officer Pierre Loti wrote, "China is dying of this poison." In 1906, a memorial to the Emperor claimed,

"China can never become strong and stand shoulder to shoulder with the powers of the world, unless she can get rid of the habit of opium smoking by her subjects, about one-quarter of whom have been reduced to skeletons and look half dead." (*China Times*, Jan. 16, 1906)

Cold Turkey   In 1907, the Dowager Empress vowed to eradicate the opium scourge within ten years. By June, all 700 opium dens in a Chinese-controlled city had been closed, and by mid 1910, China had reduced by 70 to 85 percent her domestic production of opium.

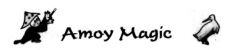

Meanwhile, Britain continued to insist that China had started the opium problem and was insincere about ending opium use.

Ironically, when impoverished Chinese farmers voluntarily torched their poppy fields, they actually boosted the profits of wealthy British traffickers by creating an opium shortage. Still, Britain mourned its alleged losses and complained about unsold stocks of opium in Shanghai and Canton warehouses. Chinese officials in Shanghai responded by purchasing 1,200 chests of opium, worth $25 million, and consigning it to the torch, evoking memories of Lin Ze Xu's conflagration a century earlier. China declared solemnly that, from that date, opium could no longer be imported legally into China. The British, old hands at smuggling, were unfazed.

On Feb. 26, 1924, a steamer hauled 180 cases of opium to Shanghai. Thousands of cases more were never discovered. Even John Campbell, representative of the Indian government, confessed that most smuggled opium "came in steamers from Liverpool and London, and steamers from the latter port arriving with 3,000 pounds of opium." He said,

> "The statistics showed beyond a shadow of a doubt that hundreds of thousands of ounces (in one year, almost 800,000 ounces) had been sent to the Far East for illicit introduction into China. China did not produce an ounce of morphia herself…"

The pleasure of what we enjoy is lost by coveting more.
Chinese Proverb

New Markets   As China tightened her borders, Britain pinned her hopes on her other Asian colonies. Opium production in the Straits Settlements (Singapore, Penang, Malacca, Labuan) rose from 353,938 pounds in 1916 to 370,688 pounds in 1920, in spite of Britain's promise at the Hague Convention to limit opium sales. In 1918, 60% of Britain's Asian income was derived from opium sales. In 1925, opium accounted for 48% of Singapore's revenue, and 100% of North Borneo's. At the 1923 Opium Conference, Mr. Campbell admitted that the British Indian government was determined to maintain high levels of both internal consumption and export, and that they,

> "controlled the production, distribution, sale, possession — every possible practical question which could arise in connection with opium—in the strictest possible manner—They had built up a complicated and highly efficient administrative system which started from the time the poppy seed was put into the ground, and did not relinquish control of the drug until it was in the hands of the consumers, or till it was actually exported."

Some wits noted wryly that the Crown did all but light the addicts' pipes.

When Indians begged Britain to abandon the opium policy, Britain responded that her opium monopoly was a humanitarian service to India (as it had been to

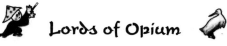

China), and that to end the trade would be "a mockery; to many millions it would be sheer inhumanity."

> History teaches us that men and nations behave wisely once they have
> exhausted all other alternatives.

Abba Eban, Israeli politician

Coming Home to Roost   Lin Zexu had warned a century earlier, "For so long as your subjects make opium, who knows but they will not sooner or later take to smoking it?" Lin was a prophet.

Even while expanding her opium trafficking abroad, Great Britain was struggling to curtail growing domestic consumption by passing the Dangerous Drugs Acts of 1920 and 1923. Desperate Western nations convened two International Opium conferences to debate the causes and cures of the worldwide opium epidemic.

Given that half of Europe's Asian profits derived from opium, the cause of the opium problem should have been obvious. But Western powers held that their mammoth opium monopolies were "*legal*" and hence blameless. While Britain exported 700 tons of opium annually, and sold 500 tons to Indian addicts, she and other Western nations agreed that the cause of the worldwide opium problem was China's domestic production of opium! And they piously shared Lord Cecil's view of Chinese opium producers as "one of the most worthless sections of the human race".

Hong Kong — Opium's Last Stand   In 1924, in a show of goodwill, Britain began an intensive campaign in HK to stop illegal (i.e., non-British) opium trade. Simultaneously, Britain expanded her own opium production. In 1922, Hong Kong's government handled 30 tons of opium, and reaped enormous profits from selling confiscated contraband opium. In spite of Hague Convention promises, in 1923 Britain asked permission to double opium imports from India, and then mounted a massive sales drive in Hong Kong to compensate for lost mainland profits. The sales drive was successful.

In 1924, a committee found that 20 to 25 percent of the Chinese adult population in HK had used opium, and the percent had been increasing for 6 to 7 years. Britain's stock response was, "It's not possible to stop opium use amongst the Chinese." But the Japanese knew better.

The Japanese Opium Experience   Japan was the only colonial power to execute faithfully the principles of opium suppression set forth at the Hague Convention in 1912, for Japan had been fighting opium addiction, at home and in her colonies, for decades. Japan persistently argued that drug trafficking was not only immoral but, in the long run, unprofitable.

One of Japan's top priorities after taking Taiwan in 1895 was to end opium use. European smugglers were impotent against the Japanese' efficient police organization and tight surveillance and investigation.   Opium-related deaths in Taiwan plummeted from 215,476 in 1908 to 38,000 annually by 1923.   Japan also suppressed opium smuggling into Korea.

At the Second Opium Conference, Mr. Sugimura of Japan complained that it "was beneath a nation's dignity to derive so much revenue from opium," and he urged Western powers to view the problem not just from a humanitarian viewpoint but from an economic one, noting that in Taiwan,

> "Even from the economic and financial point of view, a sacrifice of revenue from opium was in reality a gain, since the productive power of the nation increased."

Britain protested Japan's attacks on "the justice and fairness of the British government", but the Polish delegate agreed with the Japanese. He said that because of the smokescreen of rhetoric clouding Western opium monopolies, the world was further from eliminating opium in 1924 than it had been in 1913.

Lord Cecil finally dismissed mounting criticism by arguing that opium was "purely an Indian question...it does not appear to me to be a matter for international interference at all".

Britain clung to her Hong Kong opium monopoly right up until 1945, when postwar profits no longer justified the embarrassment.

Thankfully, opium trafficking is behind us, but not so the arrogance born of opium's easy wealth and power.

> "Mankind loves to hate. It makes us feel good and right. People feel so appallingly righteous about ideologies and faiths they have been conditioned to believe in. We need scapegoats, objects outside ourselves so that we can project our own anger and hostility. If we are to understand how we can commit barbarities, we have to analyze this need and question the whole process of demeaning and devaluing others."
> Professor Ron Baker, Holocaust survivor.

What You See   Scientists say that what you expect of people is pretty much what you get.   I think the same goes for nations.   "Japan" conjures up images of Mount Fuji and Japanese gardens, of quality cars and electronics — not of the rape of Nanjing, or the bombing of Pearl Harbor, or the enslaving of Amoy. We put Japan's atrocious past behind us, committed our resources to building a new Japan, and got one.

Germany evokes images of Beethoven and BMW, of engineering excellence — not of the millions of Jews and Gentiles massacred during the Holocaust. We put Germany's past behind us and worked to help her rebuild. We wanted a new Germany and got one.

Time (or more likely, economic success) has exonerated Japan and Germany, but we continue to view China only from the perspective of the Great Leap Forward, or the Cultural Revolution, or Mao's dental hygiene. I fear that if we

persist in painting China as the evil empire we could very well get just what we fear — a paranoid, defensive superpower.

Some people demonize China, others deify her, but she is neither demon nor deity. China is but a nation much like our own, with the same frailties and faults and hopes and dreams that we have. Chinese are a carnival glass, through which we see darkly images that, however distorted, are but of ourselves.

"Blessed are the peacemakers, for they shall be called the children of God."
The Prince of Peace

Pax Sino   Two millennia ago nearly the entire Western world was united under the Roman Peace — the Pax Romano. A strong military and stable political system kept peace as traders, using a common trade language, plied their wares along thousands of miles of stone Roman roads. It was an era of great corruption, to be sure, and mass slavery, and unimaginable immorality and depravity, but also a period of great economic, political and cultural triumphs made possible largely because of stability.

Rome fell, but China has survived for millennia because she has always sought stability above all else. Today, fully 1/5 of the world is united under a fairly stable economic and political system. Mandarin is the official tongue of the 1.3 billion people who make up the largest market and labor force in history. Domestic trade has mushroomed thanks to a network of roads so comprehensive that even a family of American devils could drive Toy Ota from Xiamen to Tibet and back in only 3 months.

China, like Rome, has the fundamentals—stability, language, and infrastructure. And Pax Sino, like Pax Romano, could as easily be a force for good as for evil. What we get is largely up to us.

Epilogue

Look Up

Time flies when you're being had!   When we slunk off the slow boat to China back in '88, we had no idea that Amoy would weave such a spell over us that we'd never leave.   Once you get Amoy in your blood, it's part of you.   (Of course, the same can be said of malaria, but who falls in love with mosquitoes?)

Amoy is a magical mix of old and new, of East and West, and home to a people who have a special gift for optimism.   Perhaps Chinese are always looking forward because they can see so far back, for as Winston Churchill said, "The farther back you can look, the farther forward you are likely to see."

Chinese can look back at least 5,015 years, give or take a few months.   And fortunately for us Laowai, Chinese learn from their past but don't dwell on it. They look up.

UP   On a crisp November morning, Susan and Matthew went shopping and Shannon and I took the road less traveled—the trail up the mountain behind the Nanputuo Buddhist monastery, past the sign that says "No foreigners beyond this sign," and over the crest.

We drank deeply of the silence as we picked our way over damp boulders covered in lichen.   We waded through ferns, and ducked beneath the grayish green moss covered branches.   At times I sunk into reverie, imagining that we were blazing trails where no man had gone before.   And every time, I was rudely yanked back into reality by the sight of Chinese characters carved deeply into the granite cliffs by ancient poets seeking immortality with a hammer and chisel centuries before Eric the Red took up real estate in Greenland.

I paused at one fork (or was it a chopstick?) in the path and asked Shannon, "Which way?"

"Up!" he said.

"Why up?"

"Because up is more fun."

It takes a decade or more for children to unlearn their inborn inclination to climb.   By adulthood, many no longer know which way is up, or care.   Yet there

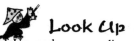

lingers a memory of Up, and a vague discontent for which we compensate by looking out, or in, but seldom Up. As Thoreau put it,

> "We seem but to linger in manhood to tell the dreams of our childhood, and they vanish out of memory ere we learn the language."

I suspect that children are a different species, a little lower than the angels and a little higher than man, given us that we may rediscover childhood's marvelous mix of ambition tempered with contentment. Of such is the kingdom.

As Shannon and I sat together on the sun-baked granite summit of the Five Old Men Mountains behind Nanputuo Temple, I penned,

> ### Up
> The simplest seed, entombed
> Ignobly on its noggin,
> Impugns the claims of gravity
> And turning, strives to gain
> The unseen sun.

Life's magic lies in looking up, but as Churchill noted, we see the future from the perspective of our past. To better appreciate our Chinese hosts' perspective, I hope you'll read the "Lords of Opium" supplement at the end of this book. And then I hope that all of us, Laowai and Laonei alike, will...

Enjoy Amoy!

Bill, Sue, Shannon, Matthew, & 🐾

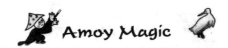
Supplement

Fujian Handicrafts （福建工艺品）
& Shopping

When you set out to explore Fujian, bring some spending money! Our province is home to marvelous craftsmen and artisans producing everything from stone and wood carvings to porcelain and Fuzhou's famous bodiless lacquerware (one of China's "**3 Treasures**";

Fuzhou is famous for wooden carvings, and exquisite paper and silk lanterns. You can also buy cheap but more durable plastic versions for your garden (I've a dozen outside our apartment) from more rural towns.

Japanese paper parasols originated from China—most likely from Fuzhou.

Fine quality **bamboo and wicker furniture** is sold throughout our province, but the best selection and lowest prices are to be had from the furniture shops beside the highway on a mountain overpass between Longyan and Liancheng 连城 (also check out their exquisite "**root sculptures**").

While in Liancheng, don't forget to pick up some famous **Xuan paper**, and while you're practicing your Chinese calligraphy, you'll of course want to sip some **Anxi tea** from the thimble-sized cups of a **Minnan teaset**. They come in every shape and size imaginable, and range from mere pennies to thousands of rmb.

With so much choice confronting you, you'll be a basket case—so buy some **baskets**. Handwoven, they come in every shape, size and color you can think of, and a few you can't.

Pick up a **Chinese puppet** or two in Quanzhou 泉州**,** the puppet capital of China. And start a collection of Xiamen's famous **beaded sculptures.**

In Xianyou 仙游 you can pick up marvelous ersatz **ancient Chinese mahogany furniture** as well as contemporary Western furniture—and a vast selection of finely detailed resin "sculptures" in the shapes of birds, animals, people, houses, castles, deng deng. While you're in the area, don't forget the drum maker, who is always seeking to drum up business.

Fujian also produces and exports a broad variety of clocks (I've always wanted a Chinese grandfather clock, but no place to put one), bicycles (Xiamen has a couple of bike factories), gold jewelry, plastic wares, electronics, canned foods, medicines, and deng deng.

You want it, we got it. Collect 'em all!

And of course, every corner of Fujian has food specialties (so does every corner of the rest of China). Try Longyan's 龙岩 spiced peanuts and dried sweet potato and Xianyou's 仙游 mushrooms, and recreate the Boston Tea Party with Anxi 安溪 famous teas. Then dine on Xiamen's seafood, Wuping County's 武平县 famous dried pig gallbladder, deng deng. Yum.

Chinese folding fans—are made in a factory right on Gulangyu Island. They're small, light, and inexpensive; we take home dozens for friends back home.

Shoushan Stone Carvings are from shoushan stone, a form of alabaster found in Shoushan mountain, north of Fuzhou. For a great selection of shoushan stone work and other Fujian arts and crafts, and good prices (they'll knock off 10% if you ask, 15% if you start to walk out the door), try Fuzhou's "Fujian Arts and Crafts Experiment Factory."

Directions: I thought of saying it's just across the street and down from a McDonalds, but nowadays what isn't? So just take a taxi to: N. May 1ˢᵗ St., #42. 五一北路 42 号 Enter the iron gate and go upstairs. Tel: (0591)754-5205.

Chinese Chops I still don't understand why Chinese value a 'chop' (stone stamp of their signature) over a signature, since chops can be copied so easily. Still, they're fun. I feel like the Emperor giving his seal every time I jab a document with my own chop, carved in shoushan stone. Chop carvers in any Fujian town will carve you a chop—in both English and Chinese if you write it out for them.

Hui'an Stone Carving. In the early Ming Dynasty, troops from Anhui's Shouxian County, stone carvers by trade, settled down and resumed their old trade, and Hui'an now produces hundreds of stone products—temple dogs, garden lanterns, Mickey & Minnie...

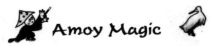
Cork Carvings I can totally lose track of time while absorbed in the minute magical detail of these miniature cork carvings of mountain scenes, temples, animals all set in exquisite glass cases. Prized the world over, these works of art come right here from Fuzhou. Exquisite, yes, but also inexpensive and light; we once bought 5 dozen small ones for about 5 Yuan each to take home as gifts.

Dehua Porcelain Dehua's a bit remote, but the scenery alone (1,800 meter mountains) is worth the drive.

Puppet Heads from Quanzhou, the puppet capital of China. A Qing-dynasty craftsman named Jiang Jinbang originated the craft, creating over 280 different puppet characters with movables eyes and mouths.

Paper Products. Bright paper parasols conjure up images of geisha girls and Japan, but they originated right here in Fujian! Paper umbrellas and intricate paper-cuts are made throughout Fujian.

"Bodiless" Fuzhou Lacquerware—one of China's "3 folk art treasures" . For more about it, please read the supplement, "Love of Lacquer".

Miniature Potted Landscapes have been around since at least 25 A.D. because they were found in Hebei's Eastern Han Dynasty tombs. (The drawing on the right of an honor maid bearing a miniature landscape is from a 1200 year old Tang Dynasty tomb).

These exquisitely crafted miniatures are a little slice of China, replete with miniature mountains, bonsai trees, fields of grass (moss, actually), tiny pagodas and bridges and people, and tiny deng deng. Some are crafted around ancient bonsai trees (like the 500 year old Chinese juniper to the right) and others on strangely twisted rocks.

5 Foot High,
500 Year Old
Chinese Juniper!

Zhangzhou's sprawling flower markets have a wide variety at fairly reasonable prices, but you can find a great assortment in Xiamen out at the giant nursery center on Lianqian Rd. 莲前路, past the airport road intersection.

Kites — next time someone tells you to go fly a kite, you're in luck. Fujian folk have been making and flying kites from time immemorial—and some of the best kites in the world are made right here in Xiamen at Pincle-Kite.

This leading kite manufacturer uses the latest technology to produce both contemporary and classical kites of terylene cloth and Fujian's famous bamboo. And you'll have no problem getting your bamboo-framed kites past customs back home because the kites are dried and sterilized under infrared light, then coated by a natural resin.

So go fly a kite!

And then see the rest of China…

图书在版编目(CIP)数据

魅力厦门/(美)潘维廉著. —2 版. —厦门:厦门大学
出版社,2003.6
ISBN 7-5615-1604-5

Ⅰ.魅… Ⅱ.潘… Ⅲ.厦门市-概况-英文
Ⅳ.K925.73

中国版本图书馆 CIP 数据核字(2003)第 043467 号

Amoy Magic
魅 力 厦 门

出版发行:厦门大学出版社
　　　　地址:厦门大学　邮编:361005
　　　　http://www.xmupress.com
　　　　E-mail:xmup@public.xm.fj.cn
印　　刷:厦门新嘉莹彩色印刷有限公司

开　本:889×1 194　1/32
印　张:13.5
插　页:6
字　数:402 千字
印　数:1-8 000
版　次:2003 年 6 月第 2 版
印　次:2003 年 6 月第 1 次印刷

定　价:30.00 元